New World Coming

New World Coming

Coming

The 1920s
and the Making of Modern America

NATHAN MILLER

DA CAPO PRESS
A MEMBER OF THE PERSEUS BOOKS GROUP

The lines from "the season 'tis, my lovely lambs," copyright © 1926, 1954, 1991 by the Trustees for the E. E. Cummings Trust. Copyright © 1985 by George James Firmage, from *Complete Poems: 1904–1962* by E. E. Cummings, edited by George J. Firmage. Used by permission of Liveright Publishing Corporation.

Designed by Colin Joh
Text set in Goudy Oldstyle

Cataloging-in-Publication data for this book is available from the Library of Congress.

First Da Capo Press edition 2004
Published by arrangement with Scribner, an imprint of Simon & Schuster
ISBN-13 978-0-306-81379-5; ISBN-10 0-306-81379-3

Published by Da Capo Press
A Member of the Perseus Books Group
http://www.dacapopress.com

Da Capo Press books are available at special discounts for bulk purchases in the U.S. by corporations, institutions, and other organizations. For more information, please contact the Special Markets Department at the Perseus Books Group, 11 Cambridge Center, Cambridge, MA 02142, or call (800) 255-1514 or (617) 252-5298, or e-mail special.markets@perseusbooks.com.

To
Joan and Stan Weiss
Myra and Jerry Barron
and their offspring

Contents

NEW WORLD
COMING

Introduction

To mention the 1920s in America immediately conjures up such personalities and events as Scott and Zelda Fitzgerald, Prohibition, the Charleston, flappers, speakeasies, "Hello, Sucker!" the Wall Street boom, and the Great Crash. In part, this is so because of Frederick Lewis Allen's compulsively readable account *Only Yesterday*. But that book has certain defects, beginning with the fact that it was published in 1931, and contains little in the way of hard data. Allen also neglected blacks and the bitter labor struggles of the period. I have tried to present the story of this rollicking decade without these defects. To frame my narrative in human terms, I have used the life of F. Scott Fitzgerald, which was at its most flamboyant in those years.

It is indeed a judgment call to select one decade to describe the warp and woof of American history, but the 1920s present themselves admirably for such treatment. They have a clear beginning at World War I and the battle for the League of Nations, and end with the stock market crash of 1929 and the resulting political explosion. To an astonishing extent, the 1920s resemble our own era, at the turn of the twenty-first century; in many ways that decade was a precursor of modern excesses. We, too, have engaged in foolishly dangerous stock market manipulations. Much of what we consider contemporary actually began in the Twenties—for example, jazz and psychiatry. Criminal conduct by business and industrial leaders was altogether too familiar then and now. As in the 1990s, one political party prevailed in the zeitgeist of the times, encouraging the high-flying mood of the nation.

I wish to thank the distinguished Civil War historian Ernest B. Furgurson for helping to make this a better book than it would have been. Similar thanks are due Gary Gerstle, professor of history at the University of Maryland and Princeton University. Dr. Jonathan Barron of the Department of English at the University of Southern Mississippi read the chapters on the literary revolution of the Twenties. Much of the data herein was drawn from Gerald Leinwand's *1927: High Tide of the 1920s*. Dr. Joseph D. Lichtenberg, an internationally known psychiatrist, commented on the chapter in which I deal with psychiatry in America.

As the Pulitzer Prize–winning historian David M. Kennedy has written of *Only Yesterday*, "Allen's field of vision, for all its comprehensiveness, was severely bound by the view from the New York editorial offices of Harper's . . . restricted geographically by the Hudson and East Rivers—or perhaps Cape Cod and the Hamptons—and restricted sociologically to his eastern urban and suburban subscribers." I have tried to look farther and deeper.

Prologue

Throughout the pale summer nights of 1919, a light always seemed to be burning in a third-floor front room of a brownstone at 599 Summit Avenue in St. Paul. Sometimes a slim figure paced back and forth across the open windows. Up there, amid the treetops, twenty-two-year-old F. Scott Fitzgerald, subsisting mainly on cigarettes and nervous energy, was working on a novel he desperately hoped would bring him money and acclaim. Not long out of the U.S. Army following the Armistice, which ended World War I, he was being supported by his parents, his career as a writer was stymied, and his girl had broken up with him because she believed he had no prospects.

To get a breath of air, Fitzgerald unlatched a screen on one of the windows and, careful not to disturb the chapter outlines pinned to the curtains, stepped out onto a small landing where he had a sweeping view up and down the boulevard. Summit Avenue crowns a bluff overlooking the Lower Town, St. Paul's business section, and is the spine of the Summit, then the city's most fashionable neighborhood. Nearby, the Roman Catholic Cathedral of St. Paul—Fitzgerald was christened there—crouched at the intersection of Summit and Selby Avenues "like a plump white bulldog." Wooden Queen Annes, Romanesque sandstones, red-brick faux châteaus with fairy-tale towers, and Renaissance palazzos lined the avenue—"a museum of American architectural failures," in his words.

As a child, Fitzgerald mingled with children whose surnames were the same as the streets on which they played—Griggs and MacKubin and Hersey. It was a good time and a good place to grow up. Scott and his companions saw the coming of the automobile and the airplane, the spread of electric lights and the telephone, and for a nickel they could pass an enchanted hour watching the first movies. Nearby, there were still fields to race across and woods in which to gather chestnuts. These were America's "Confident Years" in which Theodore Roosevelt fought trusts and political bosses at home, made the dirt fly on the Panama Canal, and sent the U.S. Navy's white-hulled battleships around the world.

Fitzgerald went to tea dances at the University Club up Summit Avenue and was invited to parties given by the daughter of James J. Hill, the railroad magnate, at her family's nearby thirty-two-room mansion. In later years Fitzgerald was contemptuous of the Summit, but there was a touch of envy in his feelings, for his family had only a tenuous hold on St. Paul society. Throughout his life, he was always haunted by the terror of slipping from the comfortable assurance of this world into poverty.

Edward Fitzgerald, his father, had claim to a past that was brighter than his present. A small, dapper man with a Vandyke and courtly manners, he had come to Minnesota from Maryland, where his family had been prominent in colonial times. Francis Scott Key, the author of "The Star-Spangled Banner," for whom he named his son, was a remote cousin of his mother, but by the elder Fitzgerald's time, the bloodline had thinned. He ran a wicker furniture business and in 1890 married Mary McQuillan, the daughter of a prosperous Irish wholesale grocer. Not long after the couple married, their misfortunes began. The Fitzgeralds' first two children, both girls, died in epidemics, and shortly after Scott's birth, in 1896, the wicker business failed.

Fortunes diminished, the elder Fitzgerald became a salesman for Procter & Gamble and peddled soap powder and other products to stores in various upstate New York towns. He enjoyed only a modest success and the morning mail often contained bills that he crumpled and threw down with a grunted "Confound it." Scott was twelve when his father, then in his fifties, lost even that job. "Dear God," Fitzgerald remembered praying, "please don't let us go to the poorhouse; please don't let us go to the poorhouse." The Fitzgeralds returned to St. Paul, where the family resources lay, to become pensioners of the McQuillans.

A rich maiden aunt paid Scott's tuition at Newman, a Catholic prep school in New Jersey, and at Princeton. Only a few years before, Woodrow Wilson, the university's president, had vainly tried to democratize the school by closing the exclusive eating clubs, but Princeton was "the pleasantest country club in America" according to Fitzgerald. Although he was a Midwesterner, he wasn't a Jew or a "poler," as grinds were known, and made Cottage, one of the more socially select clubs. At the induction party, he passed out cold for the first time in his life. With his friend Edmund Wilson he wrote skits and lyrics for Triangle Club musicals, flounced on stage as a chorus girl, and contributed to *The Tiger* and *Nassau Lit.* He neglected his studies, but had larger horizons. "I want to be one of the greatest writers who have ever lived, don't you?" he remarked to Wilson.

Fitzgerald was infatuated with Ginevra King, a beautiful debutante from Lake Forest, outside Chicago. "Flirt smiled from her large black-brown eyes," he later wrote of Ginevra's fictional counterpart. But their relationship was troubled. At a house party in Lake Forest, Fitzgerald overheard someone say, "Poor boys shouldn't think of marrying rich girls." Before long, Ginevra's letters grew less frequent and then stopped altogether. Soon after, she married a man who owned a string of polo ponies. Fitzgerald never forgot Ginevra King—he saved all her letters—and Jay Gatsby's timeless love for Daisy Fay, who also married a man with a string of polo ponies, undoubtedly had its roots in his memory of her.

On academic probation and unlikely to graduate, Fitzgerald was rescued by America's entry into World War I. He obtained a commission as a second lieutenant in the army, and went to war in a trim uniform tailored by Brooks Brothers. He reported to Fort Leavenworth, Kansas, for training, where the captain in charge of his company was a West Pointer with a broad grin named Dwight D. Eisenhower. Fitzgerald envisioned himself as a war hero, but was an inept soldier. He bumbled through close-order drill, slept during lectures on "Trench Behavior" and "The Lewis Gun," and claimed with some justification to be "the world's worst second lieutenant."

Weekends were spent in a corner of the officers club, where amid smoke, conversation, and rattling newspapers, he labored over a novel, *The Romantic Egoist,* that he had started at Princeton. In a hospital in Italy, nineteen-year-old Ernest Hemingway struggled to recover the use of a leg shattered by an Austrian mortar shell and read and reread the words a British officer had written out for him on a slip of paper: "By my troth, I care not; a man can die but once, we owe God a death. . . . He that dies this year is quit for the next." In France, Private John Dos Passos, U.S. Army Medical Corps, carried away "buckets full of amputated arms and hands and legs from an operating room." And in Baltimore, Henry L. Mencken tapped out the opening chapter of *The American Language* on his battered Corona while trucks rumbled under the window of his row house on Union Square day and night, carrying the victims of an influenza pandemic to the cemeteries.

Fitzgerald, overcome by the conviction that he was going to be killed in the war like the British poet Rupert Brooke, saw his book as a chance to leave a record behind. "I lived in the smeary pencil pages" of the novel, he recalled. "The drills, marches and Small Problems for Infantry were a shadowy dream. My whole heart was concentrated upon my book." He sent the manuscript to Scribners, who rejected it, but he received an encouraging letter from Maxwell Perkins, a young editor, suggesting revisions that might make the book acceptable.

In the summer of 1918, Fitzgerald was ordered to Camp Sheridan, just outside Montgomery, Alabama. Blond hair parted in two wings over his almost girlish features, and wearing the whipcord riding breeches and shiny boots of a general's aide, he cut a handsome figure. He met Zelda Sayre, the spoiled daughter of an Alabama Supreme Court judge, at a country club dance. She was, he told a friend, "the prettiest girl in Alabama *and* Georgia." There was something golden about her. At eighteen, Zelda—named for a Gypsy queen who had turned up in her mother's reading—had a mass of honey-colored hair, a lilting grace, and a sparkling deviltry in her eye. If a dance was dull, she would turn cartwheels around the floor to liven things up.

She was popular—the student pilots at a nearby airfield courted her by stunting their planes over her house—but soon Fitzgerald monopolized the Sayres' porch swing. He read Zelda some of his stories and part of the novel he was revising and assured her that one day he would be a famous writer. He loved her from their first meeting for her beauty, her daring, and her originality, and she was in love with him. Ever the romantic, Fitzgerald hoped to impress her with the heroic deeds he intended to perform in France, but the war ended just as his unit was being marched up the gangplank of a transport. And Scribners again rejected his novel.

Following his discharge from the army in February 1919, Fitzgerald asked Zelda to marry him, but she was reluctant to commit herself because of his lack of money and prospects. To improve them, he joined his literary friends from Princeton in New York. With a sheaf of stories under his arm, he made the rounds of the city's newspapers in search of a job as a reporter so he could "trail murderers by day and do short stories by night." No one was impressed. Fitzgerald took a position as a $90-a-month copywriter at an advertising agency, less than his army pay. His biggest success was a slogan for the Muscatine Steam Laundry in Muscatine, Iowa: "We keep you clean in Muscatine."

Bored, Fitzgerald lived in one room in "a high horrible apartment house" on Claremont Avenue in Morningside Heights, lusting after success and his elusive Southern belle. In March, he sent Zelda an engagement ring that had been his mother's. The weeks of separation stretched into months. And the stories Fitzgerald ground out in his spare time failed to sell. Every evening he raced back to his dreary room hoping to find a letter from Montgomery, only to be greeted by a fresh pile of rejected manuscripts. Soon, he had a frieze of 122 rejection slips pinned about his room. Not one contained a personal note or a word of encouragement. In June, Fitzgerald finally sold a story, "Babes in the Woods," to *The Smart Set*, which under Henry Mencken and George Jean Nathan was the liveliest magazine in America, for which he received $30. But he got little cheer from it because the story was a rewrite of one previously printed in *The List*. He spent the money on a pair of white flannels.

Mencken met Fitzgerald for the first time at a party at Nathan's apartment in the Hotel Royalton, a center of the city's artistic life. "He was a slim, blond young fellow, tall and straight in build and so handsome that he might even have been called beautiful," the editor wrote in his memoirs. "I well recall that he was still so full of Army ways when we first met, and so shy a young fellow by nature, that he not only misterred Nathan and me but also sirred us."

Unhappy with his progress, Fitzgerald suddenly announced, while lunching one day with friends at the Yale Club, that he was going to jump out the window. No one made an effort to restrain him; in fact, he was cheerfully assured that the floor-to-ceiling French windows were ideally suited for jumping. Fitzgerald quickly thought better of his proposal. Prohibition was not to begin until January 1920, and he haunted the Red Room of the Plaza and the Biltmore Bar and went to "lush and liquid garden parties in the East Sixties" with fellow Ivy Leaguers, debutantes, and party girls.

Like many provincials from "the vast obscurity beyond the city," he was enraptured by the texture and glitter of New York, of youthful forms leaning together in taxis at twilight and tea dances where the bodies "drifted here and there like rose petals blown by the sad horns around the floor." For the young man from St. Paul, the city was the fulfillment of all his dreams of glamour and money. Years later, Fitzgerald recalled that New York in 1919 "had all the iridescence of the beginning of the world."

The curtain was rising on the Jazz Age, the decade Fitzgerald named and was to make his own. Skirts were going up, young women were drinking in public, painting their faces, and puffing defiantly, if awkwardly, on cigarettes, and "all night the saxophones wailed the hopeless comment of the 'Beale Street Blues' in Harlem." Fitzgerald later wrote that the Jazz Age began at about the time of some anti-Socialist riots on May Day 1919, inspiring cynicism about a war that had not ended all wars and had not made the world safe for democracy. But he was basically apolitical even though he professed a naive Socialism, and an all-night spree of his own is a better benchmark for the beginning of the age he would chronicle.

Following an interfraternity dance at Delmonico's, the crowd adjourned to Childs all-night restaurant, on Broadway, to sober up. At first, Fitzgerald sat in a corner intently mixing hash, poached eggs, and ketchup in a derby belonging to Porter Gillespie, a Princeton friend. Next, he felt the urge to climb up on a table to make a speech and was ejected by the management. Each time the revolving door opened, he tried to sneak back in on his hands and knees. With dawn coming, Fitzgerald and Gillespie returned to Delmonico's where they appropriated the "In" and "Out" signs from the swinging men's room doors, fixed them to their stiff shirtfronts, and drunkenly insisted on introducing each other as "Mr. In" and "Mr. Out."

Then they were off in search of champagne for Sunday morning breakfast. "You buy it," Fitzgerald told Gillespie. "Your father has the money to pay for it." They were refused at several hotel bars but finally got some at the Commodore and ended up rolling the empty bottles among the legs of the early morning churchgoers on Fifth Avenue. In after years, Fitzgerald put the antics of "Mr. In" and "Mr. Out" into one of his best stories, "May Day," which also caught his feelings of frustration and failure at the time.

Not long afterward, Fitzgerald went down to Montgomery where Zelda, who had had enough of an engagement that looked every day less and less likely to lead to marriage, gave him back his ring. Fitzgerald received the blow poorly. "He seized her in his arms and tried literally to kiss her into marrying him at once," he later wrote in a story called "'The Sensible Thing,'" which incorporated his own experience. "When this failed, he broke into a long monologue of self-pity, and ceased only when he saw that he was making himself despicable in her sight." Zelda saw him off at the train station and he climbed into a Pullman; as soon as she was out of sight, he switched to a day coach, all he could afford.

Back in New York, Fitzgerald borrowed from classmates and went on a "roaring, weeping" three-week drunk. "I was a failure—mediocre at advertising work and unable to get started as a writer," he declared. Sheer physical exhaustion put an end to the binge but it had "done its business; he was over the first flush of pain" at Zelda's decision to drop him. "Since I last saw you," he wrote Edmund Wilson, "I've tried to get married and drink myself to death."

Fitzgerald quit his advertising job with relief and left for St. Paul early in July to rewrite *The Romantic Egoist* with the hope of producing a best-seller, win back Zelda, and become rich. His parents disapproved of his writing ambitions. His mother had hoped he would make a career of the army and his father wanted him to go into business. They were deeply disappointed when he turned down the offer of a "real" job as advertising manager of a St. Paul department store. Yet when he skipped meals they left sandwiches and milk at the door of his room and took his telephone calls so his friends would not distract him. Still, they kept the purse strings tight, fearing he might take off on some fresh escapade.

Working around the clock, Fitzgerald ripped the old manuscript apart. Cigarette stubs overflowed the ashtrays onto the floor of his room. When he ran out, he salvaged butts and relit them. He ruthlessly lopped out chapters and scrawled new ones in pencil. From the beginning, he seemed to write effectively only about himself and those he knew. He threw in elements of previous stories, sketches, and even a one-act play, causing a cynical friend to call the book "The Collected Works of F. Scott Fitzgerald." In the process, he developed an easy narrative style that was rich with images, a sense of comedy, and natural dialogue.

Now retitled *This Side of Paradise*, the novel is the story of Amory Blaine, who bears a sharp resemblance to his creator. Like Fitzgerald, Amory enjoys the gaiety of undergraduate life at Princeton, serves in the army, and writes advertising copy in New York while on a journey from youth to maturity. "I know myself but that is all," he proclaims in his valedictory. Rosalind Connage, Amory's great love, has touches of Zelda Sayre—"glorious yellow hair . . . the eternal kissable mouth, small, slightly sensual, and utterly disturbing . . . gray eyes, and an unimpeachable skin with two spots of vanishing color"—and she rejects Amory because he has no money. In Rosalind, Fitzgerald created the flapper: bright, beautiful, and possessing a sure sense of how to handle her men. Her tragedy was that almost any day now, she might find herself twenty rather than nineteen.

Once the manuscript was typed, Fitzgerald sent it to Max Perkins on September 3, and while waiting to hear from him, went to work roofing freight cars at the shops of the Northern Pacific Railroad. Told to wear old clothes, he showed up for work in a polo shirt and dirty white flannels, exotic gear to the other laborers. Fitzgerald's railroad career did not last long. On September 16—eight days before his twenty-third birthday—he received a special delivery letter from Perkins telling him *This Side of Paradise* had been accepted for publication. "The book is so different that it is hard to prophesy how it will sell but we are all for taking a chance and supporting it with vigor," wrote the editor.

Intoxicated, but not on alcohol, Fitzgerald dashed out into Summit

Avenue to stop pedestrians and cars and tell everyone about his good fortune. It was just the beginning. Over the next few months, his life became the concrete expression of the American Dream of easy, overnight success that is a persistent theme of the Jazz Age. He married his girl, magazine editors clamored for his stories—some even bought those they had previously rejected—and *This Side of Paradise* was adopted by his contemporaries as their Bible. The first printing sold out in twenty-four hours.

The book is flawed by a haphazard framework, the author's borrowing from other coming-of-age novels is readily apparent, its characters are inconsistent, and the writing uneven, yet it captures the rhythm and feel of its era. Flippant, ironic in tone, and drenched in alcohol and an innocent sexuality, it consigned the remnants of Victorian morality to oblivion and gave voice to the attitudes, pleasures, and self-doubts of "a new generation . . . grown up to find all Gods dead, all wars fought, all faiths in man shaken."

As he and Zelda set up housekeeping at the Biltmore in March 1920, Scott Fitzgerald sensed a new world coming. "America," he said, "was going on the greatest, gaudiest spree in history." Money, mobility, and celebrity would be the motifs of the age and it would have a perverse duality: innocent yet worldly, sentimental yet dissipated, idealistic yet cynical.

And he would be there to tell all about it.

CHAPTER I

"The Personal Instrument of God"

Wearing an old golf cap, Woodrow Wilson watched with his wife, Edith, from the bridge of the troopship *George Washington* as the pewter gray towers of Manhattan faded into the winter mists. It was December 18, 1918, little more than a month after the Armistice. Large crowds cheered the president as he left for a peace conference in Paris that was to create the new world eagerly awaited by Scott Fitzgerald and his generation. Hundreds of vessels sounded their whistles in an impromptu salute as the former German liner passed the Statue of Liberty. Six escorting U.S. Navy destroyers took up station as the huge ship reached the open Atlantic and picked up speed.

For a day, the ocean was rough and the weather boisterous, but after the *George Washington* entered the Gulf Stream, conditions moderated. Under the advice of his personal physician, Rear Admiral Cary T. Grayson, every day Wilson walked two miles about the promenade deck with the first lady at his side. Wilson's long-jawed, long-toothed face often cracked into a smile at some joke she made. A small boy, the son of the Italian ambassador, jumped up from his deck chair and briskly saluted each time the couple passed. Wilson soon assured the lad that one salute a day was enough.

Wilson and Edith Bolling Galt had married only three years before, having met following the death in 1914 of the president's first wife, the gentle Ellen Wilson. Sometimes he called Edith, sixteen years his junior, "Little Girl." The second Mrs. Wilson was a descendant of Pocahontas and the widow of a wealthy Washington jeweler.* Stylishly dressed by Worth of

---

* There was unsubstantiated gossip that she had been the mistress of the swashbuckling German ambassador, Count Johann von Bernstorff.

Paris, statuesque and vivacious, she brought a new lightness into the former professor's arid life. An amused Secret Service man reported seeing the prim Wilson leap into the air the morning after the wedding, click his heels, and burst into the popular song "Oh, You Beautiful Doll."

Wilson was the first American president to leave the Western Hemisphere while in office. Lifeboat drills and the threat of floating mines added spice to the voyage. Enjoying his moments of leisure, he put off a meeting with "the Inquiry," the group of scholars who had produced nearly two thousand reports for him on subjects likely to come up at the peace conference, until the ship was steaming past the green slopes of the Azores.

The Virginia-born Wilson was the product of two centuries of Calvinist divines. He grew up steeped in righteousness and exuded moral certainty. Wilson's father had wished his son to follow him into the Presbyterian ministry, but the young man's own ideal was William Ewart Gladstone, the British statesman and prime minister. As a child, he had practiced speechmaking before the empty pews of his father's church so he could bring great thoughts to the world. Wilson briefly practiced law and yearned for a political career but, lacking the stomach for the rough and tumble of politics, switched to teaching government and history, first at Johns Hopkins, then Bryn Mawr and Wesleyan and finally Princeton, his alma mater.

Wilson's efforts as Princeton's president to democratize the university were well publicized and in 1910, New Jersey's Democratic bosses, looking for a reformer as a front man, picked him as their gubernatorial candidate. Two years later, he was elected president when former president Theodore Roosevelt, convinced that William Howard Taft, his conservative successor, was undoing the progressive reforms made during his administration, tried to recapture the White House on the third-party Bull Moose ticket and split the Republican vote.

The Wilson administration represented the full flowering of the Progressive Era—that extraordinary wave of reform that swept the United States in the early years of the twentieth century. Although he had denounced Roosevelt's platform as dangerously radical, Wilson boldly hijacked most of it. Much to the anger of the Rough Rider, he made it the heart of his own plan for reform, the New Freedom. The Federal Reserve System, the Federal Trade Commission, lower tariffs, the income tax, direct election of U.S. senators, and votes for women—all the things reformers had long dreamed about—were enacted into law during his first term or were on the verge of approval. On the other hand, Wilson, who had grown up in the post–Civil War South, was a disappointment to American blacks. Although he had told them during the campaign that "they may count upon me for absolute fair dealing," he brought racial segregation to the federal government offices in Washington where clerks of both races had previously worked together without friction. And he dismissed every black holding a postmastership in the South on grounds that no white man should be forced to work for a black.

Socialists, anarchists, social workers, suffragettes, feminists, union organizers—reformers of every stripe—thrived in the progressive years. They spoke in terms of crusades and used words like "sinful," "wicked," and "obligation." With evangelical fervor, they waged campaigns against predatory monopolies, corrupt political machines, foul tenements, tainted food and drugs, and the evils of alcohol and child labor. The progressives created the modern state, which regulated corporations, directed the economy, and protected the interests of workers and consumers against the excesses of capitalism.*

Free-wheeling young Americans—the "moderns"—sloughed off Victorian prudery in literature, psychology, drama, and art. "Realism" was an agent of social protest. New magazines, from the Socialist *Masses* to the arty *Dial*, mixed politics and literature. Literary clubs, little theaters, and experimental schools were organized all over the country. Alfred Stieglitz's "291" gallery on the top floor of a Fifth Avenue brownstone and the Armory Show of 1913 introduced Americans to the latest art forms from Europe and the United States and signaled the decline of traditional painting and sculpture. People came to "291" to see "the craziest painters in America" and Stieglitz hectored them into becoming believers in modern art. He exhibited the work of John Marin, Abraham Walkowitz, Max Weber, Marsden Hartley, and Arthur Dove, among others. Without subsidies from Stieglitz and his friends, many of these artists would have starved.

Young people from all over the country flocked to a colorful bohemia that flourished in the neighborhood below Washington Square known as Greenwich Village, where they were free "to be themselves." Back alley

---

* By 1920 progressivism was largely a spent force for reasons still debated by historians. Its achievements proved to be ambiguous, contradictory, and often disappointing. A handful of giant companies continued to dominate the American economy. Unsympathetic to unions, the progressives left in place legal barriers that blocked the right of labor to organize until the New Deal. Regulation created a new class of bureaucrats and highly organized interest groups. And the reforms intended to curb the power of the political bosses—the referendum, initiative, and primaries—perversely increased the influence of big money and mass media on politics. Unsatisfied by the accomplishments of the progressives, the New Dealers who followed saw their task as nothing less than the redistribution of wealth.

stables became studios and decayed mansions with surrealistic plumbing provided rookeries for artists, writers, and radicals. A furnished hall-bedroom could be rented for $2 or $3 a week. Long-haired men and short-haired women pursued free love, free speech, Socialism, and politically engaged art, while joyfully assaulting the bedrock values of bourgeois culture.

Looking homeward from Europe, Idaho-born Ezra Pound foresaw an American cultural upheaval that would "make the Italian Renaissance look like a tempest in a teapot." Isadora Duncan was revolutionizing dance. Georgia O'Keeffe made an impression not only as a painter but as a model for Stieglitz's photographs and later became his wife. The American theater was infused with a fresh energy when the Provincetown Playhouse presented the early one-act plays of Eugene O'Neill in an old stable in MacDougal Street. Pretty, redheaded Edna St. Vincent Millay came down from Vassar to flout convention in her life and poetry and to burn her candle at both ends. Bohemian women slept with men they had no intention of marrying—and with other women, too. Margaret Sanger, fresh from prison where she had been jailed for propagandizing for birth control, extolled the joys of the flesh and ridiculed the traditional sense of sin. Gay men and lesbians were prominent in Village culture although male homosexuals were still largely closeted. Sigmund Freud's studies of dreams and the unconscious were endlessly discussed—if not completely understood. The idea of free love was so prevalent that one bohemian couple was too embarrassed to tell friends they were married.

The Village attracted the aspiring, the ambitious, the angry, the exhibitionist, the curious, and those along for the ride. Ideas and ambitions clashed at the tables in Polly Holliday's restaurant and in saloons like the Working Girls' Home and at the salon of wealthy Mabel Dodge, a pretty, plump heiress from Buffalo who originated "radical chic." Both the Armory Show and a giant pageant held in Madison Square Garden to dramatize a strike in the silk mills of Paterson, New Jersey, were incubated in Mrs. Dodge's drawing room at 23 Fifth Avenue.

Frequent guests at her "evenings" included muckraker Lincoln Steffens, and his protégés Walter Lippmann and John Reed (soon to be the hostess's bedmate), both of the Harvard class of 1910;* gnomelike Dr. A. A. Brill, Freud's leading disciple in the United States; Eugene O'Neill; Floyd Dell, chronicler of Village life and loves; one-eyed "Big Bill" Haywood, leader of

---

* Other members of this class included poet Alan Seeger, who found his "rendezvous with death" as a Foreign Legionnaire in France in 1916; poet T. S. Eliot; radical journalist Heywood Broun; and Hamilton Fish, later a reactionary congressman and longtime political thorn in the side of his Dutchess County neighbor, Franklin D. Roosevelt.

the radical Industrial Workers of the World, and his companion, fiery labor organizer Elizabeth Gurley Flynn; Emma Goldman, anarchist and advocate of free love; Randolph Bourne, the hideously deformed but brilliant conversationalist and essayist; artists; Vassar girls; poets; stage designers; and those who came merely for the food and drink. "Whether in literature, plastic art, the labor movement . . . we find an instinct to loosen up the old forms and traditions, to dynamite the baked and hardened earth so that fresh flowers can grow," proclaimed the writer Hutchins Hapgood. But American society could not sustain, for more than a limited time, the tension and turbulence of reform. Some of these romantic rebels were to be buried in the wreckage.

In the West, the IWW was active among the bindle stiffs, loggers, silver and copper miners, and other members of the postfrontier underclass. Unlike the conservative American Federation of Labor, an organization of craft unions and skilled workers, the IWW supported the idea of "one big union" in which in all workers, both skilled and unskilled, would be united. Mainstream Americans, however, were badly frightened by the Wobblies'* rhetoric of class warfare and reputation for violence.

Europe, in these same years, enjoyed unprecedented growth and prosperity, a circumstance made possible by an equally unprecedented degree of cooperation and integration of the economies of the major nations of the Continent and the United States. Political leaders, industrialists, intellectuals, and ordinary citizens all agreed that such cooperation made war impossible. Nevertheless, William James, the American philosopher, warned in his 1910 essay "The Moral Equivalent of War" that "modern man inherits all the innate pugnacity and all the love of glory as his ancestors." In August 1914, the wisdom of James's observation was proven when young men in European countries eagerly trooped to the recruiting stations as if they were going to a sports event.

In the United States, progressive intellectuals, as the self-appointed custodians of ideals and fundamental moral principles, were shocked by the unstoppable rush to war in Europe. The Europeans, said the New York Times on August 2, 1914, seemed to have "reverted to the condition of savage tribes." Few ordinary Americans were concerned with the outbreak of war, however. They were engrossed in the exploits of the Boston Braves, who were in last place in the National League on July 4, and then went on to win the pennant.

* The name is said to have originated when a Chinese laundryman pronounced IWW as "I Wobble Wobble."

Wilson, faithful to his party's traditional isolationism, opposed American intervention in the struggle, fearing that militarism would infringe upon the campaign for reform. Power must yield to morality, he said, and armed conflict to the force of public opinion. The tide turned when huge British and French orders for American war matériel and foodstuffs financed by private bankers—the so-called Morgan loans—boosted the depressed economy and, together with Allied propaganda about supposed German atrocities, created public sympathy for the Allied cause. Wilson continued to oppose intervention and was narrowly reelected in 1916 with the campaign slogan "He Kept Us out of War." But in April 1917, in the face of repeated German violations of American neutrality, he led the nation into the conflict "to make the world safe for democracy"—just in time to prevent the defeat of the exhausted British and French.

A mobilization designed to harness the nation's immense and sprawling economy to the needs of war created a revolution that fulfilled progressive dreams. New federal agencies regulated industry, agriculture, and the railroads, reined in the power of capital, and augmented the rights of labor—causing establishment intellectuals such as John Dewey to support the war. The war, he said, would bring about the "democratization of industry." The Food Administration, headed by Herbert C. Hoover, a brilliant mining engineer, directed the production and distribution of prodigious amounts of food. William G. McAdoo, Wilson's son-in-law and treasury secretary, overhauled the chaotic rail industry. Labor won the right to collective bargaining and an eight-hour day.

World War I was the great turning point of modern history. Over 15 million lives were lost in the struggle, including those of about 130,000 Americans. The universal presumptions of the Victorian Age—progress, order, and culture—were blown to bits. For those who had endured the savagery of the fighting and those who lost husbands, fathers, brothers, lovers, and friends, life would never be the same again. The war ushered in a world of violent change that produced the leviathan state, consumerism, mass culture and mass communications, and the global economy—an era in which America would be supreme.

With Germany's defeat looming in 1918, Wilson envisioned a liberal peace, a peace without victory, a peace that would restore Germany to its rightful place in a world of free trade and international harmony. It would be capped by an international organization—the League of Nations—to provide collective security and prevent future wars. Essentially, Wilson's plan—the Fourteen Points—was designed to project abroad the progressive and reformist ideals of the New Freedom. America, said Wilson, "is the only idealistic nation in the world," implying that the world should be remade in the American image. Wilson was also determined to prevent the spread of Bolshevism, which had seized power in Russia in November 1917 after the overthrow of the Czarist regime.

To millions of Americans war's end meant the completion of a great and noble task and the beginning of a bright future. "You carry with you the hearts and hopes and dreams and desires of millions of your fellow Americans," Stockton Axson, the brother of Wilson's first wife, wrote him as he departed for Paris. "Your vision of the new world that should spring from the ashes of the old is all that had made the world tolerable to many of us. That vision has removed the sting, has filled our imaginations, and had made the war not a tragedy but a sacrament. Nothing but a new world is worth the purchase price of a war."

Unhappily, victory fed Wilson's messianism and he had already betrayed these dreams. Although aides advised him to remain at home to avoid being pressured into hasty decisions, he insisted on going to Paris. And rejecting the political bipartisanship that had prevailed during the war, Wilson shocked the Republicans by calling for the election of a Democratic Congress in 1918 to give him a free hand in making the peace. The nation would have been far better served had Wilson asked for a bipartisan Congress of both Democrats and Republicans who would support him.

Speaking for the angry Republicans, Theodore Roosevelt rose from his sickbed to address a rally at Carnegie Hall in New York City on October 28, 1918, in which he attacked Wilson for ignoring the loyal opposition in the peacemaking process. "We can pay with the blood of our hearts' dearest, but that is all we are to be allowed," thundered the former president, whose own youngest son, Quentin, had been killed in an air battle over France only a few months before.

Roosevelt, stung by Wilson's refusal to allow him to lead a volunteer division like the Rough Riders to France as well as the pirating of his 1912 platform, had earlier denounced Wilson's "peace without victory." He urged Congress to pass a resolution demanding the unconditional surrender of Germany because it would "safeguard the world for at least a generation to come from another attempt by the Germans to secure world domination." Roosevelt was cautiously affirmative about the League of Nations—but with reservations that would prevent any international body from overriding the Constitution and such fundamental principles of American nationalism as the Monroe Doctrine. In his speech accepting the Nobel Peace Prize for his efforts to end the Russo-Japanese War, he had proposed a League of Peace that foreshadowed Wilson's League of Nations, but little attention had been paid to it at the time.

Wilson was rebuked at the polls in November as the Republicans narrowly won control of both houses of Congress—the Senate by only a single vote. Henry Ford, the automobile magnate, who had run as a pro-League Democrat in Michigan at Wilson's personal request, lost the race by only eight thousand votes.* Had Ford won, the Senate would have been tied forty-eight to forty-eight and the vice president, Thomas R. Marshall, a Democrat, would have cast the deciding vote. The Senate Foreign Relations Committee, which made recommendations to the full Senate on all treaties, would have had a Democratic chairman and majority.

The president's usually shrewd political judgment failed him. Rather than conciliating the opposition, he obstinately refused even to include pro-League Republicans such as former President William H. Taft and ex–Secretary of State Elihu Root in the American delegation to Paris. In the words of his principal biographer, Arthur S. Link, he acted "like a divine-right monarch in the conduct of foreign affairs."†

As Wilson boarded the *George Washington*, Roosevelt's imprecations resounded about his head. "Mr. Wilson has no authority whatever to speak for the American people. His leadership has just been emphatically repudiated by them." It was the old lion's last roar. Worn out by sixty years of strenuous living, Roosevelt died peacefully in his sleep on January 6, 1919. "Death had to take him sleeping," said Vice President Marshall, "for if Roosevelt had been awake, there would have been a fight." Wilson's reaction to his great rival's death, noted a reporter, was surprise, then pity, and finally "transcendent triumph."

Woodrow Wilson may have suffered a setback at home, but in Europe he was greeted by frenzied throngs who hailed him as the champion of justice

---

* In 1915, Ford, a pacifist, fell under the spell of Rosika Schwimmer, an eccentric peace activist, and announced that he was going to personally end the war and "get the boys out of the trenches by Christmas." Although he had no support from any government, Ford chartered a "peace ship" and sailed for Europe to petition for "continuous mediation." No one took his mission seriously—a wag let loose a pair of squirrels on the vessel as it sailed to symbolize the "nuts" on board. The fiasco undoubtedly cost Ford votes in 1918 and, hurt and humiliated, he blamed the failure of his peace mission and ensuing political defeat on Madame Schwimmer, a Jew. Some authorities trace his virulent public anti-Semitism to this incident.

† Link was once asked if he liked Wilson after spending years writing his multivolume biography. "I respected him," was the reply. "But did you like him?" pressed his interrogator. "I respected him," said Link.

and the apostle of peace. In remote villages, peasants burned candles before his picture. A hundred thousand people packed the Place de la Concorde in front of the Hôtel de Crillon, the headquarters of the American delegation in Paris, to cheer him, many waving tiny American flags. A U.S. Army captain named Harry S Truman later said he never again saw anything like the welcome the French gave Wilson in 1919. Critics grumbled, however, that this acclaim only fed the president's vanity and messiah complex.

Paris was in a carnival mood. The city teemed with supplicants and suitors: Macedonians, Serbs, Croats, Slovenes, Slovaks and Czechs, Arabs in flowing robes shepherded by a craggy-faced little Englishman named Lawrence; Zionists, Armenians, Azerbaijanis, and tiny men from Indochina with wispy beards—all wishing something at the expense of their neighbors. The world tingled with expectation as it awaited for a new age to be born in the Salon de l'Horloge, the gathering place of the victorious Allied leaders. Europe was in chaos. The kaiser had fled into exile; Russia was convulsed by civil war; the Hapsburgs had been deposed; and the Ottoman Empire had collapsed. Famine, typhus, and cholera stalked the Continent and the pandemic of Spanish flu that killed hundreds of thousands of people around the globe was in its final stages. And the red cloud of Bolshevism was spreading westward. "The wolf is at the door," warned Herbert Hoover, who had the task of caring for Europe's starving and dispossessed. Short-lived Communist regimes seized power in Hungary and Bavaria and the Bolsheviks boasted that all Europe would be Communist within a year.

With the intention of isolating the bacillus of Bolshevism, the Allies dispatched troops to northern Russia and Siberia to intervene in the civil war on the side of the White counterrevolutionaries. On Armistice Day 1918, a sizable contingent of American, British, and Canadian troops clashed with Red soldiers near Archangel with heavy casualties. Allied troops remained in the Soviet Union until the counterrevolution collapsed in April 1920. About 150 Americans were killed during this misadventure and it was a source of lasting hostility between the Soviets and the West.

Tension quickly flared between Wilson and the other members of the "Big Four"—David Lloyd George of Britain, Georges Clemenceau of France, and Vittorio Orlando of Italy. No agenda had been established but the American president wanted the Covenant of the League of Nations— the organization's constitution—to be the conference's first order of business. Wilson feared that if the League was not adopted early on, it would be lost in the scramble for spoils. He saw the League in apocalyptic terms—

not as a step on the road to an ultimate world order but as an effort to remake the world itself.

Wilson's partners misinterpreted his words and actions, believing they were merely intended for show. More interested in dividing up the booty of war—reparations and Germany's colonies—than the League and peace without victory, the Allied leaders were shocked and surprised to discover that Wilson actually meant what he was saying. In character, thought, and temperament, he was not so much a lawyer, a scholar, or a politician as he was, like his forebears, a theologian, and he wrapped his mission to Paris in a religious and moral intensity.

To the other leaders, he appeared priggish and self-righteous and set on crushing his opponents if he could not convince them. Wilson's great failure in Paris was his inability to understand that the art of diplomacy consists of trying to convince the other fellow that all parties to a negotiation share a common interest rather than browbeating him into submission. Wilson sacrificed considerable bargaining strength in making the League Covenant the first order of business.

Despite the promise of the Fourteen Points, with its declaration of "open covenants . . . openly arrived at," the conference met behind closed doors, and the outside world knew next to nothing of its proceedings. Each nation had its own selfish aims, most of them mutually conflicting. A good number of the Fourteen Points were ignored, violated, or compromised. Wilson tacitly accepted several "secret treaties" signed by the Allies before America entered the war that divided the spoils, although he later denied it. The haggling was intense, worse than any Congress. Sometimes, the Allied leaders met for eighteen hours on end, often holding meetings on different subjects at once in different rooms, arguing with one another as they rotated between them. As the debate dragged on, the German people continued to suffer because of the continuation of the wartime starvation blockade.

Even as Wilson was playing midwife to the difficult birth of the League, he was inundated with demands from the United States where inflation, ugly race riots, and strikes raged. Hatreds whipped up by the wartime demand for "100 percent Americanism" and fear of a Bolshevik revolution spawned a suspicion of foreigners and radicals that became known as the Red Scare. "Come home and reduce the high cost of living," cabled twenty Massachusetts state legislators. West Coast residents demanded that Japanese immigration be halted. From wives, mothers, and sweethearts came calls for the two million American troops overseas to be brought home immediately and for an end to wartime restrictions.

On February 14, 1919, Wilson appeared before the full conference to triumphantly read the Covenant of the League of Nations. "A living thing is born," he declared. That night the exhausted president boarded the *George Washington* at Brest to report to the American people and to be on hand for the opening of the new Sixty-fifth—and Republican-controlled—Congress. The ship also carried a full load of returning soldiers. Unlike the passage to France, the weather was bad and the ship rolled and pitched her way across the Atlantic.

Among the bystanders watching the negotiations were Assistant Secretary of the Navy Franklin D. Roosevelt and his wife, Eleanor. Roosevelt was returning home on the *George Washington* after overseeing the disposal of navy surplus property in Britain and France. He was a distant cousin of Theodore Roosevelt and his wife was the Rough Rider's niece.

Franklin Roosevelt hoped to discuss the Covenant with the president, but Wilson and his wife kept to themselves during most of the voyage. Eventually, the Roosevelts were invited to lunch in the presidential cabin. The conversation turned to the League of Nations and Wilson made a remark that the younger man never forgot: "The United States must go in or it will break the heart of the world, for she is the only nation that all feel is disinterested and all trust." Roosevelt learned an important lesson from Wilson's failures: foreign policy cannot be carried out in a partisan manner. When World War II approached, he brought Republican elders into his cabinet and the Republicans were encouraged to participate in creating the United Nations.

The day before the *George Washington* was due to arrive in Boston, fog rolled in and the navigator was unable to make out her position. Suddenly, bells sounded throughout the ship and the engines were put full astern. "We are almost on the beach!" someone told Mrs. Roosevelt. Legend has it that her husband dashed to the bridge and took over the helm of the *George Washington* and steered the vessel to safety, but his role was far less dramatic. Finding the ship's officers confused by the sighting of land where no land was supposed to be, Roosevelt, an experienced yachtsman familiar with these waters, said they were near Marblehead—and when the fog lifted it was discovered he was correct. The great ship and its accompanying destroyers had nearly run aground just off Cape Ann.

Wilson received a tumultuous greeting in Boston. "We could see the President and Mrs. Wilson ahead of us, the President standing up and waving his hat at intervals to the crowds which lined the streets," reported Mrs. Roosevelt, who rode with her husband a few cars back in line. "Everyone was wildly enthusiastic." Even the Republican governor of Massachusetts, the stone-faced Calvin Coolidge, was "sure the people would back the President" on the League.

Wilson confronted his critics for the first time at a White House dinner for the congressional committees dealing with foreign affairs on February 26, at which he presented an outline of what had occurred in Paris. Wilson's chief adversary was Senator Henry Cabot Lodge of Massachusetts, the new majority leader and chairman of the Foreign Relations Committee. Both men heartily detested each other. Lodge, a strong nationalist like his friend Theodore Roosevelt, charged that Wilson had betrayed America's interests in Paris. Why should the Stars and Stripes fly beneath the banner of some international superstate? Lodge had endorsed Roosevelt's plan for an international peacekeeping organization—in fact he had called it "the united nations"—so the issue at this point was not whether the nation would engage the world but on what terms.

The differences between the two men transcended politics, however. The austerely elegant Boston Brahmin had a doctorate in history from Harvard, had written several books, and, until the arrival of Woodrow Wilson on the scene, was regarded as the "Scholar in Politics."* Lodge sorely resented having to share this distinction with Wilson. The president, for his part, hated the senator with such passion that he refused to even share a platform with him at ceremonies marking the centennial of a Washington church.

Wilson's aides thought his presentation had gone well but his inquisitors were unimpressed. "I feel as if I had been wandering with Alice in Wonderland and had tea with the Mad Hatter," said Senator Frank Brandegee of Connecticut. Lodge derided Wilson's scholarship by drawling in his high, irritating voice, which sounded to some like the tearing of a bedsheet, that the president's presentation "might get by at Princeton, but certainly not at Harvard."

Nevertheless, Lodge and other Republicans were concerned that the president, a resourceful politician, might use the fight over the League as a springboard for seeking a third term in 1920. Throwing down a challenge, they published a "Round Robin" signed by thirty-nine senators—more than the one third plus one needed to reject the treaty—saying the League was unacceptable because it undermined American sovereignty. Wilson considered the Round Robin a bluff; the Republicans would not dare incur the odium of rejecting the treaty in the face of the strong popular support for it.

---

* Paradoxically, Lodge had, as editor of the *International Review*, published Wilson's first scholarly article in 1879.

Returning to Paris, the president fought over the next two months with little success for a just peace against the demands of the Allies for revenge and reparations from the Germans. Clemenceau, even though seriously wounded by an assassin's bullet, was his bitterest foe. The Fourteen Points had been a unilateral American declaration, according to the Tiger of France, and he scorned them. "Mr. Wilson bores me with his Fourteen Points," he declared. "Why, God Almighty has only Ten!" Twice in less than a half century, France had been invaded by the Germans, and the French demanded a security that could be obtained only from a prostrate Germany.

Wilson tried to convince the French that security was unobtainable by imposing intolerable burdens on the vanquished. But his health was failing. Never robust, the president had developed under the stress of wartime a twitching about one eye. Now, half his face twitched spasmodically and he may have had an undetected stroke while in Paris. He spent hours on his hands and knees on the floor of his suite poring over maps and charts, trying to master the complicated maze of facts involved in the negotiations. In contrast, Clemenceau dozed off when matters not of concern to France were being discussed. Worn out and exhausted, Wilson contracted the flu and grew thinner and his hair appeared to whiten day by day.

To Wilson, the French were greedy, the British unreasonable, and the Italians unhelpful. He was testy, failed to heed the advice of his experts, and didn't use the press effectively. And he began to act irrationally. He was obsessed with the idea that all the French servants in his quarters were spies.* He insisted that everything in his rooms be painstakingly inventoried because he suspected items were being stolen. He was overheard saying, "If I didn't feel that I was the personal instrument of God, I couldn't carry on."

Several observers were disappointed that the president failed to use the "unlimited physical power" he and America possessed to make the Europeans adopt his demand for a just peace. "Never," wrote John Maynard Keynes, an economic adviser to the British delegation, "had a philosopher held such weapons wherewith to bind the Princes of the World"—and failed to use them.

Herbert Hoover, who knew more about what was actually happening in the devastated countries of Europe than anyone else in Paris but was never

---

* Wilson was not altogether paranoid because the conference was like a giant poker game. While the major players remade the world, the respective intelligence services, like kibitzers, spied on them to obtain their fallback positions. (See Miller, *Spying for America*, pp. 205–6.)

consulted by Wilson, was slipped a copy of the still secret treaty early on the morning of May 7. "I was greatly disturbed," he later wrote. "It seemed to me the economic consequences alone would pull down all Europe and injure the United States." Hoover was so upset that he dressed and went out to walk the darkened streets of Paris to work off his agitation. "In a few blocks I met General [Jan] Smuts [the South African leader] and John Maynard Keynes," he continued. "It flashed in all our minds why the others were walking about at that time of day. . . . We agreed that it [the treaty] was terrible."

The Germans, who protested that they had surrendered to Wilson's promise of peace without victory, were dismayed by the document presented to them on the point of a bayonet. It was little more than unconditional surrender. Germany was also saddled with the guilt of having launched an aggressive war—blame that could easily have been spread among all the belligerents. The train carrying the German delegation to Versailles was forced to creep through northern France at ten miles per hour so its members would be fully exposed to the damage wrought by their armies. The ceremonies were held amid the regal splendors of the Hall of Mirrors at Versailles on June 28, 1919, the fifth anniversary of the assassination of Archduke Franz Ferdinand of Austria, which touched off the war.

France regained Alsace and Lorraine, which she had lost after the Franco-Prussian War of 1870, and was awarded a trusteeship over the rich coal mines of the Saar Valley. Germany also had to pay the victors a staggering $33 billion in reparations and was stripped of her colonies. A newly independent Poland was given part of eastern Germany and a goulash of new nations was carved out of the old Austro-Hungarian and Ottoman Empires. In the final analysis, rather than giving birth to the liberal and peaceful new world promised by Wilson, the Versailles Treaty carried within itself the seeds of World War II. Keynes passionately opposed the Versailles settlement. "Vengeance, I dare predict, will not limp" if the victors insist on impoverishing the vanquished, he declared.

Keynes was not the only one to sense the catastrophe lurking in the future. Prince Fumimaro Konoye, a young Japanese diplomat in Paris, urged his nation to reject the treaty because it failed to acknowledge resource-starved Japan's need to expand into Asia, particularly into China. Twenty years later, as Japanese premier, Konoye entered into an alliance with Germany to upset the settlement reached at Versailles. Privately, Wilson understood that errors had been made in the making of the peace, and expected them to be adjusted by the League of Nations, in which the United States would, of course, play a leading role.

"The stage is set, the destiny disclosed," the president declared in tones that resembled an evangelical sermon as he submitted the Treaty of Versailles to the Senate for ratification on July 10, 1919. "It has come about by no plan of our conceiving, but by the hand of God, who led us into this way." There was no doubt about the outcome in his mind. "The Senate is going to ratify the treaty," he grimly told a reporter.

Initially, most Americans favored ratification and some sort of international organization to maintain world peace. In fact, some political observers believed that by wrapping the treaty and the League Covenant in one "package of peace," Wilson had outflanked the opposition by a maneuver worthy of "a foxy ward politician." Despairing of defeating the treaty outright, Lodge and his allies adopted the strategy of trying to "Americanize" it by adding a number of amendments or reservations. Perhaps the stubborn Wilson would play into their hands and refuse to accept an emasculated version.

Not everyone was certain that Wilson would be taken in by this ploy. "Suppose the president accepts the treaty with your reservations," Senator James Watson of Indiana asked Lodge. "Then we are in the League." Lodge smiled confidently and spoke of Wilson's personal hatred for him. "Never under any circumstance in this world would he be induced to accept a treaty with Lodge reservations appended to it." Lodge knew his man. Asked by the French ambassador if he would accept any reservations, Wilson snapped: "I shall consent to nothing."

To allow time for opposition to build up against the treaty, Lodge staged elaborate public hearings before the Senate Foreign Relations Committee, which he had packed with anti-League men—the "Battalion of Death." He personally read the entire 264 densely printed pages of the document into the record. This consumed two weeks. Expert testimony took another six weeks. Half a hundred amendments and reservations were introduced and anybody with a grievance was allowed to appear. The senators solemnly listened to arguments for the breakup of the British Empire, for a united Ireland, for Italy's claim for Fiume, on the Adriatic, which had been given to the newly created Yugoslavia, and many similar ideas.

The struggle over the treaty was one of the most brutally partisan and bitterly personal disputes in American history. As the debate droned on in the cruel heat and monsoon rains of a Washington summer, Wilson invited the Foreign Relations Committee to the White House to meet with him.

Although he answered questions for three hours, he made little headway. Later, he observed that one of his most persistent questioners, Ohio's Senator Warren G. Harding, "had a disturbingly dull mind and that it seemed impossible to get any explanation to lodge in it."

As Lodge had forecast, disappointment and disillusionment with the treaty mounted as the details became known. Liberals were profoundly disturbed by the cynicism and land-grabbing in Paris and by what they saw as the bartering away of the Fourteen Points. Hoover urged the president to forget about "turning the Covenant into a constitution for the human race" and to make the League simply an international forum. Walter Lippmann, editor of *The New Republic* and onetime member of the Inquiry, belabored Wilson for accepting the "secret treaties" and argued that the treaty was unsound and unjust.

The "hyphenates"—German-Americans, Italian-Americans, Irish-Americans—were all affronted by some aspect of the treaty or another. Traditional isolationists were convinced that internationalism was a wicked departure from the warnings of the Founding Fathers against entangling alliances. Wealthy businessmen such as Henry Clay Frick and Andrew W. Mellon, fearful of a revived New Freedom and a possible third term for Wilson, bankrolled the opposition. On the far left, the Communists assailed Wilson as a "hypocrite and murderer" because of the intervention in Russia.

Wilson had returned from Paris a premature globalist. He saw a connection between events overseas and tranquillity and progress at home, but the vast majority of Americans were less inclined toward internationalism. Despite the war, they had not abandoned their traditional sense of American exceptionalism and isolation. Returning soldiers were unimpressed with what they had seen of the European way of life. They thought Europeans different from Americans with their kings and wars and famines and felt that they must bear the consequences of that difference. We had gone over there to fix things for them, and if they couldn't keep them sorted out, that was too bad.

The most common demand for alterations in the League Covenant was to bring it into conformance with the Constitution and American practice. Most vexing was Article X, which pledged the United States to send troops abroad to uphold the "territorial integrity" and "political independence" of any member nation. Americans saw this proposal as an infringement on congressional authority to declare war. Although critics pointed out that Wilson had accepted numerous compromises to obtain British and French approval of the League, he refused with the obstinacy of his

Scotch-Irish ancestors to give a single inch to win over moderates and iso-
late Lodge and the "irreconcilables," who refused to vote for the treaty in
any form.

Wilson blindly insisted that the Covenant was perfect, that it could not
be improved, even though he had privately expressed the need for
changes. Rather than acknowledging that the League was an experiment,
and that there was no reason to believe the Covenant to be any more perfect than the Constitution, which had been repeatedly amended, Wilson
stubbornly refused to make concessions—such as reaffirming that the
Constitution was paramount in cases where the Covenant came into conflict with it. In failing to accept any reservations, he did as much as Lodge
to ensure that the United States did not join the League of Nations. They
were collaborators in catastrophe.

Warned that the treaty was losing ground and that he would have to
accept some of Lodge's reservations, Wilson retorted: "Never! Never! . . .
I'll appeal to the country." He was an eloquent speaker and had previously
reached over the heads of his opponents with success. On September 3,
1919, he left Washington in a seven-car special train on a barnstorming
tour across the heartland of America to the Pacific Coast and back again.
At sixty-three, Wilson was weak, trembling, and worn out, and this physically punishing journey was undertaken against the advice of his wife, Dr.
Grayson, and numerous friends.

Over the next twenty-two days, Wilson covered eight thousand miles
and gave about forty speeches—some longer than an hour—plus innumer-
able talks from the rear platform of the *Mayflower*, the presidential car. At
first the crowds were lukewarm. But as Wilson got farther from Washington, enthusiasm increased. In St. Louis, storms of applause capped almost
every one of his sentences. Wilson's audience in Omaha screamed outrage
at every mention of the president's opponents. Excited crowds turned out
in Billings and Helena. His reception in Seattle was overwhelmingly positive. Wilson addressed fifty thousand people in San Diego through a
recently installed loudspeaker system. In Salt Lake City, the Mormon
Tabernacle was packed to suffocation. In Cheyenne there was a parade and
Denver was ablaze with lights. Meantime, with delicious irony, Lodge
reported that the Foreign Relations Committee had completed its work
and recommended ratification of the treaty—with forty-two amendments
and reservations.

Wilson's whirlwind tour had a downside, however. Plagued by blinding
headaches that sometimes made it almost impossible for him to speak, he

was nearly irrational in his hatred for his opponents. Pounding the rostrum, he questioned their patriotism and warned that the dissenters were doing the work of the Bolsheviks. Such irresponsible talk fed the hysteria about dangerous subversives and radicals that was sweeping the country.

Every seat and bit of standing room in the Memorial Auditorium in Pueblo, Colorado, was filled long before the president's arrival on the afternoon of September 25, 1919, and the crowd overflowed into the street. Before his appearance, Wilson, although exhausted, reviewed some ten thousand cheering people at the local fairgrounds in an open car. He appeared pale and tired when the auto drew up at the auditorium. As he climbed up the stairs to the platform, he stumbled, but Colonel Edmund W. Starling of the Secret Service, who was directly behind him, caught the president and set him back on his feet.

Wilson began in his familiar confident manner although his voice was not strong. Suddenly, after a few minutes, he faltered. "Germany must never be allowed . . ." he declared and stopped. "A lesson must be taught to Germany . . ." he began again. And again he halted. "The world will not allow Germany . . ." One of the reporters glanced at Edith Wilson and saw terror in her eyes. Starling thought the president was about to collapse and prepared to leap forward to catch him. But Wilson shook off his difficulties and pressed ahead. He spoke of a visit he had made on Memorial Day to a cemetery in France where American troops killed in the war had been laid to rest.

"There seems to me to stand between us and rejection or qualification of the treaty," he continued, "the serried ranks of those boys in khaki—not only those boys who came home but those dear ghosts that still deploy upon the fields of France." He told of seeing French women tending the graves of American soldiers—"putting flowers every day upon those graves, taking them as their own sons, their own beloved, because they had died to save France. France was free, and the world was free because the Americans had come."

Joseph P. Tumulty, the president's secretary and friend, who was standing at the side of the platform, saw both men and women in the audience dabbing at their eyes with handkerchiefs. Wilson himself was in tears as he reached the end of his speech. In words that were to be his testament, he declared:

I believe that men will see the truth, eye to eye and face to face. There is one thing that the American people always rise to and extend their hand to, and that is the truth of justice and of liberty and of peace. We have accepted that truth and we are going to be led by it, and it is going to lead us, and through us the world, out into pastures of quietness and peace such as the world never dreamed of before.

The audience rose and cheered for ten minutes. Wilson remained motionless at the podium until the first lady gently led him away. These were the last words Woodrow Wilson spoke to a public audience as president. That night, as the train rolled toward Wichita, he had a stroke. "I seem to have gone to pieces," he mumbled, the words slurred and almost indistinct. One side of his face seemed fallen and frozen. The rest of the tour was canceled and with the blinds of the *Mayflower* drawn, the train sped back to Washington. Silent crowds stood by the tracks, watching gravely as it passed.

Wilson, by the time he reached the capital, had recovered enough to walk slowly but unassisted from the train to his open car in the plaza outside Union Station. It was a Sunday morning and the streets were nearly empty, but as the president rode to the White House, aides were shocked to see him take off his hat and bow as if he were acknowledging the cheers of a vast throng. Not long after, on October 2, 1919, he had another stroke—this one nearly fatal—that paralyzed his left side and affected his power of speech.

For five months Wilson lay in the great Lincoln bed in a darkened room on the second floor of the White House, sometimes weeping, sometimes looking blankly out into space. Extraordinary precautions were taken to prevent Congress, the cabinet, and the nation from learning that he was unable to perform the functions of his office. The president had suffered a nervous breakdown, Joe Tumulty was instructed to tell the press, and with rest he would soon be on the mend. Dr. Grayson issued optimistic bulletins, yet in a memorandum not made public until 1990, he acknowledged that Wilson's condition precluded "anything more than a minimal state of recovery." Edith Wilson had little knowledge of politics or statecraft and only two years of formal schooling, but she became president in all but name, with Grayson and Tumulty the fellow members of a regency. "He must never know how ill he was; and I must carry on," she said.

In spite of the efforts at secrecy, some members of the cabinet learned just how incapacitated Wilson was, and Secretary of State Robert Lansing* sought

* The uncle of John Foster Dulles, secretary of state in the Eisenhower administration and his brother, Allen Dulles, director of central intelligence under both Presidents Eisen-

to place in effect the constitutional provisions requiring the vice president
to assume the duties of a disabled president. But Grayson and Tumulty said
they would resist any such effort. "He has been too kind, too loyal and too
wonderful to me to receive such treatment at my hands," Tumulty declared.
And Vice President Marshall, when eventually informed of Wilson's condition, made clear that he did not want to step in as president.

The great iron gates of the White House were chained and locked.
Policemen guarded its approaches as rumors that the president had gone
mad swept the country. The government all but stopped. Most domestic
matters were settled by the department heads concerned. Diplomatic
crises in Mexico and Central America were ignored. Lord Grey, the former
British foreign secretary, came over to assist in the League fight, but was
snubbed by the White House on grounds that he was weak on the Lodge
reservations. Herbert Hoover was unable to find anyone to accept his resignation as wartime food czar and simply shut up shop and slipped out of
Washington. The situation "is bad as it can be," wrote a veteran journalist.
"No government—no policies—almost every Cabinet officer a candidate
for President. . . . The Congress is chaotic. There is no leadership worthy of
the name."

To hold things together, Lansing called weekly cabinet meetings—until
February 1920, when an angry letter came out of Wilson's sickroom dismissing him from his post. Every message, every newspaper given the president passed through Mrs. Wilson's hands and she decided whether it
would upset him. If so, he did not see it. Letters to the president from the
cabinet were answered in a large schoolgirlish handwriting that mean-

---

hower and Kennedy. As a result of Lansing's influence both men were junior members of
the American team in Paris in 1919.

Allen Dulles had spent the war as an intelligence officer operating out of the American
legation in Bern, Switzerland. On April 11, 1917, he was duty officer, most of the staff having left for the day, when he received a telephone call from a man who spoke Russian-
accented German. The caller told Dulles that he was arriving in Bern late in the afternoon
and that it was vital that he speak to someone in authority at the legation. Regarding him
as one of the troublesome émigré cranks who populated Switzerland, Dulles, who had a
tennis date with a girlfriend, told him the legation would be closed then and to come the
next day. "Tomorrow," said the man, his voice rising in excitement, "will be too late."

Dulles insisted that the meeting could not take place until 10 A.M. the next day, and
kept his tennis date. The caller, Vladimir Ilyich Lenin, couldn't wait. By ten o'clock the
next morning he had already left Switzerland for Russia on the famous "sealed train" provided by the Germans, who hoped Lenin and his Bolsheviks would take Russia out of the
war. In later years, Dulles often cited the incident to new CIA recruits as an example of the
folly of failing to follow up on a lead.

dered down the left-hand margin of the original letter, then across the bottom and up the right margin and then across the top. The first lady received cabinet members in a sitting room off the president's bedroom. They explained what they wanted and she went in to see him and then returned to pass on what she said was his answer. Two replacement cabinet officers—the agriculture and treasury secretaries—were appointed after chats over teacups with Mrs. Wilson and never saw the president.

"We have no president," declared Senator Albert B. Fall, a New Mexico Republican. "We have petticoat government." Fall got himself appointed to a special senatorial committee to call upon Wilson. He claimed that he wished to discuss the case of a constituent arrested by the Mexican authorities, but his real aim was to check upon Wilson's condition.

"We've been praying for you, sir," declared the unctuous Fall.

"Which way, Senator?" Wilson shot back.

On November 19, 1919, the Senate finally voted on the Versailles Treaty. Forty-two Democrats, following the president's orders, joined with thirteen Republican irreconcilables to reject the amended treaty. Next, the Senate voted on the original treaty without any reservations: thirty-five senators, all but one a Democrat, voted to approve it; fifty-five senators voted no. By asking for all or nothing, Wilson got nothing. The Republicans were jubilant.

But the American people were not quite ready for the interment of the pact. Under the lash of public opinion, the Senate agreed to reconsider its action. As March 20, 1920, the date for the new vote, neared, Wilson's advisers pleaded with him to give in, to compromise by accepting some of Lodge's reservations in order to ensure American participation in the League. Hoover and Bernard Baruch, the chief of wartime economic mobilization, asked Grayson and the first lady to join in making such a plea, hoping their entreaties would tip the balance. Enough senators were ready to vote for the treaty with moderate reservations to win passage, they said, if only Wilson would give his approval.

"For my sake," Mrs. Wilson asked her husband, "won't you accept these reservations and get this awful thing settled?"

"Little girl, don't you desert me," replied the president, patting her hand.

When Grayson tried to add his thoughts, Wilson shook his head. "Better a thousand times to go down fighting," he declared.

Having flung health, strength, and life itself into the struggle, he was resolute. Even so, the urge for compromise was strong and only the strictest orders from the White House kept all the Democrats in line. "We can always depend upon Mr. Wilson," observed Senator Frank B. Brandegee with a grim smile. Even so, twenty-one Democrats broke ranks to vote in favor of the amended treaty and it came within seven votes of winning the two-thirds necessary for ratification. Once the votes had been tallied, Henry Cabot Lodge observed with satisfaction that the League of Nations was now "as dead as Marley's ghost."

That night, Wilson could not sleep. Grayson looked in on his restless patient from time to time and just before dawn, the president asked him to get a nearby Bible and read from Second Corinthians: "We are troubled on every side, yet not distressed; we are perplexed, but not in despair; persecuted but not forsaken; cast down but not destroyed."

"I can predict with absolute certainty that within another generation there will be another world war if the nations of the world do not concert the method to prevent it," Wilson prophesied. Liberals and internationalists claim the failure of the United States to join the League of Nations was a vital factor in the outbreak of a global war two decades later. But this judgment is questionable. In point of fact, none of the great powers was willing to give the League significant authority to accomplish all that its creator wished. Even if the United States had joined, it, too, would probably have continued to act outside the bounds of the League, especially in the Western Hemisphere. And short of an actual threat to national security of the United States, the American people were unlikely to assume an obligation to defend the territorial integrity of another nation or its political system.

Woodrow Wilson had ventured beyond the realm of reality as it was understood in the United States and around the globe in 1919. The League was a cry for restraint, but the world was not yet ready to heed it—and would not until the horrors of World War II and Hiroshima provided an incentive.

CHAPTER 2

"To the Red Dawn!"

E leanor and Franklin Roosevelt were parking their car near their home at 2131 R Street, off Embassy Row in Washington, on the night of June 2, 1919. Having just returned from a pleasant dinner at the Chevy Chase Club on the outskirts of the city, they were enjoying the soft evening air. Washington's social season with its round of formal diplomatic receptions and parties was drawing to an end and the surrounding streets were quiet. Here and there, random lights burned in the tall windows of embassies and private residences, illuminating tiny patches of sidewalk.

Suddenly, the tranquillity of Embassy Row was ripped apart by a violent explosion. Flames and a cloud of acrid yellow smoke soared into the air. Startled residents ran into the street in various stages of undress, windows were blown out, cars were damaged, and nearby trees were scorched. A bomb had ripped away the front of the home of Attorney General A. Mitchell Palmer, directly across the street from that of the Roosevelts. Palmer, leader of a postwar crusade against radicals and subversives, and his family were badly frightened, but escaped injury.

Roosevelt rushed homeward, fearing that his eleven-year-old son, James, the only one of his five children in the house that night, might have been hurt. Bloody pieces of a corpse lay on the front steps of Roosevelt's house amid shards of shattered glass. He thought it was the body of his son. "I'll never forget how uncommonly unnerved Father was when he dashed upstairs and found me standing at the window in my pajamas," Jimmy Roosevelt later recalled. "He grabbed me in an embrace that almost cracked my ribs."

Investigators determined the explosion had probably been premature. The bomber had evidently stumbled on the front steps of Palmer's home and been blown to bits by his own device. His head was found on a nearby

rooftop. The evidence indicated he was an anarchist from Philadelphia.*
His crumpled hat bore a Philadelphia hatter's mark, a return railroad
ticket to that city was discovered in the bloody rags that had been his
clothes, and a copy of *Plain Words*, an anarchist tract, was found nearby.
"We will kill," it proclaimed. "There will have to be destruction . . . we are
ready to do anything and everything to suppress the capitalist class." Some
thought him to be a former editor of *Cronaca Sovverso,* an Italian-language
anarchist paper.

The bomb was one of eight explosions that evening. In Cleveland, the
mayor's home was dynamited. The residence of a Massachusetts state legislator was damaged. A bomb exploded in the vestibule of a federal judge's
residence in New York City, killing a passerby. Other attempts were made
to kill judges in Boston and Pittsburgh. In Paterson, New Jersey, where
workers in silk mills had conducted a hard-fought strike in 1913, a bomb
wrecked the home of a mill owner. In Philadelphia, the residence of a
prominent jeweler was bombed as was the rectory of a Catholic church.

Only a few weeks before, bombs disguised as packages from Gimbel's
department store had been sent by mail to thirty-six prominent Americans, including Mitchell Palmer; financial titans J. P. Morgan and John D.
Rockefeller; Supreme Court Justice Oliver Wendell Holmes; and Ole
Hanson, the anti-labor mayor of Seattle. Only one was delivered, severely
injuring the wife of Thomas W. Hardwick, a former Georgia senator, and a
black servant. The rest were delayed in the New York Post Office where
they were detected by an alert clerk, because of inadequate postage. No
one was ever arrested for these terrorist acts, but officials and the press
blamed foreign radicals.

The bombings were probably the work of a handful of deluded individuals rather than a wide-ranging revolutionary conspiracy. But to people
inflamed by a sensation-seeking press, there was no difference between
peaceful reformers and revolutionaries. To most Americans, "Red" meant
"bomb"—and "bomb" meant a wild-eyed, bearded, foreign radical. Fear of
the spread of the Bolshevik Revolution, inflation, an unprecedented wave
of strikes—more than 3,600 in 1919 alone—the increasing presence of
blacks in Northern cities, Prohibition, and the franchise for women, had
all unsettled the public mind.

Americans had been united by a common set of beliefs. Farmers in the

---

* Parts of what appeared to be two left legs were found at the scene of the explosion,
indicating that two men were involved in the incident, but the police insisted there was
only one bomber. If he possessed two left legs, the *Washington Evening Star* dryly noted, no
wonder he had stumbled.

Nebraska heartland, miners in the West Virginia coal fields, and immigrants on the sidewalks of New York all knew that life meant struggle, sacrifice, and obligation, with the rewards falling to one's children, not to oneself. But a sharply divided vision of themselves and their future materialized in the years following World War I. While Americans took pride in the country's remarkable growth in the twentieth century, many were convinced the old moral and spiritual values were being undermined by industrialization, standardization, and mass society.

Wealth was being concentrated in ever fewer hands and discontent was rising as the social bond among classes disintegrated. Urban slums produced a new and dangerous criminal class. Racism and antipathy to blacks and immigrants were rife. Although the continent had been conquered and the frontier closed, this triumph had been accompanied by reckless and wasteful exploitation of land, forest, and water. Wartime controls had also resulted in mounting hostility to federal intervention into the lives of the American people—an issue that continues to shape policy discussions in our own time. A search for order, for conformity and homogeneity at every level of society, was under way. But as philosopher-historian Henry Adams gloomily noted, chaos was the law of nature.

Only the flimsiest of evidence was required to convince the public that the bombings were part of a Bolshevik plot. Even though Wilson's physical collapse and withdrawal contributed to the disarray, it is doubtful that even a healthy and active president could have prevented the spiral downward from the exhilaration of the Armistice to the brutal repression of 1919.

Mitchell Palmer, with the intention of winning the Democratic presidential nomination in 1920, seized control of the crusade against radicals, immigrants, organized labor, and dissenters. Wilson turned to Palmer at a cabinet meeting and admonished: "Do not let this country see red." Paradoxically, Palmer was the prototype of the Wilsonian liberal. As a congressman from Pennsylvania, Palmer fought for votes for women, helped pass laws against child labor, and was considered pro-union. Now, driven by political ambition and a fanatic's zeal, the "Fighting Quaker" saw Reds everywhere.

He charged that Bolshevism was an immediate threat to the sacred American values of religion, private property, and democracy. "Like a prairie-fire the blaze of revolution [is] eating its way into the homes of the American workman," an impassioned Palmer declared. "Its sharp tongues of revolutionary heat [are] licking the altars of the churches, leaping into the belfry of the school bell, crawling into the scared corners of American homes, burning up the foundations of society."

Following the bombing of the attorney general's home, Congress appropriated $500,000 for the establishment of an anti-radical General Intelligence Division within the Justice Department's Bureau of Investigation.* An ambitious, twenty-four-year-old bureaucrat named John Edgar Hoover—no relation to Herbert Hoover—was placed in charge. Hoover had begun his government career as a card cataloger in the Library of Congress and quickly put this skill to use by organizing a 200,000-card file containing detailed information on every suspected radical and subversive, a project he zealously pursued for the next half century.

Government agents infiltrated the Socialist Party, the IWW, and the American Jewish Congress, for the Red Scare had a strong anti-Semitic cast. Jews were seen as the masterminds behind the Russian Revolution and were a highly visible presence in radical organizations. Admiral Albert P. Niblack, of the Office of Naval Intelligence, warned of a terrorist plot led by Emma Goldman, the notorious anarchist, and her lover, Alexander Berkman—both Jews. Dredging up every bugaboo likely to arouse alarm, Niblack claimed that this uprising would be carried out by a sinister combination of Jews, Mexican bandits, and a Japanese master spy named Kato Kamoto. "The Terror will surpass anything that ever happened in this country, and the brains of the plot are already on the Pacific Coast," he averred.†

The Red Scare had its roots in wartime propaganda, censorship, and violence. "Woe be to the man or group of men that seeks to stand in our way in this day of high resolution," Wilson had warned after the declaration of war. In creating an atmosphere of total war, the administration lent credibility to blind hatreds and suspicions against foreigners and foreign ideas that lay just below the surface of American life. Chinese immigrants had been excluded from the United States since 1882‡ and Japanese settlers could not be naturalized. Old-stock Americans were disturbed by the arrival of 20 million new immigrants, mostly from Eastern and Southern

---

* It become the Federal Bureau of Investigation in 1924.

† In 1918, anti-war writer Randolph Bourne took a break on the Connecticut shore with two female friends. They were shadowed by naval intelligence and questioned when one of the women, a professional dancer, burst into free-spirited Isadora Duncan–like cavorting on the beach. She was accused of signaling to German submarines supposedly lurking offshore. A trunkload of Bourne's manuscripts mysteriously disappeared while in transit.

‡ A restriction that remained in force until 1943.

Europe. Restrictionists used the pseudoscience of eugenics to argue that the new immigrants were racially inferior to "Nordics" from Northern Europe. In 1917, Congress passed legislation, over Wilson's veto, imposing a literacy test upon immigrants, an initial step toward a total ban on all except Northern Europeans.

Once war was declared, German-Americans became the victims of American prejudices. Although previously highly respected, they were now suspected of espionage and sabotage. The German language was banned from the schools, German books were burned, Beethoven and Wagner were dropped from orchestral programs, and with patriotic zeal, sauerkraut was transformed into "liberty cabbage." In Baltimore, German Street became Redwood Street and the waiters at the city's leading German restaurant were rumored to be spies. Writers with Germanic-sounding names, among them Henry Mencken and Theodore Dreiser, were harassed. Super-patriotic vigilante groups such as the American Protective League and the National Security League rounded up supposed "slackers," pacifists, and conscientious objectors, with official approval.

IWW organizers were beaten and jailed. A man who refused to stand during the playing of "The Star-Spangled Banner" at a Victory Bond rally in Washington was shot dead by a uniformed sailor. The crowd broke into cheers. In Indiana a jury took two minutes to free a defendant charged with killing a man who had yelled "To hell with the United States!" Max Eastman, a Socialist intellectual, was nearly lynched in North Dakota when he tried to give an anti-war speech. Senator Robert M. La Follette, Sr., the Wisconsin Progressive, was charged with disloyalty for opposing the war and it took a Senate committee to clear him. Secret agents were placed among the servants of press mogul William Randolph Hearst, who disagreed with American entry into the war.

Free speech was curbed by the draconian Espionage and Sedition Acts, which made it a crime to criticize the government. Liberal and left-wing magazines closed up shop. Mail was opened and people looked over their shoulders for eavesdroppers before expressing their views to friends. Two thousand Socialists, pacifists, Wobblies, anarchists, and alleged pro-Germans were jailed while thousands of other suspects were placed under surveillance. Yet, as the radical press noted, no effort was made to curb the brutal profiteering of big business on cost-plus war contracts. Eugene V. Debs, who had received nearly a million votes as the Socialist candidate for president in 1912, was sentenced to ten years in federal prison for opposing the war.

Prohibition, long the goal of temperance crusaders, became law during this period of turmoil.* Reformers, citing the wartime emergency, argued that alcohol undermined military discipline and caused absenteeism and inefficiency in the war industries. They cannily emphasized that most of the great brewers—Busch, Ruppert, Pabst, Schmidt—were of German origin and doing the kaiser's work. The Eighteenth Amendment, banning the manufacture, transportation, and sale of intoxicants, swept though Congress on December 18, 1917, after only thirteen hours of debate. Thirty-six states quickly ratified it, five without a dissenting vote. Prohibition was to become effective on January 16, 1920.

Preoccupied with the making of the peace, Wilson had made no plans for demobilization. Without warning, without preparation, the nation stumbled leaderless into a turbulent conversion to peacetime. The first day after the Armistice, Washington residents found it almost impossible to place long-distance telephone calls because the lines were jammed by officials canceling $4 billion in government contracts. Nine million workers were almost immediately thrown out of work. Some four million servicemen were released into an already chaotic labor market with $60 each and a railway ticket home—and without any program for integrating them into civilian life.†

Progressives and liberals, buoyed by the heady wartime experience of regulating the economy, hoped the administration would make these changes permanent, but Wilson dismantled most of the wartime regulatory agencies. Reformers were particularly disheartened by his decision to abandon government operation of the railroads. A plan for joint management by the government, the operators, and the unions was branded by opponents as "a bold, bald, naked attempt to sovietize the railroads of the nation," and the lines were returned to private hands. Suspicion of the wartime bureaucracy was so great that daylight savings time was repealed. "We might soon have laws passed attempting to regulate the volume of air a man should breathe, suspend the law of gravity, or change the colors of the rainbow," said one congressman.

A postwar boom was touched off by pent-up consumer demand for hard-to-get civilian goods, easy credit, and foreign purchases of American products that lasted into 1920. Nevertheless, reconversion and demobi-

---

* Herbert Asbury argues in his book *The Great Illusion* that the dry victory was not a product of the war but was actually won in the congressional election of 1916 when the dry forces took control of Congress.

† Congress, after several presidential vetoes, approved a veterans' bonus in 1924, but it was not to be paid until 1945.

lization were accompanied by confusion and turmoil. Government clerks and stenographers who had been fired with little advance notice had to borrow money to get back to their hometowns. Haunted and lonely former soldiers wandered the streets of cities and towns vainly hunting down elusive jobs, some still in their old uniforms because they had nothing else to wear. Restless, jobless, and embittered, they searched for scapegoats, and some blamed Bolsheviks, radicals, and foreigners for their plight.

Throughout the country on May 1, 1919, ex-servicemen and civilians taunted and then attacked Socialist demonstrators celebrating May Day, the traditional international holiday for labor. In Boston, police, marchers, and veterans clashed and one policeman was killed. Rioters in New York wrecked the office of a Socialist paper, the *New York Call*, and broke up rallies and marches in the violence described by Scott Fitzgerald in "May Day." The riots reached their peak in Cleveland, where one person was killed and forty injured. The police arrested 106 Socialists but not a single anti-radical. "Cleveland recognizes but one flag. . . . It is the Stars and Stripes," proclaimed the *Plain Dealer*. Although the riots were aimed at the radicals, newspapers claimed the demonstrations were "dress rehearsals" for an approaching "Red Revolution." Senator Kenneth McKellar of Tennessee sought the deportation of foreign-born radicals and the exile of native-born radicals to a penal colony on Guam.

Fearful conservatives suspected that foreign radicals were hiding underground, and noted that some Bolshevik leaders had bided their time here before the Russian Revolution. Nikolai Bukharin had edited the paper of the Russian Socialist Federation in a dank cellar on St. Mark's Place in New York City, and Leon Trotsky, briefly in the United States in 1917, wrote for the same journal. The blood of Americans was chilled by the boast of Karl Radek, executive secretary of the newly organized Communist International, that the money expended on the uprising in Bavaria "was as nothing compared to the funds transmitted to New York for the purpose of spreading bolshevism in the United States." Russia . . . Bavaria . . . Hungary—might not America be next?

Yet, as the rest of the nation was growing more conformist, American radicals had been electrified by the Bolshevik triumph. "I have been into the future and by God it works!" proclaimed Lincoln Steffens, following a trip to the Soviet Union in 1919.* Greenwich Village bohemians such as

---

* Steffens later claimed this observation was put in his mouth by others, but he repeated it many times and novelist Katherine Anne Porter, for one, said she heard him say it. See Porter, "The Never-Ending Wrong," *Atlantic Monthly*, June 1977.

John Reed, who had chronicled the Bolshevik coup in admiring terms in *Ten Days That Shook the World,* now discovered in an anti-capitalist, anti-imperialist Communism the righteous cause their fathers had found in the progressivism of Theodore Roosevelt and Woodrow Wilson. Hardly any of these literary rebels had ever worked with their hands, but they had a romantic vision of themselves in the vanguard of the uprising of the workers of the world. "Toasts were drunk at parties 'To the Red Dawn!'" recalled Katherine Anne Porter. "'See you at the barricades!' friends would say at the end of an evening dancing in Harlem." Young and idealistic, they envisioned a world driven by altruism rather than greed and materialism. Massacres and atrocities committed by the Bolsheviks in the name of the proletariat were shrugged off as wartime necessities or capitalist fabrications.

Old-line Socialism with its emphasis upon gradualism and parliamentary reform was swept away by a shrill militancy on the left, which fed public unease. The Socialist Party, which under Gene Debs had been largely run by American-born leaders, was captured by alien radicals. Few spoke English and most were so ignorant of conditions in the United States that they thought a revolution imminent. Two thirds of the membership broke away to form rival Communist parties, one dominated by non–English speakers and the other controlled by John Reed and other native-born leaders.* They merged in 1924 as the Communist Party of the United States with an estimated membership of forty thousand to seventy thousand, according to the government, mostly foreign-born.

Raging inflation wiped out the modest gains in wages won during the war. By late 1919, the purchasing power of the dollar was less than half what it was in 1913. For the average family, it was a disaster. The price of bread, butter, and bacon doubled and potatoes had quadrupled in price. Clothing cost twice as much. Professional and salaried workers, including policemen, clerical workers, and government employees, were worse off than at any time since the Civil War. Semiskilled workers earned less than $2,000

---

* Indicted for sedition, Reed fled the United States on a false passport and was enthusiastically welcomed in Russia. He died of typhus in 1920 and is the only Harvard man buried in the Kremlin Wall. Some writers claim that he was having second thoughts about the Bolsheviks at the time of his death but offer no convincing evidence. Warren Beatty portrayed a wildly romantic Jack Reed in the film *Reds.* Diane Keaton played his mistress and wife, Louise Bryant, who later married William C. Bullitt, who in 1933 became the first American ambassador to the Soviet Union.

a year; unskilled laborers less than the $1,500 generally accepted as the poverty line for a family of five.

American labor entered the postwar period with high expectations. The unions had, with government encouragement, launched successful wartime organizing drives, with membership totaling about five million, almost a fifth of the labor force, and they anticipated further gains. Labor had shown its patriotism during the war by limiting strikes, but once the fighting was over all restraints were thrown off. Job insecurity, layoffs, and miserable working conditions—made worse by employers who thought labor needed disciplining and used the return of peace to take back benefits they had been forced to concede—made strife inevitable. A majority of workers put in a forty-eight-hour week and retirement was almost nonexistent. In good times, they worked feverishly to lay aside something against the inevitable layoffs. Few employers and no state provided any form of unemployment insurance against the day when the production line shut down or the furnaces were banked. Samuel Gompers, the conservative head of the AFL, opposed unemployment compensation on the grounds that it was Socialistic and therefore un-American.

Embittered by decades of government intervention on behalf of employers, Gompers argued that labor should shun government assistance and depend upon its own resources to wring concessions from employers. Unfortunately, labor had few such resources. Four million workers walked picket lines during 1919. Copper miners in Butte, Montana; New England telephone operators; textile workers in Passaic, New Jersey, and Lawrence, Massachusetts; New York City building trades workers and railway shopmen—all went on strike. Most of these walkouts ended in failure and strengthened the will of the corporate establishment to resist labor's demands.

The year began with a strike by 35,000 Seattle shipyard workers seeking higher wages and shorter hours. Seattle was the center of the militant labor tradition of the Pacific Northwest, and the Central Labor Council, which represented all organized labor in the area, broke from the usual tactics of American unions and called a general strike that shut down the entire city. James Duncan, the leader of the Labor Council, had ties to the IWW, and the Wobblies were blamed for the general strike. Although the strikers saw to it that essential services were uninterrupted and there was no violence, the Seattle newspapers and Mayor Ole Hanson claimed the walkout was the harbinger of a Communist takeover of America. Newspapers across the country followed the same line.

Some 1,500 federal troops were sent into Seattle at Hanson's request, and the mayor, who rode about the city in a flag-draped car, warned union leaders that unless they immediately called off the strike, he would use the soldiers to crush it. At the same time, Gompers and the top leadership of the AFL came out against the general strike, which they denounced as a weapon of European class warfare. All AFL unions were ordered to cease supporting the shipyard workers, and without their backing, the strike sputtered to an end. Ole Hanson claimed credit for a victory over the Bolsheviks, although the hostility of the AFL leadership to the general strike was the true cause of its collapse. Hanson resigned as mayor to tour the country giving hair-raising lectures on the dangers of the Red Peril—which proved far more lucrative than his elected job.

The crushing of the Seattle strike set the pattern for 1919. Business, industrial, and banking leaders claimed radicalism, not wages or working conditions, was the real issue in most labor disputes. They bankrolled super-patriotic groups that whipped up public anxiety about the Bolshevik menace whenever a strike loomed, and unions were branded "sovietism in disguise." These campaigns were eminently successful, as the public was convinced that organized labor owed its allegiance to an alien creed. Politicians quickly climbed on the bandwagon and the press found the fight against radicalism a circulation-building substitute for wartime sensationalism.

In September 1919, about three quarters of the poorly paid, miserably treated Boston police force, with greater desperation than hope, went on strike for recognition of a union affiliated with the AFL and improvements in pay and working conditions. They worked a twelve-hour shift for about $23 a week and had to furnish their own uniforms. Mayor Andrew J. Peters urged Governor Calvin Coolidge to call out the National Guard to maintain order. The cautious Coolidge passed the buck back to the mayor, contending he lacked power to intervene in city affairs.

Unlike Seattle, which had remained calm during the general strike, Boston exploded into violence. Three people were killed and shops were looted as efforts by veterans, college students, and businessmen to police the streets were ineffective. From his Western swing in support of the League of Nations, President Wilson denounced the strike as "a crime against civilization" and the strikers—mostly good Irish Catholics—were called "Bolsheviks" and "deserters."

Mayor Peters finally ordered out local Guard units and order was restored, although the strike went on. Unexpectedly, on the third day of the walkout, Coolidge took it upon himself to order additional state troops into Boston. Realizing that they had made a serious error, the strikers voted to return to work, but Coolidge would not have it. The entire police force was fired and replaced. Samuel Gompers urged Coolidge to reconsider, but the governor refused in ringing tones: "There is no right to strike against the public safety, by anybody, anywhere, anytime." Anxious Americans hailed Coolidge's words and even though he had played only a minor role in ending the Boston police strike, he became a figure of national importance.

Two days after the Boston police walked off the job, 365,000 steelworkers went on strike. They demanded an eight-hour day, six-day week, and recognition of their union. Some logged as much as eighty-four hours a week, working twelve hours a day, seven days a week for $28. This was made worse by the periodic "turnover" in which workers stood twenty-four-hour shifts. U.S. Steel's profits had grown from $135 million in 1914 to $492 million in 1919. One steelworker described his working conditions as follows:

> You lift a large sack of coal to your shoulders, run toward the white hot steel in a 100-ton ladle, you must get close enough without burning your face off to hurl the sack, using every ounce of strength, into the ladle and run, as flames leap up the roof. Then you rush out to the ladle and madly shovel manganese into it, as hot a job as can be managed.

Most steelworkers were illiterate immigrants, usually from Central and Eastern Europe, and lived in primitive conditions in drab shacks near the mills, often without running water or indoor plumbing. The steel companies employed spies and if a man was discovered talking union he was summarily fired and blacklisted. Meetings held in foreign languages were banned. Labor organizers were beaten by the police and run out of town.

Steel was the symbol of America's might and the bastion of anti-unionism in the United States since the brutal crushing of a strike at the Homestead works of Carnegie Steel in 1892. If the steel business could be unionized, the AFL was convinced the rest of American industry would fall into line. To convince the public of the justice of the steelworkers' case, William "Red Bill" Foster, the strike leader, asked Judge Elbert H. Gary, the head of U.S. Steel and the industry's spokesman, to agree to arbitration of all matters at issue. Gary, a foppish little man who professed to believe "all" of the Bible, scoffed at the idea of collective bargaining. "The officers of the corporation respectfully decline to discuss with you, as representative of a labor union, any matters relating to our employees," he coldly replied to Foster's offer. Gary also dismissed the Wilson administration's efforts to avert a strike.

Initially, there was considerable public sympathy for the workers' cause. But the companies, aided by the national press, successfully portrayed the strike as "another experiment in the way of Bolshevizing American industry" and branded Foster as a dangerous radical bent on revolution and chaos. In reality, most of the workers were deeply religious, had no interest in revolutionary ideology, and yearned desperately to be accepted as part of the American majority.

The AFL's insistence on retaining a craft union structure in an industry in which most workers were unskilled made it difficult to coordinate activities among the strikers. American-born skilled workers refused to strike along with the foreign-born "hunkies," whom they viewed with contempt. The civil authorities in the steel towns owed their positions to the companies, and local police and mounted state troopers—called "Cossacks" by the strikers—broke up meetings, cracked heads, arrested pickets, and invaded homes. They were assisted by 25,000 armed men hired by the mill owners, and in some areas there were more deputy sheriffs than strikers.

Four strikers were killed in Farrell, Pennsylvania, and eleven were badly beaten by police and company guards. In Gary, Indiana, eighteen strikers were killed and federal troops were called in to restore order. Pitting one group of have-nots against another, the mill owners imported trainloads of black strikebreakers from the South, who were eager for jobs. Rioting broke out in the steel towns when they arrived protected by armed guards, giving birth to long-lived racial hatreds.

The strike dragged on for several months, but the companies managed to keep the mills operating at 70 percent of capacity. Enthusiasm for the walkout waned and at the end of 1919, the timid AFL withdrew what little support it was giving the strikers. Savings depleted, the beaten men drifted back to the mills. The dismal failure of the steel strike was a setback from which organized labor, stranded and isolated, did not recover for a decade. The so-called American Plan—essentially a no-strike pledge in return for a job—became the rule in American industry and was held enforceable by the Supreme Court. Red Bill Foster joined the Communist Party, soon became its leader, and ran for president on the Communist ticket in 1924.

* * *

While the steel strike was fizzling out, the last of the major work stoppages of 1919 occurred in the coal fields. Unlike the steelworkers and textile workers, the miners were well organized. Working in an extremely dangerous industry, they had formed bonds that transcended the usual divisions of nationality and race that hampered American unionism. Under the leadership of John L. Lewis, a son of Welsh immigrants with the theatrical manner of an old-time Shakespearean actor, the United Mine Workers of America had a half million members, and was the AFL's largest union.

The basic problem of the coal industry was overproduction. Wartime demands and high prices had led to the opening of more mines than the nation needed, particularly in the bituminous (soft coal) fields of western Pennsylvania, northern West Virginia, Ohio, Indiana, and Illinois. In good times the miners could count on only three or four days work; in bad times they were lucky to get two or three. The miners wanted a 60 percent pay raise to match a wage increase granted the anthracite (hard coal) miners, and a guarantee of a six-hour day, five-day week. The operators rejected these demands as too costly. President Wilson said a coal strike in the face of approaching winter was "a grave moral and legal wrong," and Attorney General Palmer obtained a preliminary injunction barring a strike. Nevertheless, on November 1, 1919, 400,000 miners walked off the job. John L. Lewis calmly settled down to read Homer's *Iliad* while waiting for the operators to come to terms.

Lewis was a lifelong Republican and, aware of the condemnation of the steelworkers as Bolsheviks, had emphasized that wages and working conditions were the sole issues of the struggle in the mines. Nevertheless, the operators denounced the strike as a Bolshevik plot and charged that it had personally been ordered by Lenin and Trotsky. Telegrams and letters poured in to Washington urging action to end the strike.

The strikers' cause suffered a serious blow when the voters of Massachusetts elected Calvin Coolidge to a second term as governor by an overwhelming margin. Ordinarily a state election would have been of little national interest, but developments in Massachusetts were keenly observed because the key issue was Coolidge's conduct during the Boston police strike. Coolidge had wrapped himself in the cloak of "law and order" and his victory was hailed as a defeat for radicalism and clear evidence that the public was fed up with industrial unrest.

Four days after the Massachusetts election, a federal judge granted Palmer's motion for a permanent injunction against the strike. UMW leaders were directed to order the miners to go back to work or face fines or jail for contempt. Realizing he had made a tactical error by authorizing the walkout in the face of public hostility, Lewis called for an end to the strike. "We are Americans," he rumbled. "We cannot fight our government." To the surprise of Lewis and the operators, thousands of miners defied their leaders and the courts, and the strike went on.

Over the next month, schools closed for want of coal, factories shut down, railroad traffic was drastically curtailed, and in some areas the workday was cut to a few hours. Palmer was now convinced that the objective of the strike was to bring down the government and asked the courts to cite Lewis and eighty-three other UMW officials for contempt. At the same time, the White House issued an appeal for an end to the strike and sweetened it with the offer of a substantial wage increase. Aware that public opinion had turned against them, the insurgent miners accepted this offer although it contained no change in hours and working conditions.

Two groups of Americans, women and blacks, emerged from the war with heightened expectations and new attitudes toward their place in society. The emancipated woman was the standard-bearer of the modern age. "When the world began to change, the restlessness of women was the main cause," observed the writer Hutchins Hapgood. While mainstream feminists fought for the vote, a radical vanguard, the New Women, sought sexual equality with men, including the freedom to love and access to birth control. The war accelerated the triumph of women's rights, as it did that of Prohibition. "The greatest thing that came out of the war," said Carrie Chapman Catt, a suffragette leader, "was the emancipation of women, for which no man fought."

Writing to a Midwestern friend, Randolph Bourne, who had sympathy for the compromises women made, provided a graphic look at the New Women:

> They are all social workers or magazine writers in a small way. They are decidedly emancipated and advanced, and so thoroughly healthy and zestful, so it seems to my unsophisticated masculine sense. They shock you constantly. . . . They have an amazing combination of wisdom and youthfulness, of humor and ability, and innocence and self-reliance, which absolutely belies everything you will read in the story-books or any other description of womankind. They are, of course, self-supporting and independent; and they enjoy the adventure of life; the full reliant, audacious way in which they go about

makes you wonder if the new woman isn't to be a very splendid sort of a person.

Numerous nations preceded the United States in granting women the right to vote, the first being New Zealand, which acted in 1893, followed by Australia and Finland. One of the most curious aspects of this triumph was the minor role played by the political parties in the victory. In 1913, President Wilson rejected the idea of a constitutional amendment to enfranchise women, saying the states controlled voting rights. The suffragettes continued the struggle. "Call on God, my dear," a determined Mrs. Oliver H. P. Belmont told a young worker who was despondent about the chance for success. "*She* will help you."

Five years later, in January 1918, Wilson made an unprecedented appearance before the Senate to urge ratification of the Nineteenth Amendment, which banned sexual discrimination in voting. Women were full partners in the struggle to make the world safe for democracy. They had taken over jobs in the industrial plants and shipyards, served with the Red Cross, performed noncombat duty in the army and navy, and eleven thousand nurses had volunteered. They had helped sell Liberty Bonds and conserve food. The war had proved that women could handle such jobs as trainmen, lathe operators, blacksmiths, and riveters. "Shall we admit them only to a partnership of suffering and not to a partnership of privilege and right?" Wilson asked.

With the approval of Tennessee on August 18, 1920, the Nineteenth Amendment became part of the Constitution. An estimated 9.5 million women were added to the electorate of 17.5 million men. Nevertheless, as historian Carl N. Degler points out, "suffrage, once achieved, had almost no observable effect upon the position of women." The number of female workers doubled in the postwar years but, treated as an underprivileged minority, they were denied equal opportunity and equal pay. Feminism broke up into two distinct wings—one led by Alice Paul of the National Woman's Party, which focused on a constitutional amendment guaranteeing equal rights for women; the other turned its attention toward a clutch of causes, including pacifism, birth control, and trade unions. Some New Women charged that an equal rights amendment would nullify existing special protective laws for women. What would happen to the minimum wage for women, the eight-hour day for female workers, and penalties for rape if the amendment became law? In the meantime, for many women, the grim, everyday reality of life in industrial America was summed up by an advertisement that appeared in the *New York World* on November 2, 1919:

WOMEN

Light factory work
Experience unnecessary
Can make $15–$18

Leon H. Hirsch & Co.

World War I brought a host of new possibilities for the estimated 10.5 million American blacks. There were several reasons for such hopes, the paramount being the spread of large numbers of blacks beyond the South and the rise of more militant leadership. Before the war, Booker T. Washington, the nation's leading black spokesman, had espoused a policy that essentially consisted of waiting patiently for whites to recognize the plight of blacks and do right by them. Washington's conciliatory and humble philosophy was contested by younger, more militant rivals, chief among them W. E. B. Du Bois, a founder of the National Association for the Advancement of Colored People and editor of *The Crisis*, its journal. Du Bois, who had studied at the University of Berlin and was the first black to be awarded a Ph.D. by Harvard, said, "Mr. Washington represents in Negro thought the old attitude of adjustment and submission" that had resulted in "a distinct status of civil inferiority for the Negro."

Blacks flooded into Northern cities after Allied war orders touched off an industrial boom and a demand for unskilled labor. The war had closed off the immigration from Europe that had previously filled the gap, and beginning in 1915, desperate employers sent agents and recruiters to the South to hire black workers. Eager to escape racial prejudice, lynching, disenfranchisement,* and the economic devastation caused by the cotton boll weevil, hundreds of thousands of African-Americans streamed north to the Promised Land of New York, Chicago, Pittsburgh, Cleveland, Detroit, and Philadelphia.

The African-American press encouraged blacks to participate in what was called the Great Migration. "To die from the bite of frost is far more glorious than at the hands of a mob," proclaimed the *Chicago Defender*. Like earlier waves of immigrants, the new arrivals, once they had saved a few dollars, sent for their wives, children, and other relations. Almost

---

* The Supreme Court, in *Nixon v. Herndon*, declared unconstitutional a 1924 Texas law specifically excluding blacks from the Democratic primary. Only 5 percent of eligible black voters in the eleven states of the Confederacy were registered as late as 1940.

overnight, the racial demography of America's major cities was transformed. A million blacks may have departed from the South by the end of the war.

The closing in November 1917 of Storyville, the wide-open New Orleans red-light district, to protect the health and morals of the U.S. Navy's sailors, added a vibrant new force to the culture of Northern cities—jazz music. Many of the military bands that saw service in the war with Spain had broken up in New Orleans following the conflict, and some musicians left their instruments in pawn shops where they fell into the hands of eager and talented young blacks. Nondescript little bands began beating out lively, improvised tunes, a mixture of African rhythms, black folk chants, and syncopation. They led the funerals of girls found dead in rumpled beds and men knifed in alley brawls, moaning low with the "St. James Infirmary Blues" on the way to the cemetery, and stepping out loud and lively on the return with "Oh, Didn't He Ramble."

Jazz bands played in honky-tonks, dives, and dance halls such as Funky Butt Hall and the Come Clean Dance Hall. Musicians gathered after work, usually around 3 A.M., at a place called the Frenchman's. "It was only a back room, but it was where all the greatest pianists frequented," recalled Jelly Roll Morton, the first real master of the jazz form, who created a synthesis of blues and ragtime. "The millionaires would come to listen to their favorite piano players. . . . People came from all over the country and most time you couldn't get in." The drugstore across the street sold cocaine; newsboys peddled three marijuana cigarettes for a dime.

Jazz, near jazz, and semi-jazz was also being played beyond the Crescent City. Itinerant black piano men crisscrossed the South and West, offering various styles: ragtime, fast western, overhand bass, barrelhouse, and sock. Syncopated music was also featured by minstrel and vaudeville troupes, and there were numerous guitar pickers like Leadbelly and Blind Lemon Jefferson who earned an erratic living singing and playing blues and dance tunes. St. Louis, Kansas City, and Memphis also had their own distinctive styles of jazz and blues.

As Storyville's prostitutes abandoned the shuttered brothels with their tawdry possessions piled high on wheelbarrows, the city's massed jazz bands sent them off with a syncopated version of "Nearer My God to Thee." Some of the musicians lingered on in New Orleans playing the gin mills and riverboats. Others—Jelly Roll Morton; the virtuoso cornetist Joe "King" Oliver; his second cornetist, Louis Armstrong; clarinetist Johnny Dodds; Kid Ory; and Sidney Bechet among them—had already made the roundabout journey up the Mississippi to Memphis, St. Louis, and St. Paul and then on to Chicago and New York and across the Atlantic to Paris. One night a white youth named Bix Beiderbecke heard Louis Armstrong playing on a distant riverboat with Fate Marable's band as it glided past his hometown of Davenport, Iowa, and he promptly decided that he wanted to be a jazzman.

Suddenly there were enormous black communities in the heart of the big cities, made up mostly of unsophisticated country folk unfamiliar with the complexities of urban living and indoor plumbing. For the first time, Northern whites, unused to blacks and generally hostile to them, found themselves in close proximity to large African-American populations. Nerves were rubbed raw on both sides as the races jostled for limited housing and for jobs, on the streets and in the shops of the overcrowded cities. Whites were also convinced that black workers, who were usually paid less than whites, depressed wages and were a ready pool of scabs and strikebreakers.

Such tensions and animosities were fertile breeding grounds for a revival of the Ku Klux Klan, which had originally been organized in the South during Reconstruction to prevent the former slaves from exercising their political rights. Reborn in Atlanta in 1915, the Invisible Empire spread its tentacles well beyond the old Confederacy and appealed to white supremacists, anti-Catholics, and anti-immigrant nativists in the Northern and Midwestern states. The Leo Frank case* and the epic movie *The Birth of a Nation*, released in 1915, which glorified the earlier Klan and dwelled on the debauchery of white women by blacks, increased the appeal of the new organization, which ran recruiting notices next to newspaper ads for the film.† Plays such as *The Coon at the Door* and *The Coon and the*

---

* Frank, a New York Jew who had come to Atlanta to manage a pencil factory owned by relatives, was accused of raping and murdering a fourteen-year-old girl named Mary Phagan, an employee of the factory, on April 26, 1913, Confederate Memorial Day. Frank declared his innocence, but following a sensational trial in which mobs screaming for "the Jew's blood" surrounded the courthouse, he was convicted largely on the testimony of Jim Conley, a black janitor, and sentenced to hang. Conley was initially suspected of the crime and changed his story several times. Believing Frank a victim of hysteria and religious prejudice, Governor John Slater commuted his sentence to life. On August 16, 1915, Frank was abducted from a prison hospital by a band calling themselves the Knights of Mary Phagan and was lynched near her grave. Some fifteen thousand people flocked to see the corpse as it dangled from a tree.

† *The Birth of a Nation* was shown in the White House and supposedly hailed by President Wilson as "like writing history with lightning."

Chink were popular and the slick magazine stories of Octavus Roy Cohen, who portrayed blacks as easygoing simpletons, had a large audience.

These pressures exploded in a rash of race riots. The most vicious wartime clash occurred on July 2, 1917, in East St. Louis, Illinois, where whites protested the mounting number of blacks employed in local industrial plants. Forty-nine people—all but ten black—were shot, stabbed, and clubbed to death and the homes of some six thousand blacks were torched. A two-year-old black child was shot and hurled into a burning building. Theodore Roosevelt was one of the few white politicians to openly condemn the riots. "We have demanded that the Negro submit to the draft, and do his share of the fighting as exactly as the white man does," declared the former president. "Surely, when such is the case, we should give him the same protection by the law, that we give the white man. . . . Murder is not debatable." Woodrow Wilson remained silent.

Black leaders, nevertheless, saw the war as a major opportunity for economic advancement and an end to the racial caste system. Over 400,000 African-Americans served in the military, about a half overseas. Although the U.S. Army was rigidly segregated, Europe was a liberating experience for black soldiers. As a result, there was a heightened militancy in black America and demand for change. Also, some white Southerners, worried about losing their cheap workforce to Northern industry, talked about improving race relations. "By the God of Heaven," declared W. E. B. Du Bois in *The Crisis*, "we are cowards and jackasses if now that the war is over, we do not marshal every ounce of our brain and brawn to fight a sterner, longer, more unbending battle against the forces." This supposed new era was ushered in by the triumphant return in 1919 from Europe of the highly decorated all-black 369th Infantry—called the Hell Fighters by the Germans—which was cheered by whites and blacks alike as it marched up Fifth Avenue all the way to Harlem, led every step of the way by Lieutenant James Reese Europe's fifty-man jazz band.

African-Americans who expected improvements in their condition as recognition for their wartime service were quickly disillusioned. In the North, they were laid off as returning white veterans displaced blacks in the factories. The old rule applied—blacks were the last to be hired and first to be fired. And in the South, where black servicemen were expected to resume their "proper place" in the caste system, nervous whites met with violence efforts by the veterans to exercise the rights for which they had fought. South Carolina congressman James F. Byrnes expressed the fears of many whites when he warned of a Bolshevik-led uprising of Southern blacks.*

Seventy-six lynchings occurred in 1919, the highest number since 1908. Ten black soldiers, some still in their uniforms, were strung up. Fourteen blacks were burned publicly, according to historian John Hope Franklin, "eleven of whom were burned alive." Others were beaten, branded, or forced to flee their homes and farms. In Jackson, Mississippi, a lynching was advertised. The *Jackson Daily News* reported on June 26, 1919, the arrest of an alleged black rapist: "The officers have agreed to turn him over to the people of the city at four o'clock this afternoon, when it is expected he will be burned." Lynch law was not confined to the South. In Duluth, Minnesota, in 1920, the mother of a girl who claimed to have been raped by three black youths was asked about her daughter's condition. "She's in bed," the woman replied. This was misheard as "She's dead," and the three blacks suspected of rape were strung up on a lamppost on the town's main street. Pictures were taken of the bodies and made into postcards.†

That summer about twenty-five race riots erupted across the nation. These clashes were not confined to any particular section of the country but took place in Northern cities, small Southern towns, and rural areas of the Mississippi Delta, wherever the races rubbed against each other. Unlike past incidents, however, blacks showed a racial cohesiveness, self-respect, and a willingness to defend themselves. While these atrocities were unfolding, the NAACP pressed for federal anti-lynching legislation. President Wilson's reaction was eloquent; once again, he was silent. "Saving the world for democracy" did not apply at home.

Washington witnessed the nightmare of a race riot within sight of the Capitol in July 1919. Reports of blacks assaulting white women whipped up mobs of servicemen, some armed with pistols and clubs, who ran amok for three days. The mob dragged blacks from streetcars and shops and beat them unmercifully, some in front of the White House. Facing a mob of jeering whites, a black streetcar passenger emptied his revolver into the crowd, wounding four men. He was immediately shot dead by a policeman. An attempt to burn Southwest Washington, the black section of the city, was halted by federal troops and a torrential rainstorm. Six people were killed and scores injured before the riot ended. White newspapers charged

---

* Byrnes was to become a senator, Supreme Court justice, a chief wartime civilian adviser to Franklin Roosevelt, and secretary of state under Harry Truman.

† Years later, a native of nearby Hibbing, Minnesota, named Robert Zimmerman, who took the name Bob Dylan, wrote in the opening line of his disturbing ballad "Desolation Row": "They're selling postcards of the hanging . . ."

that the disorders were the result of Red propaganda. The *New York Times* told its readers that "Bolshevik agitation has been extended among the Negroes."

The most serious outburst of racial violence took place in Chicago. The city was a mecca to Southern blacks, who called it "the Top of the World." Within a decade, the black population had more than doubled to some 109,000 people and blacks were spreading into white ethnic working-class neighborhoods, particularly on the South Side. Whites retaliated by bombing the homes of blacks who broke the color line, and racial tensions were at the boiling point in the torrid summer of 1919. Blacks were beaten as they tried to get a cooling breath of air in the parks and on the Lake Michigan beaches, and two black men were murdered by gangs of young white toughs.

On July 27, a blazing-hot Sunday, the beaches were crowded with families seeking relief. A seventeen-year-old black youth floating on a makeshift raft drifted into waters customarily used by whites and stones were thrown at him to drive him off. Suddenly, the boy sank from sight. Several blacks grabbed a white man they accused of knocking the boy off his raft with a rock and causing his death, but a policeman refused to make an arrest. Scuffles broke out along the crowded five-block stretch of beach.

By now rumors were spreading into the surrounding streets and passions were rising: a white boy had been stoned by blacks and drowned; a white policeman was keeping rescuers at bay with his pistol as a black boy drowned; blacks and whites were clubbing and stabbing one another and the beach was red with blood. In point of fact, swimmers of both races were diving into the water trying to find the missing boy's body.*

Several policemen arrived on the scene and arrested a black man accused by a white of assaulting him. Angry blacks mobbed the police and set the prisoner free. Volleys of stones and bottles began to fall among groups of cowering, screaming women and children of both races. Whites vented their anger by attacking blacks. A black man pulled out a pistol and fired at the police and the gunman was killed by a black policeman. As night fell, carloads of white youths raced through the city's Black Belt, firing pistols, rifles, and shotguns at black homes. Barricaded inside, the residents shot back.

On Monday, whites pulled blacks from streetcars as they were returning home from work and pummeled and kicked them. Five people were killed in these clashes and others were injured. On the South Side, a band of rov-

---

* An autopsy later determined that he had drowned and the body showed no marks of stoning.

ing young blacks stabbed two white men to death. The next day, the violence spread to the Loop, Chicago's downtown, where blacks were dragged
from shops, restaurants, and railroad stations and robbed, beaten, and shot
out of hand. Black homes were vandalized and set afire and, that night, a
heavy cloud of smoke hung over the city.

By Wednesday, the exhausted police were pleading for help but neither
Mayor "Big Bill" Thompson nor Illinois governor Frank O. Lowden would
take responsibility for calling out the National Guard. Finally, the mayor
gave way and guardsmen began appearing on the streets shortly before
midnight. A heavy rain also broke the heat and kept people inside. Nevertheless, there were sporadic racial incidents over the next ten days and an
entire block of homes in a Polish neighborhood near the stockyards went
up in flames. By the time order was restored in Chicago, twenty-three
blacks and fifteen whites had been killed and 537 people were injured.
More than a thousand families, black and white, were homeless.

Over the next two months, riots occurred in Omaha, Nebraska,
Knoxville, Tennessee, and Elaine, Arkansas. In some parts of the South,
planters grumbled about "labor agents" luring off their "niggers" to jobs in
the North.

Surveying the violence and hateful prejudice sweeping America,
Claude McKay starkly expressed the bitter attitude of many black Americans:

> If we must die let it not be like hogs
> Hunted and penned in an inglorious spot,
> While round us bark the mad and hungry dogs,
> Making their mock at our accursed lot.
> If we must die, O let us nobly die

The Red Scare reached its climax in this torrid atmosphere. Victor Berger,
a German-born Socialist under indictment for violating the Espionage
Act, was elected to Congress from Milwaukee in November 1918 but
denied the seat he had fairly won. Elected again the following year, he was
again refused admission to Congress. The anti-Bolshevik Berger was
barred, it was said, because Socialism "was of the same cloth as Russian
Bolshevism."* Five Socialist members of the New York State Legislature
were expelled, and their party was declared an illegal organization. School-

* In 1920, Berger ran for Congress a third time, but lost in the Harding landslide. On his
fourth try, he was elected and allowed to take his seat. Not long after, he was struck by a
Washington streetcar and fatally injured.

teachers were threatened with dismissal unless they canceled their sub-
scriptions to *The Nation* and *New Republic*. Frederick Howe, the liberal
commissioner of immigration, was forced to resign when a congressional
investigation concluded that he had not been assiduous enough in deport-
ing alien radicals.

Following a parade on Armistice Day 1919, members of the American
Legion, a newly organized, super-patriotic veterans group, attacked an
IWW meeting hall in the lumber town of Centralia, Washington. Fore-
warned of the attack, the Wobblies had armed themselves and met the veterans with a fusillade of gunfire. Three men were killed and several
wounded in what became known as the Centralia Massacre. Pleading self-
defense, the Wobblies surrendered to the police, except for Wesley Everest,
an organizer and ex-soldier, who escaped. Everest emptied his pistol at a
pursuing posse, killing one man. He was captured, beaten, and with his
teeth smashed in by a gun butt was brought back to Centralia where he was
jailed with the other Wobblies.

That night, the lights went out all over Centralia, and under cover of
darkness, a party of men broke into the jail and seized Everest. Thrown
into a car, he was again savagely beaten and castrated by his kidnappers.
He was dragged from the car to a bridge over the Chehalis River and amid
his anguished pleas of "Shoot me, for God's sake, shoot me!" he was
thrown over the bridge rail with a rope around his neck. Twice, he was
hauled up, still alive, and dropped again. Making certain they had accomplished their ghastly mission, Everest's murderers turned on the lights of
their cars and used his corpse for target practice. It was left there for two
days. The local coroner summed up his findings as follows: "Everest broke
out of jail, went to the Chehalis River bridge, and committed suicide. He
jumped off with a rope around his neck and then shot himself full of holes."

The noose and gun were hardly the style of Mitchell Palmer and J. Edgar
Hoover. They confronted the Red menace with the law. Under the terms
of a 1903 act, aliens could be deported after only an administrative hearing
rather than a jury trial and this became the method of choice for getting rid
of radicals and suspected subversives. In November 1919, Justice Department agents raided the offices of the Union of Russian Workers in twelve
cities and detained everyone found there. Emma Goldman and Alexander
Berkman were also arrested. After perfunctory hearings at Ellis Island, 249
people, including Goldman and Berkman, were deemed deportable aliens.

All of them were crammed on the *Burford*—an old and nearly unsea-
worthy steamer that had served as a transport in the Spanish-American
War—which sailed on December 21, 1919, for Russia by way of Finland.

The "Soviet Ark" also carried 250 armed soldiers to guard the "guests." The public was convinced everyone on board was a dangerous radical because of the presence of Goldman and Berkman, but the great majority of the deportees were bewildered workingmen who had nothing to do with terrorism and did not have criminal records. Twelve left wives and children behind. When the weeping families tried to break through the Ellis Island ferry gates to join their fathers and husbands, a newspaper carried the headline: "Reds Storm Ferry Gates to Free Pals." As the ship pulled away, the indomitable Emma Goldman stood at the rail and thumbed her nose at a group of officials, supposedly including J. Edgar Hoover, who had come to gloat.

Liberals and civil libertarians were in despair. "It is forever incredible," wrote Walter Lippmann, "that an administration announcing the most spacious ideals in our history should have done more to endanger fundamental American liberties than any group of men for a hundred years." Woodrow Wilson, who was now hobbling about the White House with the aid of a stick, was silent and it is doubtful whether the news of his attorney general's excesses penetrated the wall of silence about him.

Spurred by this success and the public clamor for more deportations, Palmer and Hoover planned additional raids "to drive from our midst the agents of Bolshisvism." Hoover's informers set meetings of the radical organizations that they had infiltrated for the night of January 2, 1920. Federal agents swooped down on gatherings in thirty-three cities and towns across the nation. Mass arrests were made without warrants and some six thousand people were taken into custody. Families were separated and the prisoners held without charge or access to lawyers. In Newark, a man was arrested because "he looked like a radical"; another was seized when he stopped to inquire about what was happening. The raiders expected to find huge caches of arms and explosives but the total take was three pistols and no dynamite.

Suspected radicals who were aliens were held by the Department of Justice for deportation while American citizens were turned over to local authorities to be prosecuted under state anti-radical laws. The prisoners were treated brutally. Half the eight hundred people detained in New England were taken to Deer Island in Boston Harbor in chains and kept in primitive conditions with no heat, poor sanitation, and no legal representation. An anarchist fell five stories to his death (there were charges he was pushed), another man went insane, and two died of pneumonia. In Detroit, eight hundred people were held captive for a week in a dark, windowless corridor of the antiquated Federal Building, where there was but a single toilet. For a time, the public was dazzled by the Palmer raids, and the attorney general was hailed as the savior of the republic. "There is no time to waste on hairsplitting over infringement of liberty," declared the *Washington Post*. Most of those arrested were released for lack of evidence, and only a handful of wretched aliens were deported.

Palmer eventually overreached himself with shrill warnings of a Red coup on May Day 1920. As the fatal day neared, Hoover deployed his agents, local police went on the alert, and public officials and buildings were placed under guard. Not a single disturbance occurred and the nation was torn between rage at Palmer for creating unnecessary tensions and laughter at his failure. Palmer's presidential ambitions imploded and Henry Mencken jeered that he was "one of the most obnoxious mountebanks in public life."*

The anti-Red fever had crested, and it subsided almost as rapidly as it had developed for a number of reasons. In Europe, the spread of Bolshevism had been checked and Italy, France, and Germany did not go Communist as expected. At home, there was a dawning realization that there was never a real cause for alarm. While there was some fire behind all the smoke, the danger of a Bolshevik coup in the United States had been vastly exaggerated. Even Senator William Borah denounced "the strange lunacy . . . that you must destroy all guarantees of the Constitution in order to preserve the rights of the American people."

As the country moved further from the war, there was a change in the national temper. Turmoil and conflict were replaced by a less frenetic, less restless atmosphere. The public mind was diverted by a whole host of new fads, fashions, and concerns. The popular song of the day was "Yes, We Have No Bananas." Prohibition and the newfangled radio soon replaced the threat of Communism as the chief topic of conversation. Average Americans were now less concerned about bomb-throwing, bewhiskered Bolsheviks than what station they could pick up on their primitive crystal sets, where they could obtain a decent drink, and how they could get the money together to buy one of those shiny new Lexingtons or Overlands pouring off the production lines. And the press, especially the new tabloids, devoted less attention to political and economic affairs and served up a bubbly froth of sports, crime, and sex.

* Hoover survived the debacle by blaming everything on Palmer, and he persuaded the American Civil Liberties Union that he had been an unwilling participant in the attorney general's operations. He was appointed to head the newly named Federal Bureau of Investigation in 1924 and continued to maintain a low-key watch on radicals. By the mid-1920s, his secret file of alleged radicals had reached 400,000.

That summer, the Miss America Pageant was launched in Atlantic City, New Jersey, in an effort to draw visitors to the resort. It was based upon a baby contest held in nearby Asbury Park. A committee headed by a local cleaner, Thomas P. Endicott—"When You See a Spot Call Endicott"— asked Eastern newspaper editors to run contests to pick local winners who would compete for the title. Sixteen-year-old Margaret Gorman, a Washington, D.C., high school girl who looked like Mary Pickford, the reigning movie queen, was the first Miss America. She was five feet, one inch tall and her vital statistics were a flapperish 30–25–32.

Weeks before Prohibition became law at 12:01 A.M. on January 16, 1920, stores, hotels, and saloons were crowded with customers laying in private stocks. They carried their prizes away in cars, baby buggies, and children's wagons. The Yale Club in New York City laid in a fourteen-year supply. Magazines and newspapers suddenly blossomed with articles on how to make your own alcoholic beverages. Hardware stores experienced a run on crocks, kettles, wash boilers, and copper tubing and there were advertisements by suppliers of hops, yeast, malt, and various grains.

In New York City, where heavy snow was falling, the deadline was met with mock funeral services all over town and a mixture of resignation, melancholy, and forced gaiety. Gold's Liquors at 42nd Street and Broadway sold off the last of its stock at $1 a bottle—with an extra bottle thrown in if the customer bought a half dozen. People crowded into corner saloons, hotel ballrooms, and hot spots along Broadway. Free champagne was handed out at the Hotel Vanderbilt. A coffin was paraded about the dance floor of the Golden Glade restaurant and the customers threw in empty bottles and glasses. In Baltimore there was a mass demonstration against Prohibition. A California vintner took such a dark view of the future that he killed himself. The Coors brewery announced that it would henceforth make malted milk.

The chief architects of Prohibition gathered in Washington for a watch night service at the First Congregational Church. William Jennings Bryan, the thrice-defeated Democratic candidate for president and mouthpiece of the Anti-Saloon League, mounted the pulpit at midnight, great bald dome shining like a beacon, to proclaim that now "the nation would be saloonless forever."

Exactly fifty-nine minutes later, a truck rolled into a railroad switching yard in Chicago and out leaped six masked men brandishing pistols. They bound and gagged a watchman and after breaking into two freight cars removed $100,000 worth of whiskey reserved for medicinal use. It was the first recorded violation of the Volstead Act, the enforcing statute for Prohibition named for Andrew Volstead, the Minnesota congressman who introduced it. Another gang lifted four barrels of grain alcohol from a government bonded warehouse, while a third hijacked a truck loaded with whiskey belonging to a competitor—the first recorded instance of what was to become a standard gangster practice. No one was ever arrested in any of these forays.

Nor had political violence ended. In May 1920, two Italian immigrants, Nicola Sacco and Bartolomeo Vanzetti, both militant anarchists, were arrested and charged with the murder the month before of a paymaster and guard during a $15,000 payroll robbery at a shoe factory in South Braintree, outside Boston. Sacco and Vanzetti were hardly the naive fishmonger and shoemaker portrayed by the defense, for they had a long history of participation in anarchist causes and dodged the draft during the war. For these and other reasons, Judge Webster Thayer, who presided at their trial, was openly disdainful and prejudiced against them. While the evidence was inconclusive—raising questions about whether Sacco and Vanzetti were guilty beyond a reasonable doubt—they were convicted and sentenced to death. Several motions for a new trial on the basis of new evidence and charges that prosecution witnesses had perjured themselves were rejected by Judge Thayer. He even ruled against a motion for his removal from the case because he was prejudiced against the defendants. Today, the consensus appears to be that a strong case could be made for the guilt of Sacco, less so for Vanzetti.

Over the next seven years, the effort to save the pair from the electric chair became an international cause and riots against American "justice" swept across Europe and South America. Petitions poured in to President Calvin Coolidge but he refused to intervene. Benito Mussolini asked Governor Alvan T. Fuller for mercy. The case generated a sense of purpose and fraternity among liberals and intellectuals: Felix Frankfurter, John Dos Passos, Katherine Anne Porter, Edna St. Vincent Millay, Walter Lippmann, Heywood Broun, and H. G. Wells all took part in the fight. While liberals fought to save Sacco and Vanzetti, the Communists had more sinister motives. "Saved? Who wants them saved?" one Communist organizer told Katherine Anne Porter. "What earthly good would they do us alive?"

For a moment, Governor Fuller seemed to hesitate and convened a special commission to consider clemency. The commission held that clemency was not warranted. Some wept, some cried in anger and anguish when Sacco and Vanzetti went to the chair on the night of August 23, 1927.

Through it all, the condemned men seemed the most serene of all those involved. Vanzetti, despite his limited English, wrote the most remarkable message of the affair:

> If it had not been for this thing, I might have lived out my life talking at street corners to scorning men. I might have died unmarked, unknown, a failure. This is our career and our triumph. Now we are not a failure. Never in our full life could we hope to do so such work for tolerance, for justice, for man's understanding of man, as we now do by accident. Our words—our lives—our pains: nothing! The taking of our lives—lives of a good shoemaker and a poor fish peddler—all! That last moment belongs to us—that agony is our triumph.

The coda to the Red Scare sounded on September 16, 1920. Shortly before noon a horse and wagon drew up before the granite fortress occupied by J. P. Morgan & Co. at the corner of Wall and Broad Streets in the heart of the New York financial district, and the driver walked away. The area was crowded with tourists and clerks on their way to lunch. Suddenly, the wagon disintegrated in an awesome explosion. Thirty pedestrians were killed and hundreds of others were injured, ten of whom died later. People at windows six floors from the ground were badly burned. Only an iron shoe was left of the horse. The perpetrators of what was called "the Outrage" were never discovered, although anarchists were blamed on the basis of leaflets found stuffed in a nearby mailbox. Others surmised that the explosion was the work of a maniac. Yet, in contrast to the recent hysteria, the Wall Street bombing evoked surprisingly little public response.

By 1920, Americans were tired of Wilsonian crusades at home and abroad, tired of idealism, tired of reform, tired of controversy and instability. John Maynard Keynes spoke for them. "We are at the dead season of our fortunes," he wrote. "Our power of feeling or caring beyond the immediate questions of our own direct experience and the most dreadful anticipations cannot move us. . . . We have already been moved beyond endurance, and need rest." In an effort to find tranquillity, Americans turned to an obscure Republican senator from Ohio named Warren Gamaliel Harding, who offered a return to "normalcy." "There might be no such word in the dictionary," observed Frederick Lewis Allen, the chronicler of the Twenties, "but it was what Americans wanted."

CHAPTER 3

"We're All Real Proud of Wurr'n"

Marion, Ohio

To get there you follow U.S. 23, which runs almost as straight as an arrow up from the state capital at Columbus about forty miles to the south. Back in the summer of 1920 the road was only a narrow strip of thin blacktop, and in the raw sunlight the asphalt gleamed like water and the flatness of the land was hypnotic. Level fields of ripening corn and rich green alfalfa stretched to the horizon and fat Holsteins dotted the pastures. Every half mile or so, comfortable but unpretentious white farmhouses were set down among groves of live oaks with their big barns not far away. A steady stream of automobiles passed along on the way to Marion that summer. They were mostly Ford Model T flivvers with windshields popped open to give the illusion of speed, but there were larger and more expensive Reos, Maxwells, and Cadillacs as well.

Close in to town, the large fields gave way to smaller ones—really quarter-acre plots, on each of which stood a tiny laborer's cottage with a straight gable roof and a vegetable garden out back. Soon, the visitor was driving along brick-paved, maple-lined streets, past rows of substantial houses, each on its own lot, into the center of town, which consisted mostly of two- and three-story brick buildings. Welcome to Marion, population 27,891, county seat of Marion County and the home of Senator Warren Harding, the newly minted Republican presidential nominee and owner of the *Marion Star*. "To understand Harding," said Mark Sullivan, a leading newsman of the day, "you had to know Marion."

Harding's unexpected victory at the convention in Chicago in June 1920 brought instant fame to the town. It seemed to residents that some mysterious force had tipped the continent in their direction. Suddenly the streets and sidewalks were crowded with strangers. Party workers, volunteers, reporters, magazine writers, photographers, hot dog, ice cream, and souvenir vendors, pitchmen, political hangers-on, and curious citizens nearly doubled the population overnight. The hotels were full and even though hospitable residents threw open their homes to visitors, the overflow had to find lodging in Findlay and Toledo, which lay to the north.

The Chamber of Commerce, whose motto was "Make Marion More Marvelous," mobilized to honor the town's favorite son. Delegations arriving at Union Station were welcomed by a big sign that proclaimed: MARION, THE HOME OF WARREN G. HARDING. The Harding Welcome Wagon, manned by volunteers, shepherded the visitors along Mount Vernon Street—temporarily dubbed Victory Avenue—between a recently erected double line of white-painted wooden columns topped with gilded eagles to Harding's home in the best section of town.

A big frame structure, painted green with white trim, it was distinguished from its neighbors only by a soon-to-be famous front porch that bulged onto the lawn like a bandstand. Unlike his Democratic opponent, James M. Cox, another Ohio newspaper publisher, Harding chose to conduct his campaign from his home rather than to barnstorm the country. Visitors noted that the house was no more impressive than that of the candidate's secretary, who lived next door. The flag pole out front had been transplanted from nearby Canton, where it had graced the home of William McKinley, the last Ohioan to be elected president, whom many thought Harding resembled. Formal flag raisings took place at seven every morning—sometimes Harding himself did the honors—and always attracted a crowd.

Reporters covering the nominee camped out in a nearby bungalow and Harding came over nightly to visit them. "Usually he seated himself on the rail of the porch and after lighting a stogie or a cigarette . . . or 'bumming' a chew of fine cut, he'd say 'Shoot!'" recalled one newsman. "Then in a jolly, intimate, confidential fashion, answered without evasion any question that might be fired at him." Prohibition was the law of the land, but the journalists were adequately supplied with liquor and Harding sometimes joined them in striking "a blow for liberty."

Flags and bunting decorated almost all the stores and businesses along Main Street. The massive gray-stone courthouse—deep-graven above the front portal was the Latin admonition *Fiat Justitia, Ruat Caelum**—also blossomed in red, white, and blue bunting. Almost every house flew a flag or had a picture of Harding in the window. He was popular with most of his

---

* Let Justice Be Done Though the Heavens Fall.

neighbors, and more than a few Democrats joined the official reception committee. "We're all real proud of Wurr'n," everyone shyly told visitors.

Some professed to remember Harding's arrival in town in 1882, a dust-streaked seventeen-year-old with all his worldly possessions strapped to the sides of a balky mule. Marion was then a country village of some 4,500 people. Over the years, both Marion and Harding had prospered. He had risen to ownership of the *Star* and was a stockholder in several large enterprises and a bank. And Marion had grown apace.

Even though it retained the characteristics of a small rural community, it was home to the largest steam shovel works in the country; other plants produced gasoline engines, metal castings, and cigars. There was also a silk mill, a lumber mill, and a thriving stockyard, all providing hundreds of jobs and business for five railroads. Civic boosters bragged that nearly every worker owned his own home and, unlike the anonymity of the big cities, each knew his neighbor. Twenty-seven church bells summoned Marion's people to Sunday services and prayer meetings and its children attended fifteen schools.

Marion was mostly peopled by native-born Protestants who had come in from the surrounding farms, as the young Harding had done, and still held views formed by their agrarian past. Harding—and Marion—believed in the same simple creed: Boosting was good, and knocking was bad. Conformity was good, and dissent was bad. Free competition was good, and government interference was bad. America should be strong and stand aloof from the rest of the world. Business was good for everybody, and business would be better if it were left alone to provide good jobs at fair wages.

The big-city reporters and magazine writers who flooded into Marion portrayed it as a simple little town of the kind that many Americans looked back upon with a homesick affection, even as they fled to the cities for fuller lives. Gertrude Stein called it her favorite American small town. A *New York World* man marveled that he was able to get a complete steak dinner for 65 cents in the town's best restaurant.

Yet, even as small-town America was being romanticized, it was losing its central role in American life and fading before the implacable onslaught of urbanization, standardization, and the Tin Lizzie. America was being homogenized by national advertising, chain stores, standardized products, radio networks, newspaper chains, and mass circulation magazines—foreshadowing the rise of mass culture and the decline of regional variety. The 1920 census revealed that for the first time in the nation's history, a majority of Americans were town dwellers. The number of Americans living in incorporated towns of more than 2,500 people exceeded (51.4 to 48.6 percent) those residing in rural areas. But the trend toward urbanization can be overemphasized. More than 31 million farmers—one in three Americans—toiled on the land in the 1920s, and 44 percent of the population was still counted as rural in 1930. Most lacked indoor plumbing and electricity.

Many Americans were alarmed by the wrenching social upheavals caused by the forces of modernism. Could liberty and equality be maintained in an era dominated by technology and industrial concentration? Rural and small-town America were not yet ready to surrender to urban domination, even though all the trends were running in favor of the urbanized majority. The story of the Twenties is one of constant struggle between city and countryside for control of the nation's soul.

The countryside was the home of white, Protestant America, which saw itself as the repository of the old Puritan values of thrift, hard work, and self-denial. To these people, the industrial cities, swarming with recent, as yet unassimilated and heavily Catholic immigrants, represented a loss of community and neighborliness and embodied all that was sordid and ungodly about modernism. Almost a third of Chicago's 2.7 million residents were foreign-born; more than a million were Catholic, and another 125,000 were Jews. New Yorkers spoke more than thirty languages, and only one in seven worshipped in a Protestant church. Bigotry, religious fundamentalism, Prohibition, and the intolerant nativism that marked the era were all open manifestations of this struggle.

The virtues and defects of small-town America were being hotly debated. In 1919, Sherwood Anderson flipped over the flat rock of small-town life in his book of stories, *Winesburg, Ohio,* to reveal the grotesque secret lives Americans led behind the prim facades of their slumbering hamlets. A year later, Sinclair Lewis's best-selling novel *Main Street* satirized Gopher Prairie, a thinly disguised portrait of Sauk Center, his hometown in Minnesota, where "dullness is made God." The Chamber of Commerce boosters, the backslapping Rotarians, the lodge members in their comic regalia, and the women of the uplift societies—in fact, all middle-class America—were skewered for what Lewis saw as provincialism, emotional poverty, and lack of spiritual values. The publication of *Main Street* ranks with that of *Uncle Tom's Cabin* as one of the few literary events with a profound political or social fallout, for it established a new way of looking at small-town America.

Lewis's blast did not go unanswered. William Allen White, a well-known Kansas editor, made the opposite case in an article, "The Other Side of

Main Street," in the mass circulation magazine *Collier's*. White described the small town as close to "the Utopia of the American dream." It was prosperous and it was keeping pace with the city. There were rich and poor in the small towns, but "great wealth is as unusual as bitter poverty." The greatest difference between the city and the small town, according to White, was the "collective neighborliness" of the latter. "Death, poverty, grief, tragedy visit the city and no friends hurry to heal the wounds," he continued. "But good will in the American country town is institutionalized. In some organized way the town's good will touches every family. Men feel the strength of it, take courage from it, give themselves to it . . . and they grow in stature by what they give."

To which Warren Harding may well have added a heartfelt "Amen!" "What is the greatest thing in life?" he once asked. "Happiness. And there is more happiness in the American small village than in any place on earth." Yet, small towns like Marion were a paradox. Even as their residents gloried in smallness and neighborliness, town boosters strived for bigness.

Harding was born on November 2, 1865, in a frame house on the family farm near the village of Blooming Grove in north-central Ohio. He was the oldest of the eight children of George T. Harding, a Civil War drummer boy, farmer, and country schoolteacher turned homeopathic physician, and his wife, Phoebe, a midwife. Robust and big for his age, Warren helped out around the farm, painting barns, milking cows, and plowing. He attended a one-room school where he was an indifferent student but showed a talent for learning and spelling long words. Harding's childhood was far from idyllic, however. He grew up amid gossip that haunted him all his life: the Hardings had African-American blood. At school, Warren and the other olive-skinned Harding children were taunted as "niggers" and "coons." And later, in Marion, some neighbors slyly called the big house on Mount Vernon Street "Uncle Tom's Cabin."*

Following a meager three years of schooling at a backwoods academy, Harding taught for a year in a one-room schoolhouse for $30 a month. It was, he said later, the hardest job he ever had. Once the term was over, he immediately headed for Marion on his mule. "As I neared the town the evening bells were ringing for the mid-week prayer," Harding reminisced after becoming president. "I do not know that I have ever heard a concert

---

* Throughout his life, Harding bore these slanders silently, for the most part. He did not know if there was any truth in them. "How do I know?" he once told a friend. "One of my ancestors may have jumped the fence." (Murray, *The Harding Era*, p. 64.)

of bells that sounded so sweet." Spiritually, he never again left Marion.

Harding read law briefly and when it proved beyond his capabilities, he tried selling insurance, again without much success. Next, he turned to journalism as a $1-a-week reporter on a county weekly. People liked him and through hard work and a careless bonhomie, he succeeded so well that within a few years he was sole proprietor and editor of the struggling *Star*. The paper's editorial policy was a reflection of Harding's own genial personality: "Never needlessly hurt the feelings of anybody. Be decent; be fair; be generous. Boost, don't knock."

Bulky, virile, and with a thick shock of black hair prematurely turning silver, Harding was like a prize bull among Marion's female population. Eventually, he was entrapped by Florence "Flossie" Kling De Wolfe, the daughter of Amos Kling, the town's wealthiest man. Flossie was five years older than Wurr'n, as she called him, bespectacled and plain. At nineteen she had become pregnant and run away with her seducer, who promptly abandoned her and their son. She returned to Marion pretending to be a separated wife and taught piano. For propriety's sake, she "divorced" her common-law "husband" and accepted her father's offer to adopt her child.

What Flossie may have lacked in looks she made up for in determination. Although Harding lazily tried to ward off her advances, he was no match for her. In 1891, at the age of twenty-six, he found himself married. Old Mr. Kling opposed the union, and once accosted his future son-in-law in the street, called him a "nigger," and threatened to blow his brains out. For years after the marriage, he would not even speak to his daughter.

The marriage was childless and not happy. Mrs. Harding was shrewish and jealous of her handsome husband, and went to the *Star* office every day to keep an eye on him. She was a good businesswoman and overhauled the *Star*'s bookkeeping system and supervised the circulation department and delivery boys. They included Norman Thomas, later the perennial Socialist candidate for president. Contrary to myth, she did not make the paper a success, for it was already a going concern. One of the phenomena of Harding's rise was that other people were always stepping forward to take credit for it, as if he were not bright enough to have advanced on his own. But Mark Sullivan thought his "easy-goingness of spirit, coupled with his common sense and his touch with the common man were precisely what . . . enabled the *Star* to become what it was. . . . Marion was a growing town, the *Star* needed only to grow with it."

Harding called his wife "Duchess," treated her with deference, and, reluctant to face unpleasant situations, usually let her have her way. He sought refuge from her shrill demands in liaisons with other women. Nothing remains secret in a small town, and the wife of a reporter visiting Marion in 1920 recalled dining at the home of one of Harding's neighbors, a handsome widow, and being taken upstairs by a child who proudly showed her Harding's toothbrush. "He always stays here when Mrs. Harding goes away," the boy said.

For all his appearance of jovial good health, Harding suffered unexplained bouts of illness. He appears to have had an enlarged heart and high blood pressure aggravated by overeating and heavy smoking. Between 1889 and 1901, he went five times to be treated by the famous Dr. J. P. Kellogg at the Battle Creek Sanatorium in Michigan for what might be diagnosed today as depression and anxiety.

The Harding of these years bears a striking resemblance to Sinclair Lewis's fictional real estate salesman, George F. Babbitt. Like Babbitt, he was a backslapper and was known for his amiability and eagerness to do a favor. Mindful of the racial slurs against him, Harding wanted more than anything to be accepted by Marion's leading citizens. One of his great disappointments was the refusal of the local Masonic lodge, the apex of the town's fraternal organizations, to admit him, a bar that was not lifted until he was nominated for the presidency. A more vindictive, bitter man might have spurned the delayed offer, yet Harding accepted with alacrity and became an enthusiastic Mason. "Warren, it's a good thing you wasn't born a girl because you'd be in a family way all the time," the future president's father is supposed to have declared. "You can't say no."*

Harding played cornet in the town band and was active in the Kiwanis, Rotary, the Hoo-Hoos, the Moose, the Elks, the Red Men, and the Odd Fellows. He read little except for Zane Grey westerns and popular magazines† and devoured the "funnies." His companions were men like himself who enjoyed playing poker and cracking off-color jokes. "What d'ya know?" they greeted each other, straw boaters kicked back and thumbs in the armholes of their vests. "What d'ya know?" Sociability soon led Harding into politics, the chief diversion of the Ohio hinterland.

Harding was a political natural. Although a meandering orator, his apparent sincerity, coupled with an imposing presence, a mellifluous voice, and a gassy pomposity, made him a welcome speaker at grassroots Republican

---

* Harding is supposed to have related this story at an off-the-record session at the National Press Club in 1922. (Murray, *The Harding Era*, p. 116.)

† Harding told a group of actors who came to Marion to support his candidacy in 1920 that he was a great admirer of Shakespeare and was much moved by a production of "*Charles the Fifth*" he had once seen.

rallies. He called such appearances "bloviating." Audiences were never quite certain what Harding said, but remembered how well he said it. William G. McAdoo, Wilson's treasury secretary, said his speeches "leave the impression of an army of pompous phrases moving over landscape in search of an idea." And the poet e.e. cummings observed that Harding was "the only man, woman or child / who wrote a simple declarative sentence / with seven grammatical errors."

It was at one of these rural festivities in Richwood, Ohio, in 1899 that he attracted the attention of Harry M. Daugherty, who was to have a major influence on his life. Harding had just delivered a speech to the faithful and had lined up at an outdoor privy to relieve himself when Daugherty, next in line, mused upon what a handsome and genial-looking fellow Harding was. He was then thirty-four, a tad under six feet tall, with massive if slightly stooped shoulders, a bronzed complexion, and was fastidiously dressed. "Gee, what a great-looking president that man would make!" Daugherty said to himself—or so he later claimed. After Harding became president, Daugherty sanitized the tale to say that they had been standing in line to have their shoes shined when he was vouchsafed this vision.

Harry Daugherty was five years older than Harding and had a similar small-town background. He had held a few minor state offices but, by the time he met Harding, was primarily a lobbyist at the state capital in Columbus for an assortment of utilities and business interests. Mark Sullivan, who knew Daugherty well, wrote: "Always he knew what wire to pull; always he kept a web of wires running from his office out to all sorts of men who occupied places of leverage; always he knew how to get results."

Ohio had provided the nation with six presidents—Harding was to be the seventh—but the state's politics were a cesspool. Political control was divided between the battling forces of Mark A. Hanna, a Cleveland industrialist and éminence gris behind President McKinley, and Senator "Fire Alarm Joe" Foraker,* later exposed as being on the payroll of Standard Oil. In 1899, Harding was elected to the first of two terms in the state senate, where he made himself useful to the Foraker faction. To get along in the Ohio politics of the day a man had to "go along," and Harding went along so well that as a reward he was elected lieutenant governor. Like most Ohio politicos, he regarded graft as an integral part of the system. He accepted stock in a local brewery in return for puffing it in the *Star* and is said to have taken $10,000 from a farm implement company in return for similar services. Nevertheless, by the standards of the age, he was reasonably honest.

---

* So named because of his arm-flourishing, spread-eagle oratorical style.

Harding's roving eye had settled upon Carrie Fulton Phillips, the statuesque wife of James Phillips, a successful dry goods merchant and a close friend. For several years, neither the watchful Flossie nor Jim Phillips were aware of the torrid affair conducted by their spouses, even though the two couples socialized and traveled together to Europe and Bermuda. When they were apart, Harding wrote Carrie numerous letters and expressed his love for her in passionate poetry:

> I love your back, I love your breasts,
> Darling to feel, where my face rests,
> I love your skin, so soft and white,
> So dear to feel and sweet to bite . . .
> I love your poise of perfect thighs,
> When they hold me in paradise.

Once, the lovers were surprised by the Harding housekeeper as they copulated on a kitchen table. Eventually, Carrie tired of this clandestine affair, told her husband about it, and demanded that Harding divorce the Duchess and marry her. When he refused, she decamped to Europe.*

In the meantime, Harding's political star was rising. In 1910, he won the Republican nomination for governor, only to be soundly beaten. Two years later, he was chosen to renominate President Taft at the Republican convention. In 1914, with the Democrats badly hurt by a business slump resulting from the outbreak of World War I, Harding was easily elected to the Senate in the first election in which senators were chosen by popular vote rather than by the state legislatures. Once there, he followed the policy that "conciliation and harmony were superior political weapons to obstruction and strife." His six years in the Senate were undistinguished even in terms of the rather undistinguished body of that day. There was no Harding Act or even a Harding Amendment to an important bill to draw public attention to him. What little legislation he introduced was petty and designed to provide some advantage for a constituent or campaign contributor. When controversial matters came before the Senate, he usually avoided a roll call by being absent.

Harding was comfortable in the clubby atmosphere of the Senate,

* The cuckolded Jim Phillips eventually got his revenge in 1920 by pointedly refusing to decorate his store in honor of Marion's favorite son—thereby calling the attention of out-of-town reporters to the affair. While they soon learned the details of Harding's sexual escapades nothing was printed about them, as in the case of John F. Kennedy's affairs forty years later.

where his closest friend was New Mexico's Albert Fall, for whose intelligence he harbored an inordinate admiration. There was nothing to tax Harding's abilities or his energies. The pay was good—$5,000 a year plus allowances. Along with the $20,000 or so coming in from the *Star*, he was well off and the Hardings could well afford a $50,000 Georgian home at 2314 Wyoming Avenue. For amusement, Harding played middling golf and high-stakes poker at the socially elect Chevy Chase Club, where the members were obviously unaware of his questionable racial background. Eager as always to be accepted, he was obliging and easygoing, ready to share a drink or a story, and was considered a swell fellow.

Mrs. Harding, nervously talkative and always bustling about, was at first rebuffed by Washington society. But she was befriended by the boozy, morphine-addicted Evalyn Walsh McLean, owner of the cursed Hope Diamond and wife of Edward B. McLean, the playboy publisher of the *Washington Post*. The Hardings were frequent quests at Friendship, the McLean estate, and were invited to the home of Nick and Alice Longworth for poker. Unlike Alice, Mrs. Harding did not play and her job was to tend bar. She sought solace from her husband's compulsive adulteries in astrology and became addicted to the prognostications of Madame Marcia Champney, a clairvoyant also patronized by Edith Wilson.*

Harding, meanwhile, was enjoying the favors of a baby-faced young blonde named Nan Britton, who was thirty-one years his junior and had been infatuated with him since her teens. She later claimed that in 1919 she gave birth to a girl fathered by Harding.† He also had other affairs and resumed his relationship with Carrie Phillips, who returned to the United States after the start of World War I.

Had Harding's career "stopped with the Senate, he would have only an obscure and forgotten name preserved like thousands of others in old Congressional Directories," observed Mark Sullivan. Nevertheless, Harding was a shrewd Ohio politician and prominent enough to be considered by Theodore Roosevelt, who would have had the Republican presidential

---

* World War I was followed by an intense interest in spiritualism as the living tried to make contact with those on the "other side." *Scientific American* offered a $2,500 prize for any objective demonstration of psychic phenomena and named a distinguished committee to investigate these claims. J. P. Morgan supposedly took advice from an occult adviser and the Ouija board, which spelled out occult messages, had a popular vogue.

† It should be noted that there is some question about the truth of Nan Britton's allegations, especially as to whether Harding was the father of her child. For a discussion, see Ferrell, *The Strange Deaths of President Harding*, Chap. 3.

nomination in 1920 had he lived, as a possible vice president. Harry Daugherty, who had never forgotten his first impression of Harding, set a higher goal for his friend that year—the White House.

"We drew to a pair of deuces and filled," Warren Harding was to say of his nomination as the Republican presidential candidate in 1920. So did Charles Ponzi. When the forty-two-year-old Italian immigrant, former dealer in fresh vegetables, and convicted forger decided that he wanted to become a wealthy financier he was unfazed by the fact that he had no money. In 1919, he was a $20-a-week clerk in a Boston foreign trade house, had only $150 to his name, and no contacts in the financial world. Yet, within a few months he was handling millions of dollars of other people's money and was being hailed as a financial genius. The sleek and handsome Ponzi knew something more important than how to read a balance sheet or the difference between debits and credits, interest and dividends. He understood human cupidity and how to plumb its depths.

Quitting his job, Ponzi opened the Old Colony Foreign Exchange Company on Boston's School Street, and the firm's newspaper advertisements quickly attracted attention. Ponzi was selling promissory notes that would pay back $15 for every $10 invested for ninety days. A 50 percent dividend! It sounded too good to be true, but Ponzi explained to would-be investors that he would make money by taking advantage of differences in foreign exchange rates. He would buy International Postal Union reply coupons in countries with weak economies and then redeem them in more stable countries at higher rates. The difference in exchange rates for francs, lire, and drachmas would be profit and returned to his customers. What could be simpler or more risk-free? Even better yet, it was legal.

At first, only a slow trickle of funds came in, but as Ponzi was seen to be actually paying 50 percent interest as promised to all who brought him money—far more than any bank—his fame spread. By June 1920, money was flowing into Old Colony at a rate of $1 million a week. The staff couldn't take it in fast enough and cash overflowed counter drawers into wastepaper baskets and closets. The lines outside Ponzi's office ranged around the block as thousands of people bought his notes, with the average investment running about $300. Three quarters of the Boston police force were said to be among his investors.

Branch offices were established and Ponzi talked of opening a string of banks and brokerage houses. He claimed he could pay such high rates of interest because his own profits ran upward of 400 percent. To win additional funds and respectability, he bought control of the Hanover Trust Company and became its president. He treated himself to a lavish lifestyle, complete with a twenty-room mansion in suburban Lexington, servants, and a chauffeur-driven limousine, and he showered his wife with jewels. He bought out the company for which he had formerly worked and fired his ex-boss. Loud cheers and applause greeted him everywhere and people wanted to touch his hand to assure him of their gratitude.

"You are the greatest Italian of them all!" shouted a group of investors.

"No. No," Ponzi protested. "Columbus and Marconi. Columbus discovered America. Marconi discovered the wireless."

"Yes, yes," came the response, "but you discovered money."

Most Americans knew little about investing, having never done so until, as a patriotic duty, they bought their first bonds during the wartime Liberty Loan drives. Nearly a third of these bonds were bought by people with annual incomes of $2,000 or less. The loan drives "taught people to buy securities," states one historian. "More than 22 million individuals had discovered the magic of coupon-clipping and the desirability of bonds as a form of wealth"—and it made them fair game for Charles Ponzi.

Ponzi's instant success also attracted attention of another kind. The Boston district attorney's office launched a quiet investigation of Old Colony and another of his operations, the Securities Exchange Company. The *Boston Post* also began its own inquiry. Yet no one could pin anything on him. Ponzi had paid off all his notes as promised and not a single complaint had been filed. The break came on July 26, 1920, when the paper reported that less than $75,000 worth of postal reply coupons were printed in most years. In 1919, only $58,600 was issued. Ponzi had accepted millions of dollars and claimed to have invested the money in coupons. Where had the money gone? The *Post* also reported that Ponzi had been convicted in Canada on a forgery charge and served three years in prison.

Ponzi's house of cards began to collapse. Lenders besieged his offices, demanding the return of their money. Proclaiming his innocence, Ponzi denied everything and to prevent a panic paid off all the pressing claims without a single default. To bolster confidence, he offered to pay 50 percent interest on money invested for forty-five days, rather than the ninety days previously set. The *Post* now charged that he was insolvent but people continued to press funds upon Ponzi, who failed to realize that the key to a successful scam is to take the money and run. The end came on August 11. All of his offices were closed by order of the district attorney, never to reopen again.

In addition to the forgery conviction, Ponzi had done two years in

Atlanta for smuggling a group of Italians across the border from Canada. The investors also learned that Ponzi had no assets, and liabilities of $2.1 million. He had purchased a few coupons, but most of the money had gone to repay his early investors. Overall, Ponzi took in about $15 million in eight months from about forty thousand people; less than $200,000 was recovered. A welter of federal and state criminal and civil trials, bankruptcy hearings, and suits filed by and against Ponzi followed and five banks collapsed. Ultimately, he was convicted of mail fraud and sentenced to five years in federal prison and to seven more on additional charges filed by the Massachusetts authorities—and saw his name absorbed into American folklore as the prince of swindlers. Upon his release in 1934, Ponzi was deported to Italy. A large group of faithful supporters turned out to give him a rousing send-off.*

Several myths surround Warren Harding's nomination in 1920: that he was browbeaten into running by Daugherty and the ambitious Mrs. Harding; that he was handpicked by a Senate cabal in a "smoke-filled room" at the Chicago convention; that his nomination was purchased by tainted oil money. All are false. Daugherty created the legend that Harding was a reluctant candidate to magnify his own role in the candidate's success. Rather than pressuring her husband into seeking the presidency, Mrs. Harding looked upon the White House with superstitious dread, for Madame Marcia, her astrologer, predicted that if her husband ran he would be elected but would not live out his term. Nor did Harding win the nomination because he was handpicked by the Senate bosses or the oil interests. "Harding was the perfect expression of the instinctive choice of the great majority of those average men who made up the convention," in the opinion of Mark Sullivan.

Nor did Harding have a carefully calculated plan for winning the White House. As historian Robert K. Murray writes, he kept the door open and left "his destiny to the fates." He entered the race as Ohio's favorite son largely to keep the state Republican and thereby ensure his reelection to the Senate. In a speech in Boston in May 1920, he unveiled what was to be the theme of his campaign: "America's present need is not heroics but helping, not nostrums but normalcy, not revolution but restoration, not agitation but adjustment, not surgery but serenity."

* Once he was back in Italy, Ponzi ingratiated himself with the Fascist regime and was sent to Rio de Janeiro to head the local office of LATI, an Italian airline. He became a favorite of the business community there and a fixture of the social set. He died in Brazil in 1949 and was deeply mourned.

The senator entered only two of the twenty state primaries and did not do well in either. In Indiana, he ran fourth and although he won in Ohio, he lost eight of the state's forty-eight votes to Major General Leonard Wood, a former army chief of staff, a friend of Theodore Roosevelt, and a front-runner for the nomination. Nevertheless, Daugherty threw himself into his work with evangelical fervor. He had a simple strategy. He expected Wood and Governor Frank Lowden of Illinois to tear each other to pieces while Harding angered no one and remained quietly available as everyone's second or third choice. Harding spent only $113,109 on his campaign, about one twentieth of General Wood's expenditures. But his weakness was deceiving, for he had accumulated an enormous reservoir of goodwill during his travels around the country.

As early as February 1920, Daugherty confidently predicted how his candidate would win the nomination:

> I don't expect Senator Harding to be nominated on the first, second, or third ballots, but I think we can afford to take chances, about eleven minutes after two on Friday morning at the convention, when fifteen or twenty men, somewhat weary, are sitting around a table, some of them will say, "Who will we nominate?" At that decisive time, the friends of Harding can suggest him and can afford to bide by the result.

Later Daugherty embellished his prediction to say that the choice of the Republican standard-bearer would be made by "fifteen men in a smoke-filled room"—thereby adding a memorable phrase to American political folklore.

The Republican convention of 1920 was the first after Prohibition went into effect, but Chicago officials made certain the delegates were adequately supplied with potables. Some visitors arrived with their own stock, among them Henry Mencken and his colleagues from the *Baltimore Sun*, who brought along several cases of 100 proof Maryland rye. Their suite was crowded with delegates and journalists and resounded with rollicking song every evening. A scarfaced hoodlum newly arrived from New York named Alphonse Capone established his first bootlegging operation during the convention under the vocational mask of "secondhand furniture dealer."

Immediately after the convention was gaveled to order by its chairman, Henry Cabot Lodge, on a swelteringly hot June 8, 1920, it became a maelstrom of conflicting ambitions. Just as Daugherty had predicted, Wood and Lowden deadlocked through the fourth ballot. Harding, however, had only sixty-five and a half votes on the first ballot and slipped on the succeeding tallies. Primed by the heat and the bootleg booze, tempers flared, nerves rubbed raw, and fights broke out on the floor and in the gallery. Finally, the convention recessed on the night of Friday, June 11, so a way out of the impasse could be found off the floor before the party tore itself to pieces. The moment Harry Daugherty had forecast was now at hand.

Party leaders met in the rooms and corridors of the Blackstone Hotel well into the next morning. One such group, made up of old guard senators, gathered in Suite 404–6, which was rented by Republican National Chairman Will H. Hays and magazine publisher George Harvey. Liquor flowed freely and cigar smoke coiled about as men came and went. Wood and Lowden had knocked each other out—that much was agreed upon. But who would take their place? The names of the various possibilities were trotted out: Herbert Hoover, Calvin Coolidge, the progressive Senator Hiram Johnson of California, who had been Theodore Roosevelt's running mate in 1912, Nicholas Murray Butler, the president of Columbia University . . . and Warren Harding.

Usually, it is stated that Harding was chosen as the nominee by this Senate cabal and then called in for questioning about potential skeletons in his closet—a good story, but it never happened. Actually, the meeting broke up without reaching a decision. Harding partisans tried to get a bandwagon rolling by convincing reporters and other delegates that the convention would choose the Ohioan when it reconvened. But several of Harding's Senate colleagues thought themselves better qualified than he to be the nominee. Thirteen of the sixteen senators in Chicago voted against Harding when the convention reconvened on Saturday morning. Lodge even tried to organize a "Stop Harding" movement. Nor was there an immediate swing to the Ohioan on the early ballots.

Nevertheless, the rumors of Harding's impending nomination circulated by his partisans convinced reporters and delegates, always eager for hints of conspiracy, that the Senate leadership had indeed fingered him and that his nomination was inevitable. The Ohioan's share of the votes mounted steadily until he was nominated on the ninth ballot with 692 ½ votes, and his victory was declared unanimous amid scattered cries of "No! No!" Mrs. Harding was unhappy with the outcome. "I cannot see why anyone should want to be President," she told a newsman, perhaps with Madame Marcia's prediction in mind. "I can see but one word on the head of my husband if he is elected, and that word is 'Tragedy.'"

Party leaders put forward the moderately progressive Senator Irvine L. Lenroot of Wisconsin as the vice presidential nominee to balance the conservative Harding. Thinking the choice a perfunctory matter, Senator Lodge, the permanent chairman, handed over the gavel to Senator Frank B. Willis of Ohio and left the rostrum. But the delegates, as a result of all the talk about the "smoke-filled room," saw this as another attempt by the "Senate cabal" to force one of their colleagues down their throats. When Lenroot's name was presented to the convention, one delegate shouted, "Not on your life!"

In the tumult, an Oregon delegate stood on his chair and began shouting "Coolidge! Coolidge!" Willis lost control of the convention as other delegations picked up the chant and the name of the prim-looking law and order Massachusetts governor was placed in nomination. Coolidge won on the first ballot by a landslide vote of 674 to 146 while the shocked Senate leaders gasped. The entire process took only about ten minutes. Having approved the most conservative platform written by a Republican convention in two decades and a pair of conservative candidates, the exhausted delegates streamed out of Chicago.

In the final analysis, Harding's nomination was logical. Modest and unassuming, the convivial senator was the candidate who best expressed the mood of the delegates—and the nation. He had no political enemies, was from a pivotal state, had voted for Prohibition and female suffrage, and, unlike the intellectually arrogant Woodrow Wilson, would not browbeat business or Congress. There would be no grandiose reform plans under Harding; there would be no global crusades. The bucolic small-town America invoked by him may never have existed but it was what most Americans wanted. "The times," said Senator Frank Brandegee, did not require "first-raters."

"Take wine, women and song, add plenty of A-No. 1 victuals, the belch and bellow of oratory, a balmy and stimulating climate and the whiff of patriotism, and it must be obvious that you have a dose with a powerful kick in it." So wrote Mencken in fond memory of the 1920 Democratic convention in San Francisco. Mitchell Palmer, James Cox, and William McAdoo were the front-runners, but progressives such as Franklin Roosevelt and Supreme Court Justice Louis D. Brandeis thought Herbert Hoover worthy of the nomination—until he revealed himself a Republican.

The tragic shadow of Woodrow Wilson lay over the convention. He called upon the party to make the campaign "a solemn referendum" on American participation in the League of Nations, and despite his physical incapacity and the no-third-term tradition gave every indication of wanting the nomination. Wilson obviously believed that the delegates would be unable to agree on a nominee because Democratic conventions required a two-thirds majority, and would turn in the end to him.

Palmer's star, damaged by the excesses of the Red Scare, quickly fizzled, leaving McAdoo and Cox to contest the nomination. McAdoo would have probably been the party's strongest candidate. Vigorous-looking and commanding in a Lincolnesque way, he was able, progressive, a strong dry (pro-Prohibitionist), and popular in the South and West and with labor as well. But not only had he served as Wilson's treasury secretary, he was married to the president's daughter, and the Democratic city bosses detested Wilson and all his works. The bland and cautious Cox, who had served a pair of mildly progressive terms as governor of Ohio and whose major appeal to urban Democrats was his opposition to Prohibition, was finally nominated on the forty-fourth ballot. Franklin Roosevelt was chosen as his running mate as a sop to the Wilsonites, and because of his famous name.

Cox and Roosevelt went to Washington to pay their respects to the president and were shocked by what they found. Ushered out onto the South Portico of the White House, they found him in a wheelchair, looking frail and shriveled. Despite the stifling heat of a Washington summer, his left shoulder was covered with a shawl, which concealed his paralyzed arm. Wilson did not, at first, seem to realize the presence of his visitors until Cox approached and warmly greeted him.

"Thank you for coming," the president replied weakly. "I am very glad you came."

A few minutes of desultory conversation ensued during which Wilson's head was bowed on his chest. And then Cox said: "Mr. President, we are going to be a million percent with you and your Administration and that means the League of Nations."

"I am very grateful," Wilson replied in a barely audible voice. "I am very grateful."

Following this dramatic meeting, Cox, who heretofore had not taken a strong position on American participation in the League, issued a statement committing the Democratic candidates to making the League the paramount issue of the campaign. The Republicans were delighted. They intended to appeal to extreme nationalism and "America First." But the election was not a referendum on American participation in the League, or upon Wilson, or even on idealism and progressivism. It was a referendum upon Warren Harding—and the voters liked what they saw.

The campaign itself was anticlimactic. Most of the American public responded to it with a yawn. They were much more interested in Babe Ruth's first assault on the major league home run record. Harding set the style for his campaign. He remained for the most part in Marion, serenely projecting confidence and affability. Coolidge, whom Harding called the "Little Feller," made a few less than successful forays onto the campaign trail and then subsided into silence. Legend has attributed Harding's front porch strategy to Senator Boies Penrose, Pennsylvania's sardonic Republican boss. "Keep Warren at home," he is supposed to have said. "Don't let him make any speeches. If he goes on a tour, somebody's sure to ask him questions and Warren's just the sort of damn fool that'll try to answer them." Penrose's advice, if actually given, merely coincided with Harding's own inclinations.

As his first task, Harding had to unify the various warring factions of the party. Sensing victory in the offing, progressives and conservatives, pro- and anti-League Republicans made the pilgrimage to Marion where Harding worked both sides of the political street, telling everyone what they wanted to hear. Always a skillful compromiser and pacifier, he showed, as was to be said in a later day of Richard M. Nixon, that "he could campaign in Scylla and Charybdis and carry both precincts."

The candidate was backed by a well-oiled political machine run by Will Hays and Albert Lasker, a brilliant Chicago advertising man, who had a war chest of over $8 million to work with, four times that of the Democrats. Potential voters were brought to Marion in droves—some 600,000 in all—where Harding greeted them with canned platitudes while Lasker peddled him to the rest of the country as if he were toothpaste or mouthwash. The Chicago Cubs came to Marion for an exhibition game with a local team, thereby providing the candidate the opportunity to assume a presidential stance as he threw out the first ball.

Lasker added a new twist to political campaigning. For the first time, Broadway and Hollywood celebrities visited a presidential nominee and were photographed with him. Singer Al Jolson produced a campaign song he had written: "We need another Lincoln / To do this country's thinkin' / Mis-ter Harding / You're the man for us." Taking no chances on a last-minute scandal, Lasker gave Carrie Phillips $20,000 plus a monthly stipend and put her on a slow boat to Japan.

Cox and Roosevelt actively stumped the country while Harding remained on his front porch. Sometimes Cox spoke as many as twenty-six times a day and tried mightily to pin Harding down on the issues, especially the question of America's adherence to the League. But he found himself flailing futilely against his rival's clever straddling. Harding all but ignored Cox and clouded difficult issues in "Gamalielese," as Mencken labeled Harding's grandiose oratory. No one knew exactly where the candidate stood. Senator William E. Borah told the voters that Harding opposed America's entry into the League; former president Taft said he supported it. Liberal intellectuals such as Walter Lippmann threw up their hands and decried the campaign between two "provincial, ignorant politicians" as a depressing spectacle.

The Democrats were badly divided. Western farmers complained that Wilson's agricultural policies had favored Southern cotton over Western wheat. Drys protested Cox's wet stand on Prohibition. Fundamentalists attacked him for being a divorced man. Hyphenated Americans turned against the Democrats because of Wilson's refusal to meet the demands of their homelands during the making of the peace. Cox was also saddled with the abrupt collapse of the postwar economic boom in the summer of 1920. Resulting in part from the deflationary policies of the Federal Reserve, the ensuing recession brought layoffs and plummeting agricultural prices. As the election neared, every straw poll forecast a Republican victory.

"We move toward a lofty ideal," wrote Mencken. The "great and glorious day" is approaching when "the plain folks of the land will reach their heart's desire at last, and the White House will be adorned by a downright moron."

Only the isolated figure in the White House believed in a Democratic victory. When Navy Secretary Josephus Daniels told Wilson that Cox had no chance, the incredulous president asked, "Do you mean that it is possible that the American people would elect Harding?"

"It is not only possible," replied Daniels, "but they are going to do it."

Three weeks before the election, the Harding camp was stunned by an "October surprise" in the form of crudely printed circulars reviving the old charge that the candidate had Negro blood and offering dubious proof of that claim. They were the work of William E. Chancellor, a professor at Wooster College in Wooster, Ohio, and a rabid racist, who claimed that Harding's nomination was a plot to impose black rule upon America. Although Cox declined to touch the circulars, less fastidious Democrats saw to it that they were widely distributed. The press warily refused to repeat the actual charges but the oblique references in some papers, including the *New York Times*, to the "odious propaganda" against Harding piqued public interest. Tongues wagged and the word spread, inspiring "jokes" such as the following:

Sambo: Did yo' heah the big news, Ephrum? Dey done nominated
   Mistah Harding in Chicago.
Ephrum: Sho! Who'd de white folks nominate?

Republican strategists feared the charges would adversely affect the
female vote—women were voting for the first time—and would wipe out
any chance of a Harding victory in the South as well. Mrs. Harding was
"red-eyed from weeping," reported Evalyn McLean, and the candidate was
so angry he had to be restrained from going "over to Wooster and [beating]
Chancellor up." In an effort at damage control, Lasker issued an elaborate
lily-white Harding genealogy. The Hardings, once anger had cooled,
decided to maintain a dignified silence. Senator Penrose also added his
advice: "Don't say a thing about it. From what I hear we've been having a
lot of trouble holding the nigger vote lately."*

Election Day—November 2, 1920—was Harding's fifty-fifth birthday,
and the American people gave him the greatest gift in their possession: the
presidency. He won 60.3 percent of the popular vote, the largest popular
majority in history up until that time, and he carried thirty-seven of the
forty-eight states with 404 electoral votes to 127 for Cox. The returns were
broadcast for the first time by KDKA, a radio station that had only recently
gone on the air in Pittsburgh. The Republicans also won control of both
houses of Congress by wide margins. "It wasn't a landslide; it was an earthquake," moaned Joe Tumulty. Even Henry Mencken confessed to having
voted for "the numskull, Gamaliel" after a night spent, as he put it, on his
knees in prayerful meditation. Ninety-five percent of the blacks who cast
ballots voted for Harding. Women voted overwhelmingly for him, too,
although less than half those eligible turned out. They were obviously not
yet used to the idea of voting.

Gene Debs—Federal Prisoner No. 9563—won nearly a million votes on
the Socialist ticket even though he was behind bars in the Atlanta penitentiary. Many of these ballots were undoubtedly cast not for Debs and
Socialism but in protest against the bleakness of choice between the major
party candidates.

* Chancellor was sacked from his job at Wooster College, but in 1921 he produced a little book reiterating his charges, which was sold surreptitiously. The plates and all but a
handful of copies were seized and destroyed by Department of Justice agents at the order of
Harry Daugherty, who was attorney general in Harding's cabinet—an illegal act in time of
peace.

CHAPTER 4

"Gee, How the Money Rolls In!"

The *tap-tap* of a cane on the marble floor could be heard from a long way off. President-elect Harding, the fur-swathed Mrs. Harding, and the members of the Congressional Inauguration Committee looked up expectantly as Woodrow Wilson struggled into the Blue Room of the White House, leaning on a steel-banded blackthorn stick and the arm of his wife, Edith. It was Inauguration Day—March 4, 1921. Wilson moved slowly, pushing his right foot forward, and dragging the paralyzed left foot along afterward. His face was twisted into a permanent grimace and his hair was sparse and white. Only the eyes imprisoned in the ruined face seemed alive.

There was a brief exchange of greetings and then everyone prepared to go out onto the portico where a line of autos waited to carry them to the Capitol. Harding stepped forward to offer his predecessor his arm and Wilson leaned upon him heavily. Once they were outside, the president was lifted by White House servants as if he were a sack of potatoes and placed in an open limousine, while Harding entered from the other side. Fifty policemen blocked photographers so no pictures were taken of Wilson's ordeal.

Spectators lining Pennsylvania Avenue thought the contrast between the incoming and outgoing presidents startling. Harding, who bowed and waved his tall, silk hat at the cheering crowds, was glowing with health, while the solemn and seemingly distracted Wilson looked as withered as an autumn leaf. Yet, two and a half years later, Wilson was to attend Harding's funeral services.

To make conversation on the ride to the Capitol, its majestic dome etched against the steel gray sky, Harding talked about the various pets he had over the years, including his current one, a shaggy Airedale named

Laddie Boy. He added that he had always wanted to own an elephant, to which the president dryly replied: "I hope it won't turn out to be a white elephant!" Harding, pleased to have found a topic that seemed to interest his solemn companion, related a story he had heard from his sister, Carolyn, a missionary in Burma. It concerned a dying elephant that moaned inconsolably for its keeper. When the man came, the beast hugged him with its trunk and seemingly died happily. Much to Harding's alarm, Wilson began to weep uncontrollably and tears flowed down his withered cheeks. Harding wondered whether he should reach over with a handkerchief and wipe the president's eyes, but just as the car drew up at the Senate side of the Capitol, Wilson got control of himself.

Harding walked up the marble steps, vigorously waving his hat to the crowds. Wilson was driven to a nearby freight entrance, where an elevator took him up to the ornate President's Room to sign or veto last-minute legislation. Senators, cabinet members, and friends greeted him there. As Wilson slipped off his overcoat, he momentarily lost his balance and former Boston mayor John Fitzgerald steadied him.* When he had laboriously put his signature to a few bills, he looked up as the dry voice of Senator Lodge, in his role as majority leader, announced that Congress had completed its business and stood ready to adjourn unless the president had any further measure to communicate. Joe Tumulty feared an explosion but Wilson kept himself under control.

"I have no communication to make," he replied with an icy contempt. "I appreciate your courtesy. Good morning, sir!"

Wilson intended to be present at the inauguration ceremony but had already exhausted his limited reserves of strength. The always kindly Harding told him that he would not consider it a discourtesy if the outgoing president did not appear. With that, Harding was swept away to attend the inauguration of Calvin Coolidge as vice president in the Senate Chamber. Wilson and his wife were driven away to their new home, a Georgian mansion on S Street, on the fringes of downtown Washington.† Some two thousand people waited to greet him there, completely blocking the street.

*   *   *

* "Honey Fitz" Fitzgerald was the grandfather of the then nearly four-year-old John Fitzgerald Kennedy.

† The S Street house, which cost the then considerable sum of $150,000, was bought by the Wilsons with the assistance of ten friends and supporters who each put up $10,000, which would be more than frowned upon today. It is now a museum and almost unchanged from the time when the former president and his wife lived there.

"I, Warren Gamaliel Harding, do solemnly swear . . ."

With his noblest-Roman-of-them-all profile turned toward the crowd, right arm raised and left hand on the Bible used at George Washington's first inaugural, Harding took the oath of office as twenty-ninth president of the United States from Chief Justice Edward D. White in a clear, resonant voice. A reporter saw Mrs. Harding's lips moving silently along with his as if she were repeating the words. As he uttered the valedictory "So help me God," the band crashed into "The Star-Spangled Banner."

Harding looked out over the forty acres of spectators crowded shoulder to shoulder in the plaza between the Capitol and the Library of Congress and adjusted a pince-nez before launching into his inaugural address. It was vintage Harding—a distillation of decades of *Marion Star* editorials, overlaid with the promise of a return to normalcy and assurances that America would engage with the rest of the world only on its own terms. No eloquence of phrase or glint of original thought brightened the polar darkness. Clichés abounded.

"Our supreme task is the resumption of our onward normal way," Harding declared. "Reconstruction, readjustment, restoration—all these must follow. We must strive for normalcy to reach stability." He restated his opposition to "entangling alliances" such as the League of Nations and said the United States would not be party to agreements that would subject "our decisions to any other than our own authority." On the home front, his proposals smacked of McKinleyism: reduced taxes and spending, governmental economy, tariff protection, full employment, and an end to government interference with business. "We want less government in business and more business in government."

This was the first inauguration to be carried by a public address system and the new president's words were heard all over the plaza and widely applauded. "We have had Wilson for eight years, and I have not understood him," said one woman in the crowd. "I understand Harding already." Henry Mencken almost salivated as the words of Harding's speech trailed out on the frosty air like "a string of wet sponges." That night, back in Baltimore, he assessed the new president in a column tapped out while sitting in his drawers, as was his habit: "No other such complete and dreadful nitwit is to be found in the pages of American history."

In selecting his cabinet, Harding, obviously aware of the questions about his ability to govern, stated that he would rely upon "the best minds" in the country. Charles Evans Hughes, the frosty, bearded former governor of

New York, Supreme Court justice, and narrowly defeated Republican candidate for president in 1916, was named secretary of state.* Herbert Hoover was appointed secretary of commerce. In picking him, Harding showed independence, for Hoover was opposed by party regulars as a Wilsonian and too progressive for their taste. Before taking the post, Hoover turned down what was then one of the most lucrative job offers in American history. The Guggenheim family had offered him a yearly salary of $500,000 to manage its mining interests.

Andrew Mellon, whose fortune rested on control of Gulf Oil and Alcoa and who was the third richest man in the nation, was chosen as treasury secretary. He resigned directorships in sixty companies to take the job. Mellon was a sad-eyed wisp of a man who looked like a village undertaker; his only passion was his art collection, one of the largest in the world. Henry C. Wallace, editor of *Wallace's Farmer*, a respected farm journal in the progressive mold, became agriculture secretary.† Although these appointments were well received, they were accompanied by others that inspired ironic jokes about Harding's concept of the "best minds."

Prohibition was in its early stages and several wartime fraud cases were pending, so the post of attorney general required a person of the utmost integrity. Harding gave the job to Harry Daugherty. "It won't be long before Daugherty is selling the sunshine off the Capitol steps," observed a cynic. To the concern of conservationists and the delight of the oil barons, Harding appointed his senatorial friend, Albert Fall, as secretary of the interior. The choice of Edwin N. Denby, a dull-witted, conservative ex-congressman, as secretary of the navy was another tragic blunder. John W. Weeks, the new secretary of war, was a former senator and, like Mellon, a heavy campaign contributor. James "Puddler" Davis, a onetime ironworker better known as director-general of the Loyal Order of the Moose, was named labor secretary. Will Hays was rewarded for his work during the campaign with the job of postmaster general, the chief dispenser of patronage.

Having settled on his cabinet, Harding remembered his friends from Ohio. Dr. Charles F. Sawyer, a Marion homeopath and favorite of Mrs. Harding, was appointed presidential physician despite questionable qualifications and given the rank of brigadier general. Donald R. Crissinger, a boyhood friend whose financial experience consisted of a few months in a

* Justice Brandeis described Hughes as "the most enlightened mind of the eighteenth century."

† He was the father of Henry A. Wallace, who served as secretary of agriculture, secretary of commerce, and vice president under Franklin Roosevelt and was the Progressive Party candidate for president in 1948.

small-town bank, was named comptroller of the currency and later held the important post of governor of the Federal Reserve Board. Another old crony, Ed Scobey, who had never risen above sheriff of Pickaway County, was named director of the mint. The post of supervisor of federal prisons was removed from civil service and given to the Reverend Heber H. Votaw, Harding's brother-in-law.

To head the newly formed Veterans' Bureau, which had enormous funds at its disposal, the president chose Colonel Charles H. Forbes, a smooth-talking confidence man and adventurer he had met on a senatorial junket to Hawaii. Twenty-three of the top diplomatic posts were reserved for cam-paign contributors and friends, among them George Harvey, who was named envoy to London. The alcoholic Ned McLean was delighted to receive the badge and secret code of a special agent of the Justice Depart-ment and his *Washington Post* was soon known as the Harding administra-tion's "Court Journal."

Harding defended these appointments on the grounds of loyalty to old pals. "God," he is supposed to have said, "I can't be an ingrate!" In his insis-tence upon loyalty to political friends, Harding resembles Harry Truman, another postwar president who got into trouble because of the misdeeds of his cronies, but the resemblance ends there. Truman had a flinty integrity and a boundless capacity to expand his horizons.

Trailing in Harding's wake was what was to be called the "Ohio Gang." Big-bellied and good-natured, they set up offices all over Washington, where they trafficked in government jobs and contracts, from which they took kickbacks, and shared in the profits of political fixing and bootleggers. Among them was a curious, loose-limbed character named Jess Smith, who followed Daugherty around like a friendly puppy. Although Smith had a small office at the Department of Justice near that of the attorney gen-eral, no one seemed to know what he did there.*

Jess Smith frequented a house at 1625 K Street near the White House, where Howard Mannington, an Ohio lobbyist and Daugherty's longtime friend, operated a combination speakeasy, gambling house, and brothel for the Ohio Gang. Open for business day and night, the "little green house on K Street" was said to be the place to arrange protection for bootleggers, withdrawal permits from federal alcohol stocks, appointments to office, and the purchase of paroles, pardons, and privileges. No one ever saw the president there.

* Daugherty and Smith shared bachelor's quarters at the fashionable Wardman Park Hotel. Some people suggested that they were homosexual lovers but no evidence was offered.

Charlie Forbes, the head of the Veterans' Bureau, later claimed that he had seen Mannington studying a Justice Department file of applications for federal judgeships that he said had been sent over to be auctioned off to the highest bidder. "Gee, how the money rolls in!" Jess Smith cheerily hummed to himself—and with good reason, for he was the bag man for the Ohio Gang.

The gates of the White House, padlocked since President Wilson's stroke, were immediately thrown open following Harding's inauguration. Upon her return from the Capitol, Mrs. Harding found the staff drawing the curtains in the East Room to prevent the people outside from peering in at a reception and ordered them to stop. "Let 'em look if they want to," she said. "It's their White House!" The gesture was more than symbolic. Thousands of visitors thronged the old mansion—part grand hotel, part museum—for a reception the next day.

The Hardings, with their "just folks" small-town ways, were popular with the American public after the austerity of the Wilson years. Mrs. Harding had the public and private rooms filled with flowers. The traditional Easter egg roll on the South Grounds was held for the first time in four years and Harding revived the custom of having the Marine Band give concerts on the lawn. Garden parties and receptions were resumed. Anyone who passed the Secret Service's test of respectability and harmlessness could shake the presidential hand any day in a time set aside before lunch. "I love to meet people," Harding proclaimed. Over the course of his presidency, he is estimated to have shaken the hands of a quarter of a million people. For all his faults, he was a likable man and was regarded as the most genial of presidents.

Among Harding's most popular acts was to order the release of the aging Gene Debs from the Atlanta penitentiary on Christmas Day 1921. A vindictive Woodrow Wilson had called the Socialist leader "a traitor to his country" and said he would never release him from a ten-year term for opposing the war. As America's foremost political prisoner prepared to leave the prison, the warden suspended the rules and 2,300 convicts crowded around the front gate to cheer him. Debs stood motionless before them, hat in hand, tears in his eyes. He had intended to return immediately to his home in Terre Haute, Indiana, but Harding asked him to call first at the White House.

The president bounded out from behind his desk as the gaunt-looking Debs was ushered into the Oval Office. "Well," said Harding, shaking his hand, "I have heard so damned much about you, Mr. Debs, that I am now very glad to meet you personally." Following the private meeting, reporters asked Debs what he thought of the president. "Mr. Harding appears to me to be a kind gentleman, one whom I believe possesses humane impulses," he replied. "We understood each other perfectly." Over the next few months, Harding freed those political prisoners who had not engaged in violence, including twenty-three members of the IWW.

Woodrow Wilson had bequeathed Harding a morass of problems: a disintegrating presidency, a rebellious Congress, a foreign policy in chaos, an economy in shambles, and a society festering with hatreds and turmoil. Farmers were the worst hit by the collapse of the postwar economic boom. To meet wartime needs, they had put marginal land under the plow and mechanized their farms to increase production. By May 1921, crop prices had dropped to only a third of what they had been the year before. In 1919, a bushel of corn would buy five gallons of gasoline; in 1921, the same bushel would buy little more than a gallon. Land values collapsed and rural bank failures tripled. Nearly a million farmers lost their homesteads to foreclosure and freeholders became tenants. Five million Americans were jobless— about 20 percent of the workforce—levels not seen since the depression of the 1890s. The gross national product, which stood at a record $88.9 billion in 1920, dropped to $74 billion. Wages fell, consumer spending plunged, and foreign trade was off 40 percent from the previous year.

The failure of the Senate to ratify the Versailles Treaty had left the United States technically in a state of war with Germany, and the conflict had to be liquidated. Even more important, a way had to be found for the United States to have contact with the rest of the world without becoming involved in the League of Nations. In the first year of the Harding administration, the State Department did not even acknowledge communications from the League. Japan was also perceived as a rising threat to American interests in the Pacific and Far East. And instability plagued the nations of Latin America.

In his relations with Congress, Harding followed a conciliatory view. As a candidate he had sworn to restore the balance between the White House and Capitol Hill that had been upset by the struggle between Wilson and the Senate over the Versailles Treaty, and it governed his view of the presidency. His ideal was McKinley, not Roosevelt or Wilson. A strong presidency would, in his view, lead only to the abuse of power and to contentious relations with Congress.

Eager to be thought worthy of his office, Harding was among the most hardworking presidents. He was usually at his desk every morning by 8 A.M.

and was sometimes still there at midnight. But nothing in his career had prepared him for being president. Intellectually limited, his thinking bounded by the clichés, well-worn maxims, and certitudes of small-town America, he lacked understanding of the forces at work in the postwar United States: a mix of social change and moral crisis; economic opportunity and massive economic dislocation. Where should power reside in the complex industrial and bureaucratic society that America had become? In the states or the federal government? Rather than seeking long-range, large-scale solutions to these questions, normalcy meant a turning back of the clock to a more primitive approach to dealing with national problems.

Harding was well aware of his inadequacy. "I am not fit for this office and I should never have been here," he complained to Nicholas Murray Butler. He paced the corridors restlessly, day and night, trying to get a grip on the problems facing him. He found it difficult to make decisions and often temporized. Once a knotty tax matter was dropped on his desk and he threw up his hands in desperation, telling a secretary:

"John, I can't make a damn thing out of this tax problem. I listen to one side and they seem to be right and then—God!—I talk to the other side and they seem just as right, and here I am where I started. I know somewhere there is a book that will give me the truth, but hell, I couldn't read the book. I know somewhere there is an economist who knows the truth, and I don't know where to find him, and haven't the sense to know and trust him when I find him. God, what a job!"

Foreign affairs were also a puzzle to Harding. When a *New York Tribune* correspondent dropped by the White House after a trip to Europe and offered to fill him in, the president called Judson Welliver, his secretary, into the office and told the journalist, "I don't know anything about this European stuff. You and Jud get together and he can tell me later; he handles these matters for me."

If Harding was confused by the day-to-day decisions required by his office, corporate America was ready to guide him. Under Harding and his successor, Calvin Coolidge, government became an instrument for funneling favors to business. "Never before, here or anywhere else," beamed the *Wall Street Journal*, "has a government been so completely fused with business." In supporting business, Harding was in step with the country, for in the 1920s, business thinking dominated American society as it was to do again during the boom of the 1990s. Although Sinclair Lewis lampooned him in *Main Street* and *Babbitt*, the businessman, from the Wall Street baron to the small-town merchant, was treated with respect and looked upon for leadership. "The successful businessman . . . enjoys the public respect and adulation that elsewhere bathe only bishops and generals of artillery," noted Mencken. One of the most successful books of the era was Bruce Barton's *The Man Nobody Knows*, which re-created Christ as a modern go-getting businessman.

Harding was in office only four days when he made his first move to support American business interests. The rise of the automobile and the conversion of the world's navies to oil placed a premium upon an assured supply of petroleum.* At the same time, there were widespread if erroneous fears that oil reserves were running out. European nations vigorously supported the efforts of private companies based in their nations to monopolize new oil fields in the Middle East, Latin America, and Africa, and American producers, led by the Rockefeller interests, demanded similar support from their government.

The Senate was pressed to ratify a long-stalled treaty designed to make amends to Colombia for the way Theodore Roosevelt had engineered the independence of Panama from Colombia in 1903 and then built a canal across the isthmus. "I took Panama," Roosevelt had proclaimed with a toothy grin. But Colombian animosity resulting from the Panama affair made it difficult for Yankee oilmen to get a foothold in the area. With the Rough Rider safely dead, the apology was sweetened with $25 million of the taxpayers' money. Although the payment was assailed as "an indirect subsidy to the oil interests," it was quickly approved by the business-oriented Senate.

Herbert Hoover was the key figure in the Harding cabinet. Still basking in his wartime popularity, he served not only as secretary of commerce but as a troubleshooter with a voice on foreign trade, agriculture, and labor under both Harding and Coolidge. Some observers joked that he was actually the president. To many Americans, according to Charles Michelson of the *New York Times*, Hoover was "an almost supernatural figure whose wisdom encompassed all branches, whose judgment was never at fault, who knew the answers to all questions and could see in the dark."

Every morning he ate the same breakfast of bacon and eggs, dressed in the same color suit and tie, and hurried to his office, where he smoked twenty big, black cigars a day and tried to impose his views on the government. Under Hoover, the Department of Commerce became a player in

---

* Automobile registration in the United States increased from 468,500 in 1910 to 9,239,161 in 1920.

Washington, equal to the State and Treasury Departments. Everything from children's health to housing standards to the regulation of radio and commercial aviation came under Hoover's control. Bureaus were reorganized, deadwood was cut away, salaries were raised. Hoover helped make second mortgages a new vehicle for home financing by persuading Julius Rosenwald of Sears to issue them at 6 percent interest. Banks, which had been demanding 15 percent on such loans, followed. Countermanding the orders issued by Woodrow Wilson, he desegregated the Commerce Department.

Hoover was a master of public relations—the first major politician with an appreciation of this new art—and mixed good works with ambition. It was no accident that he was the most heralded public official in the country. Over time, he had several "personal assistants"—paid for by Hoover out of his own pocket—to cultivate the press. Magazine and newspaper editors were showered with press releases, articles, statistical studies, and copies of Hoover's speeches. One reported receiving at least one missive from the Commerce Department every day while Hoover was in office. He also enjoyed friendships with such leading journalists as Walter Lippmann, Mark Sullivan, and William Allen White.

Hoover was zealous in his pursuit of international trade opportunities for American business. The Bureau of Standards tested consumer products, the Bureau of Census gathered data helpful to the marketing of American products abroad, and the Bureau of Fisheries established programs designed to capture world markets for fish exports. He negotiated a treaty with Canada that thirty years later would lead to the construction of the St. Lawrence Seaway.

Although a firm believer in free enterprise, Hoover dreamed the progressive dream of managing social change and achieving prosperity through cooperativism and voluntarism—not through government interference. Having observed the benefits of cooperation between government and business during the war, Hoover tried to apply this principle to peacetime. Business, he argued, assisted by the government and guided by scientific principles, could create greater freedom and prosperity by cooperation rather than competition. Individual producers were urged to establish trade associations that would allow firms engaged in like-minded endeavors to reduce costs, eliminate waste, and increase profits without facing the threat of antitrust suits.

To Hoover's anger, however, some businessmen saw his proposals merely as a green light to fix prices, rig markets, and engage in other activities barred by the antitrust laws. He rejected such illegal collusion—which caused his critics to shake their heads in disbelief. However in 1923, Hoover did succeed in pressuring the steel industry to grudgingly reduce the working day for most employees from twelve to eight hours. He also played an important role in shaping the Railway Labor Act of 1926, which granted the railroad unions collective bargaining rights and established mediation procedures if a rail strike threatened.

Harding did little to alleviate the plight of the farmers and the five million unemployed. Like most Americans, he regarded the slump as a temporary natural phenomenon that would work itself out just as the fourteen depressions, recessions, and economic downturns since the Civil War had resolved themselves. Efforts by farm bloc congressmen to raise commodity prices by having the government purchase surpluses and then dump them abroad failed because a majority of Republicans regarded government intervention in the economy as unacceptable.

Hoover's proposal for an accelerated program of public works for the unemployed was also too radical for Harding and the Republican leadership. Warning that he "would have little enthusiasm for any proposed relief which seeks either palliation or tonic from the public treasury," Harding cut rather than increased spending. He went before the Senate to oppose a veterans' bonus and received a letter of "personal thanks" from J. P. Morgan for this "extremely courageous action."

As part of his effort to reduce federal expenditures, Harding established the Bureau of the Budget, which was his administration's most important domestic contribution. Under Charles G. Dawes, the Chicago banker who headed the agency, business methods were brought to government.* For the first time, a budget was established for the entire executive branch of the federal government and funds were allocated to the various departments on a planned schedule. Dawes was hailed for reducing federal spending by about a billion dollars a year. The General Accounting Office was also established as a congressional watchdog to make certain government funds were not misused.

Harding also supported Andrew Mellon's view that it was immoral to tax the wealthy. The sixty thousand families at the top of the economy were worth as much as the 25 million families at the bottom—and it was to these sixty thousand that Mellon appealed. To the anger of labor, farmers,

---

* Dawes, a brigadier general in charge of supply during World War I, was known as "Hell'n Maria" Dawes for his angry reply when persistently questioned by a congressional committee about the fabulous prices paid for supplies. "Hell'n Maria!" he finally exploded. "We were winning the war, not keeping books!" Dawes's bravura performance went over so well that the investigators never found out where the money had gone.

and veterans, the treasury secretary repealed a surtax on upper incomes. To win the support of leading Democrats, Mellon raised the exemption for the head of a family from $2,000 to $2,500, and cut taxes on lower incomes as well. Nevertheless, the major beneficiaries of the 1921 reduction were wealthy individuals and large corporations. Other tax cuts came in 1924, 1926, and 1928, all aiding business and the rich.

Mellon believed that if the wealthy kept a larger portion of their incomes, they would invest more, and the average worker and consumer would benefit through the availability of more jobs and lower prices.* Republicans defended this position by arguing that people with yearly incomes in excess of $100,000 paid a larger proportion of the total tax bill in 1929 than they had paid in 1920, while taxes for those with incomes under $5,000 were almost eliminated. While this was true, Mellon's new tax laws made it possible for the wealthy to avoid taxes through loopholes. Jack Morgan and other prominent bankers and businessmen paid no taxes at all. To make up for the loss of revenue from the reduction of taxes on the upper brackets, Mellon sought an increase in the price of postal cards, a 2 cent tax on every check cashed, and a federal tax on automobiles. Critics described Mellon's program as "feeding the sparrows by stuffing the horses."

The progressives still had some muscle in Congress and Mellon's cuts were trimmed. Nevertheless, over the years, he succeeded so well in reducing the tax burden on corporate America that $3.5 billion in refunds and rebates were handed out to large corporations, including those controlled by the Mellon family. Not surprisingly, businessmen were soon hailing him as "the greatest secretary of the treasury since Alexander Hamilton."

Chemicals and other new industries developed during the war—known as "war babies"—also clamored for protection against foreign competition. Even though the United States had become the world's largest creditor nation and one of its biggest exporters, all the old arguments for picking the consumer's pocket were trotted out: high tariffs protected the jobs of American workers and the American standard of living and nurtured self-sufficiency. The resulting Fordney-McCumber Act of 1922 imposed the highest tariff rates in U.S. history, with increases ranging from 60 to 400 percent on some items. Dismayed, the European nations claimed they were unable to pay the $10 billion in war debts owed the United States

---

* Similar arguments were advanced by President George W. Bush in 2001 for a massive $1.6 trillion cut in income taxes, most of which was tilted toward those in the upper brackets. After all, Bush pointed out, they paid most of the taxes.

because they could not sell goods in this country due to the high tariffs.*

Harding wholeheartedly supported efforts to curb foreign immigration into the United States. By the summer of 1920, immigration was almost up to prewar levels as record numbers of Eastern European Jews fled Russian pogroms and the civil war between the Bolsheviks and Whites. Nativists warned that the populations of the ghettos of Poland and the Ukraine were about to be dumped on American shores and that they would steal the jobs of native-born Americans. "You have it in your power to keep out of our country [the] criminal hordes of Europe," Senator Tom Heflin of Alabama told his colleagues.

In 1921, Congress, at the urging of the resurgent Ku Klux Klan, the Daughters of the American Revolution, and the American Federation of Labor,† passed the Emergency Immigration Act, which restricted immigration to 3 percent of the number of foreign-born from each European country residing in the United States in 1910. Intended to favor immigrants from Northern Europe, it reduced the number of entering aliens from 805,228 in 1920 to 309,556 the following year. British and Irish immigration fell only 19 percent but arrivals from Eastern Europe and Italy plummeted 90 percent.

On the other hand, Harding, perhaps haunted by his own shadows, raised the hopes of blacks by being the first president to speak out for civil rights for African-Americans while in the South. "I want to see the time come when black men will regard themselves as full participants in the benefits and duties of American citizens," he told a rigidly segregated audience in Birmingham, Alabama, on October 26, 1921. "We cannot go on, as we have gone on for more than a half century, with one great section of our population . . . set off from real contribution to solving national issues, because of a division on race lines."

There were cries of approval from blacks while whites sat in stunned silence. Whatever hopes that were inspired by these words were soon dashed, however. While Harding originally supported an anti-lynching bill, he cast the measure adrift when it ran afoul of a Southern filibuster in the Senate, out of fear that the long, angry debate would be harmful to

---

* Harding surprised one reporter by saying, "We should adopt a protective tariff of such a character as will help the struggling nations of Europe to get on their feet."

† Samuel Gompers, the head of the AFL, was a Dutch-born Jew, but like many Jews from Western Europe he was embarrassed by the backwardness of his brethren from Eastern Europe and ignored their plight.

other administration projects.* No effort was made to abolish segregation in government offices, nor did he appoint blacks to important posts. Some disappointed black leaders discussed the possibility of abandoning the party of Lincoln, but with the Democrats led by Southern racists, they had no place to go.

Harding's words about improving the lot of African-Americans came against the background of what has been called the most devastating race riot in American history. Only a few weeks before, on June 1, 1921, Greenwood, a prosperous black enclave in Tulsa, Oklahoma, was torched. Estimates of the number killed vary. Tulsa officials said 36 people died; the Salvation Army put the total at 150; NAACP head Walter White said 200 to 250. Hundreds were injured.† Greenwood seemed an unlikely place for such violence. Following the discovery of oil in Oklahoma, black migrants flowed into the state and Greenwood, with a population of fifteen thousand people, became the "Negro Capital of the Southwest." The neat rows of comfortable homes were occupied by small businessmen, teachers, doctors, and lawyers who thrived on hope and hard work. Even so, blacks faced an uneasy situation in Oklahoma where the Ku Klux Klan was active and lynchings routine.

The holocaust was touched off by the allegation that a nineteen-year-old black youth named Dick Rowland, who earned his living shining shoes, had assaulted a white elevator operator. Although Rowland claimed that he had lost his balance and merely reached out to steady himself, the girl, Sarah Page, panicked and he was arrested. Within hours, some one thousand whites aroused by inflammatory press accounts of the incident gathered at the jail. Rumors of a lynching spread and a force of armed blacks assembled to protect Rowland. Fighting broke out between the two groups and a white mob raced across the railroad tracks to burn and loot homes in Greenwood. Firemen were prevented by armed men from putting out the fires and Greenwood went up in flames. Tulsa city authorities, it was charged, tacitly and directly supported the mob as it looted, burned, and

---

* Between 1918 and 1927, there were 454 lynchings in the United States. Thirty-eight victims were white and 416 black. Eleven were black women, three of whom were pregnant. Forty-two were burned alive and eight victims were either hacked or beaten to death. (White, *Rope and Faggot*, pp. 34–35.)

† A recent study contends that as many as three hundred African-American men, women, and children may have died in the rioting: "The Tulsa Lynching of 1921—a Hidden Story," a documentary shown on Cinemax on May 31, 2000, written and directed by Michael Wilkerson.

killed. The police armed some five hundred deputies, all white, except for one light-skinned black man, who was mistakenly enlisted. He reported that the deputies were told: "Now you can shoot any nigger you see and the law will be behind you."

Women, trying to drag children to safety, ran screaming down the streets of Greenwood under a hail of bullets. Whites burst into black homes and set them on fire, sometimes before the residents could flee. A black war veteran put on his uniform and stood at attention in front of his home with the pathetic hope that this would save it, but to no avail. Some 1,200 houses were destroyed along with schools, churches, and businesses. The rioting was eventually put down by the arrival of four companies of national guardsmen who imposed martial law.

Only smoking piles of bricks and rubble marked where Greenwood had stood, and the ruins disclosed the still sizzling remains of victims, blackened and twisted like badly burnt pretzels. Most blacks fled or were herded into detainment camps. While the rampage was spontaneous, it was also calculated. Once it had begun, telegraph and telephone lines were cut and trains blocked from entering Tulsa to prevent outside interference. A survivor recalled that the air was heavy with the scent of honeysuckle and burnt flesh. "After that we distrusted every white person," she said.

Paradoxically in view of its nationalist ideology, the Harding administration's most important achievements were in foreign policy. Within a month of taking office, the president requested Congress "to establish a state of technical peace" with Germany. On July 2, 1921, a joint resolution was approved declaring the end of hostilities, and slickly reserving to the United States all the rights and reparations due the other victorious nations under the Versailles Treaty. Thus, America claimed the fruits of the treaty without shouldering any of its responsibilities. Harding was summoned off a golf course to sign the resolution. He glanced over the document, put his signature to it, and returned to the links.

Harding began dismantling the crude interventionist policies that had clouded relations with the nations of the Western Hemisphere under Roosevelt, Taft, and Wilson. Relations with Mexico were normalized for the first time since the beginning of the Mexican Revolution in 1911, and the regime of General Alvaro Obregón was recognized in 1923 in return for Mexico's pledge to compensate Americans whose property had been seized during the upheaval.

The most dangerous foreign problem facing the new administration was a debilitating naval race between Britain, Japan, and the United States. While the Western nations had been otherwise engaged, Japan had made demands upon China, and the British were concerned about the safety of their Far Eastern empire despite a long-standing alliance with Japan. The Americans were upset by what they saw as Japanese attempts to close the "Open Door" in China and by Japan's seizure of the formerly German-held Caroline and Marshall island groups, which lay athwart the line of communications between Hawaii and the Philippines. For their part, the Japanese were angry about discrimination against Japanese immigrants in the United States. All three nations continued to build new battleships at a fast pace for several years after the end of World War I.

With the horror and waste of the conflict fresh in the public mind, revolt flared against what was seen as a senseless arms race. Overwhelmed by the cost of building a new fleet, Britain put out diplomatic feelers to Washington for a disarmament conference and indicated that they would accept parity in naval strength with the U.S. Navy for the first time—both a truly historic step and a recognition of existing reality. Eager to show that he was for peace and arms reduction despite the rejection of the League of Nations, Harding supported Secretary of State Hughes's decision to adopt the British initiative as America's own.

The Washington conference for the limitation of naval armaments convened on November 12, 1921—the day after the interment of America's Unknown Soldier—amid high emotions and a sense of noble purpose. Some 1,300 spectators crowded the boxes and galleries of Constitution Hall, as Harding opened the conference by bluntly declaring that "one hundred million [people] frankly want less armament and none of war!" Having learned from Wilson's fatal mistake, he had included Democrats as well as Republicans in the American delegation. "Of all the human conclaves I have ever witnessed the gathering of the Disarmament Conference in Washington furnished the most intensely dramatic moment," observed William Allen White.

Hughes surprised everyone with a proposal that exploded among the delegates with the force of a sixteen-inch shell. He called for a moratorium on the building of battleships and the scrapping of existing vessels, which would leave the navies of the United States, Britain, and Japan with a tonnage ratio of 5:5:3. Sixty-six battleships and battle cruisers were to be sent to the scrap yard—"more than all the admirals of the world had sunk in a cycle of centuries," a British observer wryly noted.

The Japanese were unhappy with the inferior position allotted the Imperial Navy—"Rolls-Royce:Rolls-Royce:Ford" they called it—and some delegates feared they might walk out of the conference. But the code breakers of the State Department's "Black Chamber" were monitoring the Japanese delegation's communications with Tokyo and discovered that despite their seeming bellicosity, the Japanese were not yet ready to offend the West. A deal was worked out of the basis of Hughes's proposal.* Two other agreements came out of the conference: a nine-power treaty designed to preserve the territorial integrity of China, and a four-power pact in which the United States, Japan, Britain, and France agreed to respect one another's rights in the Pacific. The latter allowed Japan to save face following the abrogation of the Anglo-Japanese alliance, which had become an embarrassment to the British as they sought to improve relations with the United States. Although the results of the conference were mixed, tensions in East Asia were reduced for a decade.

For the Democrats, the post-Wilson years were a time of general despondency. The party lapsed into sectionalism, split between its urban Eastern wing and the predominately rural South and West. Franklin Roosevelt, the defeated vice presidential candidate in 1920, observed that "every war brings after it a period of materialism and conservatism; people tire quickly of ideals and we are now repeating history." He thought the solution lay in creating a vigorous national party that was moderately progressive in outlook. As part of this rebuilding effort, Roosevelt planned to run in 1922 for governor of New York or senator.

Having reestablished himself in business and the law, Roosevelt joined his vacationing wife and children in August 1921 at the family place on Campobello Island in New Brunswick in eastern Canada. Like Eleanor Roosevelt's Uncle Ted, he was a believer in the strenuous life and led his brood on a vigorous round of swimming, tennis, sailing, and rock climbing. On August 10, while out sailing, they spotted a forest fire and joined in fighting it. This was topped off by a plunge into the icy waters of the Bay of Fundy, which Roosevelt usually found invigorating. Much to his surprise, he found that he "didn't feel the usual reaction, the glow I expected."

Back at the family cottage, he found the mail had arrived bringing fresh newspapers, and he sat down on the porch in his wet bathing suit to read

---

* It was an article of faith among American naval officers that the Washington Treaty was an unmitigated disaster for the U.S. Navy. They charged that the United States scrapped modern vessels and newly laid down hulls while the other nations did little more than junk worn-out vessels or tear up blueprints. In reality, the U.S. Navy fared better at the conference table than was thought at the time. The vessels that it retained were newer than most of those in the British and Japanese fleets and incorporated developments in firepower and armor protection that had resulted from wartime experience.

them. After a while, complaining of chills and aches, he went to bed. The next morning, when Roosevelt swung out of bed, his left leg was weak. "I tried to persuade myself that this trouble with my leg was muscular, that it would disappear as I used it," he said. "But presently, it refused to work, and then the other."

"I don't know what's wrong with me," Roosevelt muttered a few days later to his friend and political adviser, Louis M. Howe, his face etched with pain, "I just don't know." Dr. E. H. Bennett, the country doctor summoned by the worried Eleanor, diagnosed his illness as a heavy cold and was puzzled when the patient's condition rapidly deteriorated. Severe pains spread through Roosevelt's back and legs, and soon he was unable to move the muscles of his lower body. Howe and Dr. Bennett scoured resorts in nearby Maine in search of a vacationing specialist. One came, concluded Roosevelt was suffering from a blood clot on the lower spinal cord, prescribed massage, and sent Eleanor a bill for $600.

For two nightmarish weeks, she slept on a cot in her husband's room, nursing him night and day. She bathed him, fed him, and tried to keep up his spirits, while her own anxiety was made worse by the inability of the doctors to determine the nature of Roosevelt's illness. The Roosevelt children were not immediately told of their father's illness and were sent to stay with friends. For a time, Roosevelt lost control of his bodily functions. Following the specialist's misguided advice, Eleanor and Howe massaged his limbs for hours, only to later learn that besides being painful, it damaged his weakened muscles.

Roosevelt was undergoing mental as well as physical anguish. Overnight, he was transformed from a lithe, active man of thirty-nine with a brilliant future into a bedridden cripple completely dependent upon others for even the simplest service. Lying in bed through those waning summer days, he was spiritually crushed. Many years later, he told his friend and labor secretary, Frances Perkins, that he was in "utter despair" and feared "God had abandoned him." Nevertheless, his buoyant spirit prevented him from giving up and before long he was bantering in his usual cheerful manner with his wife, children, and Howe.

There had been a poliomyelitis scare that summer and several weeks after Roosevelt was stricken, an uncle, suspecting polio, sent a specialist to Campobello. An examination confirmed that he had indeed contracted the disease. The doctor thought the case a mild one and assured Eleanor that her husband's chances for a full recovery were excellent. In mid-September, Roosevelt was transferred to Presbyterian Hospital in

New York City in a private railroad car. Further examination proved the earlier optimism unwarranted. Not only would Roosevelt never walk or stand up by himself again, said the doctors, it was doubtful whether he would even be able to sit up unassisted.

Some of Roosevelt's contemporaries regarded him as little more than an amiable country squire, but he had hidden reserves of courage. Visitors found that he brushed off any hint of sadness. Perspiration streamed down his face as he concentrated for hours on trying to wiggle a big toe. Both his arm and back muscles became stronger, and the day came when he could sit up. By the time he was discharged late in October, he could, with the aid of a strap suspended from the ceiling, swing himself from his bed into a wheelchair. Still, there was a certain finality about the last entry on his hospital chart: "Not Improving."

Poker was Warren Harding's primary form of recreation and relaxation and he usually invited friends in twice a week for a game in the presidential study. The regulars included Daugherty, Jess Smith, Albert Fall, Evalyn and Ned McLean, Charlie Forbes, Doc Sawyer, and Albert Lasker, now head of the Shipping Board—all sourly described by Herbert Hoover as Harding's "playmates." Hoover was invited once, but his Quaker sensibilities were offended by the idea of gambling in the White House and he was not asked back. Mrs. Harding fluttered in the background, chattering and mixing drinks. Every kind of liquor was available, but the poker parties were hardly the orgies portrayed by some writers. Harding rarely had more than a single drink or a glass or two of ale, according to Colonel Starling, his Secret Service bodyguard. Once, the president showed journalist Louis Seibold a pearl stickpin that the newsman estimated was worth $4,000 or $5,000. Harding said he had won it playing poker.

Forbes provided an account of one session. "I remember that it was very hot and Albert Lasker took his coat off, displaying red suspenders two inches wide. I won $397 and Will Hays won. The losers all payed up promptly. During the game Ned McLean announced that Jack Johnson, the black prizefighter, was to be discharged from the Federal penitentiary at Leavenworth, and either Ned or Lasker exclaimed, 'Why his old mother used to work for me and he has a fine of $1,000 hanging over him and can't pay it.'* Ned McLean said: 'Albert, I'll give $500 and you give $500 and we

---

* Johnson, probably the greatest American prizefighter of all time, won the heavyweight championship by knocking out Tommy Burns in 1908 and confirmed his title by defeating former champion Jim Jeffries in 1910. Both men were white and race riots erupted in sev-

will pay his fine.' The President spoke up: 'Don't let that worry you; I'll remit the fine.' And the game went on."

Mrs. Harding probably enjoyed being first lady far more than her husband enjoyed being president. Within the limits of her era, she was a modern and innovative presidential wife. She lobbied for more federal jobs for women, sought equal treatment of women in sports, business, and education, advocated prison reform, sought improved care for wounded veterans—"my boys," she called them—talked freely to newsmen, invited Hollywood stars to the White House, made speeches, and edited some of the president's. The black velvet neck band she wore to hide wrinkles became a fad among flappers who called it a "flossie" after her nickname. Although often ailing because of kidney problems, she delighted in the unconventional. She was the first first lady to fly in an airplane, brought a jazz band to the White House even though jazz was denounced in some quarters as "invented by demons for the torture of imbeciles," and tried the Charleston. Sometimes she surprised tourists by pulling them out of the regular line of sightseers and taking them on a private tour of the mansion. "Mrs. Harding has been a success in her first year in the White House," said the *Philadelphia Public Ledger*. "She has personified the new American woman."

Evalyn McLean remained her closest confidante, even after Mrs. Harding learned from Alice Longworth that the president used Friendship, the McLean estate, for assignations. In ignoring her husband's obsessive womanizing, Mrs. Harding uncannily prefigured Hillary Rodham Clinton. Out of love and desire to protect her Wurr'n, she poured his drinks and looked the other way when it came to adultery. "A man's heart is like a filing cabinet," she once observed. "Each section is complete in itself."

Among those present at a garden party in May 1921 was a pretty young blonde identified on the guest list as "Miss Elizabeth Britton."* Nan Britton later claimed she often saw Harding in the White House. On her first visit, she said that he took her "to the one place where, he said, we might share kisses in safety. That was a small closet . . . [where] . . . we repaired . . . many times in the course of my visits to the White House, and in the dark-

---

eral parts of the country after Johnson's victory over Jeffries. Whites were especially angered by Johnson's insistence on flaunting his white girlfriends and he was convicted on a trumped-up morals charge in 1913. Sentenced to a year in jail, he fled and lived abroad until 1920, when he returned home and served out his term. By then, his career in the ring was over.

* Oddly enough, this was the name of the illegitimate daughter that Nan Britton claimed had been fathered by Harding.

ness of a space no more than five feet square the President of the United States and his adoring sweetheart made love."

Booze might flow freely in the private quarters of the White House, but the common attitude was expressed by John F. Kramer, the first Prohibition commissioner. "This law will be obeyed in cities large and small, and in villages, and where it is not obeyed it will be enforced." The Anti-Saloon League estimated that enforcement of the Volstead Act would not cost more than $5 million a year, so eager, it claimed, were Americans to embrace the dry utopia. Congress provided a slightly larger sum to establish an enforcement group of 1,500 agents to prevent 125 million Americans from buying anything stronger than near beer. In the first flush of optimism, a large section of the Chicago City House of Correction and the alcoholic ward of Cook County Hospital were closed, as, it was said, they would no longer be needed.

One of the great myths of the Twenties is that the nation was immediately inundated by a torrent of illegal beer and booze. In reality, during the early years of Prohibition, the amount of liquor consumed actually decreased substantially. From 1911 to 1914 the average amount was 1.69 gallons per head. Under wartime restrictions, consumption dropped to 0.97 gallons in 1918 and 1919. At the outset of Prohibition in 1921 and 1922, there was a further decrease to 0.73 gallons. Nor was Prohibition all that unpopular. A poll conducted by the *Literary Digest* showed:

For Enforcement	356,193	38.6 percent
For Modification	376,334	40.8 percent
For Repeal	189,856	20.6 percent

Nevertheless, claims that America was going dry were all too premature—at least for the largest cities. Private houses and run-down buildings in back streets and alleys became scenes of sudden activity. Speakeasies and gin mills, catering to every pocket and style from the seedy to the opulent, blossomed along with stills and breweries to supply them with illegal liquor and beer. The typical speakeasy had an anonymous, blank facade entered by a basement door with a peephole or sliding panel, or was hidden behind a grocery, a shop, or in a tenement. The magic words leading to entry were either a prearranged password or "Joe sent me" or the equivalent.

New York's most notable concentration of speakeasies occupied the old brownstones along 52nd Street between Fifth and Sixth Avenues, not far from the palazzo of Mrs. Cornelius Vanderbilt III. Most of the higher class places operated as private clubs such as the Bombay Bicycle Club or the Town and Country Club, and issued membership cards. The Twenty-one Club, also known as Jack and Charlie's and housed in an opulent mansion, was the most exclusive. Broadway and Hollywood stars and the cream of New York society were among its patrons. Drinks were expensive—cocktails were a dollar and champagne was $25 a quart.

Speakeasies introduced women other than prostitutes to bars. An alliance was created between their proprietors and the gangsters who provided them with liquor and protection against the police and rival bootleggers. Some, such as Twenty-one, outlasted Prohibition. Federal officers made their first raid on a Chicago speakeasy, the Red Lantern at Clark and Kinzie Streets, shortly after midnight on February 1, 1920, two weeks after the beginning of Prohibition. Forty surprised and well-dressed men and women were hauled off to the police station in paddy wagons.

Jane Addams, the pioneer social worker, noted that the poor but respectable Chicago working-class neighborhood surrounding her headquarters at Hull House quickly began to change for the worse with the advent of Prohibition. Speakeasies opened, families broke up, children hero-worshipped the petty gangsters and bootleggers, and drunks began appearing with regularity in the once orderly streets. With a seasoned eye she observed:

> The "stuff" is moved sometimes in a dilapidated old grocery wagon, sometimes in a motor truck. In our neighborhood it is usually handled in two-gallon cans. The inhabitants of a street near the settlement [house] were accustomed to seeing a man sitting on a front seat beside the driver of an old Ford truck with a shotgun wrapped in newspaper lying across his knee; another armed man would walk casually along the pavement. This was to secure protection from hijackers as well as from police interference. . . . Our neighborhood was filled with bootleggers coming from various parts of the city, added to those from our own vicinity, because the local police captain had the reputation of being easy to deal with.

Prohibition quickly received several setbacks. A federal judge ruled that it was legal for physicians to issue prescriptions for whiskey to be used for medicinal purposes, making the neighborhood doctor an important source for alcoholic beverages. Before Prohibition ended, an average of 10 million such prescriptions were issued each year. Some doctors did a brisk business by selling books of prescription blanks outright. Congress declined to make the purchase of alcoholic beverages a crime and five states refused to enforce the Volstead Act.*

Breweries were still open to make legal near beer and it was not difficult to recharge the stuff. This was usually done by spiking near beer with wood alcohol either in the cask or in the glass. Chicago pioneered the production of wort, or green beer, the result of the brewing process being suspended before the addition of yeast. To bring it up to mark, a cake of yeast would be dropped in the cask at the speakeasy, which allowed it to ferment on the scene. The liquids that went by the names of whiskey, gin, and brandy were nightmarish. A Chicago city chemist spilled a little of an impounded shipment of hooch on the laboratory sink and it ate away the enamel. Twelve people in the Red Hook section of Brooklyn died from drinking whiskey made from wood alcohol.

Even in the cities of the Bible Belt, it was not hard to find a drink. A youthful Ralph McGill, later one of the ablest of Southern journalists, was working for the *Nashville Banner* and was sent to interview Edna St. Vincent Millay, "the unrivaled embodiment of sex appeal" of the day, who was in town to read her poetry. She told him she would like some gin for Orange Blossoms. McGill went directly to Fouch's all-night drugstore, where a pharmacist handily whipped up a concoction of alcohol, oil of juniper, and glycerin and put it in a bottle labeled witch hazel.

Standing only five feet five and weighing over 250 pounds, bald and double-chinned, Izzy Einstein looked as harmless as a teddy bear. But along with his partner, Moe Smith, he was the terror of bootleggers and speakeasy operators, and these two unlikely federal Prohibition agents in New York City helped give the Twenties its reputation for zaniness. Izzy was a $40-a-week postal clerk living on the Lower East Side when the Volstead Act went into effect. With a wife, four children, and an old father to support, he applied for the slightly better paying job of dry agent and brought an unusual grab bag of talents to the job. In addition to English, he spoke Yiddish, Hungarian, Polish, and German, knew a little Russian, French, Spanish, and Italian and even a few words of Chinese.

Izzy's first target was a Brooklyn speakeasy. It was easy to spot because people were going in and out rather brazenly. Waddling up to the bar, he ordered a legal near beer. "Wouldn't you like a lollipop on the side," sneered the bartender to the merriment of the regulars. Izzy said he was

* They were Maryland, Montana, Nevada, New York, and later Wisconsin.

new to the neighborhood and wanted a pint of whiskey if the price was right. As soon as the bartender produced the bottle, Izzy pronounced in a melancholy voice the words that became his signature refrain: "There's sad news here. You're under arrest."

After a number of solitary coups, Izzy persuaded his old friend Moe Smith, an ex-boxer, to join him. Lean and taciturn, he was the perfect foil for Izzy. They developed a repertoire of more than a hundred disguises, not one of which, they claimed, was ever penetrated. On St. Patrick's Day, they were unlikely Irishmen, scattering "Begorras!" right and left. They invaded Harlem in blackface. They entered a gin mill near the Fulton Fish Market with a string of fresh-caught fish as a prop.

The newspapers, especially the tabloids, loved Izzy and Moe and soon the entire country was laughing at their escapades.* Once Izzy met Albert Einstein and asked him about his line of work. "I discover stars in the sky," said the famous mathematician. "I'm a discoverer, too," replied Izzy, "only I make my discoveries in the basements." Unlike some Prohibition agents who made themselves obnoxious to the public by barging into restaurants and sniffing glasses and snatching bottles off tables, Izzy and Moe had no interest in molesting the ordinary hip-flask toter. Izzy once estimated the number of speakeasies in New York at 100,000; Grover Whelan, the city's police commissioner, put the number at a more modest 30,000.

Over five years, Izzy and Moe confiscated five million bottles of booze worth $15 million, plus thousands of untallied gallons in kegs and barrels, and broke up hundreds of illicit stills and breweries. They made 4,392 arrests and a phenomenal 95 percent resulted in convictions. Ultimately, professional jealousy on the part of their chiefs put an end to their enforcement careers.

"You get your names in the newspapers all the time," one superior complained, "whereas mine hardly ever gets mentioned." The partners were told to tone it down and in 1925, they were abruptly dismissed. A spokesman solemnly declared that "the service must be dignified. Izzy and Moe belong on the vaudeville stage."† It was just as well, for by then Prohibition was no longer a laughing matter anyway.

---

* For an example, see "Einstein, Rum Sleuth" in the *New York Times*, March 26, 1922.
† Both men went into the insurance business and did well. Izzy died in 1938; Moe in 1960.

CHAPTER 5

"My God, This Is a Hell of a Job!"

One day early in 1923, a White House visitor with an appointment to see President Harding was directed to the Red Room to wait until the chief executive was ready to receive him. As he approached the chamber, the visitor heard a voice that sounded as if it were choking with anger. Entering, he was astonished to see the president with a tight grip on the throat of a man huddled against the wall.

"You yellow rat!" Harding was shouting. "You double-crossing bastard! If you ever—"

The visitor blurted out something in shocked surprise, and Harding whirled about. He immediately loosened his grip on the other man, who staggered out, his face discolored and distorted with fear.

"I am sorry," the president curtly told his visitor. "You have an appointment. Come into the other room."

On his way out of the White House, the caller asked a doorman for the name of the man who had left just after he came in.

"That was Colonel Forbes of the Veterans' Bureau, sir."*

Harding had only recently learned that Charlie Forbes had all but backed a truck up to the Veterans' Bureau and looted it. The betrayal was especially bitter to the president and his wife because they were determined to do something for the human debris cast up by Woodrow Wilson's war to end wars. No preparations had been made to treat the thousands of wounded and disabled veterans and they were shunted to poorhouses, insane asylums, and other inadequate private institutions, and some were receiving no treatment at all.

---

* The witness was a confidential representative of Adolph Ochs, the publisher of the *New York Times*. See Ferrell, *The Strange Deaths of President Harding*, pp. 32 and 174, note 5.

Harding created the Veterans' Bureau from a half dozen or so overlapping agencies to deal with the problem and provided it with a budget of a half billion dollars, one fifth of all government expenditures. The fast-talking Forbes easily convinced Harding that the men who had served the nation were receiving the care they needed and deserved. On several occasions, the president cited the excellent work being done by the Veterans' Bureau under Forbes's dynamic direction as an example of the accomplishments made by all sectors of his administration.

In reality, Forbes solicited "loans" from companies bidding for contracts to build hospitals, took rake-offs on these contracts, and emptied vast government warehouses of medical equipment and supplies, which he sold to private contractors at a fraction of their cost. In all, Forbes disposed of supplies worth upward of $7 million for only $600,000 while disabled veterans lacked bandages, bedding, and drugs. In any place but Warren Harding's Washington, the free-spending Forbes would have come under suspicion long before he did, for he cut a wide swath across the social scene on a salary of $10,000 a year. He gave elaborate dinner parties and took over a floor at the Hotel Traymore in Atlantic City for the lavish entertainment of government officials, Broadway and Hollywood stars, and other celebrities.

Doc Sawyer, who had never liked Forbes, was informed of the situation by the Public Health Service and took these facts to Harry Daugherty. Undoubtedly angered by Forbes's failure to share the loot, the attorney general informed Harding of Forbes's trespasses. Forbes was immediately summoned to the White House for what turned into a violent "interview" with the president.

Forbes was allowed to flee to Europe, from where he submitted his resignation. Harding was satisfied to have kept the lid on the scandal and did nothing more, but a Senate investigating committee began looking into Forbes's stewardship of the Veterans' Bureau. The inquiry took a surprising turn when Charles Cramer, the California lawyer brought in by Forbes to serve as the agency's general counsel, shot himself in the head while locked in his bathroom. A newspaper clipping about the Senate inquiry lay on his desk in the adjoining bedroom. Cramer was suspected of having shared in Forbes's loot.

This was the only scandal to break while Harding was alive but there were lightning flashes of others on the horizon. In addition to fraud in the Veterans' Bureau, Harding's legacy was to include conspiracy in the Interior Department, criminal stupidity in the Navy Department, and graft in the Alien Property Bureau, while under Harry Daugherty the Department of Justice became known as the "Department of Easy Virtue."

Albert Fall was the first to pick the pockets of his fellow countrymen. Born in Kentucky in 1861, Fall went west as a youth to become a cowboy, prospector, self-taught lawyer, territorial judge, and in 1912, when New Mexico became a state, its first U.S. senator. With his drooping mustache, snakelike eyes, and wide-brimmed black hat, he looked like the crooked sheriff in a western movie. He suffered financial reverses and by 1920, the Senate was a luxury he could no longer afford. The taxes on his ranch at Three Rivers had not been paid for eight years; the fences were broken and his cattle herd depleted. Fall saw the job of interior secretary as a life-line and was so eager for it that he sent Harding a telegram in Harry Daugherty's name urging the appointment—and charged it to Daugherty's account.

Once firmly in the saddle at Interior, Fall launched a campaign to get control of the public domain. Agriculture Secretary Henry Wallace was alert and stubbornly and successfully resisted his efforts to pry loose the national forest lands. But they were a mere bagatelle compared to his main objective: the petroleum reserves set aside for emergency use by the U.S. Navy, which was making the shift from coal to oil. These reserves, at Elk Hills, California, and Teapot Dome in Wyoming, had long been the target of developers. Josephus Daniels, Wilson's navy secretary, later wrote: "I remember one night toward the end of a [congressional] session that Mr. [Franklin] Roosevelt and I remained at the Capitol all night long watching the legislation of closing hours, fearing that some act might be passed that would turn over these invaluable oil reserves to parties without decent show of title."

Fall easily convinced Harding by a hocus-pocus of expert testimony that there was a drainage problem in the reserves: oil from the government lands was draining away underground to the private holdings surrounding them, so the oil ought to be used up before it disappeared. The complaisant Harding agreed. Next, Fall exercised his wiles on Edwin Denby, the navy secretary, who seems to have had little interest in his department except to administer it with minimal effort. Denby readily agreed to turn over control of the reserves to Interior on the grounds that Fall's department could better handle the leakage problem than the navy.

On May 31, 1921, Harding signed, no questions asked, an executive order placed before him by Fall that formally turned over stewardship of the reserves to Interior. Two months later, Fall awarded drilling rights to Elk Hills to the Pan-American Petroleum and Transport Company, headed by Edward Doheny, an old friend from Fall's prospecting days. In return, Doheny was to build storage tanks at Pearl Harbor, the navy's new base in Hawaii, and fill them with 1.5 million barrels of fuel oil.

"I'm just an ordinary old-time, impulsive, irresponsible, improvident sort of a prospector," Doheny once declared. Unlike most old prospectors, however, he was worth more than $100 million. In 1892, he had discovered the Los Angeles City Oil Field near what much later became the site of Dodgers Stadium. Not long after obtaining the Elk Hills drilling rights, Doheny sent Fall a little black bag containing $100,000. "We will be in bad luck," the oil baron gleefully told an associate, "if we don't get one hundred million dollars in profit."

Fall turned drilling rights to the Teapot Dome reserve over to Harry Sinclair and received $233,000 in Liberty Bonds and $70,000 in cash. Sinclair also estimated his potential profit at $100 million. A onetime Kansas pharmacist turned financial buccaneer, Sinclair had interests around the globe and possessed a fortune of nearly $380 million. In 1924, Albania asked Sinclair to become its ruler, but by then he had his own problems and turned down the throne. Thus, in exchange for about $400,000 in bonds and cash, Fall had disposed of navy petroleum reserves estimated at the time to be worth several hundred million dollars.*

Rumors that something was amiss with Fall's stewardship of the petroleum reserves surfaced almost immediately. Harry A. Slattery, a Washington lawyer with a strong interest in conservation, picked up hints about the deal from friends, while a Standard Oil executive warned Albert Lasker that the Teapot Dome deal "smells" and that he should tell the president. "This isn't the first time that this rumor has come to me," was Harding's reply, "but if Albert Fall isn't an honest man, I am not fit to be President of the United States." In the meantime, Fall's New Mexico neighbors noted a surprising change in his fortunes. Back taxes on his ranch were paid, the house and fences were repaired, and blooded stock appeared on his range.

Wisconsin's Senator La Follette, supplied with information dredged up by Slattery, introduced a Senate resolution calling for a full investigation of the leases, and Senator Thomas J. Walsh, a Montana Democrat, began probing for details. Fall defended the leases as perfectly legal and was sup-

---

* Elk Hills was sold to the Occidental Petroleum Corporation for $3.63 billion in 1997. (*New York Times*, October 7, 1997.)

ported by Harding. The investigation directed him to forward all documents relevant to the inquiry to the Senate—and he did so with a vengeance. Fall must have chuckled to himself as he dictated the letter of transmittal. "My casual estimate of the number of pages being forwarded to you is that the aggregate will be between 10 and 15,000."

Fall remained in the cabinet until March 1923, when he submitted his resignation. Harding told the press that he had offered to appoint his friend to the Supreme Court, but Fall chose to return to private life. Herbert Hoover sent his retiring colleague a cordial note expressing the wish that Fall would soon return to Washington. "In my recollection," he said, the Interior Department "has never had so constructive and legal leadership as you gave it."

Rumors of illegality in the Justice Department began circulating almost as soon as Harry Daugherty took office. The always genial attorney general was suspected of being at the center of a web of graft that reached into every corner of the administration. The word in Washington was that war fraud and profiteering cases could be settled out of court if the "proper" approach was made—through Jess Smith. One bootlegger claimed to have given Smith $250,000 for immunity; another was said to have paid $20,000 for a permit to withdraw liquor from a bonded warehouse.

The most notorious case to which Daugherty was linked concerned the Alien Property Bureau, which held property seized from German interests during the war. Smith received $224,000 in exchange for "expediting" a dubious $7 million claim through the bureau. Later it was discovered that he had deposited $50,000 in a joint account he maintained with Daugherty—"Jess Smith Extra No. 3"—in a bank operated by the attorney general's brother in their Ohio hometown. Daugherty claimed this account was established for funds collected for political purposes. The truth or falsity of this claim could not be verified because Daugherty burned all the records when he came under investigation.

In the face of demands for his ouster from office, Daugherty stood fast. "I wouldn't have given thirty cents for the office of attorney general, but I won't surrender it for a million dollars," he declared. In 1923, Congress took up a resolution calling for his impeachment, a move that spurred Daugherty to defensive action. William J. Burns, the private detective brought in by the attorney general, a boyhood friend, to head the Bureau of Investigation, and his shady chief operative, Gaston B. Means, investigated the investigators.

The cherub-faced Means is one of the more spectacular rogues of

American history. A practiced perjurer, he was charged with and acquitted of murdering a Chicago heiress he had been hired to protect and was a German agent before the United States entered World War I. Private homes and offices were burglarized by Burns and Means in search of information and the telephones of critics were tapped. An attempt was also made to frame Daugherty's chief inquisitor, Senator Burton K. Wheeler, a Montana Democrat, on a morals charge.

Although the legal bloodhounds were baying loudly at his heels, Daugherty maintained his equilibrium, but the strain took its toll on Jess Smith. He was nervous and jumpy and Daugherty exploded at his bumbling and lugubrious manner. There are also reports that Harding told Daugherty to get Smith out of Washington. On a visit home, Smith seemed to his ex-wife to be in a state of terror. Usually, he bubbled over with tales about his success in Washington, and once he showed her a money belt containing $75,000. Now, he asked her to help him destroy a batch of bank records, canceled checks, and other papers. "I don't think I have long to live," he told a friend.

Smith returned to Washington and the Wardman Park apartment he shared with Daugherty, but the attorney general was staying at the White House. Aware of Smith's agitated state, Daugherty asked his secretary, William E. Martin, to keep him company. Early on the morning of May 30, 1923, Martin heard a shot and found Smith lying on the floor of the living room with his head in a metal wastebasket, a pistol nearby and a gaping wound in his head. Martin summoned Billy Burns, who conveniently lived on the floor below, and he took control of the investigation. When the police arrived, the pistol could not be immediately found because Burns said he had misplaced it. No autopsy was done and Smith's death was written off as a suicide. Poor health, his impending banishment from Washington, and Daugherty's rejection were all presumed contributing causes. The president and Mrs. Harding sent a bank of flowers for the coffin. Rumors soon spread that Smith had been murdered to keep him quiet. Alice Longworth joked that he had died of "Harding of the arteries."*

---

* Record No. K279123 in the Department of Deeds and Records of the District of Columbia lists Jess Smith as a suicide on May 30, 1923, at 6:40 in the morning and states: "Wound of entry on left side of head shows powder burns, considerable damage to the right side of head at hole of exit. Heavy laceration under left cheekbone. Verdict suicide."

His ex-wife insisted that Jess Smith was right-handed. It would be extremely difficult for a right-handed man to shoot himself in the left side of the head. (See Werner and Starr, *Teapot Dome*, p. 100.)

* * *

By mid-1922, Harding would have been justified in feeling that everything was going wrong. Mrs. Harding almost died from an attack of hydronephritis, a form of kidney disease, and her recovery was slow. Congress spurned his offers of cooperation and rejected his pet proposal for federal subsidies for the nation's merchant fleet. Moreover, the Senate blocked his proposal for American adherence to the World Court, Harding's substitute for membership in the League of Nations. Although the economy was improving, crop prices seemed permanently depressed. In the South, where cotton had fallen to a dime a pound, night riders were burning down cotton gins to keep crops off the market.

There was another race riot, this one in Rosewood, a black hamlet in the pine woods of northern Florida, where in January 1923 a white woman charged that she had been assaulted by an unidentified black man. Some three hundred armed whites converged on Rosewood in search of a suspect. When the vigilantes tried to search their houses, the black residents resisted and a gun battle erupted in which several people were killed on both sides. In revenge, the whites set fire to the church and store as well as twenty-five to thirty houses while the black residents fled to the swamps. Eight people were killed—six blacks and two whites—over the next week. Some blacks later claimed that the woman had actually been beaten by a white lover and she had covered up by telling her husband that her assailant was a black man.

Organized labor, even though pounded into submission in 1919, sought to roll back wage cuts ordered in the wake of the recession. The unions also struggled against a conservative Supreme Court—with the liberal justices Oliver Wendell Holmes and Louis Brandeis usually dissenting—that blocked almost every effort at social reform. Boycotts to force unionization were declared illegal and picketing was drastically limited. When Congress passed a law levying prohibitive taxes on products manufactured by child labor, the court declared it unconstitutional (*Bailey v. Drexel Furniture Company*). It also threw out a District of Columbia minimum wage law for women (*Adkins v. Children's Hospital*).

Sixty thousand New England textile workers struck in February 1922 against a proposed 20 percent wage cut that followed a 22.5 percent slash imposed only a year before. Management also wanted to extend the workweek from forty-eight to fifty-four hours, a move deemed necessary to meet the competition of low-cost Southern mills. The strike lasted nine months before a compromise was reached: the 22.5 percent wage cut was rescinded but the increased workweek went into effect.

Another coal strike broke out in April when the United Mine Workers closed down the pits in protest against a plan by the Northern mine operators to reduce wages. Since 1898, the United Mine Workers had insisted on a single national contract but the operators now wanted to negotiate individual contracts to meet the competition from nonunion mines. Violence quickly erupted, especially in Williamson County, Illinois—known as "Bloody Williamson" because of its violent labor history.

One mine owner tried to resume operations with strikebreakers protected by armed guards. The guards killed three striking union miners and, in revenge, nineteen strikebreakers were seized and massacred. Some were forced to crawl on their hands and knees to the graves dug for them in a cemetery and were shot before a cheering crowd. Others had their throats slit. A Williamson County jury failed to convict anyone of these gruesome murders.

Anti-union forces denounced the UMW's complicity in this atrocity and it cost the strikers public sympathy. Unable to maintain the walkout in the face of government and public opposition, John L. Lewis cut a deal. Wages remained at 1920 levels but the union gave way on a national contract. Thousands of western Pennsylvania miners, who were living in tents and shacks because they had been evicted from company housing, were abandoned by their leaders. Union membership plummeted from 600,000 in 1920 to 100,000 by 1929, and those with work earned only about half what they had made in 1920. Lewis grew increasingly dictatorial and charged that opponents to his leadership had sold out to the Communists. Many of the miners who abandoned the coal fields took jobs in the automobile and tire plants of Detroit and Akron where they became the spearhead of unionization in the next decade.

Four hundred thousand railroad shop workers—electricians, boilermakers, carpenters, and machinists, among others—went on strike on July 1, 1922, against wage cuts, stringent new work rules, and attempts to form company unions. Even though the operating brotherhoods, the locomotive engineers, firemen, and brakemen, refused to support it, the walkout was the first big railway strike since 1894. Herbert Hoover advised the president to remain neutral, and at first Harding complied. But Harding's pro-business bias came to the fore and Daugherty convinced him that the strike was not only damaging economic recovery but was a Bolshevik conspiracy. "So long and to the extent that I can speak for the government of the United States," the attorney general declared, "I will use the power of the government to prevent the labor unions of the country from destroying the open shop."

Without consulting anyone else, Harding authorized Daugherty to obtain a restraining order against the union, even though the strike was on its last legs because of the refusal of the operating brotherhoods to support it. The injunction handed down by Judge James Wilkerson in Chicago has been described as the most sweeping in the stormy history of American labor. The union was ordered to cease "picketing or in any manner by letters, circulars, telephone messages, word of mouth, or interviews encouraging any person to leave the employ of a railroad."

Several cabinet members denounced the injunction and Harding, taken aback, ordered Daugherty to modify some of its most obnoxious terms. Nevertheless, the president's unthinking decision earned him the reputation of an enemy of labor and the full effect was felt in the midterm congressional elections of 1922. Incumbent parties usually lose seats in such elections, but Republican losses went beyond that: seven seats in the Senate and seventy in the House—a defeat blamed on the administration's mishandling of the railroad strike, the tariff, and the veterans' bonus. Some of these seats were won by Farmer-Labor Party candidates, giving the progressives the balance of power on certain issues. Several of Harding's advisers now feared that the popular automobile magnate Henry Ford might oppose him for the Republican presidential nomination in 1924.

In the face of continuing white racism and violence, some blacks rejected the integrationism preached by W. E. B. Du Bois, the other light-skinned leaders of the NAACP, and their white liberal allies. They found their Moses in Marcus M. Garvey, a magnetic African nationalist who preached black pride and racial separatism. Garvey, who was born in Jamaica in 1887, emigrated to London where he worked for several years as a printer. Returning to Jamaica, he led a printers' strike that failed, lost his job, and came to the United States. Impressed by Booker T. Washington's call for blacks to pull themselves up by their own bootstraps, Garvey told his mostly dark-skinned followers that American blacks would achieve power and dignity only when they had reclaimed Africa from the white colonials. "The hour has come," he declared, proclaiming a form of black Zionism, "when the whole continent of Africa shall be reclaimed and redeemed as the home of the black peoples."

In 1914, Garvey organized the Universal Negro Improvement Association, beginning among West Indian immigrants in Harlem, and it spread to black communities across the country. The first mass movement aimed at working-class blacks, UNIA operated a chain of cooperative grocery stores, a laundry, a publishing house, and a restaurant. Garvey's newspaper, the *Negro World,* was the most widely read black paper in the country. The capstone of his empire was the Black Star Steamship Line, which was designed to promote worldwide trade and unity among blacks. Laborers and domestics invested their meager savings in Garvey's grand schemes. By the early 1920s, UNIA claimed a membership of upwards of two million people on four continents. Garvey glorified blackness, and he claimed both God and Jesus were black. His followers believed white racism and not black inadequacy was responsible for their poverty and powerlessness and sublimated their current despair and disillusionment in the promise of a better future. In explaining the origins of his movement, Garvey wrote:

> I was determined that the black man would not continue to be kicked about by all the other races and nations of the world. . . . I saw before me then, even as I do now, a new world of black men, not peons, serfs, dogs and slaves, but a nation of sturdy men making their impress upon civilization and causing a new light to dawn upon the human race.

Garvey petitioned the League of Nations to transfer the former German colonies in Africa to his control. Failing that, he designated himself president of a new black republic with a militia and a full panoply of titles and a flag: red for the blood that must be shed, black for the color of their skin, and green for the vegetation of the motherland. Wearing snappy uniforms, the Garveyites attracted admiring attention as they paraded through black neighborhoods to the strains of

> Ethiopia, thou land of our fathers
> Thou land where the gods loved to be,
> As storm cloud at night sudden gathers
> Our armies come rushing to thee!

Unfortunately for Garvey, he also attracted the enmity of both the NAACP and J. Edgar Hoover. Fearing that Garvey was a threat to their organization, mainline NAACP leaders derided his teachings as pie-in-the-sky, back-to-Africa separatism and attacked him with a wrath usually reserved for the Ku Klux Klan. They waged a "Garvey must go!" campaign and sneered at his followers as "universally ignorant Negro savages." Du Bois described Garvey as "a little fat black man, ugly but with intelligent eyes and a big head"; Garvey called Du Bois a "lazy dependent mulatto."

The NAACP urged Attorney General Daugherty to look into Garvey's activities.

Having already concluded that Garvey was as great a menace to the social order as the Communists and anarchists, Hoover needed no encouragement. Over the next two years, his agents infiltrated UNIA and combed through its records. Garvey was no businessman and the chaotic state of the Black Star Steamship Line resulted in an indictment for mail fraud. He was convicted at a trial in which the judge carried an NAACP card, and in 1925 Garvey was sentenced to a five-year term in Atlanta.

UNIA did not long survive his imprisonment, but the *Amsterdam News* prophetically observed that his influence would be felt in the future. "Marcus Garvey made black people proud of their race," the paper declared. "In a world where black is despised, he taught them that black is beautiful."

When—if ever—Warren Harding realized his administration was honeycombed with corruption is an unresolved question. By the spring of 1923, enough evidence had piled up to arouse questions in the mind of any prudent person. Charlie Forbes's outrageous grafting, the suspicious deaths of Cramer and Smith, the rumors about Harry Daugherty's questionable relations with the Alien Property Bureau, and the rumblings from Albert Fall's handling of the oil leases were too much to be ignored.

"The president has aged perceptibly during the last 18 months," wrote Charles G. Ross of the *St. Louis Post-Dispatch*. "There is more gray in his hair, more bagginess under his eyes." Although Harding was only fifty-eight, he looked much older. That winter he was exhausted by a battle with the flu and showed signs of cardiovascular problems. He weighed nearly 240 pounds and found it difficult to breathe and sleep unless he was propped up by pillows. He all but gave up golf because he could not complete an eighteen-hole round. Frequently, he felt pains in his chest, which Doc Sawyer diagnosed as chronic heartburn and indigestion. Despite the indications that the president was suffering from something more severe, no one contested Sawyer's competence or the accuracy of his diagnosis.

A drained and confused man, Harding resorted to a familiar remedy—he would travel about the country and "bloviate." He had long planned a trip to Alaska and decided to turn the journey into a two-month "Voyage of Understanding" in which he would meet the people. Before leaving Washington, he took a pair of actions that raised the possibility that he might have had a premonition about the future: he sold the *Marion Star* for $550,000 and wrote a new will. Shortly before leaving, Mrs. Harding summoned Madame Marcia to the White House for guidance. The clairvoyant spoke of "death stalking the air we breathe in Washington," which terrified the first lady. "You must take back what you predicted to me!" she shouted. "You must!" Madame Marcia stuck with her earlier prediction that the president would not live to the end of his term.

Sixty-five people accompanied Harding and his wife as they left Washington by special train on June 30, 1923. Significantly, Harry Daugherty was not among them, causing observers to wonder if he had fallen out of presidential favor. Frequent stops were made on the way to the West Coast for hand shaking and speeches—Harding delivered fourteen speeches in two weeks—and as in the case of Woodrow Wilson four years before, the farther the president got from Washington, the greater his popularity. The accompanying newsmen thought he was doing an excellent job of laying the groundwork for a run for reelection in 1924.

But the shadow of scandal fell across his path. In Kansas City, Albert Fall's wife, looking worried and wan, talked privately with Harding for nearly an hour. What they talked about was never revealed, although Mrs. Fall later claimed she did not discuss the oil leases with the president. The next day, Harding told William Allen White: "My God, this is a hell of a job! I have no trouble with my enemies. I can take care of my enemies all right. But my damn friends, my God-damn friends . . . they're the ones that keep me walking the floor nights!"

Harding was the first president to visit Alaska. He and his wife enjoyed themselves as the specially refurbished navy transport *Henderson* poked its way along the spectacular glacier- and mountain-edged coast. Several relaxed visits were made to picturesque wooden settlements and to Russian churches adorned with onion-shaped domes. But Harding could not shake off the problems he had left behind in Washington. Wireless messages brought the news that wheat had dropped below a dollar a bushel on the Chicago market . . . Talk of Henry Ford for president in 1924 was growing . . . In Minnesota, the candidate of the radical Farmer-Labor Party soundly beat the regular Republican candidate for senator in a special election . . . Senator La Follette said the election made it clear that a farm revolt was spreading across the West. Moreover, Harding was beset by financial woes. He had been playing the stock market, using a blind account under an assumed name, and had lost $180,000.

Shortly after the *Henderson* left Alaskan waters, Harding appears to have suffered a nervous collapse. Washington state senator C. C. Dill later recalled that the president "tearfully lamented the betrayal of two of his Cabinet members, Interior Secretary Albert Fall and Attorney General

Harry Daugherty." Herbert Hoover also related that Harding called him to his cabin and said there was a great scandal brewing within the administration. Should it be aired or covered up?

My natural reply was "Publish it, and at least get credit for integrity on your side." He remarked that this method might be politically dangerous. I asked for more particulars. He said he had received some rumors of irregularities, centering around Smith, in connection with cases in the Department of Justice. Harding gave me no information about what Smith had been up to. I asked what Daugherty's relation to the affair were. He abruptly dried up and never raised the question again.

To fight off whatever nightmares may have haunted him, the "nervous and distraught" president played bridge day and night. The other players sat in shifts so that one of them might have a break. The atmosphere was so tense that once the trip was over, Hoover could never again bring himself to play bridge.

Harding was not feeling well when the *Henderson* reached Vancouver, but as the first American president to visit Canada, he forced himself to go through the formal welcoming ceremonies. Doc Sawyer diagnosed his problem as "a slight attack of ptomaine" probably resulting from eating tainted crabmeat. Early the next morning, as the ship steamed through a heavy fog, she sliced into the accompanying destroyer *Zeilen*. The grinding crash was accompanied by the command "All hands on deck!" The *Henderson* was only lightly damaged but the destroyer had to be beached to prevent it from sinking.

Arthur Brooks, the president's valet, hurried to his cabin and found him lying in bed, with his face covered by his hands. Harding asked what had happened and Brooks told him that there had been a collision but he needn't go on deck. The president continued to lie there motionless with his face still hidden. "I hope the boat sinks," he sighed.

When the *Henderson* arrived in Seattle on July 27, Harry Daugherty suddenly turned up, according to Hoover, and he and Harding had an hour-long private conversation. Harding felt well enough to give a speech before forty thousand people gathered under a bright sun in the University of Washington stadium. Written by Hoover but edited by the president, who added "his usual three-dollar words" and sonorous phrases, the speech was a surprisingly strong endorsement of the conservation of Alaska's natural resources.

Harding promised that they would not be allowed to fall into the hands of exploiters to be looted "as the possibility of profit arises." Americans must "regard life in a lovely wonderful Alaska as an end not a means." Several times during the speech, he slurred his words, called Alaska "Nebraska," and dropped the pages of his speech. Those seated near the president were shocked by his flabby skin, puffy eyes, and appearance of utter exhaustion.

Now convinced that Harding had enough, his advisers canceled a stop in Portland and the presidential train sped straight through to San Francisco, arriving there two days later. Harding disdained the wheelchair brought up for him and insisted on walking to a waiting limousine, which took him to the Palace Hotel, where he immediately went to bed. Sawyer issued an optimistic bulletin about the president's health, but other physicians who examined Harding thought he had suffered a heart attack. There were also signs of pneumonia. No effort was made to keep Vice President Coolidge informed of Harding's condition or to recall him from his vacation at the family homestead in Vermont.

On the evening of August 2, 1923, Harding was resting comfortably in Room 8064 of the Palace as the first lady sat by his bed and read from a friendly article in *The Saturday Evening Post* entitled "A Calm Review of a Calm Man." The article suggested that Harding was doing a good job as president despite all the criticism. "That's good," he said. "Go on, read some more." When Mrs. Harding finished she went to her own room across the hall. The president remained as she left him, sitting propped up in bed, his eyes shut and his head back on the pillows, with a nurse in attendance. Suddenly, at about 7:30 P.M., he had a galvanic seizure, his mouth fell open, and his head fell lifelessly to the side.

Sawyer and the other doctors issued a statement saying Harding died of apoplexy, a term then used for a stroke, but modern studies indicate a massive heart attack. The actual cause was never ascertained because Mrs. Harding did not permit an autopsy and the body was immediately embalmed. A year later, Sawyer died unexpectedly while Mrs. Harding was visiting him at his sanatorium. Within six months, she was dead, too. This string of deaths, as final as the end of a Shakespearean tragedy, touched off rumors of foul play.

In a book published in 1930, *The Strange Death of President Harding*, Gaston Means spread the lurid tale that the president had been poisoned by his wife, possibly with the collusion of Sawyer, to spare him from public disgrace. The book was sheer fiction but sold over eighty thousand copies in its first weeks.* People believed a conspiracy had put Harding in the White House, so it was only natural that a conspiracy should put him in his grave.

A national outpouring of genuine grief greeted Warren Harding's unexpected passing. The American people were still largely unaware of the scandals brewing behind the facade of his administration, and his popularity was high. As the funeral train moved across the country to Washington, the tracks were lined with mourners singing his favorite hymns. When the cortege reached the White House, Mrs. Harding had the coffin opened and sat beside it for hours as the president's body lay in state in the East Room. Putting her face close to that of her husband, she was heard to say, "No one can hurt you now, Wurr'n."

There is no evidence that Harding stole so much as a nickel, but his name is forever linked with an era of unbridled graft and corruption. For Republican leaders, his death was a godsend. It allowed them to pass off to him culpability for Teapot Dome and all the other scandals soon to be made public, forever burying Harding's reputation in muck, despite subsequent efforts by revisionist writers to restore it.

At first, Albert Fall treated the Teapot Dome investigation with amused contempt. He accepted full responsibility for the leasing of the naval petroleum reserves at a hearing of the Senate Committee on Public Lands and Surveys, contended the transfer was based on sound business principles, and claimed the oil storage facilities constructed by Doheny at Pearl Harbor more than doubled the U.S. Navy's fighting capacity. And he flatly denied having received any payments from Doheny and Sinclair. The two tycoons backed him up, saying the leases were saving the American people millions of dollars lost by drainage from the petroleum reserves.

Press coverage waned and some newspapers called the inquiry a Democratic witch hunt. The *New York Times* found it "humiliating to think that we have come to the point where every idle tale and gratuitous suspicion must be given resounding publicity." The telephone of Senator Thomas Walsh, the head of the inquiry, was tapped, his past was raked over by Billy

---

* This was hardly the last of Gaston Means. After several other swindles and brushes with the law, in 1932 he convinced Evalyn Walsh McLean that he was in contact with the kidnappers of the baby son of Charles A. Lindbergh and she gave him $100,000 to ransom the child plus another $4,000 for expenses. Means was eventually convicted of grand larceny and sentenced to fifteen years in prison where he died in 1938. The $100,000 was never found.

Burns's agents, his mail was opened, and his office ransacked. Still, with bulldog intensity, Walsh persisted. Where had Fall gotten the money to make improvements at his ranch while his neighbors were experiencing hard times?

Walsh's persistent digging began to exact a toll on Fall. Friends told him that he had to account for the source of his newfound prosperity to save his reputation. Again summoned before Walsh's committee, he declined to appear because of poor health but sent Walsh a long, rambling letter in which he claimed that he had borrowed $100,000 from Ned McLean. The playboy-publisher dodged an appearance before the committee by claim-ing to be too ill to return to Washington from Florida to testify.

Walsh went himself to Palm Beach to personally take testimony from McLean. In December 1921, he said, Fall had asked for a loan of $100,000 and he had given him several checks—he couldn't remember how many—on several banks. Not long after, Fall told him that he had made other arrangements and returned the uncashed checks. No, he did not have any check stubs to support his story. Walsh put no stock in this tale because he had already inspected McLean's checking account and determined he had never kept enough in it to cover a $100,000 check. As soon as he returned to Washington, Walsh told the press that Fall had obviously lied to the committee.

This was the turning point of the investigation. Conflicting testimony about oil drainage and storage tanks was pretty tame stuff, but a cabinet officer who lied to a Senate committee, a playboy with $100,000 in missing checks, and a mysterious "loan" was a sensation made to order for the tabloids. Amid all the rumors afloat about the source of Fall's sudden wealth, Doheny voluntarily agreed to testify. He disclosed that he had lent his old prospecting friend $100,000 in December 1921, and received a promissory note. When the non-interest-bearing note was produced, it was found that the signature was torn off.

Doheny explained that he had torn Fall's name off the note himself as a safety precaution in case he died unexpectedly and his estate tried to collect the note. He described the "loan" of $100,000 as a trifle, "no more than $25 or perhaps $50 to the ordinary individual."

"I can appreciate that on your side," Walsh commented dryly, "but looking at it from Senator Fall's side, it was quite a loan." Another senator asked Doheny about the possibility that the interior secretary might favor him in the award of the leases because of the loan, the oilman replied: "I don't think he is more than human"—a remark greeted by a wave of laughter.

Bristling under a barrage of questions from Democratic senators, Doheny disclosed that Fall was not the only former cabinet member to benefit from his largess. Democrats had also taken his money. He revealed that he had paid William McAdoo, Wilson's treasury secretary and son-in law, $250,000 for legal services. This created a sensation, for McAdoo was the front-runner for the Democratic presidential nomination in 1924. Hastening before the committee, McAdoo testified that his law firm had indeed been retained by Doheny for a much smaller sum to deal with matters that had nothing to do with the oil leases. But the damage to his reputation was done. So pervasive was the smell of oil in the 1920s that anyone who came in touch with it was, in the public mind, automatically guilty.

In the end, Fall was convicted of conspiracy to defraud the government by transferring Elk Hills and Teapot Dome to Doheny and Sinclair in exchange for $400,000 in bribes, and was sentenced to a year in jail—the first cabinet member to meet such a fate. The oil barons who did the bribing escaped punishment. There was talk of impeaching Edwin Denby, the blundering navy secretary who had turned the petroleum reserves over to Fall without asking any questions. The charges were dropped after Senator Walsh damningly observed: "Stupidity is not a ground for impeachment as far as I can learn."

High-flying Charlie Forbes eventually returned from Europe to be convicted of bribery and conspiracy. He was sentenced to two years in Leavenworth and fined $10,000 but got away with some $2 million in swag. To no one's surprise, Harry Daugherty tried to brazen his way out of his troubles. He was finally ousted as attorney general by Calvin Coolidge, Harding's successor, when he refused to supply Senate investigators with documents bearing on bootlegging, oil deals, and the sale of prosecutorial favors. Indicted along with allied property custodian Colonel Thomas Miller on charges of defrauding the government, Daugherty declined to take the stand, implying that he was protecting the late president's memory and creating—as was probably intended—the widespread impression that somehow President Harding was involved in the scandals. These suspicions were heightened when Max D. Steuer, Daugherty's attorney and a prominent criminal lawyer of the day, remarked that "if the jury knew the real reason for destroying the ledger sheets [of the Jess Smith Extra No. 3 bank account] they would commend rather than condemn Mr. Daugherty."

· After deliberating for sixty-five hours, the jury convicted Miller, who served thirteen months in prison, but failed to agree on a verdict on Daugherty. As The Nation observed, "The jury decided that a president's good name was at stake." Brought to trial for a second time, Daugherty once again refused to take the stand, and again the jury was unable to agree on a verdict although all but one juror were in favor of conviction. Thus, Daugherty could say "no charge against me was ever proven in any court"—but it was a hollow victory. He had escaped justice only at the cost of Harding's reputation.

The final nail was hammered into Harding's coffin by Nan Britton, who sought money from the Harding family for the support of the illegitimate daughter she claimed was his. Rebuffed, she published a memoir, *The President's Daughter*, in 1927 that recounted her version of her relations with Harding. The book was "dedicated with understanding and love to all unwed mothers, and to their innocent children" and was an instant bestseller.

Sometime after Harding's death, a committee to select a design for a memorial at Marion for the late president and his wife met to consider a proposal from John Russell Pope, a distinguished architect. Having arrived late, one member took a glance at the model and threw up his hands.

"My God, gentlemen! You're not going to build *this!*"

"Why not?" demanded the chairman.

"Stick a handle on here, and what have you got? A teapot!"

CHAPTER 6

"I Thought I Could Swing It"

Not long after Harding's death, Henry Mencken recalled a strange incident. Following Calvin Coolidge's nomination as Republican candidate for vice president at the tumultuous 1920 Chicago convention, Mencken had gone down into the arena's catacombs in search of a drink. "In one of the passages I encountered a colleague from one of the Boston papers surrounded by a group of politicians, policemen and reporters. He was making a kind of speech, and I paused idly to listen. To my astonishment, he was offering to bet all comers that Harding, if elected, would be assassinated before he had served half his term. . . . 'I know Cal Coolidge inside and out,'" bawled out the Boston newsman. "'He is the luckiest son-of-a-bitch in the whole world!'"

On the stiflingly humid evening of August 2, 1923, the object of this prediction strolled into the general store in his hometown of Plymouth Notch in rural Vermont, and ordered a cold Moxie, a popular soft drink. "Hot night," observed the vacationing vice president with his usual taciturnity.

Coolidge and his wife, Grace, went to bed early because they were leaving first thing in the morning on the next stage of their holiday trip. He had followed newspaper reports of President Harding's illness like most Americans and seen no cause for alarm. Shortly after midnight, John Coolidge, the vice president's seventy-eight-year-old father, was awakened by pounding on the door and went downstairs in his nightshirt to see what the commotion was all about. "What's wanted?" he asked.

"President Harding's dead!" replied a messenger. "I have a telegram for the vice president."

The report of Harding's death on the other side of the continent had arrived at the nearest Western Union office, in Bridgewater, about ten miles away. Unable to reach Coolidge by telephone—the general store that contained the Notch's only phone had already closed for the night—the messenger raced over the winding mountain roads in the dark in a Model T. Voice trembling, the elder Coolidge called out the momentous news to his son.

"I was awakened by my father coming up the stairs calling my name," Coolidge recalled. "I noticed that his voice trembled. As the only time I had ever observed that before was when death visited our family, I knew that something of the gravest nature had occurred."

Coolidge was stunned but not shaken. He and Grace dressed quickly and knelt briefly by their bed to pray. He sent a telegram of condolence to Mrs. Harding and issued a brief statement to the few reporters covering the vice presidential vacation. Attorney General Harry Daugherty telegraphed, urging him to take the oath of office immediately. By now, the lights were on in every house in the Notch and Coolidge consulted by telephone with Secretary of State Charles Evans Hughes, who agreed but warned that the oath should be administered by a government official. "Father's a notary," said Coolidge. "That's fine," replied Hughes.

The new president was sworn in at 2:47 A.M. by his father in the family sitting room by the flickering yellow light of a kerosene lamp. He took the oath with a hand on a worn Bible that had belonged to his late mother and with his wife beside him.* A head taller than his son, the elder Coolidge had put on a shirt over his nightshirt but was not wearing a collar or tie. The inauguration's informality was one example of Coolidge's luck. Had Harding died a day later, he would have taken the oath at the baronial home of a wealthy friend, Guy Currier, at Peterborough, New Hampshire, and the ceremony would have lacked its telling symbolism. Reproductions of a drawing of the historic tableau soon appeared in numerous American homes.

The rural simplicity of Coolidge's inauguration was perfect because the nation's thirtieth president appeared to be a reluctant refugee from the previous century. William Allen White dubbed him a "Puritan in Babylon" and he had all the virtues of a small-town New England bank clerk. He was honest, thrifty, austere, punctual, conscientious, frugal, cautious, conservative, and moral. Needle-nosed and with thin pursed lips, carroty hair, and a Vermont twang—it was said he pronounced the word "cow" with three syllables—Coolidge seemed embarrassingly out of place in a world of

---

* The elder Coolidge's authority was restricted to state matters so the ceremony was repeated in Washington.

flappers, get-rich-quick schemes, bootleg booze, and easy sex. He looked as if he had smelled something off-color, and appeared to Alice Longworth to have "been weaned on a pickle." Congressman Lewis Douglas said he was "much like a wooden Indian except more tired looking." But to a nation rocked by scandal, Coolidge soon stood for rectitude.

The Lincolnesque trappings of his coming to power—the simple homestead, the kerosene lamps, the family Bible—were all seen as evidence that the old-fashioned virtues still existed despite widespread cynicism and spiritual doubts. Many Americans found Coolidge an ideal leader to preside over the nation in the hyperactive Twenties, a time when they were pushing the outer limits of self-indulgence, yet feared that traditional values were being lost. By 1923, wrote Scott Fitzgerald, the flappers' elders, "tired of watching the carnival with ill-concealed envy, had discovered that young liquor will take the place of young blood and with a whoop" joined in the dance.

Someone asked Coolidge what his first thought had been upon learning that he was now president of the United States. "I thought I could swing it," he answered. Nevertheless, as an "accidental president," he faced several challenges. He had to assure the American people of the stability of the government, deal with the rising stench of the Harding scandals, and if he wished to be elected to the presidency in 1924, to build a political base. With no support of his own, he had to maneuver among the Republican Party's contending factions to win backing for his candidacy.

Coolidge consecrated himself to stability. "Whatever his [Harding's] policies were are my policies," he told his first press conference. The ablest members of Harding's cabinet—Hoover, Mellon, and Hughes—were asked to stay on. By emphasizing consistency in policy and in the cabinet, he conveyed a need for political stability—which, he intimated, would best be achieved by avoiding a factional struggle and agreeing upon him as the party's standard-bearer in 1924.

Coolidge had made little impression in his two and a half years as vice president. Harding allowed him to sit in on cabinet meetings but if he made any contribution, it went unrecorded. He and Grace lived in two rooms at the Willard Hotel and he spent most of his time quietly presiding over the Senate. Three nights a week, he dined out as the White House representative at official dinners.* Usually, he said nothing, ate sparingly,

---

* Not long after he became vice president, Coolidge received a letter from Washington's exclusive Cosmos Club notifying him that he had been elected a member and enclosing a bill for the initiation fee. He declined to pay.

and quickly disappeared. "Got to eat somewhere," he replied when asked why he bothered. He wrote a few magazine articles including a series on "Enemies of the Republic" in which readers learned that dangerous Reds had infiltrated the women's colleges. A booking agent who tried to arrange speeches for Coolidge had few takers and there were reports that Harding had intended to drop the "Little Feller" from the ticket in 1924.

Nor were party leaders impressed by the way he had come to prominence. Mark Sullivan related the joke that Coolidge "got his first base on balls, stole around second (police strike) to 3rd (V.P.) on an error and reached home because the catcher fell dead." Coolidge quickly altered this image. "In a week," said Clinton Gilbert, a veteran Washington correspondent, "the only things there were in common with Mr. Coolidge, the vice president, and Mr. Coolidge, the president, was his name."

The contrast between the new president and his predecessor was striking. Coolidge did not drink, play cards, chase women, or consort with those who did. Under Grace Coolidge, who presided over the White House with charm and dignity, the fumigation was complete. The first time Alice Longworth visited the Coolidge White House she found it as different from the Harding days "as a New England front parlor is from the backroom of a speakeasy."

Wary of rocking the boat, Coolidge took his time in jockeying the scandal-tainted Harry Daugherty and Edwin Denby, the hapless navy secretary, out of the cabinet. Some observers called the president's initial reluctance to move against Daugherty "cautious immobility." The shaky electoral prospects of the Republicans in 1924 forced his hand. Because of the gusher of scandals, they were so dim that one senator observed, "The question is not so much whether the Republican party will be defeated as to whether it will survive." Perhaps in jest, perhaps not, a Democratic leader suggested that his party run on a simple platform: "Thou Shalt Not Steal!"

The Democrats were outmaneuvered by Calvin Coolidge—and not for the last time. Daugherty was finally replaced as attorney general by Harlan Fiske Stone, a former dean of the Columbia Law School whom the president had known at Amherst. Two special co-consuls were also appointed to investigate every aspect of Teapot Dome: Owen J. Roberts, a Republican and former professor at the University of Pennsylvania Law School and, like Stone, a future Supreme Court justice; and Atlee Pomerene, a one-time Democratic senator from Ohio. "Let the guilty be punished," Coolidge now proclaimed. Having wrapped himself in pristine Yankee virtue, he reaped accolades for fighting corruption. As Franklin Roosevelt, who was edging his way back into politics while struggling to move about with crutches and painful steel braces on his useless legs, wryly noted, it was a repetition of the Boston police strike, when the canny Coolidge had won credit for the accomplishments of others.

One of the chief amusements of Americans is to rapidly change amusements and in the Twenties the country was periodically swept by fads. Publicity and ballyhoo had a lot to do with the spread of these novelties across the country. For about two years, Mah-Jongg, a game imported from China that was played with decorated tiles, was the rage even though it required calculations "as intricate as an income tax blank." As many as 1.6 million sets of tiles were sold, costing anywhere from less than a dollar to $100. Mah-Jongg was briefly more popular than bridge, but the influence of China was soon replaced by that of Egypt when the discovery of the nearly undisturbed tomb of Tutankhamen inspired a fad for Egyptian-style clothing and decor.

Next came marathon dancing, in which contestants competed for cash prizes by dancing day and night until all but the winning couple had collapsed. A record was set by a couple in Cleveland who dragged themselves about the dance floor for ninety hours and ten minutes in April 1923. A reporter for the *New York World* described the scene of a marathon as follows:

> The dingy hall, littered with worn slippers, cigaret stubs, newspapers and soup cans; reeking with the mingled odors of stale coffee, tobacco smoke, cold broth, chewing gum and smelling salts, was the scene of one of the most drab and grueling endurance contests ever witnessed. There is nothing inspiring in seeing an extremely tired pretty girl in a worn bathrobe, dingy white stockings in rolls about scruffling felt slippers, her eyes half shut, her arms hung around her partner's shoulders, drag aching feet that seemed glued to the floor in one short, agonizing step after another.*

Flagpole sitting soon replaced marathon dancing. The craze began in 1924 when Alvin "Shipwreck" Kelly, a professional stuntman, took to a small platform atop a flagpole on the roof of a Los Angeles hotel for reasons unknown and remained there for thirteen hours and thirteen minutes.

---

* Marathon dancing returned with a vengeance during the Great Depression when poverty-stricken Americans were desperate for a way to make a few dollars. For a graphic account, see Horace McCoy's novel, *They Shoot Horses, Don't They?* or the Jane Fonda movie made from it.

Kelly repeated the feat all over the country, setting new records. By his retirement he claimed to have spent 20,613 hours aloft, including 47 in snow, 1,400 in rain or sleet, and 210 in subfreezing conditions. One day, a man observed Kelly on his pole and said, "He's nothing but a damn fool." A young woman defended the flagpole sitter and slapped the man's face. Upon hearing the story, Kelly insisted she be brought to the base of his perch for a chat. They were married not long after he came down.

A visit by Kelly to Baltimore inspired a fifteen-year-old boy named Avon Freeman to climb a pole and announce that he intended to stay there until he broke the "juvenile record"—whatever it was. The boy's father, an electrician, rigged up spotlights so the crowds could view his son at night as well as day. Mayor William F. Broening, a noted gasbag, presented "Azey" with a testimonial and hailed his achievement as an example of "the grit and stamina so essential to success in the great struggle of life."[1] After remaining atop his pole for ten hours and ten minutes, the boy decided the juvenile record had been broken and came down. Within days, flagpoles from ten to twenty feet high were erected in backyards and empty lots all over Baltimore. At one time there were fifteen children roosting on poles with the intention of setting a new record. The city fathers rose to the occasion by requiring flapoles to be inspected for safety and charging a license fee of a dollar for each.

Americans have always been great believers in self-help, and when Dr. Emile Coue arrived from Paris in 1923 to spread his new system for curing mental and physical ills by autosuggestion, or self-hypnosis, he was greeted by eager audiences. Coue told them that if they constantly repeated his mantra—"Every day, in every way, I am getting better and better"—they would come to believe these words. And if they believed them, then they would make them come true. Coue's book, *Self Mastery Through Conscious Autosuggestion*, one of the first in a long line of self-help books gobbled up by Americans over the decades, was a best-seller.

Suntans were also suddenly fashionable. Victorian and Edwardian women had avoided the sun, for a pale, unblemished skin was the mark of gentility, but things began to change under the influence of Zelda and Scott Fitzgerald and their Riviera friends, Sarah and Gerald Murphy. A tanned body was now the symbol of the good life. "I love those beautiful tan people," Zelda wrote in her novel, *Save Me the Waltz*. "They seem so free of secrets." Zelda herself had "a gorgeous body" and was brown all over, said a friend. Those who could not afford a trip to the south of France got the required tan from sun lamps, which were first advertised in *Vogue* in 1923.

There was also a craze for visiting European royalty. The handsome if weedy Prince of Wales (later the Duke of Windsor) stole the hearts of shopgirls during a tour in 1924. He did the Charleston and took the place of the drummer with a dance band and seemed "a regular guy." Two years later, Queen Marie of Romania created an even greater stir on the first of several visits in which she waged a relentless campaign for the limelight, while Americans went wild over the presence of "a genuine live queen" in America.

By far the biggest craze to sweep the United States in the Twenties was for the crossword puzzle. Crossword puzzles originally appeared in the *New York World* in 1912 but attracted only a modest number of devotees. One day in 1924, two fledgling publishers, Richard Simon and M. Lincoln Schuster, visited Simon's aunt, who asked them if they knew of a book of crossword puzzles. No, they didn't—and decided to publish one themselves. *The Crossword Puzzle Book* was an instant success, touching off a new mania. For some reason, while a single puzzle was of no great moment, a book of them seemed irresistible. A second book followed and then a third; millions of copies were sold. There were biblical crossword books, crossword books for children, and crossword books in Yiddish. Each book came with a sharpened pencil—ready for action. For several years afterward, the Egyptian sun god "Ra"; "eel" ("a snakelike fish"); the "Oo" bird of Hawaii; and the printer's measures of "em" and "en" were among the most used words in the English language.

Two American presidents have died on the Fourth of July—Thomas Jefferson and John Adams, both within hours of each other in 1826—but John Calvin Coolidge is the only one born on the national holiday, in 1872. Coolidges had lived in the Green Mountains since the Revolution but, as Yankee yeomen, were only distantly related to the Coolidges of Boston's codfish aristocracy. Satisfied with what God in his infinite wisdom had given them, they were disinclined to look beyond the next ridge or to leave their granite hills.

The president's father, also John Calvin Coolidge, was a prosperous farmer, storekeeper, and public official. From him, Young Cal inherited his taciturnity, frugality, and interest in public affairs. Virginia Moor Coolidge, his mother, was also a native Vermonter. She was a pretty and sensitive but frail woman with a touch of "mysticism and poetry." She loved "to gaze at the purple sunsets and the evening stars," according to her son. Virginia Coolidge died at the age of thirty-nine, probably of tuberculosis, when Calvin was twelve, leaving a void in the boy's life that was never filled. For the rest of his days, he carried a picture of his mother in his watch case and often talked of it. The care of Calvin and Abbie, his younger sister, devolved upon their paternal grandmother.

Even though the Coolidges were prosperous by the standards of Plymouth Notch, life was not easy. As soon as he was old enough, Calvin had chores to do: tapping maple trees, mending fences, piling up wood for winter, and plowing by himself by the time he was twelve. Although not often punished, punishment was terrible when it came; he was locked up alone for hours in a dark, cobweb-filled attic. A frail child, he was sometimes seized by sneezing and coughing attacks traced to several allergies. These resulted in an unusual quacking quality in his voice that grated on people's nerves. The famous indolence of his later years may have resulted not from a lack of energy but ill health.

Perhaps because of his odd voice and ailments, he had few friends as a child. Looking back later in life, he recalled:

> In politics, one must meet people, and that is not easy for me. . . . When I was a little fellow, as long ago as I can remember, I would go into a panic if I heard strange voices in the kitchen. I felt I just couldn't meet the people and shake hands with them. . . . I was almost ten before I realized I couldn't go on that way. And by fighting hard I used to go through that door. I'm all right with old friends, but every time I meet a stranger, I've got to go through the old kitchen door—and it's not easy.

When he could be spared from his chores, Calvin attended the local one-room schoolhouse. In 1886, at the age of fourteen, he was sent to Black River Academy, a Baptist-supported school in Ludlow, about a dozen miles from his home, which his parents had also attended. Shy and lonely, he was an average student and took no part in school activities or athletics. Life brightened when he was joined by Abbie, a pretty, vivacious girl of thirteen and an outstanding student. Little more than a year later, she died of a burst appendix. "It is lonesome here without Abbie," Calvin wrote his father from school soon after her death. For a Coolidge, this was an outpouring of emotion.

Calvin was the first of the family to attend college and he was influenced toward Amherst, just over the line in Massachusetts, by one of his teachers. The taciturn and withdrawn freshman yearned for acceptance without knowing how to achieve it. Fraternities were important at

Amherst but none bothered to rush him. "I don't seem to get acquainted very fast," he wistfully told his father.

By his senior year, Calvin had won a measure of acceptance. A friend who had been pledged by a new fraternity insisted that he be taken in, too. Coolidge also came under the influence of Charles E. Garman, who stressed the doctrine of service in his philosophy course and may have helped guide the young man toward a political career. Some of his classmates had also become aware of the dry wit that lay below his granite exterior, and he was chosen to give the Grove Oration, the Class Day humorous address. He won a $150 gold medal for first prize in a national essay contest on the causes of the American Revolution sponsored by the Sons of the American Revolution. In 1895, he graduated cum laude.

No soaring ambitions filled Coolidge as he faced the future, and he had no desire to move beyond the familiar hills that had always limited his horizon. He considered storekeeping and the law as careers and chose the latter. When a college friend asked where he planed to settle, Coolidge tersely replied, "Northampton's the nearest courthouse." Rather than attending law school he read law in the primitive manner of the early republic with a pair of prominent local attorneys. He sat in the outer office learning to prepare writs, deeds, and wills while reading lawbooks in his spare time. He received no salary. Coolidge spent twenty months there, an unobtrusive, inscrutable, and silent figure. Then, one morning, his table was clear of books and papers and he was gone. Having learned enough to pass the bar examination in 1897, he used a small inheritance to open an office of his own. Not long afterward, he began an active role in local Republican politics.

Northampton, Massachusetts, was a town of some fifteen thousand people with its industry tempered by Smith College, which had been founded two decades before. The old-line professional and business class was solidly Republican, while the numerically superior Irish and French-Canadian textile workers were Democrats. Coolidge, however, had qualities that allowed him to overcome this disadvantage. Besides being inordinately lucky, he had, despite his taciturnity, the knack of winning the goodwill of working-class voters. In fact, he felt more at ease with the barber, cobbler, even the tavern keeper, than with Northampton's elite. Some even abandoned their traditional party loyalty to vote for him.

Elected to the city council in 1898, Coolidge began his rise up the Massachusetts Republican escalator. Coolidge was no boat rocker and pro-

gressed to city solicitor, circuit court clerk, and then to the lower house of
the state legislature, the General Court. In Boston, he took a dollar-a-day
room in a dingy hotel and showed an interest in such progressive issues as
votes for women, a six-day workweek for laborers, and limits on the hours
worked by women and children. With his neat black suit, prim manner,
and pinched face, he was at first mistaken for an undertaker.

In Northampton, Coolidge lived a quiet life in a rented room on Round
Hill, across from the Clarke Institute for the Deaf. Now and then he
stopped at a beer garden for a glass of beer, but he spent most of his
evenings reading biography, history, and law in his room. He also worked at
his own translation of Dante's *Inferno* into English. He did not dance or
play cards and despite the opportunities afforded by the presence of Smith
College, was too shy to approach women.

One day in 1904, Grace Goodhue, an attractive, black-haired teacher
of lip reading at Clarke, was watering the flowers outside a school building
when she glanced up at an open window of a nearby house. She saw a
strange sight—a young man shaving in front of a mirror while wearing
long underwear and a felt hat—and burst into laughter. Startled,
Coolidge caught a glimpse of her as she turned away in embarrassment.
He sought a more formal meeting at which he explained to Grace that he
had an unruly lock of hair that got in the way when he shaved and wore
the hat to anchor it.

Like Coolidge, Grace Goodhue was of old Vermont stock, but as the
daughter of a Burlington mechanical engineer, was a cut above him on the
social ladder. They were attracted to each other although they made a
strange pair. Grace, a Phi Beta Kappa graduate of the University of Vermont, was vivacious and liked by everyone who knew her. Her friends could
not understand what she saw in this old-maidish, dry stick of a lawyer.
Coolidge tried to please her by learning to dance—not very successfully—
and by squiring her to church socials and parties. It was his hope, he joked
in his pinched way, "that after having made the deaf to hear, Miss Goodhue
might perhaps teach the mute to speak."

Following a prolonged and rather silent courtship, Coolidge proposed in
his usual straightforward manner during a walk in the woods, "I am going
to be married to you," he declared. Grace accepted him, and he walked on
without another word for fifteen minutes. When she asked him if he had
anything else to say, he replied that perhaps he had already said too much.
Although Grace's mother disliked her prospective son-in-law and opposed
the marriage, it took place on October 4, 1905. Coolidge was thirty-three;
Grace twenty-eight. They went on a two-week honeymoon to Montreal,

which Coolidge terminated after a week, saying he wished to return home to show off his "prize."

The newlyweds rented half of a two-family house on a maple-shaded Northampton street that was to be home to them and their two sons until they went to Washington. The monthly rent was $36, and Coolidge stoked the furnace. His telephone was on a party line, and he did not own a car until he became vice president. Grace was quickly introduced to her husband's oddities. She discovered that he had what must have been the largest collection of socks in the state, almost all with holes in them. One day, he gave Grace a bag containing fifty-two pairs to be darned. She asked him if he had married her to get his socks mended. "No," he replied, "but I find it mighty handy." He never discussed politics with Grace and all she knew about his activities she read in the papers. "He did not trust my education," she wrote later.

In 1909, Coolidge ran for mayor of Northampton. Suppressing his shyness, he went from door to door in every ward of the city, introducing himself and saying: "I want your vote. I need it. I shall appreciate it." He won by a wide margin, even carrying the city's normally Democratic working-class wards. Coolidge served two terms as mayor, in which he emphasized honesty, efficiency, and economy in government. Upon one occasion, the Coolidges entertained a Baptist preacher who was in town to conduct a revival meeting. The guest ate sparingly, explaining that abstinence improved his ability to preach. Later, Coolidge gave Grace a succinct critique of his performance. "Might as well have et."

Three terms in the state senate followed, and during the last, Coolidge served as president of the body. With the Democrats in control of the governorship and lieutenant governor's office, he was the ranking Republican official in the commonwealth. In 1915, he announced his candidacy for lieutenant governor. During this period, he acquired the backing of two powerful patrons, Frank Stearns, a wealthy Boston merchant and Amherst trustee, and Dwight Morrow, an Amherst classmate and now a partner in the House of Morgan. Stearns put the full weight of his advertising department and his influence among Massachusetts businessmen behind Coolidge. As a reward, he was later allowed to sit on the White House portico with Coolidge while they smoked their cigars in utter silence.

Traditionally, lieutenant governors served three one-year terms before moving up to governor. Biding his time, Coolidge reached the governor's chair on schedule in 1918. In twenty years in politics, he had achieved little in the way of a record, but had antagonized no one. "What is your hobby?" a newspaper writer asked the new governor. "Holding office," declared Coolidge. In fact, he did little more than that. Every morning he saw a few visitors and signed letters, had lunch at the Union Club, usually alone, and strolled back to the office. With his feet up on his big desk, he smoked a cigar as he read the early edition of the *Boston Transcript* and dozed off for several hours. And then the Boston police strike propelled him onto the national scene.

Congress was not to meet until December and Coolidge had four months to put his stamp upon the government. In this period he showed one of his most important characteristics: the capacity to adapt quickly to changed circumstances. As a state legislator and governor in progressive times, he was a mild progressive; as president in more conservative times, he was conservative. Coolidge was for sound money, high tariffs, low taxes, prompt payment of the war loans that the European nations owed the United States, and against all forms of activism or reform.

Coolidge's approach to public problems rested upon a few broad homilies: America's social and economic order was sound; its critics were either misguided or radicals; private enterprise was the backbone of the nation, and the United States, by virtue of its superior institutions and enlightened moral sense, held a special place among the nations of the globe. For a man who had spent most of his adult life on the public payroll, Coolidge had a narrow view of the capabilities and responsibilities of government. He believed its only real justification was to help business and pledged early on to usher in a "new era" in the relationship between government and business.

"If the Federal Government should go out of existence, the common run of people would not detect the difference," said the president. Government was nonproductive in Coolidge's view and money diverted to it could be better invested in private industry. "The chief business of the American people is business," was his most quoted observation, made a few months after he became president.* Many Americans agreed with Coolidge on the need for limited government, yet at the same time they demanded new roads for their automobiles.

Under Coolidge, regulatory agencies and boards were packed with eco-

---

* It should be pointed out that in this speech, to the American Society of Newspaper Editors in January 1924, Coolidge also emphasized that the amassing of wealth was not the chief end of man. Instead, wealth should be the means of achieving worthwhile goals— "the multiplication of schools, the increase of knowledge, the dissemination of intelligence, the encouragement of science, the broadening of outlook, the expansion of liberties, the widening of culture. . . . So long as wealth is made the means not the end, we need not greatly fear it."

nomic conservatives and representatives of the businesses they were supposed to regulate. He appointed the attorney for the lumber industry to the Federal Trade Commission—a man who had once described the agency as "an instrument of oppression." The U.S. Shipping Board, filled with industry representatives, sold 104 vessels to private operators for one tenth of their cost. Numerous antitrust suits were filed—primarily for show—and most were lost or settled behind closed doors for fines as low as $2,000. When Attorney General Stone threatened to file an antitrust suit against Alcoa, a firm controlled by Andrew Mellon, he was kicked upstairs to the Supreme Court.

Cheeseparing economies resulted in fewer food, drug, and meat inspectors. The budget of the Interior Department, which was responsible for the management of the public lands, had its budget cut from $48 to $32 million. Mencken, even though he had tagged Harding as an "ignoramus," credited the late president with having greater social impulses than Coolidge. And Lincoln Steffens observed that under Harding, the federal government was the kept woman of business; under Coolidge, Wall Street and Washington married.

The age of ballyhoo and public relations was dawning at the time Coolidge entered the White House, and he made political capital of two traits that were in vivid contrast to most politicians—he was tight-lipped in public and tight with money. Reporters and comedians told stories that underscored these characteristics, some true, some exaggerated, some invented, which transformed this fundamentally colorless man into a national character. "Every time he opens his mouth," noted an observer, "a moth flies out of it." It was said he prowled the White House in his nightshirt, spindly legs showing, turning off unnecessary lights.

Coolidge went along with the game but he was no buffoon. He re-created himself as "Silent Cal"—the sly and laconic Yankee rustic who was cleverer than he appeared—because that was what the public wanted. He allowed himself to be photographed unsmiling in full Indian headdress and fishing in a three-piece suit and waders. "In public life it is sometimes necessary in order to appear really natural to be actually artificial," he confided in his *Autobiography*.

In private, however, Coolidge was often garrulous—as the texts of his press conferences make abundantly clear. One reporter went to what he thought was an interview with the president only to be harangued for two hours on everything from trout fishing to the cost of cigars. Even though he tried diligently, he never managed to get in a question. Coolidge gave more formal speeches than Wilson—twenty-eight in 1925 alone, while Wilson gave only seventeen in his best year—and met the press more often than any previous president. Written questions were submitted in advance by the dozen or so members of the White House press corps who gathered in his office twice a week, and he chose which to answer. He could not be quoted directly and his remarks were attributed to a wraithlike White House spokesman. He warned reporters not to transcribe the conferences in shorthand.

Coolidge, not Franklin Roosevelt as is usually stated, was the first president to use radio effectively. He had a thin, reedy voice that was a handicap on the stump but worked well on radio. Even with his twang, he sounded conversational. In all, he gave sixteen radio speeches as president, and they were well received. And unlike Harding's bloated prose, his formal messages were brief and well crafted. Even Henry Mencken noted that he had "a natural talent for the incomparable English language."

Higher profits for business was Coolidge's recipe for national prosperity, but unlike modern Republican supply-siders he cut federal spending to reduce the need for increased taxes. "I am for economy," he declared. "After that I am for more economy." The White House set the example for what he called "orderly retrenchment." Paper drinking cups were replaced by old-fashioned glass tumblers, the number of towels in the lavatories was reduced, and reporters were told to buy their own pencils.

Nevertheless, Coolidge kept the presidential yacht, the *Mayflower*, in commission, for he enjoyed weekend cruises on the Potomac. The vessel's half-million-dollar annual cost was concealed in the Navy Department budget by classifying the craft as a warship. Otherwise, the army and navy largely stagnated during the Coolidge era. Informed that both services wanted to buy new aircraft, the president supposedly replied, "Why can't they buy a plane and take turns using it?"*

Following the stock market crash in 1929, which occurred little more than six months after Coolidge left the White House, his reputation went into a free fall but it has, in recent years, been on the upswing, notably among conservative advocates of limited government. Ronald Reagan, who was a teenager when Coolidge was in the White House, admired him so much that in 1981 he ordered a portrait of Thomas Jefferson removed

---

* Prospects for promotion were so poor that the members of the Naval Academy graduating class of 1923 were told that they would be lucky if they reached the rank of lieutenant commander before retiring with twenty years of service.

from the Cabinet Room to make way for one of Coolidge. "Look at the record," said Reagan. "He cut taxes four times. We had the greatest growth and prosperity that we've ever known." There was no mention of the day of the locust that followed the Coolidge Prosperity.

For the most part, Coolidge's relations with an independent-minded Congress were a continuation of the struggle between the White House and Capitol Hill of the Harding years. He twice vetoed the McNary-Haugen Bill, an effort by the farm bloc to raise the income of American farmers by having the government purchase surpluses and then dump them abroad. Instead, he urged farmers to voluntarily cut back on acreage and lower production to raise their prices.

While he praised the veterans for their patriotism, Coolidge vetoed a congressional plan for payment of a bonus in 1925. Congress overrode his veto. The president also quashed Herbert Hoover's plans for elaborate federally financed river control projects for the parched West, on grounds that they cost too much. He blocked a $68 million increase in the notoriously low Post Office salaries. Senator James Couzens of Michigan told Coolidge that a postman could not raise a family on a salary of $1,500 a year but the president replied: "In Northampton, Massachusetts, you can have a first-rate house to live in for $30 a month."

"That's no argument!" said Couzens. "All our postal employees can't live in Northampton, Massachusetts."

"I had an uncle in Northampton," the president continued. "He sent his children through high school and college and he never made more than $1,500 a year in his life."

"That's the trouble with you, Mr. President!" said Couzens, banging his fist down on Coolidge's desk. "You have a Northampton viewpoint, instead of a national viewpoint!"*

Coolidge, who liked a glass of beer now and then and opposed federal interference in people's lives, looked with disfavor on Prohibition. Nevertheless, he did not serve liquor in the White House and took the position that inasmuch as Congress had passed the Volstead Act, he would enforce it. But he added, "Any law that inspires disrespect for other laws—the

---

* Along about this time, U.S. postal inspectors sought the dismissal of the postmaster of the University of Mississippi in Oxford, a young man named William C. Faulkner, on grounds that he spent most of his time writing, drinking, loafing, playing bridge with friends, and reading his customers' magazines. Large bundles of undelivered mail were found in the trash and stuffed in closets.

good laws—is a bad law." In this oblique way, he made his stand clear.

Coolidge did not have "an international hair on his head," remarked an observer. But he was no isolationist and during the fight over the League had been a mild reservationist. He supported Harding's proposal for American participation in the World Court, opposed recognition of the Soviet Union until the Bolshevik regime learned to act in a civilized manner, and was against cancellation of the war debt. To his small-town New England mind, payment of a debt on schedule and in full approached religious dogma. When the Allies argued that these debts should be considered part of America's contribution to victory, Coolidge refused. "Wal, they hired the money, didn't they?" he supposedly drawled.*

The presidency was vastly different in 1923 than it is today. Coolidge was the last president to spend hours in the White House lobby shaking hands with touring visitors. He was the last president to have only a single secretary and no other aides. Coolidge had no telephone on his desk: there was one in a little booth outside his office but he never used it. "The president should not talk on the telephone," he explained. "In the first place, you can't be sure it is private, and, besides, it isn't in keeping with the dignity of the job."

Probably no president was less impressed with his exalted status than Coolidge. Upon entering the White House, he placed a rocking chair on the elegant portico and sat there in full view of tourists on Pennsylvania Avenue, rocking and contentedly puffing on a cigar. Coolidge smoked 50 cent Coronas; White House guests were offered nickel stogies. He did not indulge in such traditional presidential recreations as golf, tennis, bowling, billiards, or horseback riding; the only horse in the White House was a mechanical one. For amusement, he liked to window-shop the stores on nearby F Street.

"Mr. Coolidge's genius for inactivity is developed to a very high point," wrote Walter Lippmann. "It is far from being indolent inactivity. It is a grim determined alert inactivity." Like Reagan and George W. Bush, he was a master of delegation. "There are many things you . . . must not tell me," he said to his cabinet. Other presidents have talked of sleepless nights in the White House as they worried over problems but Coolidge slept nine hours a night plus a two-hour afternoon nap. One evening he went to the theater to see the Marx Brothers in *Animal Crackers* and Groucho spotted him in

---

* This statement is not found in the transcripts of his press conferences and some authorities believe the pronouncement to be apocryphal, but it certainly sounds like vintage Coolidge.

the audience. "Isn't it past your bedtime, Calvin?" he slyly inquired from the stage.

Grace Coolidge's mother, who did not like her son-in-law, attributed much of his success to the first lady. Donald McCoy, the ablest of Coolidge's biographers, thought she had a point. Grace "was a perfect helpmate to a loving but often cranky husband. . . . Where he was dull, she shone. Where he was rude, she displayed strikingly good manners. Where he irritated people, she ingratiated herself with them. Where he turned men sour, she made them smile. Where he chilled women, she warmed them. In short, when he needed help, she supplied it."

The new president had an acid wit. On one occasion, he told a press conference that he was going to visit a country fair. Would he speak there? "No," he replied, "I'm going as an exhibit." Some breakfast guests were surprised when he poured cream into a saucer but they followed suit. When he picked up the dish as if to slurp it, they did the same. Instead, Coolidge placed the saucer on the floor for the family cat and then looked blandly about the table as his guests held their plates before their lips.

A typical exchange took place with a White House guest. "You must talk to me, Mr. President," she said. "I made a bet today that I could get more than two words out of you." "You lose," he replied. Foreign diplomats were warned that Coolidge "can be silent in five languages." Before leaving office, he gave Hoover, his successor, some advice on how to deal with long-winded visitors. "If you keep dead still, they will run down in three or four minutes."

In an age of material success, Coolidge's frugality—or stinginess—became the stuff of legend. He was probably the only president to save money in the White House.* Snooping about the kitchen one day, he complained to the housekeeper about the unwarranted extravagance of providing a half-dozen hams for a dinner of sixty persons. The cook finally quit because of his parsimony. Coolidge was annoyed when he gave an aide a dime to buy a magazine and did not get back his nickel change. Colonel Starling recalled that as Coolidge prepared sandwiches for them in the White House pantry after an afternoon walk, the president grumbled that he had to pay for the cheese. At the end of his presidency, he refused to make the customary purchase of the chair he had used in cabinet meetings; Hoover and Mellon bought it for him.

Coolidge also had a boorish side that showed itself in practical jokes

* Coolidge's estate totaled over $700,000 at the time of his death in 1933, a princely sum in the throes of the Great Depression and in view of the fact that he had spent most of his adult life in government.

with an undertone of sadism. Ike Hoover, the longtime chief usher of the White House, noted that "he always seemed to be watching, rather suspicious lest something be 'put over' on him." Sometimes he polished off his dessert at state dinners and left the table while his astonished guests were still eating theirs. Family members, White House aides, and servants who crossed him were treated to storms of abuse or frosty silence. He intentionally tripped the White House alarm and then hid behind the curtains as the frantic guards searched for the intruder. A Secret Service agent who baited the president's hook on a fishing trip swore that Coolidge deliberately snagged him. And while Harding had pardoned Gene Debs, Coolidge ordered the deportation of Marcus Garvey, the radical black nationalist.

CHAPTER 7

"My Country 'Tis of Me"

Nose up like a clumsy bird settling into its nest, the small gilded biplane bounced several times before rolling to a stop on a grassy meadow outside Kokomo in central Indiana. It was late in the afternoon of July 23, 1923, two weeks before Calvin Coolidge became president. As the propeller ticked over, a solidly built man, hooded and in a purple silk robe with gold piping and mystic symbols, jumped out the rear cockpit to the ground. A huge crowd, many wearing the flowing white robes of the Ku Klux Klan and estimated at some 100,000 people, watched as an official delegation filed out to greet him.

"Kigy," he said.

"Itsub," they solemnly replied.*

David C. Stephenson, an ex-soldier, itinerant Texas printer, and newly anointed Grand Dragon of Indiana, was escorted to a mound in the middle of the field—called the "mount"—and flung back his hood. Men and women cheered and applauded and bobbed up and down to get a look at "the new Messiah." Previous speakers had already exhorted them to smite the devil and there had been allusions to the "Prince, the Sermon on the Mount and the Nativity." Some of the multitude raised their arms to him and shouted prayers of thanksgiving. Parents hoisted their children up on their shoulders so they could have a better view. With an imperious gesture, Stephenson signaled for silence and began to speak:

"My worthy subjects, citizens of the Invisible Empire, Klansmen all, greetings. It grieves me to be late. The President of the United States kept me unduly long counseling upon vital matters of state. Only my plea that

---

* These were Klan code words formed from the first letters of the words "Klansmen, I greet you" and "In the sacred, unfailing bond."

this is the time and place of my coronation obtained for me surcease from his prayers for guidance." President Harding was on his Alaskan travels and not even Stephenson's gilded plane could have gotten him there and back, but no one doubted the veracity of the story and a buzz of approval swept the crowd.

Stephenson flourished his commission, signed by Imperial Wizard Hiram Wesley Evans, naming him as Grand Dragon of Indiana "by Virtue of God's Unchanging Grace." And then he preached the virtues of white supremacy, and urged his audience to fight for "one hundred percent Americanism" and to thwart "foreign elements" that were trying to control the country. As he stepped back, a silver dollar sailed through the air and landed at his feet. Someone threw another. Rings, money, jewelry, watches, anything bright and valuable followed as demonstrations of fealty and love. When the offering slackened, Stephenson had his retainers sweep it all up as he met with his Hydras, Great Titans, Furies, Giants, Kleagles, King Kleagles, Exalted Cyclopses, and Terrors. Later, it was announced $50,000 had been collected.

The gathering was a tri-state Konklave of Klan members from Indiana, Ohio, and Illinois, but for several days, bumper-to-bumper lines of cars had poured into Kokomo from every point of the compass. Some were draped in flags and decorated with placards: "America for Americans"; "The Pope Will Never Rule America"; "Trade with Klansmen Not Jews." Kokomo had become the focus for those who saw themselves as the custodians of the Cross and Flag—the front line in the defense against evil, diversity, and modernism. The meeting was the nearest thing to a national convention ever held by the Klan.

The Konklave was clear evidence of the hooded organization's growing strength and influence. A force to be reckoned with in Maine, Indiana, Texas, Oklahoma, Colorado, Florida, and Oregon, the Klan enforced its will with midnight intimidations, whippings, brandings, and tar-and-featherings. In Texas, alone, forty-three people, including a white woman, were tarred and feathered. The initials "K.K.K." were branded into the forehead of a black bellboy. An elderly farmer was whipped by a mob. Police and sheriff's deputies in many places were Klansmen.

That night, there was a torchlight parade along Kokomo's Main Street, with thirty bands, but there was no music, only the measured beating of a big bass drum as the Klansmen marched along, four abreast, in a ghostly silence. People with no contact with the Klan thought it could be laughed out of existence because of its ridiculous rituals and comic mumbo jumbo, but few thought so after witnessing a Klan parade.

"The column extended, in the glare of one street lamp after another, as far as there was any visibility," wrote Morton Harrison, of the *Atlantic*. "White-robed figures with heads and faces covered with pointed hoods, bodies completely draped in loose flowing cassocks. . . . In the great mass of marchers there was not an eye or a face or a hand in sight, nothing to read but a broken ripple of old shoes—square-toed, cracked, run-over at the heel—shuffling in and out of the shadows cast by the robes." When the last hooded figure had disappeared into the darkness, a towering cross, twenty-four feet high, was set afire to mark the end of a great day in the Klan's history.

The revived Klan had been organized in 1915 by an obscure Methodist preacher named William J. Simmons in a ceremony atop Stone Mountain, outside Atlanta. Simmons had to mortgage his home to keep the organization alive and it did not reach its zenith until five years later, when he took on two skilled publicists, Edward Y. Clarke and a pretty widow named Elizabeth Tyler. Having previously raised funds for such organizations as the Red Cross, Near East Relief, the YMCA, and the Anti-Saloon League, they were impressed with the possibilities in the white supremacy doctrines of the Klan. Clarke named himself King Kleagle, or second in command to Imperial Wizard Simmons, and he and Mrs. Tyler put religious and racial bigotry on a business basis. They realized that contrary to the conventional wisdom, the Klan was not a grotesque abnormality in America; nativism and racism were part of the national consciousness.

Recruiters, or Kleagles, who received $4 of each $10 initiation fee, or Klecktoken, fanned out through the South and West and were told to "play upon whatever prejudices were most acute in the particular area." After the regional Grand Dragon and local officials took their rake-off, the remaining $4.50 went to national headquarters in Atlanta. Robes, newspapers, magazines, and tracts were marketed to members at a considerable markup. A women's auxiliary, the Kamellia, was also organized. The pope was a special target of the Klan, and it claimed he was preparing a move to Washington. Photographs of the Episcopal Cathedral under construction on Mount Alban, the city's highest point, were circulated and it was described as the new Vatican, the site selected because artillery mounted there would command the capital.

Klan membership mushroomed because the organization fed not only on distrust, suspicion, and fear; it also appealed to the joiner instinct of average Americans. The Klan offered fraternalism and camaraderie and its fantastic rigmarole of hoods, robes, and fiery crosses, Wizards, Dragons, and Goblins provided relief from the dreariness of ordinary life. Within a year, Simmons bragged that the Klan had well over 100,000 dues-paying members and the national treasury was netting about $40,000 a month. It was also responsible, according to an exposé published in the *New York World* in September 1921, for four murders, five kidnappings, and other assorted atrocities. A fruitless congressional inquiry followed, in which the Imperial Wizard denied all the charges. The investigation provided free publicity for the Klan and new members signed up at a record rate. "Congress made us," chortled Simmons.

The *World* also reported that King Kleagle Clarke and Mrs. Tyler had once been arrested in their bedclothes in an Atlanta disorderly house operated by the lady. Rank-and-file Klansmen were shocked by this moral breach and demanded the couple's ouster from the movement. Simmons resisted, insisting their organizational skills made them indispensable. Weakened by the scandal, he was deposed in November 1922 in a palace coup engineered by David Stephenson, and was replaced as Imperial Wizard by Evans, a pudgy dentist who was Grand Titan of the Texas Province and the self-proclaimed "most average man in America."

Under the leadership of Evans and Stephenson, the Klan boosted its membership to five million and offered a broader base than merely being anti-black, anti-Catholic, and anti-Jew. It tapped into inchoate grievances of the underclass against big business and economic exploitation. Echoing the old Populist platform of the 1890s, it was now strongly pro-farmer, pro–working class and anti–Wall Street. The Klan was the champion of Prohibition, guardian of the purity of Christian women, and opponent of international Jewish bankers, who, it was charged, had started the war for their own profit.

The typical Klansman lived in a small town or rural area in the South or Midwest. As the influence of the organization spread, it attracted displaced sharecroppers and tenant farmers who had taken jobs on the factory production lines of Detroit and in the mills of Cleveland. Small-town businessmen, desperately trying to maintain their status against the growing influence of chain stores and monopoly, were also a ripe source of recruits. Nervous about the present and fearful of the future, these people believed themselves and their ideals mocked by the nation's social and economic elite and sought revenge.

"We are a movement of the plain people, very weak in the matter of culture, intellectual support, and trained leadership," Imperial Wizard Evans declared in explaining the growth of the Klan. "One by one all our traditional moral standards went by the boards, or were so disregarded that they ceased to be binding. The sacredness of our Sabbath, of our homes, of chastity, and fidelity, and finally even of our right to teach our own children in our own schools fundamental facts and truths were torn away from us. Those who maintained the old standards did so only in the face of constant ridicule."

Both Texas and Indiana were represented in the U.S. Senate by Klansmen, about seventy-five members of Congress owed their seats to the Klan, and the governors of Indiana, Georgia, Alabama, California, and Oregon had been elected with its support. In Oregon, where there were over 100,000 Klansmen in a population of 850,000, the Klan elected the mayor of Portland and would have succeeded in outlawing Catholic schools except for a ruling by the Supreme Court.

Stephenson was the key man in the organization. A pathological liar, a heavy drinker, and a drifter, he was a supreme hustler. Having seized power from Simmons's appointee as Grand Dragon of Indiana, he set up headquarters in Indianapolis—Klanapolis—and was the strongest political force in the state. "I am the law," he proclaimed—and no one contested him. Known as the "Old Man," he controlled recruiting operations in twenty-three states, published his own paper, The Fiery Cross, and pulled the strings of the governor and legislature. The paper hailed him for his "unselfish devotion, sterling integrity, honor and loving personality." The mayor of Indianapolis promised to appoint no one to office not approved by the Grand Dragon. As befitted the chief executive of a large corporation, Stephenson spent weekends sailing a ninety-four-foot yacht on Lake Huron.

Upper-class Americans wrinkled their noses at the Klan's grotesqueries, but they, too, were firmly convinced that the United States was in danger of becoming the dumping ground for Europe's "scum." President A. Lawrence Lowell of Harvard led the Ivy League universities in imposing quotas for Jews while the top banks, publishing houses, law firms, and corporations refused to hire them. If prejudice against Jewish students was rife, it was even stronger against faculty. The teaching staffs of Yale, Princeton, Johns Hopkins, and the universities of Georgia, Chicago, and Texas each had one Jew. There were two each at Columbia and California and three at Harvard. There were fewer than a hundred Jews on liberal arts and sciences faculties throughout the nation in the 1920s, and not many more a decade later.

Racism and antipathy to foreigners, bordering on paranoia, created a demand for even tighter restrictions on immigration than those erected in 1921. The Dearborn Independent, a weekly newspaper owned by Henry Ford, fueled the outcry with inflammatory anti-Semitic articles. Ninety-one consecutive issues were devoted to "The International Jew: The World's Problem." The paper circulated *The Protocols of the Wise Men of Zion*, a document faked by the czarist secret police that outlined a supposed Jewish conspiracy to take over the world. Not only were the Jews unscrupulous bankers, the union-hating Ford also charged that they were behind efforts to organize the workers. "Unions are organized by Jewish financiers," he declared. "They are a scheme to interrupt work. A union is a neat trick for a Jew to have in hand when he wants to get a clutch on an industry."

In 1927, Ford was sued for libel by Aaron Sapiro, a Jewish attorney who had been attacked by name in the *Independent*. Worried about being forced to testify and ridiculed about the effect of a Jewish boycott of his cars, the old man apologized and settled out of court. The *Independent* was closed and Ford claimed its editor had full responsibility for what it printed and that he was completely unaware of the attacks on the Jews. To change its founder's image, the Ford Company spent $150,000 in advertising in the Jewish press and Ford made frequent appearances at testimonials for distinguished Jews. But historian Allan Nevins, author of a company history, observed that "the idea that he did not know the content of the anti-Semitic articles [in the *Independent*] is absurd" and Ford continued his anti-Semitic ravings in private.*

Restrictionists argued that a disproportionate share of the people convicted of violating the Prohibition laws were of Eastern and Southern European background, as were the inmates of the mental hospitals and similar institutions. Sacco and Vanzetti were cited as examples of this riffraff. "There is little or no similarity between the clear-thinking, self-governing stocks that sired the American people and this stream of irresponsible and broken wreckage that is pouring into the lifeblood of America," declared Representative Fred S. Purnell, an Indiana Republican. Evangelist Billy Sunday denounced immigrants as drinkers and papists. The *Chicago Tribune*'s expert on gangsters claimed that 85 percent of the top bootleggers in that crime-ridden city were Italian-born and another 10 percent were Jews.

---

* Oddly enough, some of Ford's best friends actually were Jews. Albert Kahn, the son of a rabbi, was his architect and they remained close. And he presented a Detroit rabbi named Leo Franklin, whom he admired, with a new Model T every year. When the rabbi returned the car after the *Independent* articles began appearing, Ford was shocked. "What's wrong, Dr. Franklin?" he asked. "Has anything come between us?" And there were never fewer than three thousand Jews in the Ford workforce during these years. Both Ford's wife and son tried to convince him to drop his anti-Semitic campaign.

These prejudices were fed by a rash of pseudoscientific studies that elevated "Nordics" above the "mongrel" races, which, it was said, threatened to turn the melting pot into a cesspool. Madison Grant, a founder of the New York Zoological Society and trustee of the American Museum of Natural History, was the Marx of this master class. His magnum opus, *The Passing of a Great Race*, based upon the racial superiority doctrines of Count Gobineau and Houston S. Chamberlain, who also influenced the thinking of an obscure Munich rabble-rouser named Adolf Hitler, had a wide readership and went through numerous editions.*

Seventy years before Patrick Buchanan, Lathrop Stoddard, Grant's major disciple, warned in *The Rising Tide of Color* that America not only faced a threat from the dregs of Europe but was besieged by the yellow, black, and brown races as well.

Unsatisfied by merely reducing the flow of immigrants, the restrictionists were now determined to turn off the tap altogether. The resulting National Origins Act of 1924 was primarily the work of Representative Albert Johnson, a Washington Republican. An admirer of Madison Grant, he had built his political career as a Red-baiter and on blatant appeals to the anti-Japanese prejudices of his constituents. The new law pushed the base period for measuring the number of immigrants in the United States from 1910 back to 1890, giving Northern Europeans an even greater advantage, and reduced the quotas from 3 to 2 percent of the foreign-born in the country at that time.

Statisticians discovered that the 1890 census was too vague on national origins to be usable for setting quotas, so the 1920 figure was to be substituted until 1929. Even so, the number of immigrants admitted annually was reduced from 357,803 to 161,184, mostly from Northern Europe. To accommodate pressure from the West Coast where anti-Japanese sentiment was strong, Japanese immigrants were completely excluded. Local legislation prevented Asians from owning or even leasing land in some areas. A Seattle group calling itself the Anti-Japanese League explained that the Japanese "constantly demonstrate their ability to best the white man at his own game in farming, fishing and business. They will work harder, deprive themselves of every comfort and luxury, make beasts of burden of their women, and stick together, making a combination that Americans cannot defeat." Similar complaints were registered against other hardworking immigrant groups—and are still heard.

* Hitler visited Chamberlain as he lay upon his deathbed in 1927, and kissed his hand. He also got some of the material used in *Mein Kampf* from the *Dearborn Independent*. Henry Ford is praised in the book and is the only American mentioned.

Immigration had few defenders. Liberals such as Senators Robert La Follette and George Norris, who were so outspoken on other issues, remained silent. Walter Lippmann, an upper-class German Jew, supported the Johnson Act on grounds that the public schools could not hope to "assimilate successfully a great mass of children with very different social backgrounds from the great mass of the American people." Organized labor and some black leaders embraced the restrictionist cause on the grounds that the new immigrants were taking the jobs of their followers. The congressional opponents of restriction were drawn mostly from big-city districts that had large immigrant populations, with Fiorello La Guardia, a maverick Republican who represented New York's heavily Italian East Harlem, the most outspoken anti-restrictionist.

La Guardia was a walking melting pot; his father, Achille, was an Italian immigrant who served as a U.S. Army bandmaster on the Western frontier, his mother was Jewish, and he was a practicing Episcopalian. He tweaked Southerners for their hypocrisy about Prohibition and mocked that there were more illiterates and law breakers in Kentucky than in New York City. When a restrictionist congressman declared that "we cannot make a well-bred dog out of a mongrel by teaching him tricks," La Guardia remarked: "My dog comes from a distinguished family tree, but he is still only a son of a bitch."

A major reason for the success of anti-immigration legislation was the withdrawal of business and industry from the anti-restrictionist coalition. Before World War I, industry supported open immigration to provide a continuing supply of cheap labor, but the war had forced them to seek out other sources of workers and to increase the pace of mechanization. Southern blacks, women, and Mexican peasants fleeing revolutionary turmoil at home took up the slack and industry no longer had need for immigrants from Europe. To ensure a steady flow of Mexican harvest workers, the Western Hemisphere nations were exempted from the quotas established by the 1924 legislation.

As the very embodiment of old Puritan stock, President Coolidge was on record as saying "America must be kept American." Yet he was no racist. He had courted the votes of French Canadians and Irish Catholics in Northampton and privately abhorred the Klan. He spoke out in favor of civil rights for black Americans. "There should be no favorites and no outcasts, no race prejudice in government," he declared. "America opposes special privileges for anybody and favors equal opportunity for everybody. . . . As a plain matter of expediency the white man cannot be protected and as a plain matter of right . . . justice is justice for everybody."

Yet Coolidge never took the next logical step, naming black Americans to important federal posts. He received several memos from Theodore Roosevelt, Jr., the Rough Rider's son, urging him to do so, and aides told Roosevelt the president was impressed. But he never did anything about these suggestions. Nor did he publicly denounce the Klan or give more than lip service to the passage of anti-lynching laws.

Nevertheless, anti-restrictionists looked upon Coolidge as their last hope. Secretary of State Hughes was concerned about the insult to Japan inherent in the Johnson Act, a nation much concerned about "face," and urged a veto. Coolidge might have made a case for giving the Japanese the same token quota allowed Southern and Eastern Europeans immigrants, but the Japanese government blundered. Tokyo issued a protest note that threatened "grave consequences" if the exclusion went into effect, which angered the Senate and made compromise impossible. Even though the president had misgivings, he again demonstrated his lifelong unwillingness to take political risk, and signed the bill. The American flag was burned in several Japanese cities, a movement to boycott American goods was launched, and one man disemboweled himself near the U.S. embassy in Tokyo.

The Johnson Act—which remained in effect until after World War II— ended an epoch in American history. The "golden door" was slammed shut and the United States was no longer a beacon for the world's oppressed.*

Calvin Coolidge's arrival in the White House coincided with the revival of the American economy and the beginning of what came to be called Coolidge Prosperity. Every economic barometer was moving upward but no one guessed—just as no one guessed in 1991—that the country would soon experience an astonishing boom. The gross national product increased from $69 billion in 1921 to $93.1 billion in 1924—a growth rate of 9 percent. At the same time, the consumer price index fell from 53.6 to 51.2, removing the threat of inflation, and the jobless rate plummeted from 11.7 to 5 percent.

Wages were going up after the postwar slump, although at a slow rate. The pay of the average federal employee climbed from $1,375 a year in 1920 to $1,515 in 1924. Construction worker wages had dipped from $1,924 in 1920 to $1,459 two years later but by 1924 had climbed back to

* The Johnson Act had disastrous consequences for the Jews. Had the 1921 quota been kept, it is estimated that as many as 300,000 Eastern European Jews would have been eligible to come to the United States between 1924 and 1929. Most of these might-have-been immigrants probably perished in the Holocaust. (Goldberg, *Discontented America*, p. 164.)

$1,822. Ministers of the gospel earned $1,428 in 1920, and $200 more in 1924. There were exceptions, however. Textiles and coal mining continued to lag, and while the lot of wheat and dairy farmers improved, the plight of most farmers remained grim. The average wage of the farmworker, which had climbed to $830 in 1920, slipped back to $551 in 1924.

Hard times and low prices drove farmers from the land in record numbers between 1919 and 1924, yet fewer farmers produced more food and fiber. Thirteen million acres were taken out of production during those years yet output increased by 5 percent annually. This paradox is explained by the fact that the family farm was giving way to the large corporate farm, especially out on the Great Plains, where the tractor and the combine revolutionized agriculture. There was a tenfold increase in the use of tractors during the decade, and the frontier for corn and wheat was pushed into the semi-arid belt that lay to the west—a development that was to have catastrophic results.

The boom had many fathers. Europe's economy had been ruined by the war, leaving the United States for a time the only truly healthy industrial power in the world. In 1914, the nation was the world's largest debtor, owing others more than $3.8 billion. Through loans and sales, America became Europe's creditor, by $12.5 billion. Industry and business benefited from benign government policies, among them protective tariffs, favorable tax schedules, and the easing of regulatory and antitrust pressures. The Federal Reserve, beginning in 1921 under the tutelage of Benjamin Strong, its most influential member, steadily reduced its discount rate from a peak of 7 to 3 percent, resulting in a dramatic thaw in interest rates.

New technology helped propel the boom. Industries such as automobiles, road construction, movies, radio, and home appliances helped create the world's first consumer economy. The U.S. Patent Office had not issued its millionth patent until 1911; by 1925, it had issued another million. One of the most startling developments was the growth of electric power. In 1912, only 16 percent of American households had electricity; by the mid-1920s, 63 percent of households were electrified and the United States was generating more electric power than all the rest of the world put together.

For the first time, people had the money to buy things other than the necessities of life and time to use them due to a shorter workweek. The postwar years ushered in an age of consumerism with a broader base of participation than had ever existed before in America or anywhere else. Throughout the previous centuries, the problem had been to produce enough of the goods that men wanted; now, it was to make men—and increasingly women—want and buy the great cornucopia of things that were suddenly available as a result of mass production and the growing efficiency of industry. Massive advertising campaigns were launched to encourage consumers to buy, to use, and buy again.

The first large advertising and publicity agencies—N. W. Ayer and J. Walter Thompson—appeared well before the war. Some of New York's best writers got their start on Madison Avenue, including humorist Robert Benchley and Dorothy Parker, who created the one-line caption. "Brevity Is the Soul of Lingerie" she wrote in an ad for women's underwear. Wartime propaganda techniques and the use of psychological studies of the buying public brought a new sophistication to the trade. Walter Thompson stated that the average consumer had the mentality of a four-teen-year-old and was a creature of whim, gullible and infinitely capable of being manipulated. Edward L. Bernays, the son of Sigmund Freud's sister Anna and a Broadway press agent turned public relations counselor, urged businessmen to make use of basic human impulses to sell products. He suggested using attractive girls in ads because they "appealed to the sex drive." Bernays retained Dr. A. A. Brill, Freud's leading drumbeater in America, to examine an advertising campaign designed for Lucky Strike cigarettes. Brill cautioned against an ad in which a woman offered a smoke to two men because "the cigarette is a phallic symbol to be offered by a man to a woman."

Advertising men now saw themselves as more than salesmen. It was no longer considered enough to merely display a product, tout its features, and tell where it could be bought. Now consumers were encouraged to buy goods for the glamour and prestige that rubbed off on the purchaser. The goal of advertising, said Bruce Barton, a founder of the Madison Avenue firm of Batten, Barton, Durstine & Osborne and author of *The Man Nobody Knows*, "is to arouse desires and stimulate wants, to make people dissatisfied with the old and out-of-date and by constant iteration to send them to work harder to get the latest model—whether that model be an icebox or a rug or a new home."

While advertising fanned the flame of desire for new goods, new forms of credit—most notably installment buying—enabled consumers to buy them. "Ride Now, Pay Later," trumpeted auto manufacturers. Advertising raised expectations and fostered a belief among Americans that they were entitled to an ever-rising standard of living. In the past, most people had thought it immoral to go into debt. Now, they were inspired by advertising to seek instant gratification. Old-fashioned notions of thrift and self-restraint were replaced by the urge to consume.

Financed by installment payments, the sale of automobiles, refrigerators, sewing machines, radios, and washing machines exploded. Over 85 percent of the furniture, 80 percent of phonographs, 75 percent of washing machines, and the greater part of household goods sold in the United States were bought on credit. By 1927, consumer debt amounted to about $3 billion.

In the 1920s, advertising emerged as a big business when the amount of money spent for it more than doubled to nearly $4 billion annually. General Motors alone spent $20 million a year on advertising. Newspapers and magazines relied almost entirely on ads for the bulk of their revenue. More was spent on advertising than on education, noted economist and social critic Stuart Chase. It created, he said "a dream world" of "smiling faces, shining teeth, school girl complexions, cornless feet, perfect fitting union suits, distinguished collars, wrinkleless pants, odorless breaths, regularized bowels . . . perfect busts, shimmering shanks [and] self-washing dishes."

Advertising also created a pre-Orwellian world of euphemism in which words were changed to make them sound better. Secondhand cars became "previously owned" automobiles; the installment plan became the "deferred-payment plan"; real estate agents became "Realtors" and the undertaker a "mortician" who operated a "funeral home." In politics, the "short ballot" became the attractive way of saying most jobs were appointive rather than elective while advocates of the vote for women preferred to call it "equal suffrage."

Slick advertising campaigns trumpeted the virtues of such soon-to-be familiar products as Scotch Tape, Welch's grape juice, and hair color rinse in ten shades. The slogan "Breakfast of Champions" was coined for Wheaties for the cereal's introduction in 1924. That same year, a scientist named Ernst Mahler developed a disposable handkerchief that was introduced as "Cellu-wipes." The name was later changed to Kleenex Kerchiefs and then simplified to Kleenex.* Clarence Birdseye, a Brooklyn-born naturalist, had discovered while living in Labrador that fish caught and instantly frozen retained their taste when thawed. Why not freeze vegetables and meat and poultry for later use?

Listerine was merely an all-purpose antiseptic until George Lambert discovered something called "halitosis" that could only be combated by gargling with his product. Lemonade-mix salesman Frank Epperson accidentally left a glass of lemonade with a spoon in it on the windowsill

---

* Previously, Mahler had developed a cotton substitute made of wood cellulose for the Kimberly-Clark company that was used to make bandages during the war. Learning that Red Cross nurses had pressed these bandages into service as sanitary napkins, the firm developed a new product, called Kotex, which was put on the market in 1921.

overnight. The lemonade froze and gave Epperson the idea for the Popsicle. The American Florists Association awarded Major P. F. O'Keefe a gold medal for creating the slogan "Say It with Flowers."

Even such a simple act as shaving was revolutionized. The safety razor and disposable double-edged blade had been patented by King Gillette in 1901, but did not come into common use until the U.S. Army issued safety razors to the troops. The straight razor received another blow when Colonel Jacob Schick patented the electric shaver in 1924. Wristwatches replaced the pocket watch during the war and condoms were first widely distributed by the military. The slide fastener was demonstrated at the Chicago World's Fair in 1893 and metal teeth were added in 1913. But the device did not catch on until Gilbert Frankau, an English novelist, gave it a name when he exclaimed at a demonstration in 1926: "Zip! It's open. Zip! It's closed."

Public relations, the handmaiden of advertising, appeared during the early years of the century when a coal mine owners association hired a former *New York Times* reporter named Ivy Lee to keep the press filled in on their version of events during a strike. It was a revolutionary move. Press agents had been active in promoting popular entertainment but most business tycoons usually adopted a "public be damned" attitude when it came to dealing with press coverage. Lee's initial statement of purpose established the fundamentals for all public relations work: "This is not a secret press bureau. All our work is done . . . in the open . . . to supply news. . . . [This is] not an advertising agency . . . any editor will be assisted most cheerfully in verifying any statement of fact." Organized labor did not look kindly on Lee's efforts in this and future strikes and to the unions he became known as "Poison Ivy" Lee.

New York's Consolidated Gas Company, the Equitable Life Assurance Company, the Pennsylvania Railroad, the Rockefeller interests, and numerous other firms hired public relations men to improve their image, ward off angry customers and stockholders, and deal with the undesirable consequences of government regulation. The motto of American business now became "the public must be taken into account." Before the war, the Women's Christian Temperance Union had showed remarkable agility in using public relations to sell Prohibition. And during the war, the Wilson administration established an immense internal propaganda machine that served as a model for the modern public relations industry.

CHAPTER 8

"Coolidge or Chaos"

One day early in June 1924, Moses Smith, a tenant farmer on the Roosevelt estate at Hyde Park, came upon Franklin Roosevelt sitting on a blanket in a field, dictating to Missy LeHand, his secretary. "Moses, what do you think I'm doing?" Roosevelt called out in greeting. "I'm writing a nominating speech to nominate Al Smith for President." The speech to the Democratic National Convention, meeting later that month in New York City, was the idea of Roosevelt's chief political adviser, the gnomelike Louis Howe. The time had come for Roosevelt to show that he had emerged victorious from his ordeal with polio. An extra bit of drama was to be added to convince doubters: Roosevelt planned to walk to the platform on the arm of his son James, and then propel himself to the podium under his own power.

Roosevelt and Howe were not at all certain that Smith could win the nomination in a fight with William McAdoo, the son-in-law of Woodrow Wilson and his treasury secretary. McAdoo was well ahead in pledged delegates, particularly in the South, and Smith was vulnerable because of his Catholicism, and his "wringing wet" position on Prohibition. But they had little alternative except to go along with New York's favorite son. Besides, Howe, operating with his usual deviousness, saw an opportunity to advance Roosevelt's political fortunes.

Smith's closest advisers, Judge Joseph M. Proskauer and Belle Moscowitz, convinced the candidate to name Roosevelt to head up the campaign because he would give it balance and broad appeal. Roosevelt, after running for vice president in 1920, had a national reputation, carried the Roosevelt name, was free of the taint of the Tammany Hall machine, was an upstate Protestant, had antagonized no one on the Prohibition issue, and could appeal to liberals suspicious of McAdoo. Proskauer and Moscowitz also felt that the crippled Roosevelt would be unable to interfere with the actual direction of their campaign. Like Al Smith, they viewed the genial patrician with contempt, regarding him as little more than a handsome piece of window dressing.

Smiling benignly at Proskauer and Moscowitz, Roosevelt accepted the offer, but he had no intention of sitting idly by and allowing them to run the show. By assuming the chairmanship of Smith's campaign, Roosevelt was able to plunge back into national politics and to broaden the contacts he had made in 1920. Howe maintained a wide-ranging correspondence with political leaders all over the country—whether they supported Smith or not—and his intelligence network reached deep into each state. Only a handful of delegates were won for Smith in the process, but it added to Roosevelt's stature, particularly when he called upon Smith campaign workers to refrain from stirring animosities that would leave scars after the convention.

The campaign also marked the first appearance of Eleanor Roosevelt in a leadership role in Democratic politics. She was named chief of the Women's Division of the Smith organization and headed a subcommittee assigned to draft planks for the party platform on social welfare legislation. Overcoming her shyness, she spoke before women's clubs, parent-teacher groups, and statewide welfare conferences. Louis Howe took an interest in her activities and accompanied her to a few meetings. He sat in the back of the audience and later provided a personal critique of her performance. To break Eleanor of a nervous giggle, he imitated it so she could see how it sounded. "Have something you want to say, say it and sit down," he told her. Under Howe's sometimes abrasive tutelage, she developed a less tense manner and a highly refined reportorial skill. The information she brought back was invaluable to him and his machinations on Franklin Roosevelt's behalf.

While the politicos maneuvered before the convention, Americans in the summer of 1924 were avidly following the details of the shocking murder of Bobby Franks, the fourteen-year-old son of Jacob Franks, a wealthy Chicago real estate investor. Bobby was last seen on the afternoon of May 21 while walking home from Harvard Preparatory, a school much favored by the well-to-do Jewish families in the then fashionable Kenwood section of the city. Another Harvard student saw him walking a short distance ahead and also noticed a Willys Knight automobile cruising slowly down the street. The boy stopped to examine some tulips in a flower bed. When he looked up Bobby had disappeared and the car was speeding away. One minute he was there; the next he was gone.

When Bobby had neither come home from school by six-thirty that evening nor called to explain his delay, his parents began to worry. Jacob Franks thought his son might have stayed late at school and been accidentally locked in, and went with one of the boy's teachers to look for him there. They found nothing. Back at the Franks's home, the phone rang and Mrs. Franks answered.

"Your son has been kidnapped," a voice said. "He's all right. There will be further news in the morning."

"What do you want?" Mrs. Franks screamed. "What do you want?"

The line went dead and Flora Franks fainted dead away.

Following a night spent in agony in which no further word was received from the kidnappers, the elder Franks went to the Chicago police, who told him to await further developments. That morning a typed special delivery letter arrived in the mail, demanding a $10,000 ransom for Bobby's safe return. Franks was told to prepare a package containing the money and he would be contacted again later that day.

Even as efforts were being made to deliver the ransom, workers discovered the nude and battered body of a boy stuffed into a waterlogged culvert in a marsh about twenty miles south of Chicago. One of the crew also found a pair of eyeglasses nearby, which were turned over to the police. The body was identified as that of the missing boy. That afternoon, one of Bobby's teachers ran into two friends, Nathan F. Leopold, Jr., and Richard A. Loeb. They were carrying copies of the latest newspapers. "Isn't that terrible what happened to poor Bobby Franks," said Loeb, "He used to play tennis all the time on our court."

Loeb and Leopold had murdered the boy for the thrill of it and with the intention of committing the "perfect crime." The eighteen-year-old "Dickie" Loeb and "Babe" Leopold, nineteen, were the sons of wealthy families—Loeb's father was second in command at Sears Roebuck—and graduate students at the University of Chicago. Loeb had recently graduated from the University of Michigan, one of the youngest graduates in its history, while Leopold set a similar record at Chicago. Loeb had an IQ of 160; Leopold's was 210 and he was to enter Harvard Law School in the fall. They were a study in contrasts: Loeb was handsome and debonair while Leopold was lumpy and socially ill at ease. Although the crime had been planned for months, the murderers did not choose a victim until they spotted Bobby Franks, Loeb's cousin, on the street. Invited by Loeb into the car for a ride, Bobby accepted.

The question of whether Loeb or Leopold actually killed the Franks boy was never cleared up because each accused the other of having done it.* As one drove with Bobby beside him, the other, who was in the back seat, bludgeoned the boy on the head from behind with a taped steel chisel. When this did not kill him, the victim was dragged over the front seat into the rear of the car. A gag was stuffed into his mouth, which caused him to suffocate. The pair stripped the corpse, poured hydrochloric acid over it, and pushed it into the culvert. Leopold later said he had no more feeling than "an entomologist . . . impaling a beetle on a pin." And then they cold-bloodedly telephoned the dead boy's parents with the ransom demand.

Yet Leopold and Loeb, despite their vaunted intelligence, stumbled badly. The glasses, which had fallen from Leopold's pocket, had unique hinges on the frames and were traced to him. He claimed they must have fallen from his pocket during a bird-watching expedition to the area. Loeb was questioned after Leopold gave police his name as an alibi witness. He broke quickly and implicated his friend. Next, the typewriter used to type the ransom note was traced to Leopold. Neither young man showed any remorse for murdering Bobby Franks. The fact that each identified the other as the actual murderer didn't really matter, the politically ambitious prosecutor, Robert E. Crowe, told the press. Both were equally guilty of murder and kidnapping.

The Leopold and Loeb case was the first of the so-called crimes of the century that gripped the nation through the mass media. Crime was certainly no stranger to Prohibition-era Chicago. Bombings, shootings, extortion threats, and kidnapping were common as mobsters sought to control the city's profitable illegal liquor trade. During the previous year, there were 267 deaths by shooting alone in Cook County and 177 killings in the first six months of 1924, including one a day in June. But the "thrill killing" of Bobby Franks was something new. It created a nationwide sensation because of the bizarre nature of the crime, the prominence and wealth of the families involved, and the accuseds' cold lack of remorse. The murder could not be explained rationally—and to some observers it was one more sign of the breakdown of morals in postwar America and a harbinger of a murderous era.

The case was made to order for Chicago's highly competitive newspapers. They offered excitement, titillation, diversion, and entertainment and served up great gobs of crime and scandal. Reporters peeped through

* Clarence Darrow, in his memoirs, identified Loeb as the actual murderer. (*The Story of My Life*, p. 228.)

keyholes, wiretapped, impersonated policemen, stole evidence, and committed burglary to get scoops. Circulation wars raged in which thugs were hired by various papers to terrorize newsdealers, newsboys, and even readers into taking their papers. Ben Hecht, a onetime Chicago newsman and co-author of the rollicking play *The Front Page*, observed: "Each publication sent stern and muscled minions through the rush hour street-cars to snatch . . . rival newspapers out of passengers' hands, and, on resistance, toss the reader into the gutter."*

There was no question of Loeb's and Leopold's guilt and the Chicago papers cried for blood. The murder of Bobby Franks sent a wave of anguish through Chicago's Jewish community where all the families involved were well connected. How could Loeb and Leopold, two young men with such brilliant futures, have committed such a crime? Yet there were also silent prayers of relief that their victim was Jewish. Had they murdered a non-Jew, the crime, with its overtone of ritual murder, would certainly have fanned the anti-Semitism prevalent in 1920s America. Even as it was, there was an undercurrent of such feeling. As soon as the confessions were made public, cynics doubted the two rich Jewish boys would ever hang—especially after they hired Clarence Darrow.

The Loeb and Leopold families turned to Darrow, Chicago's leading defense attorney, with the hope of saving the young men from the gallows. "Get them a life sentence instead of death," begged Jacob Loeb, Dickie's uncle. Darrow's legal career was built on defending the underdog. He took cases involving labor leaders, such as Eugene Debs, and unions at a time when they were ill-regarded by the courts. Tall, big-boned, and slouching at sixty-seven, Darrow hardly looked like a lion of the courtroom. He had limp hair, cavernous blue eyes, a rutted face, and the rumpled look of a country lawyer. But he had a passionate hatred of capital punishment and an enviable record in murder cases—helping 102 clients escape the death penalty. Rumor had it that Darrow was offered a million-dollar fee, but in reality he accepted less than one tenth of that.

Sunlight poured through the tall windows of a hot, stuffy chamber on the sixth floor of the Criminal Courts Building as the trial began on July 21, 1924. Thousands clamored to get into the courtroom but newsmen filled most of the three hundred seats. Darrow immediately approached the bench and told Judge John R. Caverly that his clients wished to change

---

* Twenty-seven people were killed during a circulation battle just before the war and many more were injured.

their plea from innocent to guilty. A shock wave swept through the court-room and reporters bolted for the door. The prosecution was caught com-pletely off guard. State's Attorney Crowe had expected a plea of not guilty by reason of insanity. In preparation, the prosecution's psychiatrists—called alienists in those days—had examined the defendants and were ready to testify that they were sane within the standards established by the law.

Darrow had quickly realized he had no defense. But his aim was not to exonerate Loeb and Leopold but to save them from the hangman. By switching to a guilty plea, they avoided a jury trial. Judge Caverly, alone, would determine whether they would hang or spend the rest of their lives in prison. Darrow knew that no defendant as young as his clients who pleaded guilty had ever been hanged in Chicago, and he gambled that the pattern would continue. Had the defendants taken an insanity plea, they would have faced a vengeful society in the form of a jury that would prob-ably have wasted no time in meting out the death penalty.

Darrow's aim was to shift the trial's focus from the cold-blooded nature of the crime to the motivation for it and the condition of the defendants' minds. Once the prosecution had made its case for the death penalty, he called the first of a team of prominent psychiatrists who were to testify that Loeb and Leopold were victims of a mental and moral breakdown rather than ordinary criminals. Crowe immediately leaped to his feet, protesting that this was an improper attempt to attach an insanity defense onto a guilty plea. Looking Judge Caverly squarely in the eye, Darrow observed, "I don't believe there is a judge in Cook County that would not take into con-sideration the mental status of any man before they sentence him to death." Caverly agreed to hear the witnesses—a major defense victory.

Three psychiatrists testified that Loeb had exhibited criminal tenden-cies when he was only eight or nine. Fantasizing that he was a criminal mastermind, he stole money and objects from relatives and friends and shoplifted for the thrill of it. When caught, he lied and showed no signs of guilt. Leopold served as an accomplice to Loeb's burgeoning criminal activities as part of a "compact," although he had no criminal tendencies himself. In exchange for limited homosexual favors—Leopold was allowed at certain intervals to insert his penis between Loeb's legs—he participated in crimes planned by Loeb. Leopold, according to the psychiatrists, saw himself as both a Nietzschean superman because of his intelligence and the slave of the handsome Loeb. Over time, the pair graduated from small-scale theft to stealing cars to arson and burglary—and finally to the fantasy of the perfect crime.

Once the psychiatrists had finished, Darrow began a stunning and emotional summation that lasted nearly twelve hours over two days, in which he tried to put a human face on the testimony of the experts. Thumbs in his suspenders, voice rising and falling for dramatic effect, he pleaded for the lives of his clients. Using Freudian theory, he argued that despite their great intelligence, the pair were driven by forces beyond their control to perform senseless acts of aggression and destruction. "Brains are not the chief essential in human conduct," Darrow noted. Instead, unconscious impulses determined action. Normally, the ethical and moral habits instilled in childhood were enough to hold the beast below in check, but the minds of the defendants were "diseased" and they could not suppress their dark and senseless urges.

> All the testimony of the alienists . . . shows that this terrible act was the act of immature and diseased brains, the act of children. Nobody can explain it any other way. No one can imagine it any other way. It is not possible that it could have happened in any other way. . . . The easy thing and the popular thing to do is to hang my clients. I know it. Men and women who do not think will applaud. The cruel and thoughtless will approve. . . . But, Your Honor, what they ask should not count. . . . I know the future is with me, and what I stand for here. . . . I am pleading for life, understanding, charity, kindness, and the infinite mercy. . . . I am pleading that we overcome cruelty with kindness, and hatred with love. I know the future is on my side.

On the morning of September 10, 1924, a pale and worn Judge Caverly was driven from his apartment to the Criminal Courts Building in a heavily guarded motorcade. There had been several threats against his life and that of his wife from both those who demanded the execution of Loeb and Leopold and those favoring life imprisonment. At 9:30 A.M. he began to read his decision. "The testimony in this case reveals a crime of singular atrocity," he declared. "It was deliberately planned and prepared for during a considerable period of time. It was executed with every feature of callousness and cruelty." Leopold later said that when he heard those words, he was convinced that he was going to hang. But the judge had more to say.

"It would be the path of least resistance to impose the extreme penalty of the law. . . ." Leopold's head jerked upward. Did this mean that he and Loeb were not going to be sentenced to death? Caverly quickly confirmed it. "In choosing imprisonment instead of death, the court is moved chiefly by consideration of the age of the defendants. . . . Life imprisonment may not at the moment strike the public imagination as forcibly as would death

by hanging; but to the offenders, particularly of the type they are, the prolonged suffering of years of confinement may well be the severer form of
retribution and expiation." Gazing unsmilingly into the faces of the defendants, he sentenced each to life for murder and ninety-nine years for kidnapping, with the recommendation they never be paroled.*

With the economy booming, Coolidge easily locked up the Republican
presidential nomination well before the party's national convention
opened in Cleveland on June 10, 1924. He handily dispatched his two
leading rivals—Governor Gifford Pinchot of Pennsylvania and Henry
Ford—well before the convention. And most of the old guard senators
who might have opposed him had passed from the scene or been stripped
of power. The Republican Party still had bosses but they did not possess the
influence of previous years.

Governor Pinchot, a founding father of Theodore Roosevelt's Progressive Party, had hoped to burnish his credentials for the Republican presidential nomination by settling an anthracite coal strike just as Roosevelt
had done in 1902. Coolidge, knowing full well that whoever was responsible for the settlement would "remain a hero until the coal bills come in," as
Mencken put it, slyly let him assume the task. Pinchot fell into the trap. He
settled the strike by awarding the miners a 10 percent wage increase, a
union checkoff, and an eight-hour day. The president sent "heartiest con-
gratulations" and waited for the fallout. As Coolidge had expected, the
settlement alarmed conservatives, among then Andrew Mellon, a power
in Pennsylvania politics who owned coal mines, and Pinchot's candidacy
was nipped in the bud.

Straw votes showed that Ford was the first choice for president of many
voters even though he had failed to win a Senate seat in 1918. Ford for
President clubs were springing up all over the country and the carmaker
really seemed interested in the White House. In a ghostwritten article in

---

* The two men remained friends and established a school for uneducated inmates. Loeb
was slashed to death in 1936 by another prisoner who claimed that the victim had made
homosexual advances toward him. "Richard Loeb, a brilliant college student and master of
the English language, today ended a sentence with a proposition," wrote Edwin A. Lahey, of
the Chicago Daily News. Leopold, who had volunteered to test an experimental malaria
vaccine, was paroled in 1958, after thirty-three years behind bars. To avoid press harass-
ment, he went to live in Puerto Rico. A devoted ornithologist, he published The Birds of
Puerto Rico and worked for various humanitarian causes. He married a former social worker
from Baltimore in 1961 and died ten years later from a heart attack. To the end, Leopold
insisted that it was Loeb "who had originated the idea of committing the crime, he who
planned it, he who had largely carried it out."

Collier's, he outlined what he would do "If I Were President." He thought that running the country would be rather like running his auto plant: he would make all the big decisions while trusted aides did the day-to-day work. But following a meeting with the president in December 1923, Ford unexpectedly announced his support for Coolidge. "I would never for a moment think of running against Calvin Coolidge for president on any ticket whatever," he declared. Why the sudden change?

Ford had for some time been eying a complex, built by the government during the war on the Tennessee River at Muscle Shoals in Alabama, that included a dam that generated cheap electricity and a plant producing nitrates for explosives. He saw it as an ideal place for the production of fertilizer and electric power, even the site of a new Detroit. "My purpose in taking over Muscle Shoals is not to benefit us or our business," he declared. ". . . My one purpose is to do a certain thing that will benefit the whole world." It is believed that Coolidge agreed to back the sale of Muscle Shoals to Ford, and in exchange the industrialist disavowed any presidential ambitions.

Ford offered $1 million for Muscle Shoals, which had cost the government some $90 million to build, later raising his bid to $5 million. As Coolidge had undoubtedly expected, Ford's plan ran afoul of Senator George Norris of Nebraska and other progressives and public power proponents. They saw Muscle Shoals as the centerpiece for government development of the resources of the impoverished Tennessee Valley. Norris pointed out that the hundred-year lease Ford wanted for electricity generated by the dam would yield him a profit of $15 billion. "No corporation ever got a more unconscionable contract," he added. Fought to a standstill, Ford dropped the plan—and Muscle Shoals was one of the few progressive triumphs of the era.

In 1928, Norris managed to push through legislation that permitted the federal government to operate an experimental fertilizer plant at Muscle Shoals and sell surplus power to nearby municipalities, but Coolidge allowed it to die without his signature. Herbert Hoover vetoed a similar plan but it became the foundation for the massive and far-reaching Tennessee Valley Authority when Franklin Roosevelt, a longtime advocate of public power, became president.

The Republican convention in Cleveland—the first to be broadcast on the radio and the first to be outfitted with a loudspeaker system—was humdrum. The Republicans deftly avoided taking a stand on the two great moral issues of the day: Prohibition and the Klan. Grand Wizard Evans and some sixty Klan leaders looked on benignly as the Klan problem was brushed aside with a "general tolerance" platform plank that did not mention the organization by name. On Prohibition, the party simply followed Coolidge's position that the law of the land would be enforced.

Once Coolidge was nominated by all but acclamation on the first ballot—there were thirty-four dissenting votes for La Follette—the only work left for the delegates was the choice of a vice presidential nominee. Coolidge wanted Senator Borah but the Idahoan, not at all certain that Coolidge could win because of the Harding scandals, opted to run again for his Senate seat. Besides, it was no secret that he considered himself better qualified for the presidency than the nominee. When Borah was approached to join the ticket, he supposedly asked: "At which end?"

The nomination finally went to Charles "Hell'n Maria" Dawes, Harding's able director of the Bureau of the Budget. Herbert Hoover received three hundred votes even though he had not sought the nomination. Dawes was chief architect of a new plan to rescue the German economy. To meet American claims for payment of the war debt, Britain and France had insisted on wringing from Germany the reparations awarded them under the Versailles Treaty. Wild inflation and a crippled economy sent Germany into default. The French seized the Ruhr in retaliation, aggravating the unhappy nation's plight and assisting Hitler and the Nazis to crawl out of obscurity.

Under the Dawes Plan, American banks extended enormous loans to the Germans, enabling them to make their reparations payments to the British and French, who in turn used these funds to repay their war debt to the United States.* Germany and the rest of Europe entered a period of relative stability and prosperity and Dawes, who was hailed as a hero, shared the Nobel Peace Prize in 1925. Something of a maverick, he was, in addition to being a successful banker and bureaucrat, an amateur composer. One of his compositions, "Melody in A Major," with lyrics added, became the popular song "It's All in the Game."

Two weeks after Coolidge's nomination, the Democratic convention opened in Madison Square Garden in New York City with storm warnings

---

* Some critics pointed out that it would have made better sense to just move the money from one set of books to another rather than paying the fees and interest to the bankers. Moreover, the rescue plan was viable only so long as American banks and corporations were able to pump large amounts of money into Germany. Any disruption of this flow would bring the whole house of cards down on everyone. Such warnings were, for the most part, disregarded.

flying. A masterpiece by architect Stanford White, the Garden was located in the block bounded by 26th and 27th Streets and by Madison and Fourth Avenues, and was considered the most beautiful building in New York when it opened in 1890. Its most imposing feature was a ten-story tower topped by Augustus Saint-Gaudens's gilded statue of Diana. In 1906, White was shot and killed in the rooftop garden by Harry K. Thaw, an erratic millionaire playboy who objected to the architect's attentions to his wife, a beautiful former chorus girl named Evelyn Nesbit. She is said to have posed nude for the statue of Diana. The Democratic convention was the last event held in Madison Square Garden. It was torn down immediately afterward and replaced by the tower of the New York Life Insurance Company.

For all practical purposes, the Democratic Party that gathered in New York was a purely regional party. It had elected only two presidents between the Civil War and 1920—Grover Cleveland and Wilson—and its only certain electoral base was the "Solid South." To this was added the votes of the immigrant populations of the Northeastern cities plus those of the residents of the southern regions of Ohio, Indiana, and Illinois, who had migrated from the Old South and had Southern views. There was not a single black delegate or alternate at the convention. Self-made men like Al Smith and Mayor James Michael Curley of Boston, who had fought their way out of the Lower East Side and Roxbury slums, found themselves in uneasy alliance with cotton state barons such as Senator Pat Harrison of Mississippi and rural Texans like John Nance Garner. Liberals such as Harvard Law School professor Felix Frankfurter coexisted with populist demagogues such as Louisiana's Huey Long.

Every prejudice, every animosity in American society simmered in the unbearably humid hall, ready to explode into the open. The two leading candidates were lightning rods for the regional rivalries and conflicting moralities that divided the Democratic Party and the nation. William McAdoo was the standard-bearer of the "Old America" of the rural South and West, ardently dry and Protestant. He had the endorsement of the Klan—and refused to disavow it. Smith epitomized the "New America" of the cities and their immigrant masses. A product of the Fulton Fish Market and Tammany Hall, Smith was a wet, a Catholic, and with his ever-present brown derby, cigar, and rasping New York accent, everything rural America hated and feared.

Shortly after the convention was gaveled to order on June 24, 1924, the expected explosion occurred over a platform plank put forward by Smith's supporters denouncing the Klan by name. Angry words, fistfights, and shouted obscenities punctuated the bitter debate. By mistake, the band struck up "Marching Through Georgia," the anthem of Sherman's raiding troops, and it unleashed a paroxysm of anger from McAdoo delegates. Pro-Klan Texas delegates even tried to burn a cross on the floor. The anti-Klan plank fell short by a single vote, and only the presence of a special detail of a thousand New York City policemen prevented a full-scale riot. A substitute in which all secret organizations were denounced without mentioning any by name, similar to the one approved by the Republicans, also failed. "If you say 'K.K.K.' to the elephant it answers, 'Ain't the moon beautiful,'" said a jokester. "If you say it to the donkey, it kicks itself all over the lot."

When the time came to nominate Smith, Roosevelt began the ordeal of propelling himself to the rostrum from his seat under the eyes of all the delegates. "As we walked—struggled really—he leaned heavily on my arm, gripping me so hard it hurt," his then sixteen-year-old son Jimmy Roosevelt recalled a half century later. "It was hot, but the heat in that building did not alone count for the perspiration which beaded on his brow. His hands were wet. His breathing was labored. Leaning on me with one arm, working a crutch with the other, his legs locked stiffly in his braces, he went on his awkward way." Thunderous cheers greeted Roosevelt's arrival on the platform and flashbulbs flickered about the Garden like heat lightning.

Relaxing his grip on his son's arm, Roosevelt took up his other crutch and swung himself forward, step by step, as delegates and spectators held their breath, fearing that the gallant figure might stumble or fall. He reached the rostrum and, bracing himself against it, cast aside the crutches. With a toss of his classic head, he drew himself erect and smiled triumphantly into the glaring spotlights. The crowd went wild. Several minutes passed before the cheering stopped.

Roosevelt began with a plea for unity. "You equally who come from the great cities of the East and from the plains and hills of the West, from the slopes of the Pacific and from the homes and fields of the Southland, I ask you in all seriousness . . . to keep first in your hearts and minds the words of Abraham Lincoln—'With malice toward none and charity for all.'" And then he turned to praise of Al Smith. "He has a power to strike at every error and wrongdoing that makes his adversaries quail before him. He has a personality that carries to every hearer not only the sincerity but the righteousness of what he says. He is the Happy Warrior of the political battlefield."

The demonstration for Smith lasted for an hour and thirteen minutes. After this display of courage, Roosevelt was probably more popular than any of the candidates and many observers thought the image of the Happy

Warrior better suited him than Smith. Some were convinced that if he had been proposed as a compromise candidate, Roosevelt would have carried the convention. But no single speech could prevent the Democrats from committing suicide in 1924, and the deadlocked convention became the classic political calamity.

The balloting droned on for two weeks, day and night, with neither Smith nor McAdoo able to cobble together the 732 votes needed to win under the two-thirds rule. "This thing has got to end," Will Rogers wearily observed after a week. "New York invited you people here as guests, not to live." The McAdoo delegates attacked Smith's religion and his stand against Prohibition, while the galleries were packed with Smith supporters who set off fire engine sirens and screamed "Oil! Oil! Oil!" at every mention of McAdoo's name—a reference to his connection with Teapot Dome.

Red-eyed, unshaven, and drunk with bootleg booze and fatigue, the delegates took out their frustrations by fighting among themselves. To add to the misery, a merciless heat wave brought out the animal smells left behind by a circus that had previously occupied the Garden. The cry that began every roll call—"Alabama casts twenty-four votes for Oscar W. Underwood!"—resounded over the radio and across the nation like a drumbeat. For years afterward, the popular synonym for grit was to be "as steady as Alabama for Underwood."

On July 4, as the delegates sweltered through another day of balloting, some twenty thousand Klansmen from Pennsylvania, New Jersey, and Delaware and their families rallied against Smith in Long Branch, New Jersey. An effigy of the New York governor, whose left arm cradled a whiskey bottle, was battered to a shapeless pulp. A bevy of Klan weddings and baptisms was held and the outing ended with a torchlight parade by four thousand hooded Klansmen.

McAdoo climbed to 530 votes but stalled and his support began to fall away to other candidates. Following the ninety-third ballot—Smith had 355½ votes and McAdoo 314—Roosevelt came to the rostrum to announce that although Smith was leading, it was clear that neither of the front-runners could win the two-thirds vote needed for nomination. Smith would withdraw for the sake of party unity if McAdoo would do likewise. But McAdoo stubbornly refused to give way.

Looking for a compromise candidate, the groggy delegates accepted a deal brokered by James Cox and other party chieftains and switched to John W. Davis of West Virginia. Tall, handsome, and with a ruddy face topped by a shock of white hair, Davis was a prominent Wall Street lawyer and had been Woodrow Wilson's solicitor general and envoy to Britain. He received the now worthless nomination on the 103rd ballot. Charles W. Bryan, the governor of Nebraska and quirky younger brother of the Great Commoner, was chosen as the vice presidential nominee to appease the West and South, angry over the choice of the attorney for the House of Morgan to head the ticket.*

Radio and newspapers had carried the hatreds and passions of the Garden into the homes of the voters and whatever hopes the Democrats had of capturing the White House had evaporated even before the campaign opened. Nothing that Calvin Coolidge might have said or done could have caused more damage. Besides, the American people liked Silent Cal. They found his small-town, cracker-barrel philosophy agreeable, believed in his honesty, and had the same respect he had for big businessmen.

The real opposition to Coolidge was offered by "Fighting Bob" La Follette, who ran on the insurgent Independent Progressive ticket, an alliance of old-time progressives such as Jane Addams and Justice Brandeis, farm-bloc Republicans, Socialists, the railroad brotherhoods, and mavericks like Fiorello La Guardia. La Follette charged that the two major parties had turned their backs on the farmer and working man, and launched a bitter attack on the trusts and monopolies that he said controlled the government. Henry Mencken announced that he would vote "unhesitatingly" for the Wisconsin senator despite whispers that his pockets were "stuffed with Soviet gold. . . . He is the best man in the the running, *as a man*." Although a spellbinder on the platform, La Follette did not come over well in the new age of radio. His voice wavered on and off and his stock of gestures was of no use.

Coolidge took little part in the campaign, not only because he had little inclination to do so, but because of the unexpected death that summer of his younger son, sixteen-year-old Calvin Jr. The boy, a student at Mercersburg Academy in Pennsylvania, blistered a toe while playing tennis on the White House lawn in sneakers without socks, and blood poisoning set in. Antibiotics were then unavailable and the president and his wife watched helplessly as their son weakened. Coolidge remembered that young Calvin loved animals, and one day he captured a small brown rabbit on the grounds. He carried it to the sickroom where it produced a wan smile from the dying boy. The Coolidges were devastated by his passing and the presi-

* In 1954, Davis unsuccessfully argued before the Supreme Court in the case of *Brown v. Board of Education* in favor of continuing school segregation in the United States.

dent lamented: "When he went, the power and glory of the presidency went with him. . . . I don't know why such a price was expected for occupying the White House."

As Coolidge grieved in private, the dynamic Charles Dawes conducted a one-man whirlwind campaign. He delivered more than a hundred speeches in four months and traveled fifteen thousand miles by special train. Dawes was said to be "the only man in the world who when he spoke could keep both feet and both arms in the air at once." The Republicans emphasized that Coolidge stood for peace and prosperity, and contrasted current conditions with the recession and confusion they inherited from Wilson. The alternative facing the voters, according to Republican speakers, was "Coolidge or Chaos."

The Democrats decried the Harding scandals and government for, and by, big business, but to little avail. A frustrated Davis vainly tried to draw Coolidge into a debate. In one speech he described his opponent's position this way: "If scandals break out in the government, the way to treat them is—silence. If petted industries make exorbitant profits under an exorbitant tariff the answer is—silence. If the League of Nations . . . invites us into conference on questions of worldwide importance, the answer is—silence. If race and religious prejudice threaten our domestic harmony, the answer is—silence." Coolidge answered in his own bleak way. "I don't recall any candidate for president that ever injured himself by not talking," he said.

Davis failed to take advantage of the growing dissatisfaction of African-Americans with the Republicans. Although he rendered lip service to protecting the civil rights of blacks when speaking in the Northern cities, he cautiously protected his base in the South. Black organizations such as the NAACP denounced both major parties for insensitivity on matters of concern to them, but La Follette gave so little attention to black issues they saw no advantage in turning to him.

Backed by big business, the Republicans possessed unlimited resources and acknowledged collecting $4 million in campaign funds. Even though Davis had strong corporate ties, the Democrats fared far less well, amassing little more than a quarter of that. La Follette mounted a shoestring effort, spending only $211,000 on his campaign.

Only about half the eligible voters went to the polls on Election Day—slightly more than in 1920 but well behind the 70 percent who voted in 1916. Women again failed to turn out in large numbers. Those who did vote joined their men in choosing by an overwhelming majority to "Keep Cool with Coolidge." Sailing to an easy victory, the Republican ticket amassed 15,718,211 popular and 382 electoral votes; Davis had 8,395,283 and 136; La Follette 4,831,470 plus the 13 electoral votes of ever-faithful Wisconsin. Ninety percent of Northern blacks voted for Coolidge. The Republicans also won substantial majorities in both houses of Congress, depriving the Republican insurgents from the farm states of their balance-of-power status they had won in the 1922 off-year elections. "In a fat and happy world, Coolidge is the man of the hour," said William Allen White.

La Follette's followers took solace in the fact that his total vote was the most ever won by a third-party candidate, and liberal historians usually interpret this as a sign of the liveliness of a supposedly dormant progressivism. In reality, it was merely a sign of the discontent of a minority with the conservative ascendancy in both major parties. The La Follette vote was only 15 percent of all those cast while Theodore Roosevelt's 4.1 million votes in 1912 represented 30 percent of the total. Some congressional Democrats who had been relatively progressive in the first years of the decade took the defeat as a rejection of reform and became more conservative after 1924. Moreover, the few progressives remaining in Congress found themselves increasingly isolated. Not long after, La Follette died and was succeeded in the Senate by his son, Robert Jr.

Davis carried only the eleven states of the Old Confederacy plus Oklahoma and trailed both Coolidge and La Follette in eleven states, including California. "I was quite prepared . . . for an unfavorable result," said a chastened Davis, "although I confess, I did not appreciate the magnitude of the disaster that was impending." Franklin Roosevelt glumly surveyed the wreckage and shook his head. "We Democrats may be the party of honesty and progress [but] the people will not turn out the Republicans while wages are good and the markets are booming."

And Calvin Coolidge?

"I don't anticipate to change very much," he declared.

Grace Coolidge carried on with her usual charm, but after the election, she began to crochet a bedspread. Insiders noted that it was eight squares long and six squares wide—a square for each month until the president's term was over.

CHAPTER 9

"We Loved Every Rattle"

"The world broke in two in 1922 or thereabouts," observed Willa Cather, who won the Pulitzer Prize that year with her novel *One of Ours*. Much of what Cather and many Americans cherished—a traditional agrarian order based on solid traditions—was crumbling as the nation eagerly pursued the material benefits of Coolidge Prosperity. Life was unfolding at an ever faster clip, altering the way in which people perceived the world about them. Everything, noted Cather, was becoming mechanized, packaged, and tinned. "Nobody stays at home anymore; nobody makes anything beautiful anymore."

Such a view was probably overdramatized, but there was something in the wind. In 1905, Albert Einstein published his theory of relativity and exploded the mechanistic universe. The reliability of engineering was giving way to the "uncertainty principle" of physics. In 1909, Sigmund Freud came to Clark University in Worcester, Massachusetts, to lecture and to show Americans that nothing was as it seemed. Ordinary Americans were being subjected to the microscopic examinations heretofore reserved for African bushmen and South Sea islanders. Robert S. and Helen Merrell Lynd, a husband-and-wife team of sociologists, went to Muncie, Indiana, which they called Middletown, to study the day-by-day life of a mid-continent small city. And Harry L. Hollingworth, a Columbia University psychologist, drew a picture of the average American based on tests administered by the army to some four million men during World War I. Hollingworth's portrait was unflattering. While acknowledging that the "average man" was an abstraction, he concluded:

—The life span of the average man is about fifty-three years.
—He weighs 150 pounds and is 67 inches tall.

—The average man's vocabulary includes about 7,500 words.

—The average man leaves school after the eighth grade. He has a smattering of local geography and knows a little about history, and a few elementary facts about physiology. He has little knowledge of science, politics, or literature.

—Following the example of his father, if the average man is a Democrat, he is likely to be a Methodist; if a Republican, he is probably a Baptist.

—The average man is employed in the skilled trades but is unlikely to have an occupation superior to that of his father.

—The average man does not take much interest in religion, although he has concrete ideas about morality.

In summary, said Hollingworth, the average man is "superstitious, ill educated, conventional and mentally equal to a fourteen-year-old."

The Lynds made a more rigorous and penetrating study of Middletown. They examined the way in which its residents earned their livings, reared and educated their children, worshipped their God, governed themselves, and made use of their leisure. "We . . . are probably living in one of the eras of greatest rapidity of change in the history of human institutions," the Lynds concluded. Middletown was in a state of conflict between the past and present. As the sociologists conducted their interviews and surveys, and studied a formidable array of graphs and statistics, a longtime Middletown resident snorted in disdain. "Why on earth do you need to study what's changing this country?" he asked. "I can tell you what's happening in just four letters: A-U-T-O!"

In 1924, there were about 17.5 million cars and trucks registered in the United States. Only a decade before the nation had been dominated by a horse culture. As late as 1909, two million horse-drawn vehicles were produced.* In fact, a hazard of urban life was the large amount of horse dung in the streets. Pedestrians had to exercise extreme caution to keep their shoes and sweeping dress hems clean. A study of New York City street cleaners in 1917 revealed that 80 percent suffered from some sort of disease, usually bacterial infections resulting from the ever-present manure. No one yet realized that automobile exhaust was going to prove even more detrimental to public health than "horse exhaust."

Parking was already a problem in the downtown areas of most cities. *Life* proposed in 1922 a complete ban on parking autos on Manhattan's streets, on the heretical ground that making the cities more convenient for cars

* By 1923, the number had dwindled to 10,000 carriages annually.

only attracted more cars. Traffic jams were commonplace; the average speed on Fifth Avenue on a late afternoon weekday was three miles an hour. Nationwide, auto fatalities were going up: from 5,400 in 1919 to 9,800 in 1924. The first signal lights were installed in New York in 1923, with the red, yellow, and green warnings adopted from railroad signals.* The first shopping center with an adjoining parking lot opened for business in Kansas City in 1924, and the first ramp garage opened five years later in Detroit. In Boston and San Francisco, parking garages were being hollowed out from under parks and squares. There were so many cars that popular magazines earnestly asked, "Is the auto market saturated?"

The great boon of the car was freedom of movement—especially for the farmer. In 1924, there were 4.5 million autos and trucks on the nation's 6.5 million farms. Rural Free Delivery, the telephone, and mail order shopping had already broken the isolation of the farm family, but the car gave it true mobility. Now, they could shop in large towns where the stores offered lower prices and a better selection of goods, enjoy a restaurant meal, or see a movie. A farm wife who was asked why her family had an automobile but not a bathtub had a ready answer: "You can't go to town in a bathtub."

The car was also the driving force in breaking down the barriers between town and country. The crowded streets of the nation's business districts heralded downtown's vibrancy, but also foretold its demise. A busy downtown meant prosperity, yet large crowds tied up traffic and commerce and drove businesses, workers, and shoppers to the city's outskirts. Leaving the urban hurly-burly behind, the middle class moved to new suburbs made practical by the automobile and commuted to their jobs in town. Shaker Heights, outside Cleveland, grew by 1,000 percent between 1920 and 1930; Grosse Pointe, a suburb of Detroit, grew 724 percent; and Beverly Hills by 2,485 percent.

Housing design now had to conform to the needs of the car. Homes were built closer to the curb and lawns and shrubbery were sacrificed to the driveway and the garage. The availability of school buses led to the opening of large consolidated schools with yearly changes of teachers for each grade, libraries, laboratories, and gymnasiums in place of the primitive one-room schoolhouse. The automobile also changed the sexual practices of the young. There was no room for a chaperone in the rumble seat of a roadster. And it spawned vast new areas of bureaucracy and law. These ranged from driver's licenses and speed limits to new forms of tort liability to cover the injuries and damages inflicted by cars.

* The traffic light was invented by William Post, a Detroit policeman, in 1920.

By the mid-1920s, the automobile industry was the linchpin of the American economy. Auto manufacturing had in little more than a decade created about a million and a half relatively high-paying jobs, triggered the massive construction of highways, and was the main consumer of petroleum products, glass, rubber, nickel, steel, and machine tools. An estimated $1 of every $5 spent by consumers, excluding rent and insurance, went for automobiles. New words and phrases came into the language as a result of the auto: "joyride," "flat tire," "spark plug," and "taken for a ride," among others. Trucks were replacing other forms of transportation for hauling freight. The need for roads resulted in higher taxes and a golden cornucopia for the politicians. Thanks to the automobile, visitors to the national parks jumped from 198,606 in 1910 to more than 2.7 million in 1930. The automobile was to the Twenties what television would be to the Fifties and computers and the Internet to the Nineties.

First a novelty and then a convenience, the auto rapidly became a necessity, irrespective of personal budgets. A Middletown high school boy who couldn't take a girl to a dance in a car was a social pariah, the Lynds reported. Rather than attend church services, Americans families took Sunday trips into the country in a spirit of adventure. The national mania for the car stemmed partially from the boost it gave the owner's psyche. It was the ultimate status symbol because of the feeling of mastery and power it conferred. The make of car indicated the owner's status as much as his clothes, his job, or his home. "To George F. Babbitt," Sinclair Lewis wrote of his fictional Realtor, "as to most prosperous citizens of Zenith, the motor car was poetry and tragedy, love and heroism." People mortgaged their homes to buy cars and a union leader in Middletown told the Lynds that 65 percent of the members were working to buy cars, while only 10 percent were working to buy homes. "I'll go without food before I'll give up the car," said the wife of an unemployed worker.

Henry Ford did more to put America on wheels than anyone else. One out of every two cars sold in the United States in 1924 was one of his slab-sided yet cheap and efficient Model Ts. Ford did not invent the automobile. Tinkerers all over Western Europe and the United States had produced serviceable versions of the horseless carriage well before he built his first working vehicle in 1896. Such words as "automobile," "chauffeur," and "garage" betray the European influence on early automotive technology.

Ford's genius was to build motorcars for the multitudes. He introduced mass production to an industry that was largely producing luxury, hand-built machines for an elite. The Model T, first introduced in 1908, was as rugged as a Mongolian war wagon and remained basically unchanged except for the addition of a self-starter and gas gauge until it was outsold by more stylish competitors and production ceased in 1927.* Originally priced at $950, it eventually cost $350 as mass production and volume sales brought prices down—and you could have any color you wanted, the joke went, as long as it was black. A used flivver could be had for $60 outright, or in $5 monthly installments.

Ford became a legend, a folk hero. He ranked in the American pantheon with Alexander Graham Bell, Thomas Edison, and Orville and Wilbur Wright. Yet he also represents the paradox of America in the 1920s. On the one hand, he was a visionary, builder and bulwark of a modern, technologically advanced society. He was worth an estimated $1.4 billion and the richest man in the nation, possibly the world. On the other hand, he was a backward-looking, unsophisticated, ill-educated mechanic with the simple beliefs and prejudices of late-nineteenth-century rural America. He was a man of genius, yet he was a crank—narrow, ignorant, and mean-spirited. He carried a gun, believed in reincarnation, loved square dancing, was a diet faddist, and hated bankers, doctors, Jews, Catholics, fat people, and liquor and tobacco. Yet he had a compelling vision of the new age and fathomed the answer to the dilemma of modern capitalism: Who was going to buy all the goods flowing from America's booming factories? Ford's answer was that low prices and high wages would bring these products within reach of the workers who created them and turn them into consumers.

In the spring of 1919, the city fathers of Dearborn, Michigan, announced that because of the mounting number of automobiles, the town's streets would have to be widened for a new highway. In one of several ironies, the Ford family homestead, where the industrialist had been born in 1863 and spent his early life, was one of the structures earmarked for destruction. Henry Ford decided to move the old building out of harm's way and to make a shrine of it as well. Eventually, the Ford homestead became the nucleus of Greenfield Village, Ford's 252-acre homage to the rural America of his youth—a world he did more to destroy than anyone.

Greenfield Village, named for the Michigan hamlet where his mother grew up, includes, among other structures, the courthouse where Abraham Lincoln practiced law, a country tavern, Edison's laboratory, a gristmill, the

---

* In 2001, an estimated 300,000 Model Ts were still running in various parts of the world. (New York Times, December 27, 2001.)

Ohio cycle shop where the Wrights developed their flying machine, and a replica of Independence Hall in Philadelphia. To fill these buildings, Ford became the largest purchaser of antiques in the country. The Village has a grassy common, the streets are paved with gravel, the lamps are lit by gas, tourists travel in horse-drawn wagons, and the guides wear period clothes. Altogether, a striking project for a man whose most quoted expression is "History is bunk."*

The Dearborn of Ford's childhood was a simple farming community, only a generation removed from the frontier. On both sides, his parents were Irish Protestants, whose families had fled the horrors of the potato famine for America. Ford prided himself on being a poor boy who pulled himself up from nothing, but by the time of his birth, Mary and William Ford, his parents, were prosperous by the standards of rural Michigan.

Young Henry led a typical farm boyhood with one exception—he was fascinated by gadgets, an interest he may have inherited from his father, who had worked as a railroad carpenter and kept a full set of tools on his farm. "When we had mechanical or 'wind-up' tops given us at Christmas," related his sister Margaret, "we always said, 'Don't let Henry see them! He just takes them apart!'" Ford claimed to have nearly lost a fingertip while examining a threshing machine, and a steam boiler exploded once and blew a hole through his lip.

When he was seven, Henry was enrolled in the one-room Scotch Settlement School in Dearborn. All the grades from one to eight were crammed together and taught by a single teacher. With its moralistic McGuffey Readers, American flag on the wall, dunce's cap, and willow switch, the school was typical of rural America. Ford received his entire education there. Even though some critics later dismissed him as a functional illiterate, he learned to read, write, and do sums reasonably well, although his spelling was always shaky. "I don't like to read books," he said in later life. "They muss up my mind." Nor did he think much of colleges, and refused to let his only legitimate son, Edsel, attend one.

Henry was close to his mother and from her he learned not to smoke, drink, gamble, or go into debt. The boy was nearly thirteen when his life was forever changed by the death of Mary Ford. She went into labor with her eighth child in March 1876, but something went wrong and the baby was lost. Twelve days later, she died at the age of thirty-seven. Ford never

---

* "History is more or less the bunk," is what Ford actually said. "It is tradition. We don't want tradition. We want to live in the present, and the only history that is worth a tinker's damn is the history we make today."

forgot the grief and shock of her passing. He felt, he said later, as if "a great wrong had been done to me." Without her, home and family life seemed "a watch without a mainspring."

Ford later told his authorized biographers that following his mother's death he was at odds with his father. He claimed the elder Ford disapproved of his interest in mechanical things, and said he ran away from home at the age of sixteen to escape this unhappy situation. According to his account, he walked the eight miles to Detroit and secured a job as an apprentice at the Drydock Engine Company. This story was part of his attempt to skew the accounts of his early life to emphasize his rise from the bottom. In reality, William Ford not only supported his son's mechanical interests, he obtained his first apprenticeship for him and personally took him to Detroit.

A pall of thick smoke already hung over Detroit. The town was booming and its wealth was based upon proximity to the virgin forests and mineral riches of Upper Michigan. Mills refined the iron, copper, and lead brought in by Great Lakes steamers, and factories and machine shops fashioned finished products from them. Shipyards and chemical plants flourished. Ten railroads served the town, and the D. M. Ferry Company shipped seeds, first to the pioneers, and then around the world. The city was a veritable Tower of Babel with two dozen languages spoken within its confines. In nearby Battle Creek, Charles Post and the Kellogg brothers were creating a new industry based on the humble cornflake.

Ford completed his apprenticeship in three years. Surprisingly, instead of seeking work in Detroit, he returned to Dearborn, but not to be a farmer. A machine persuaded him to forsake the city. Every autumn during his apprenticeship, he had gone home to help his father bring in the harvest, and he had become fascinated with a Westinghouse portable steam engine purchased by a neighboring farmer to run his thresher and bailer. The farmer was frightened of the puffing and shaking monster and hired Ford to operate it. The owner leased the engine out to other farmers when he had completed his harvest, and Ford traveled from farm to farm, threshing crops and performing other chores. He received $3 a day, then a good wage.

Westinghouse soon hired him as its chief demonstrator and repairman in southern Michigan. Ford loved the job of wandering mechanic—an early version of the home appliance serviceman—and remembered those years as idyllic. But these were far from idyllic years for America's farmers. Falling crop prices, overproduction, inflation, and high interest rates led to a farm revolt in which railroad tycoons, Eastern bankers, middlemen, Wall

Street, and Jews were blamed for the farmer's ill fortune. Ford absorbed these populist views as he traveled the Michigan hinterland with his satchel of tools, and they remained his core beliefs throughout his long life.

To the staid farmers of Wayne County, Henry Ford seemed shiftless, a tinkerer, a moonlighter, but he was ready to settle down. On New Year's Day 1885, the young man attended a country square dance at Greenfield, and was immediately taken with a small, vivacious girl with bright, dark eyes named Clara Jane Bryant, the daughter of a neighboring farmer. "I knew in half an hour she was the one for me," he later declared. They were married three years later. Ford's father gave him forty acres of land, and the young man built a comfortable white house there but let hired men do the farming. He busied himself by cutting down and selling the surrounding woodland. Bored by farm life, he leaped at the offer of an engineer's job from the Edison Illuminating Company. In 1893, despite Clara's protests against leaving her family, the young couple moved to Detroit, where Ford took over management of a power-generating station.

Operating a power station is largely a matter of making certain that the generators are properly set up. Once that is done they will, with routine maintenance, run themselves, and Ford had plenty of time to work on his own projects. He was fascinated with a small internal combustion engine he had seen and began building one from the instructions in a magazine. He planned to use it to propel a mechanical buggy similar to those just appearing about town and frightening the big brewery horses and sleek pacers. Some municipalities had already passed laws requiring men with red flags to walk in front of automobiles to warn the public of their approach.

The credit for producing the first practical automobile is shared by Gottlieb Daimler and Karl Benz, two German craftsmen who produced their vehicle in 1885 or 1886. The Duryea brothers, Charles and Frank, were the first to publicly demonstrate a successful automobile in the United States—at Springfield, Massachusetts, in September 1893. Ford tested his first car early in the morning of June 4, 1896, in the empty streets of Detroit. The primitive vehicle had four spindly bicycle wheels, the driver sat on a box that covered the motor, it steered with a tiller rather than a wheel, had no brakes or reverse gear, and power was transmitted from the engine to the rear wheels by a length of chain. An ordinary doorbell screwed to the front served as a horn. The car ignominiously broke down in front of the Cadillac Hotel and Ford and a friend were hooted at by a group of late-night revelers as they made repairs. Not long afterward, following modifications, Ford ventured out to Dearborn in his new contraption to show it to the home folks.

A newspaper writer took a ride with "Mr. Ford the automobileer" and told his readers what it was like:

> Mr. Ford the automobileer began by giving his steed three or four sharp jerks with the lever at the right-hand side of the seat; that is, he pulled the lever up and down sharply in order, as he said, to mix air with gasoline and drive the charge into the exploding cylinder. . . . Mr. Ford slipped a small electric switch handle and there followed a puff, puff, puff. . . . The puffing of the machine assumed a higher key. She was flying along about eight miles an hour. The ruts in the road were deep, but the machine went with dreamlike smoothness. There was none of the bumping common even to a streetcar. . . . By this time the boulevard had been reached, and the automobileer, letting a lever fall a little, let her out. Whiz! She picked up speed with infinite rapidity. As she ran on there was a clattering behind, the new noise of the automobile.

In the years between 1900 and 1908, no fewer than 502 American companies were organized to manufacture automobiles. Not all utilized the internal combustion engine; some used steam or battery power. Most failed. A mastery of the details of production and marketing separated the tinkers from the carmakers. Ford twice tried to sell cars of his design but both efforts were unsuccessful. Meantime, he publicized his vehicles by racing them and won renown as a race driver. One car, the seventy-horsepower 999, was the most powerful auto yet built in America. Ford wanted Barney Oldfield, a daredevil professional bicycle racer, to drive her, and Oldfield was willing. But there was a problem: Oldfield didn't know how to drive. Ford taught him in a couple of days. He won his first race at a speed of nearly sixty miles an hour, giving birth to the phrase "going like sixty."

In June 1903, Ford organized his third company—the Ford Motor Company—which was capitalized at $100,000, but with only $28,000 paid in. He contributed no cash but as the mechanical brain of the company received 25.5 percent of the stock and a salary of $3,000 a year. Together with A. Y. Malcolmson, a well-to-do Detroit coal dealer, he had majority control. James Couzens, Malcolmson's chief clerk (and later a U.S. senator), put in $2,500, of which $1,500 was a promissory note. In 1919, when he sold his 11 percent interest, Couzens received $29,308,858 for his shares.

The first cars produced by Ford were assembled from parts made by others. For example, the Dodge brothers, John and Horace, supplied the engines in exchange for stock in the new venture. The cars were built in batches of four, with two or three men working on each. When these vehicles were finished, the team moved on to another four cars. Over the next five years, Ford built several models with varying degrees of success. All the while he was thinking of a cheap, light car intended for the masses. "It will be so low in price," he said, "that no man making a good salary will be unable to own one, and enjoy with his family the blessings of hours of pleasure in God's open spaces."

The idea was not unique to Ford. Other carmakers had tried to produce a cheap automobile, the most successful of them Ransom E. Olds, whose small cars had been popularized by a well-known song, "In My Merry Oldsmobile." Olds turned out five thousand cars in 1903 alone, before his financial backers took the company upmarket. Malcolmson and some of the other stockholders insisted that cheap cars would be unprofitable, but Ford, clearly showing he was no country bumpkin, slickly outmaneuvered them and took over the company. The first Model T—so named because it was the twentieth design produced by Ford—rolled out of his Piquette Avenue factory in October 1908.

The Model T offered a combination of innovation and reliability, ruggedness and power never before seen in a reasonably priced automobile. Although derided as the Tin Lizzie, the car was built of strong yet lightweight chrome-vanadium steel, which Ford's experts perfected after their chief picked up a sample from a wrecked French racer. Because of its lightness the car got twenty-five miles on a gallon of gasoline compared to the ten miles of heavier vehicles. The vehicle's four-cylinder, forty-horsepower engine, which gave it a top speed of forty miles per hour, semiautomatic planetary transmission, and magneto, which supplied power for the spark and lights while doing away with heavy storage batteries, were all new designs.

As unadorned and utilitarian as a plow, the Model T came without a speedometer, windshield wipers, or even doors, and the gas gauge was a long thin stick the owner had to find for himself and insert into the tank. It was a favorite of the farmer. With a truck bed substituted for the rear seat, it carried crops and milk cans to market. The front end could be jacked up, a wheel taken off and, with a power belt fitted over the hub, it could run a churn, a thresher, or a cider press. Bootleggers found that the Model T had room for ninety one-gallon jars of liquor.

Operating a Model T was an art. The writer E. B. White, just out of Cornell in the early 1920s, drove across the country in search of work and adventure in an old Ford he called *Hotspur.* Starting the car called for a special ritual, he recalled, for you had to remember to be careful about putting your thumb around the starting handle; if you did not, you risked breaking an arm or a wrist.

The Model T was exactly what was needed by a restless population engaged in filling a continent. With its crude yet strong transverse springs, high clearance, and wobbly, almost double-jointed wheels, the car was ideally suited to rutted mud and gravel roads. It was the covered wagon of the twentieth century.

Popular demand for the Model T soon outpaced production—18,664 cars in 1909–10 and 34,528 in 1910–11. The cars were made in groups of fifty; the frames rested on cradles and teams of workers swarmed about them. This was not fast enough for Ford; there had to be a more efficient way to turn out automobiles. He noted that reapers, sewing machines, and firearms were already being produced on primitive assembly lines, Frederick W. Taylor had outlined the principles of scientific management and time and motion study, and Ransom Olds had taken the first steps to apply these techniques to cars. Why not build autos on a continuously moving conveyer belt that would bring the vehicle to the worker, who would perform a single, specific task, and then move it on to the next procedure? The job would be brought to the man, not the man to the job.

Ford hired Albert Kahn, a pioneer in the use of reinforced concrete construction, to design and build a giant new factory at Highland Park, a former racecourse on the outskirts of Detroit. With its open floor plan, fireproof construction, and wide expanse of windowpanes, the plant was ideally suited to Ford's plans. The first experiment in mass production was made in the spring of 1913 in the magneto department. Assemblers had previously worked at benches, building individual magnetos. Now, production was divided into twenty separate operations, each performed by an individual worker as the magneto passed along a conveyer belt. Production time was reduced from fifteen minutes apiece to less than five. By degrees, this process was applied to the building of the entire car, and Highland Park was soon filled with a network of belts, overhead chains, cranes, and movable platforms from which dangled engines, beams, and transmissions as they journeyed along to the next stage in the assembly line amid an eardrum-shattering din.

"The man who places a part doesn't fasten it," exulted Henry Ford. "The man who puts in a bolt does not put on the nut; the man who puts on the nut does not tighten it." He boasted that any job could now be learned in little time, with nearly half requiring only a single day. Labor costs were reduced because there was no need for skilled workers. Before the introduction of the assembly line, it took twelve hours to build a car; in 1914, the time dropped to ninety-three minutes.

Model Ts poured from the new assembly lines at a record rate of 300,000 in the first year. But the work was repetitive and stupefyingly dull, and the labor turnover was brisk. Men had became cogs in a vast impersonal machine, and respect for craftsmanship was lost. "Ford employees are not really alive—they are half-dead," said a Detroit labor official. They were forbidden "to sit, whistle, sing, lean against the machinery, smoke or talk while working"—and company spies informed on those who disobeyed these rules. The typical job was described as "put nut 14 on bolt 132, repeating, repeating, repeating until the hands shook and the legs quivered." Workers developed what was known as "Ford Stomach" due to the tensions engendered by the pressures of the tightly scheduled assembly line.

In 1914, Ford astonished the world by offering his fourteen thousand workers a wage of $5 a day for an eight-hour shift compared to the $2.34 being paid for a nine-hour day. Originally, women workers were excluded from the plan, but following complaints, this omission was rectified.* Ford claimed that by raising the wages of American workers, a whole new market would be created for his cars. A more likely reason for this largess was the need to add a third shift to increase production and the inability of the company to hold workers because of the sheer boredom of most jobs. Turnover at Highland Park reached 380 percent in December 1913, which meant Ford had to hire 983 men to keep a hundred.

Nevertheless, Ford's reputation as an industrial statesman was assured. The *New York Evening Post* called the $5 day "a magnificent act of generosity" and radicals like John Reed hailed it as revolutionary. But there were strings attached—the production line was speeded up, lunch breaks were cut to fifteen minutes, and trips to the toilet were limited to three minutes. Nor was it generally noted that the basic wage remained unchanged at $2.34 a day; the additional $2.66 was paid as a "profit-sharing bonus" only to those who remained on the job for six months and pledged to use the

---

* Ford employed more women than most Detroit employers, but he was an unreconstructed male chauvinist. "We expect the young ladies to get married," he said. More blacks worked at Highland Park than at any other auto plant and he paid them the same wages as white workers. And he hired ex-convicts without prejudice. Ford liked to talk to them when they were hired, his favorite question being: "Now, tell me how you got into it. I'll bet it was a woman, wasn't it?"

additional funds wisely.* Inspectors from a newly created Sociological Department made unannounced visits to Ford workers' homes, questioning wives and neighbors, to make certain the extra money was not being frittered away. "It will cost a man his job to have the odor of beer, wine, or liquor on his breath or have any of these intoxicants in his home," Ford employees were warned.

Today, it is impossible to fully comprehend the effect of the $5 day upon American workers. In 1914, it created a bigger sensation than the outbreak of World War I, which occurred later that year. The economy was in recession and men were only too glad to work for only a dollar or two a day at any job—if they could find a job. Ford needed about four thousand new workers, but by the time hiring began on a freezing January morning, ten thousand job seekers huddled at the Highland Park plant's gate amid raw gusts of snow. Ford agents mingled with the crowd, handing out hiring slips to likely hands. Thousands of men milled about during the next week in hope and desperation. Some had come hundreds of miles and more were on the way. The announcement that all the jobs had been filled was greeted with angry chants and jeers, bricks were thrown, and the crowd tried to break through the factory gates and rush the plant. Police and company guards turned fire hoses on the throng despite the nine degree temperatures. Soaked and shivering, the army of unemployed was soon in full retreat in every direction.

Transcending the role of mere automobile manufacturer, Ford became the symbol of the new industrial age. He was the most widely known American the world over. "Machinery," declared Ford, "is the new Messiah." The Germans coined the word *Fordismus* to describe the revolutionary process of mass production with which his name was associated. He was respected even in the Soviet Union. Some college students listed the Flivver King third among history's greatest figures, ranking him only behind Napoleon and Jesus Christ. In 1920, he achieved his dream of turning out a new car every minute of the working day. And still he was unsatisfied. On October 31, 1925, he turned out 9,109 cars, one every ten seconds. This was the high point, for competition was challenging the Model T's preeminence.

The Highland Park factory was inadequate to meet such ambitious production goals. Having unburdened himself of the Ford Motor Company's

---

* Ford also promised his customers their own form of "profit sharing"—a $50 rebate—if sales exceeded 300,000 that year.

six other stockholders in 1919—in return for an investment of $41,500, they received $105,820,894, plus the $39,425,000 in dividends previously paid out—Ford built a new super-plant on the Rouge River. Ford saw the Rouge complex as a crucible, where raw materials flowed in at one end and finished cars came out the other. He controlled every part of the process, from source to production to distribution. Ford's own fleet of ore ships brought coal and iron from his mines in Upper Michigan to his blast furnaces, which produced steel for his cars. Rubber from his own plantations, glass from his own factory, wood from his own forests flowed in, while long trains carrying finished cars streamed out of the Rouge on their way to dealers tightly controlled by Ford.

The Rouge, however, had numerous built-in inefficiencies. Although it was a superb technological achievement, the production line was inflexible and had high fixed costs. Even minor changes could be introduced only at great expense. More importantly, the plant was turning out a product—the Model T—that was obsolete. The public wanted sleeker and more stylish cars that could be had in any color, and after the invention of fast-drying pyroxylin varnishes, Ford's two chief rivals, General Motors and Chrysler, met the demand. In 1926, GM's sales were up 40 percent; Ford's were down 25 percent. The mass society Ford had done so much to create was no longer satisfied merely with price and reliability. It wanted style and glamour.

General Motors was a product of the leading trend in American business in the 1920s: industrial reorganization, combination and consolidation, and a wave of mergers. Small firms disappeared before the urge to bigness. By the end of the decade, eight thousand small mining and manufacturing companies had been swallowed up by larger corporations and five thousand utilities had disappeared, mostly into giant holding companies. In 1920, the Supreme Court gave the green light to corporate cannibalism by dismissing the Wilson administration's effort to break up U.S. Steel.

Under Harding and Coolidge, the Sherman and Clayton Antitrust Acts were dead letters. Large-scale manufacturers took over the control of the distribution of most products from the wholesalers and retailers who had previously controlled it. Local merchants, heretofore the symbol of the American free enterprise system, floundered and vanished as national chains cornered more than a quarter of the nation's food, apparel, and general merchandise markets by offering cheaper prices and a wider selection of goods.

The Great Atlantic and Pacific Tea Company had some 17,500 grocery stores by 1927 and did an annual business of $750 million. Chains such as Safeway and Kroger provided competition for A&P and Piggly-Wiggly pointed the way to the future by introducing the supermarket. There, the customer could roam the aisles with his shopping basket, compare products, make selections at leisure without dealing with a grocery clerk, and pay for what was selected at a central checkout. The F. W. Woolworth Company, with 1,600 stores that sold a wide array of dry goods, was second only to A&P with sales of $250 million.

In some industries, power resided in so few hands that competition all but vanished—a situation known to economists as oligopoly. Four rubber companies controlled two thirds of the market. U.S. Steel, the nation's largest corporation, had such a stranglehold on the industry that all its competitors combined were known as "Little Steel." Cement makers combined to fix prices. General Motors, Ford, and Chrysler dominated the automobile business. General Electric, which began by selling only one product—the incandescent electric bulb—now made half its profits from household products unknown before 1919. Eventually, these giant corporations controlled not only their own industries but many related, and ultimately unrelated businesses.

General Motors was a classic example of this method of growth. William C. Durant, its founder, was born in Boston in 1861. A born salesman, by the time he was twenty-one he was the owner of an insurance company. Next, he took over a carriage- and wagon-making business in Flint, Michigan. Billy Durant was not a pioneer tinkering in oil-stained coveralls, but the kind of man inventors turned to, the one who knew how to promote their inventions and turn them into money. Before he was forty, he was producing 150,000 vehicles a year and was a millionaire.

Others scoffed at the automobile, but Durant assumed control of Flint's foundering Buick Motor Car Company in 1905 and made it one of the largest automobile producers in the United States. While Ford, the utilitarian, concentrated on one model, Durant believed that to be successful an auto manufacturer had to offer a wide array of cars at every price level. In 1908, he organized General Motors, which drew a dozen makes together under one management, including Buick, Cadillac, Oldsmobile, and Oakland (now Pontiac), as well as the manufacturers of auto parts such as spark plugs and axles. "He never thought in dollars and cents," said a Detroit newsman. "Always in millions."

Durant choreographed his companies to offer a carefully graduated range of models that appealed to every customer. In its first year, GM accounted for one fifth of the cars sold in the United States. There was a downturn in sales in 1910 and Durant, now badly overextended, was forced to go to the bankers for financing. As soon as they held a substantial stock interest, a group headed by James J. Storrow, a Boston banker, ousted him from control of the company.*

Durant bounced back with the Chevrolet, a rival of the Model T named for Louis Chevrolet, a famous French racing driver. Backed by Delaware's Du Pont family, which was making enormous profits from the manufacture of explosives during World War I, he regained control of GM in 1916. The Du Ponts' investment of $43 million later produced dividends of $20 million annually. Over the next five years, Durant, in a spectacular surge of expansion, added Chevrolet and several other carmakers, Frigidaire, a maker of electric refrigerators, and Fisher Body to his stable. At one point, the dynamic Durant bought a new company every thirty days. GM became a billion-dollar corporation, only the second—U.S. Steel was the first—to reach such lofty heights.

Durant's most revolutionary move was to organize the General Motors Acceptance Corporation to finance car purchases on the installment plan. Installment purchases of sewing machines and furniture were already common but Henry Ford had insisted on selling his cars for cash. By 1927, two thirds of America's cars were being bought on the installment plan, usually with a 25 percent down payment required. An officer of a Middletown finance company told the Lynds that a working man earning $35 a week usually earmarked a week's pay each month as payment for his car. GMAC would one day be worth more than the firm's carmaking divisions.

Rather than exercising one-man dictatorial control of the company as did Ford, Durant, who believed tight controls destroyed initiative and led to abuses of power, permitted his various companies to operate semiautonomously. He paid little attention to efficiency, however, and some GM divisions were in wasteful competition with others for raw materials and customers. Although GM captured an even larger market share, primarily at Ford's expense, the company floundered as sales dropped during the postwar slump. As GM tottered, Durant tried single-handedly to prop up the company's stock with his own money, but once again, the money men ousted him and Pierre S. Du Pont replaced him as president. He founded Durant Motors, but there was no bounce back this time and the company failed in the aftermath of the 1929 stock market crash. Before the

---

* Ford avoided having to go to the despised "Jew bankers"—really gentiles—during the slump by financing his operations on the backs of his dealers. He raised the quota of cars each dealer had to take, irrespective of their ability to sell them, and insisted on being paid upon delivery. Any dealer who balked was threatened with loss of his dealership.

crash, Durant's assets were estimated at $120 million; when he declared bankruptcy a few years later, he had only $250 worth of clothes to his name. Several other ventures failed and Durant died in 1947, the forgotten man of American automobile history.

To bring order out of the administrative chaos left behind by Durant, Du Pont turned to Alfred P. Sloan for assistance in reorganizing GM. Sloan, who became president in 1923, had been head of the Hyatt Roller Bearing Corporation, which Durant absorbed in 1918, and was something new in the automobile industry. Unlike Ford the mechanic or Durant the promoter, he was a graduate of the Massachusetts Institute of Technology and a trained engineer and manager. Sloan immediately imposed centralized management upon the company, creating in the process one of the first modern corporations. The GM he built could run itself, independent of the whims of one man.

Under Sloan, General Motors retained the separate divisions created by Durant, but there was tighter control from the top. The division managers continued to control their own production, marketing, purchasing, and engineering, but a new general office, free of day-to-day responsibilities, directed planning and coordination and exercised overall control. Through the use of the same parts and supplies for different models, Sloan had the advantage of economy of scale over Ford. Market researchers made systematic analyses upon which future production goals, costs, prices, and employment were established. By 1925, GM was flourishing. Its share of the market rose from 19 percent in 1924 to over 43 percent in 1929. A Chevrolet cost $510; an Oldsmobile $750; an Oakland $945; a four-cylinder Buick $965; a Buick 6 $1,295; and a Cadillac $2,985. LaSalle was added to fill the gap between the big Buick and the Cadillac.

As cars poured off the assembly lines, the problem faced by auto builders was not only to persuade people without cars to buy them, but to entice the man who already had a car to buy another. Sloan resolved it by making marketing as important as production. Early cars had been patterned after horse-drawn carriages; they were open to the elements and sat high up off the ground because of poor roads. Customers were now offered stylish and comfortable all-weather, closed models, while improved roads permitted sleeker, racier-looking vehicles. The new cars had self-starters, wind-up windows, automatic windshield wipers, full instrumentation, powerful six-cylinder engines, balloon tires, interior dome lights, and better finishes.

Excitement, sex appeal, and glamour replaced reliability as selling points. Ford's strategy had been to build a car that would last for years, but GM's Sloan instituted yearly model changes to create "planned obsolescence." He launched massive advertising campaigns to persuade buyers that each new model represented a substantial improvement over the old one. Higher prices were the inevitable result of such "progress." To make it easier to buy the latest model, customers were allowed to trade in old cars on new ones, expanding the supply of used cars and lowering the entry level for auto ownership.

With autos easier to drive and maintain, women were an increasing presence in the dealers' showrooms and car advertising was targeted at them. The Model T had been the domain of men because few women wished to chance breaking an arm while cranking up a Tin Lizzie or to deal with its complicated system of shifting gears or setting the spark. Now, a car owner did not have to worry about what was under the hood. For women, carburetors and gaskets were less important than the texture of the vehicle's upholstery and whether it could be purchased in such exotic colors as Dove Gray or Arabian Sand. Chrysler ads boasted that their cars were "all that a woman wants in a modern automobile."

The third of the Big Three auto companies, Chrysler was founded in 1924 by Walter P. Chrysler, who was born in Kansas in 1875, the son of a Union Pacific Railroad engineer. As a boy, he swept floors in a roundhouse for 10 cents an hour. Taking a 50 percent pay cut, he became an apprentice in the railroad's machine shop. At twenty-one, Chrysler finished his apprenticeship and vagabonded around the country, earning a living by playing the tuba and working on every type of machine he could find. He rose to chief mechanic of the American Locomotive Company in Pittsburgh at the then substantial salary of $12,000 a year.

In 1911, Chrysler switched from steam to gasoline engines and, again taking a 50 percent cut in wages, went to work for Billy Durant, who put him in charge of the Buick plant. He was so successful that when Durant regained control of GM, he raised his salary to $10,000 a month plus a share of the profits. In 1919, Chrysler resigned to become a troubleshooter to ailing auto companies. Four years later, having taken over Maxwell Motors, he introduced the first Chrysler, which featured a high-compression engine that other automakers had believed impossible to make for an inexpensive car.

Following the General Motors strategy, Chrysler bought out the Dodge brothers, and added the De Soto and the low-priced Plymouth to his line. In 1929, Chrysler factories produced a quarter of the new cars manufactured in the United States. By then, the auto had become standardized and there was little difference in quality, performance, and price among the Big Three. To flaunt his success, Chrysler built the hypodermic-needle-tipped

Chrysler Building in Midtown Manhattan, the tallest building in the world up to then and an Art Deco classic. His mechanic's tools were displayed in a glass case in the lobby.

Shortly after Henry Ford personally drove the fifteen millionth Model T out of the factory on May 26, 1927, he closed the assembly line down to retool for a new model. He had finally given in to the public's demand for a shinier, more sporty car. Some sixty thousand workers were thrown out of their jobs in Detroit alone, twenty-three regional assembly plants were shut down, and Ford's ten thousand dealers were forced to eke out an existence by selling old stock and spare parts. Designing and building a new car from scratch was a massive project. Some sixteen thousand machine tools had to be refurbished or rebuilt, another four thousand were purchased, and the entire assembly line was reorganized. In all, the changeover cost Ford $250 million.

Hints and rumors about the new car—named the Model A—swirled about the country and America eagerly awaited its unveiling. Dealers pleaded for details and were rebuffed. The public waited and held off buying new cars until they saw what "ol' Henry" had to offer. The pent-up suspense exploded on December 2, 1927. Ford showrooms were mobbed. Some 100,000 people milled about a special display in Detroit, the police were called out in Cleveland, and in New York the crowds started gathering at the showroom on Broadway at three in morning. By Christmas, Ford dealers had taken a half-million orders, each backed up by a cash deposit—all on blind faith, because hardly anyone had tested the new car.

The Model A did not disappoint. It was cleaner-looking and more attractive than its predecessor, faster, safer, and in tune with the times. Gear shifting was easy, the car had a self-starter, wind-up windows, hydraulic shock absorbers, and came in numerous colors. At its heart was a well-designed engine, which although it had only four cylinders, could out-accelerate more powerful competitors. Moreover, at a basic price of $495, the Model A was cheaper than the comparable Chevrolet. Production problems slowed down deliveries at first, but in 1929 Ford sold 1.5 million cars, a market share of 34 percent. But the triumph was only temporary, for Chevrolet surged into the lead the following year and kept it throughout the 1930s.

Travelers who left the major cities in an automobile for a long trip in the early 1920s were intrepid adventurers. Paved roads were limited—in 1914, there were only 750 miles of concrete highway in the entire country. Most roads were merely dirt or gravel tracks, and were often washed out or quagmires. Maps of rural America were almost nonexistent as was information on road conditions. Signs were scarce and drivers relied on the *Automobile Blue Book* for directions. It mentioned no route numbers and told motorists to follow the road they were on for 3.2 miles and then go left at the fork after the barn advertising 666 malaria cure. "You can't get there from here," people joked. Bridges were rickety and designed for the horse and carriage. Guardrails were the exception in mountainous areas.

In 1919, Major Dwight Eisenhower led a convoy of autos, trucks, and ambulances across the country in a test of vehicles and the nation's highways. The convoy averaged fifty miles a day and the trip of 3,242 miles took two months. On his rounds as a county commissioner in rural Missouri, Harry Truman ballasted his car with concrete blocks to avoid being capsized by potholes.

Originally, road maintenance and construction were the responsibility of local communities, but road districts, townships, and counties were incapable of dealing with the demands being made upon them and the state legislatures took over. The highway problem was a national problem, however, and the Federal Highway Act of 1916 offered money to states that would organize highway departments and match federal grants. This act appropriated $75 million over five years for highway construction, but World War I hamstrung efforts to build roads. In 1921, Congress appropriated $75 million annually—which amounted to $600 million by 1929—for the creation of a national highway system that would connect all cities of fifty thousand people with paved roads. The states' share was to be paid for by gasoline taxes. The work itself was done by private contractors, which created a giant new industry and fresh employment opportunities.

The automobile made Los Angeles not only the fastest growing city in the nation but the largest west of Chicago. In 1910, the population totaled 319,000 and the town was overshadowed by San Francisco, its northern rival. Within a decade, the population had nearly doubled, and by 1926 had doubled again to some 1.2 million.

Venturesome motorists accepted the challenge of coast-to-coast travel and in 1923, about 180,000 cars chugged across the Great Plains and Southwestern deserts. Others headed for Florida, where the state agriculture commissioner set the tone for future tourist brochures by inviting Northerners to come on down, stretch out in a hammock, "and drink in the beauties of tropical verdure, while fanned by balmy breezes from the bosom of the Gulf Stream." These modern knights of the road lashed pasteboard suitcases and extra gasoline cans to the running boards of their battered, mud-splattered vehicles—and were off.

A new form of advertising appeared alongside America's roads—the Burma-Shave sign. The shaving cream company placed a series of small signs at intervals so the people in a passing auto could read them even at high speed. This lighthearted approach to advertising amused motorists for more than forty years until the last signs disappeared in the 1960s. An example:

> A peach looks good
> with a lot of fuzz
> but man's no peach
> and never was
> Burma-Shave

Four years after the postwar road building campaign began, in the summer of 1923, the Statler hotel chain informed tourists that the highway up into Michigan from Chicago and Detroit was safe for use. The first automotive parkway in the country, the Bronx River Parkway, opened that same year, running from the North Bronx just outside New York City to White Plains in Westchester County. The Bronx River, with its limited access, four lanes, prohibition against trucks, and accommodation to the natural landscape of hills and valleys, set the pattern for future parkways. In 1927, the Holland Tunnel was opened between Manhattan and New Jersey.

Trekkers carried everything they needed for long-distance traveling— food, fuel, water, spare tires, inner tubes, and air pumps. Hot, dirty, and near exhaustion at the end of the day, they broke out tents and camped beside the road or in a nearby field. Enterprising farmers, seeing the opportunity to make a dollar or two, offered travelers the use of outhouses and access to fresh water for a fee. Some threw together a few shacks, each containing little more than a table and a few chairs, and rented them out by the night. Beds were not provided because customers were expected to sleep on the floor in their own bedrolls. A makeshift store and lunch counter offering hot dogs, sandwiches, basic groceries, and soda pop followed. The gas pump was moved from the mechanic's garage in town— usually a converted blacksmith shop—to a location across the road that was called a filling station.*

Soon, more upmarket establishments called tourist or motor courts

---

* Precisely when and where the first filling station opened in the United States is a matter of argument, but by 1915, there were thirty of them in the Detroit area and a year later there were two hundred in Los Angeles. By 1929, there were 121,500 filling stations in the United States, some individually owned and some the property of the oil companies.

blossomed on the outskirts of towns in shady groves away from the noise of the highway, first on the way to Florida and California, and then elsewhere. Prospective patrons were wooed by attention-getting roadside signs that advertised cleanliness and comfort at bargain rates. Mostly mom-and-pop operations, their cabins were usually deployed in a three-sided rectangle with the owner's office-residence at the end closest to the road. They offered beds, bathrooms, small kitchen facilities, and a rigid policy of pay-in-advance. The term "motel" first appeared in 1925 on a cheerful complex of Spanish-style cottages in San Luis Obispo, on Route 101 in California. Such places were soon to be immortalized in the Academy Award–winning Clark Gable–Claudette Colbert film, *It Happened One Night*.

By the end of 1926, there were some two thousand tourist courts/motels in various parts of the country. Some went beyond merely being a rest stop for the weary traveler, however. They offered a place for a discreet assignation. With the relaxation of sexual standards during the 1920s, more people were popping into bed with someone who was not their spouse— and the "hot pillow hotel" outside town was the ideal place to do it. It offered anonymity and the car waited just outside the door for a fast getaway. "Mr. and Mrs. John Smith" were the most frequent guests to sign the register in such places; they had no luggage and rarely stayed for more than an hour or two.

While the automobile gave Americans a physical mobility that was previously unknown, motion pictures, which developed at the same time, provided an easy escape into a fantasy world. Audiences were introduced to the lifestyles of cowboys, criminals, the modish, and the rich. Like the automobile, movies allowed the audience to overleap barriers of caste and class, and time and geography as well.

Thomas Edison invented the motion picture, which he called the Vitascope, in 1894 and introduced it to the public by showing three brief films at a vaudeville theater on New York City's Herald Square. But no one was certain as to how this invention was to be used. Was it merely an amusing curiosity? Or could money be made from it? Edison followed up with the Kinetoscope, basically a bulky, coin-operated peep show viewer for a single customer, which showed a continuous film loop that rotated in front of a shutter and light. Lines of these primitive machines appeared first in arcades on Broadway and then spread across the country. They presented one-minute-long images of a man and woman kissing, Gentleman Jim Corbett boxing, and Annie Oakley shooting targets.

The Kinetoscope was followed by nickelodeons, or storefront theaters for larger audiences. Longer films were projected on a white sheet stretched across the back wall before rows of chairs, sometimes borrowed from the local undertaker. By 1907, there were seven thousand nickelodeons across the country, dingy places that showed short films depicting familiar scenes of urban life, onrushing trains, police and firemen in action, and the like. They catered mostly to poor and working-class audiences, especially immigrants, who did not have to know English to enjoy them.

As crude as they were, the "flickers" were enormously popular, and attracted businessmen who built larger theaters. Most had a piano player, perhaps the owner's wife or the local music teacher, who played musical clichés to suit the scenes on the screen: "Pony Boy, Pony Boy" or the "William Tell Overture" for western chases and "O Promise Me" when the hero and heroine clinched in the finale. New production companies were established, such as the Edison Company, Biograph, and Vitagraph, that turned out hundreds of short films. Europeans, particularly the French, made numerous advances in film technique and production that were adopted by the Americans. Movies also increased in length and took on fluid narrative forms. One of the most important was *The Great Train Robbery* of 1903, Edwin S. Porter's fourteen-scene, ten-minute-long restaging of a real-life heist, which was the first narrative film with a story line.

Some of the biggest names in the movie industry got their start as nickelodeon proprietors and investors: Adolph Zukor, Marcus Loew, Jesse Lasky, Samuel Goldwyn, Harry, Sam, and Jack Warner, Carl Laemmle, William Fox, and Louis B. Mayer. All were Jews, all had come to the United States from the ghettos of Eastern Europe, and all had an idealized view of their adopted country that, when put into their films, proved so powerful it ultimately shaped the myths, values, and traditions of America itself.

In 1908, the Edison and Biograph companies led the way in the organization of a monopoly, the Motion Picture Patents Company, designed to control the growing industry by pooling patents to protect profits and prevent pirating. The MPPC threatened sanctions against exhibitors showing movies made by producers who did not pay royalties to the trust. Most films up until this time were made in studios in New York City and Fort Lee, New Jersey, but independent producers now sought locations beyond the reach of the MPPC. Some went to Cuba and Mexico, but Southern California became the independents' preferred base. The mild climate made year-round production possible, and cheap land and exotic locations were readily available.

Fifteen producers were making movies in Hollywood by 1912 and the Los Angeles suburb was on its way to becoming the film capital of the world—and remained so even after the federal government went to court to break up the MPPC monopoly. Most Hollywood pictures were ground out like automobiles on a production line, and there were no stars. Actors were reluctant to work in the movies because of the poor quality of the product, and those who did often used assumed names or appeared anonymously. Producers also feared that if the public showed a fancy for some of the more significant actors, they would demand higher salaries. Eventually, however, the moguls realized the potential of the star system and certain players were given prominent billing and publicity buildups. Early movies were usually two-reel cowboy shoot-'em-ups or slapstick comedies, which ran for about twenty minutes, because no one thought the public would watch a film for much longer.

Nevertheless, D. W. Griffith and a few others, such as Thomas Ince, were trying to stretch the minds of their audiences. Ince created the concept of the studio system in which dozens of films were made cheaply under a tightly scheduled regime, but he still turned out important pictures such as the 1916 epic *Civilization*. Griffith, on the other hand, had the eye of an artist and the profligate habits of Louis XIV. With G. W. "Billy" Bitzer, his talented cameraman, he revolutionized filmmaking by varying camera positions during each scene, invented the fadeout, explored the use of backlighting, introduced crosscutting, and experimented with color. The film was tinted to match the action: red for violence, green for jealousy. Griffith also created and trained his own company of "players"—including such future stars as Mary Pickford, the Gish sisters, and Lionel Barrymore.

Prompted by Italian productions of *Dante's Inferno* and *Quo Vadis?*, which had numerous reels, Griffith decided to make a masterwork of his own. *The Birth of a Nation* still resonates today because of its energy, epic sweep, and technical brilliance, even without the cultural controversy surrounding it. It was made without a script. Griffith "carried the ideas in his head," said Lillian Gish, "or should I say in his heart." Before *Birth of a Nation* movies rarely lasted more than a half hour or cost more than a nickel; *Birth* ran three hours and tickets were priced at $2. Worried by the charges of racism leveled at him after the film, Griffith followed it up with *Intolerance*, an equally ambitious plea for human understanding, but it was a flop at the box office. Griffith went into a slow decline, and within a few years, the father of the modern cinema was working with run-of-the-mill scripts prepared by others. Soon, he could get no work at all and died an alcoholic recluse in 1948.

* * *

In the years following World War I, films grew more polished and the emphasis was on historical extravaganzas, melodramas, biblical epics, and swashbucklers starring the dashing Douglas Fairbanks. The war had destroyed the film industries of France and Italy, and American films dominated the world screen. Hollywood had also already assumed many of the features of its Golden Age: the star system, tight studio control of production that limited artistic creativity, the ownership of theaters by production companies, and domination of the studios by the money men. Movies were big business and Wall Street had the final say. Some seven hundred films were made every year and the industry was pulling in $2 billion in receipts annually. Forty million people went to the movies in 1922 and the audience more than doubled over the next eight years. There were over 22,500 movie theaters—half in towns with fewer than five thousand inhabitants—with a seating capacity of 18 million.

Better quality films broadened the audience, and middle-class patrons now thronged to the luxurious movie "palaces" that had been built in the downtowns of the big cities. In small towns, the movie theater was likely to be the community's most impressive building. Women, who made up a large part of the audience, were pampered by the new theaters. "When she comes home" a woman "will perhaps clean spinach and peel onions, but for a few hours attendants bow to her, doormen tip their hats, a maid curtsies to her in the ladies' washroom," said one observer. "She can let her fancies slip through the darkened atmosphere to the screen, where they drift in rhapsodic amours with handsome stars."

Movies provided Americans with a unifying cultural experience. Everyone, no matter what section of the nation in which he or she lived or their social and economic status, saw the same movies, admired the same stars, imitated their dress, mannerisms, and hairstyles, and shared an interest in the same celebrity gossip. Feeding this curiosity resulted in the creation of the fan magazine, which became an industry in itself. Some magazines were deluged with as many as eighty thousand letters a year, some of a deeply personal nature.

No director had the creative control over his work of a Griffith or an Ince. A few gifted men such as Erich von Stroheim and Ernst Lubitsch might be able to slip sophisticated touches into a film, but many directors were little more than glorified factory foremen turning out the prescribed daily footage. Tried-and-true formula plots prevailed and most actors and actresses were chosen on the basis of box office appeal rather than their acting skills. Audiences wanted to see their favorite stars in the same roles over and over, and Hollywood obliged. A successful film was likely to inspire a sequel. Rudolph Valentino's romantic and tempestuous *The Sheik* was of course followed by *The Son of the Sheik*.

Rodolfo Alfonzo Raffaelo Pierre Filibert Guglielmi di Valentina d'Antonguolla was born in Italy in 1895, the son of a veterinarian. He came to the United States at the age of eighteen and held a variety of jobs: gardener, dishwasher, dancer, gigolo, movie extra, and actor in minor stage roles. Handsome young Rodolfo was also trailed by rumors of homosexuality and blackmail. He was offered a secondary role in *The Four Horsemen of the Apocalypse* after being spotted in a Broadway show and stole the picture with a sexy tango. Valentino, as he was now known, embodied the fantasies of women all over the world.

While Valentino turned most women into quivering jelly, some newspapers claimed that he was effeminate. Bewildered and angry about these charges, the actor sought a meeting with Henry Mencken in 1926 to ask him how he should deal with the press. Should he challenge the editors to a succession of duels? The two men had a long talk in which Mencken told him to ignore the snide remarks, because anything he did would only worsen his problem. To his surprise, Mencken saw a great vulnerability as well as "an obvious fineness" in Valentino, and deemed him a "gentleman." The actor unexpectedly died the following month of a perforated ulcer and other complications at the age of thirty-one.

Most films of the Twenties were sheer hokum, yet there were also some first-class pictures. Emerson Hough's popular novel *The Covered Wagon* was made into a highly regarded western. King Vidor's World War I epic, *The Big Parade*, presented both the horrors and adventure of war. *Wings* recreated the thrill of aerial dogfights over the Western Front. Stroheim's *Blind Husbands*, a tale of infidelity among the idle rich, used subtle shots and detail to show high passion. In contrast, Cecil B. DeMille's *Male and Female* tackled the same theme by showing Gloria Swanson in her bath. Three European pictures, the surrealistic German fantasy-horror film *The Cabinet of Dr. Caligari*, which presented reality through the eyes of a madman, the Russian *Battleship Potemkin* with its famous Odessa Steps scene, and Abel Gance's visually revolutionary *Napoleon*, all advanced the art of cinematic storytelling.

Rin-Tin-Tin, a handsome German shepherd, was the most popular star of the mid-1920s. At the height of his fame, he earned $6,000 a month, was insured for $100,000, and had his own valet, chef, car, and driver. An orchestra played mood music while he worked and he wore a diamond-studded collar. Even his death was that of a star. The dog was playing with his trainer when he suddenly collapsed. Blond bombshell Jean Harlow was passing by, according to Jack Warner, the studio owner. "Sobbing, she took Rinty into her arms. She cradled the great furry head in her lap, and there he died."

The most enduring classics of the silent screen, however, were its comedies. Such gifted comics as the Keystone Kops, Laurel and Hardy, Buster Keaton, and Harold Lloyd all drew laughs, but Charlie Chaplin was King of Comedy. A superb pantomimist and master of timing who had learned his trade on the English music-hall circuit, Chaplin could, with a mere shrug or a tentative smile, speak volumes. "All I need to make a comedy," he said, "is a park, a policeman, and a pretty girl!" The little tramp, whom he introduced as his alter ego in 1915, was, within a few years, the best known figure not only in the United States but in the rest of the world as well.

Chaplin's comedy is immortal. Who can forget the bittersweet scene in City Lights in which the tramp, who has helped a blind girl regain her sight, anxiously awaits her reaction as she sees him for the first time. And there is the gourmet meal the starving tramp makes of a shoe in The Gold Rush. He delicately twists the shoelaces around a spoon as if they were spaghetti and sucks on the nails as if they were the most succulent chicken bones.

Chaplin's films are leavened by a biting commentary on the absurdities and brutalities of modern life. Nameless and seemingly without a past, the tramp symbolizes the ordinary man who struggles against the indifference and inequalities of society. Yet, even though he is buffeted by forces over which he has no control, he maintains his dignity. No matter what misfortunes befall him, the tramp picks himself up, brushes himself off with an elegant fastidiousness, and proceeds on his way while insouciantly twirling his cane. He is "a poet, a dreamer . . . always hopeful of romance and adventure," said Chaplin.

CHAPTER 10

"A Lost Generation"

Harold E. Stearns was addicted to a "nauseous" bootleg sherry so vile that even the ombibulous Henry Mencken, having ventured to taste it, absolutely refused to touch the stuff again. He took his favorite tipple in "frequent long stoups" and lived in a basement apartment in an old townhouse at 31 Jones Street that was squalid even by the standards of Greenwich Village. "He dressed so badly," said Mencken, "that he always looked dirty." A Harvard graduate and contributor to intellectual journals, the thirty-year-old Stearns was, in the spring of 1921, putting the final touches on *Civilization in the United States*, a symposium by thirty-three contributors that ranged over the breadth of American society.

To no one's surprise, these writers took a bleak view of the subject. Many had been suggested by Mencken, who was contemptuous of American culture, and Van Wyck Brooks, a literary critic who held that a joyless puritanism had a stranglehold on the American psyche. Life in the United States, said the contributors, was colorless, standardized, tawdry, uncreative, repressive, and given over to the worship of wealth and machinery. The nation's moral conscience had been drowned in bathtub gin, and Americans could express human feelings only in the lyrics of pop tunes. America offered no new horizons, no more promises.

Lewis Mumford wrote that the city was an index of the nation's material success and spiritual failure. The average congressman "is not only incompetent and imbecile, but is incurably dishonest," thundered Mencken. George Jean Nathan said that in no other country "is there among playwrights so little fervor for sound drama." The press was corrupt and controlled by its advertisers, according to John Macy. "Business morality" is a term without meaning, wrote Garet Garrett. Graduate students in American universities are "specialists in the obvious," concluded Robert M.

Lovett. "What immediately strikes one as one surveys the history of our literature during the last half century, is the singular impotence of its creative spirit," Brooks declared. Only a handful of the contributors offered suggestions for correcting the blemishes they saw.

"What should a young man do?" asked Stearns in a contemporaneous article in the *Freeman*. World War I and the Red Scare had destroyed the Village scene of the prewar moderns. Some radicals had been deported while others, such as John Reed, had chased the revolution to Russia. Censorship had closed most of their magazines. Feminism had given way to the flapper and premarital sex was no longer shocking. A recently opened subway stop at Sheridan Square disgorged slumming sightseers who crowded the old Village haunts. Fashion and advertising people were paying exorbitant rents for apartments and studios that had been previously occupied by struggling artists and writers. *"What should a young man do?"*

Stearns's answer to this question was simple and uncompromising. The young intellectual had no future in a country of hypocrisy and repression. Like Byron shaking the dust of England from his boots, he should take the next boat for Europe where people knew how to live. Yet, as with almost everything else about the Twenties, there was a duality in Stearns's message. Even as he scorned the emotional and aesthetic sterility of American society, he concluded his essay on "The Intellectual Life" in *Civilization in the United States* with a passionate, Whitmanesque tribute to America and a manifesto for intellectual revolution:

> Climb to the top of the Palisades and watch the great city [New York] in the deepening dusk as light after light, and rows of lights after rows, topped by towers of radiance at the end of the island, shine through the shadows across the river. Think, then, of the miles of rolling plains, fertile and dotted with cities, stretching behind one to that other ocean. . . . Must all these things . . . be reduced to a drab uniformity because we lack the courage to proclaim their sheer physical loveliness? Has not the magic of America been hidden under a fog of ugliness by those who never really loved it, who never knew our gaiety and high spirits and eagerness for knowledge? They have the upper hand now—but who would dare to prophesy that they can keep it?

Immediately after turning the manuscript of the book over to the publisher, Stearns sailed for France on July 4, 1921, after issuing his own declaration of independence. This was no ordinary departure, and reporters flocked to the *Berengaria* to jot down the valedictory of the archetypical young intellectual, who announced he was going to Europe to write books of bold consequence in a more congenial atmosphere.*

Civilization in the United States created "a tremendous pother in its day," Mencken later recalled, and Carl Van Doren, literary editor of *The Nation*, deemed it important enough to devote an entire book section to it. Nevertheless, the writers included in the volume had a blinkered vision of the civilization they evaluated so bitingly. Mostly Easterners, they ignored what Scott Fitzgerald called "that vast obscurity beyond the city." They knew nothing about rural or small town life and most of the country west of the Hudson "where the dark fields of the republic rolled on under the night" was terra incognita. They had no insight into the lives of either the wealthy or the industrial proletariat. Nor was there any mention of jazz or the movies—America's twin cultural accomplishments. More people talked about the book than read it, for only 4,991 copies were sold in the first two years after publication. The average royalty check was $81.38.

Ironically, at the very time when intellectuals proclaimed that the arts could not flourish in America, literature, art, and music were undergoing the greatest period of creativity in the nation's history. Eugene O'Neill was revolutionizing the theater. Gifted black writers such as Zora Neale Hurston, Jean Toomer, and others were being published. Ring Lardner's stories were appearing. George Gershwin was incorporating jazz rhythms into opera and symphonic music. In art, Georgia O'Keeffe was painting her stark portrayals of the New Mexico desert, Edward Hopper was producing his haunting, pre-noir urban landscapes and investing them with a romantic glow, while Joseph Stella, Charles Sheeler, and Niles Spencer brought fresh energy to Cubism. William Zorach, Arnold Bonnebeck, and Robert Garrison were adapting Expressionism to American sculpture. Even classicism received a shot in the arm from Daniel Chester French's sublime, brooding Lincoln, whose classical memorial temple was dedicated in 1922. And, reversing the trend, the French-born Gaston Lachaise brought his chisel to the United States because "the soil most fertile for the continuity of art—is here."

---

* In Paris, Stearns wrote little and drank much and became a racetrack tout and handicapper for the Paris edition of the *Chicago Tribune* under the name "Peter Pickem." Mencken later described him as "the champion drunk of the American colony." Someone seeing him passed out at a café table joked: "There lies civilization in the United States." He appears briefly in Ernest Hemingway's *The Sun Also Rises* as Harvey Stone, a drunk and a deadbeat.

* * *

The gravitational pull of Europe upon American writers has always been strong, and those who left for Paris and the south of France at the beginning of the Twenties were following a trail blazed by Nathaniel Hawthorne, Bret Harte, Henry James, Edith Wharton, T. S. Eliot, Ezra Pound, Gertrude Stein, and others. Mencken, however, remained "on the dock, wrapped in the flag." Asked why he stayed in a country whose culture he found so repulsive, he had a sardonic reply: "Why do men go to zoos?"

The French Line pier was on the Hudson River side of Greenwich Village and there, in increasing numbers, young and footloose artists, writers, poets, and their girlfriends bade farewell to America. These self-exiles claimed they could write or paint better in France, where bluenosed puritanism did not exist. Besides, the dollar went further in Montparnasse than in the Village. If you were careful, you could live well on $5 a day. Prohibition did not exist and the French ignored the strange antics of the foreigners plopped down among them. Malcolm Cowley, who chronicled the exiles' adventures, wrote:

> "I'm going to Paris," they said at first, and then, "I'm going to the South of France. . . . I'm sailing Wednesday—next month—as soon as I can scrape together money enough to buy a ticket." Money wasn't impossible to scrape together; some of it could be saved from one's salary or borrowed from one's parents or one's friends. Newspapers and magazines were interested in reports from Europe, two or three foundations had fellowships for study abroad, and publishers sometimes made advances against future royalties for an unwritten book. . . . "Goodbye, so long," they said, "I'll meet you on the Left Bank. I'll drink your health in good red Burgundy, I'll kiss all the girls for you. I'm sick of this country. I'm going abroad to write one good novel."

Ernest Hemingway was twenty-two when he arrived in Paris at the end of 1921 with his new wife, Hadley Richardson, a pretty redhead, to teach himself to write. Powerfully built, he sometimes reinforced his words with right and left hooks in the air, as if he were sparring with the person to whom he was talking. Not long after, he grew a clipped mustache and took on the look of a British army officer. He had letters of introduction to Gertrude Stein and Ezra Pound from Sherwood Anderson and a commission from the *Toronto Star* for feature articles to be paid for at penurious space rates if printed. Hadley had a small trust fund, but to save money so they could eat and drink well and travel, the young couple lived in a threadbare apartment above a sawmill in the rue Nôtre-Dame-des-Champs. The editors back in Toronto liked Hemingway's work and put him on salary and expenses, and sent him to cover diplomatic conferences and a nasty little war between the Turks and Greeks in Asia Minor.

Most mornings, Hemingway went to a café on the Place St.-Michel, where he was unlikely to meet other Americans, and wrote in longhand in cheap notebooks, his back to the wall, honing each word of his stories until they had the precision and power of poetry. He wrote about what he had seen as a boy in Upper Michigan, as a newspaper reporter in Kansas City, in Italy during the war where he was severely wounded, and as a correspondent in postwar Europe. Laboriously, he created his own style with the advice of Stein and Pound: simple words strung together in short, punchy sentences with the adjectives and emotions edited out as if he were sending the reader a telegram. Writing, insisted Hemingway, must be like an iceberg, with the most significant part unseen but understood by the reader. In 1925, he published his first collection of stories, In Our Time, and his fame was assured.

Stein's apartment at 27, rue de Fleurus, with its astonishing collection of paintings by Renoir, Gauguin, Matisse, and Picasso, was a literary center for the Americans in Paris. At her salons, she monopolized the writers while their wives and girlfriends talked to her tiny, ever watchful companion, Alice B. Toklas. "You are all a lost generation," Stein told Hemingway one evening. "All of you young people who served in the war. You have no respect for anything. You drink yourselves to death." This catchy bit of bombast was not original. Stein had picked it up from a French garage owner's diatribe against a young mechanic who failed to take proper care of her beloved Model T.*

In his fictionalized memoir of the Paris years, A Moveable Feast, Hemingway wrote that he angrily rejected the idea that a generation could judge the one that followed. As he walked back to his flat, he was still seething. "The hell with her lost-generation talk and all the dirty, easy labels," he muttered.†

Nevertheless, "a lost generation" became the unofficial badge of the literary generation of the Twenties because it so aptly evoked the alienation, disillusionment, and cynicism so fashionable during those years. Moreover,

---

* Stein, who attended the Johns Hopkins Medical School for four years without graduating, had driven the car through the mud of Flanders as a medical volunteer with the French army during World War I.

† Even so, Hemingway thought of calling his first novel The Lost Generation and made the phrase famous by using it as an epigraph for the book, finally entitled The Sun Also Rises.

the postwar intellectuals relished its romantic image of doomed youth. But like all such labels, it was only partially true. While some young people drifted aimlessly and without purpose from bar to bed and bed to bar, others worked hard at establishing themselves as writers, poets, and artists. Besides, a generation that produced *The Sun Also Rises, A Farewell to Arms, The Great Gatsby, Tender Is the Night, The Sound and the Fury, The Maltese Falcon,* and the trilogy *U.S.A.* can hardly be said to be "lost." Rather, as the poet Archibald MacLeish noted, the Twenties was "the greatest period of painting and music, literary and artistic innovation since the Renaissance."

John Dos Passos captured the excitement of the Paris that greeted these young Americans. "We were groggy with theater and Picasso was to rebuild the eye, Stravinsky was cramming the Russian steppes into our ears, currents of energy seemed breaking out everywhere as young guys climbed out of their uniforms, imperial America was all shiny . . . in every direction the countries of the world stretched out starving and angry, ready for anything turbulent and new."

The war was the unifying force that tied this group of writers together, and gave them a fund of common experiences and emotions. Born shortly before the turn of the century, they grew up in the good years before World War I when America seemed to have unlimited possibilities. Mostly Ivy League educated, they drove ambulances during the war,* and were experimenting with literary modernism. Having come to maturity during a period of violent change, they had little in common with their elders, creating the first generational gap of the twentieth century.

The previous generation had, they contended, made a mess of things. They wanted to make a clean break with the past so a better America could emerge, which led to the rejection of the nation's sacred literary gods. Longfellow and Whittier were ridiculed, while Whitman was accepted with the qualification that poetry had to go beyond his "barbaric yawp." The Genteel Tradition was rejected out of hand. Talented women of the earlier generation, such as Edith Wharton and Willa Cather, still had a popular audience—both won Pulitzer Prizes in the early 1920s—but

---

* An estimated 2,500 young men volunteered to drive ambulances for the American Field Services, the Red Cross, and other units during the war, of whom 151 were killed. Most joined because they wanted to be in the center of action but had physical handicaps that barred them from military service. Hemingway had defective vision in his left eye and Dos Passos was so myopic he couldn't read the top line of the eye chart without thick glasses. Thus, a casualty transported in Dos Passos's ambulance faced the additional peril of being carried to a hospital by a half-blind driver.

their reputations were diminished. On the other hand, the neglected Herman Melville, whose *Moby-Dick* had been regarded as a mere adventure tale for boys, won newfound acclaim. And the Dada movement, with its aura of wonderful nonsense and lack of respect for the cultural monuments of the past, had momentary shock value.* A hit song of 1924 was the Dadaist-sounding "Does the Spearmint Lose Its Flavor on the Bedpost Overnight?"

The expatriates lived, drank, made love, and wrote on the Left Bank, the traditional bohemia of Paris. To save money, they took rooms in the cheap hotels that lined the twisting old streets off the boulevards St.-Michel and St.-Germain. They drank and talked and waged vendettas at the marble-topped tables of the popular cafés—the Select, the Dôme, and the Rotonde. To be young and talented and in Paris, with a drink on the table and money in your pocket for another, was the best of all possible worlds. As word of the transatlantic good life spread, the creative artists were inundated by what Hemingway called "the scum of Greenwich Village," who were escaping Prohibition and boredom. Paris was even more attractive because the franc was falling against the dollar, skidding from 9.3 cents in 1920 to only 3.4 cents in 1924. By then, some 32,000 Americans were residing in Paris. Harold Stearns observed that you could be living in New York "except for the fact some people stubbornly persisted in talking French." College students back home drank and smoked and talked like Hemingway characters and the ironic closing words of *The Sun Also Rises* became a favorite comment: "Isn't it pretty to think so?"

For gays and lesbians, who kept a low profile back home, Paris in the 1920s was explosively different. Fashion made androgyny the mode. Coco Chanel used flapperish flat-busted, narrow-hipped models with helmetlike coiffures to show off her latest line of suits and dresses. The literary scandal of the day was a novel called *La Garçonne* (*The Tomboy*) whose nineteen-year-old heroine planned to have a baby and then dismiss the entire male sex. Its author was kicked out of the Legion of Honor. The lead in Jean Cocteau's production of *Antigone* shaved her head and plucked her eyebrows bare.

A salon held each Friday afternoon by Natalie Barney, an American heiress, was the epicenter of this world. The "Popess of Lesbos," Barney

---

* Marcel Duchamp, a French artist who lived part-time in the United States and whose *Nude Descending a Staircase* created a stir at the Armory Show, best expressed the free spirit of Dada by painting a goatee and mustache on a reproduction of the *Mona Lisa* and calling it *L.H.O.O.Q.* When pronounced with a French accent, this translates roughly into "She's got a hot ass."

wore a cape and black riding boots and claimed to have seduced at least forty women. There, in her high-walled garden in the rue Jacob, one might encounter André Gide, Cocteau, Ezra Pound, Raymond Radiguet, Djuna Barnes, Romaine Brooks, Edna St. Vincent Millay, and Radclyffe Hall. Hall made Barney the barely disguised heroine of her novel *The Well of Loneliness*, a *succès de scandale* of the era. Other lesbians who played prominent roles in the literary community included Gertrude Stein; Sylvia Beach, owner of the bookshop Shakespeare and Company and the first to dare to publish James Joyce's *Ulysses*; Jane Heap, editor of *The Little Review*; and Janet Flanner, who as "Genet" was the longtime Paris correspondent of *The New Yorker*.

People came and went, but Hemingway, Scott Fitzgerald, Dos Passos, e.e. cummings, Malcolm Cowley, Thomas Wolfe, Kay Boyle, Thornton Wilder, Djuna Barnes, Matthew Josephson, Robert E. Sherwood, and Archibald MacLeish, among others, spent considerable time in Paris. Yet, most never wavered in their loyalty to America and from a distance wrote about Upper Michigan and Blue Juniata. They didn't leave the country so much as back up and broaden their view of it. "Living abroad has intensified my Americanism," noted Stephen Vincent Benét, who was working on what was to become *John Brown's Body*. This group also included writers who resisted the siren call of Paris but were in internal exile at home. Ring Lardner, Sinclair Lewis, Dashiell Hammett, William Faulkner,* and Hart Crane were all repelled by the cold, materialistic culture of commerce they said permeated the United States during Coolidge Prosperity. As e.e. cummings said:

> the season tis,my lovely lambs,
> of Sumner, Volstead Christ and Co.
> the epoch of Mann's righteousness
> the age of dollars and no sense.†

---

* Faulkner spent a few months in Paris, accomplished little except for growing a beard and watching the old men sailing their toy boats in a pond in the Luxembourg Gardens, and went home. Years later, his work achieved wide popularity in France.

† John S. Sumner was secretary of the New York Society for the Suppression of Vice, which targeted allegedly obscene books, magazines, and plays. Andrew Volstead was the father of the Volstead Act, which enforced Prohibition. James R. Mann created the Mann Act, designed to abolish the white slave trade, but it was so loosely worded that a man could be jailed if his girlfriend accompanied him from Manhattan to Westport, Connecticut, for the weekend, and he paid her fare.

The war left these writers with an unbridled hatred of authority and of the "old men" who had bumbled into World War I, perpetrated its butcheries, and then bungled the peace. "If we only governed the world instead of the swagbellied old fogies that do," wrote Dos Passos. With the "old swagbellies" still in power, the young turned away from all forms of public concern. In fact, one of the remarkable things about the 1920s is the dearth of new political talent. Until the Wall Street crash, talented young men and women devoted themselves almost entirely to the self-directed objectives of getting rich and becoming famous.

Universal contempt was expressed for the "big words" and lofty sentiments used by "Professor Wilson" to trumpet his war. Young men had been slaughtered, wrote Ezra Pound in *Hugh Selwyn Mauberley*, "For an old bitch gone in the teeth, / For a botched civilization." Similar views were expressed in Dos Passos's *Three Soldiers;* Hemingway's *A Farewell to Arms; What Price Glory?*, a play by Laurence Stallings and Maxwell Anderson; and later, from the German side, *All Quiet on the Western Front* by Erich Maria Remarque. Heroism, if at all possible in the American postwar novel, consisted of making a "separate peace"—a personal retreat into oneself. For Hemingway's antiheroes, it took the form of preserving individual dignity and self-respect in the face of disaster. Instead of ranting or crying, Lieutenant Henry walked out into the rain after the death of his lover and child. In the same vein, Lady Brett Ashley decided not to be "a bitch" and let go of the young matador with whom she had an affair. Faulkner's most successful characters—primarily blacks and women—proved the resilience of the human spirit. Three decades before Existentialism formally appeared as a philosophy, the writers of the 1920s had adopted the concept.

In a chaotic world of cruelty, danger, and injustice, the most a man could hope for was the courage to meet whatever life had to offer with dignity—"grace under pressure," as Hemingway put it. Heroes as varied as Theodore Dreiser's Clyde Griffiths in *An American Tragedy*, Quentin Compson in Faulkner's *The Sound and the Fury,* and Jay Gatsby discovered the obsessive pursuit of a dream—whether it be true love, money, or respectability—led to catastrophe. No one was allowed to get away with anything.

T. S. Eliot's *The Waste Land* and Joyce's *Ulysses*, both published in 1922, had more influence on the postwar generation than any other literary works. In each, the author pushed beyond the mountains and discovered new territories for the coming generation to explore. Even though many readers, including Hemingway, did not understand Eliot's poem and thought it pretentious, they were pulled in by his vision of a world materially and spiritually devastated by the war. The theme was established by a quotation in the notes from Hermann Hesse: "Already half Europe, at least half of East Europe, is on the way to chaos [and] stumbles drunkenly in a holy delusion toward the abyss."

Eliot, a native of St. Louis and member of Harvard's notable class of 1910, had gone to England as a budding academic and closet poet to study philosophy at Cambridge. Told by a friend to look up Ezra Pound, he showed him his work, including "The Love Song of J. Alfred Prufrock." Pound was amazed at the quality of Eliot's writing and urged it upon *Poetry* magazine in Chicago, for which he was a scout. Eliot stuck it out in England throughout the war as an ill-paid schoolteacher and bank clerk.

When America entered the conflict in April 1917 he volunteered for the U.S. Navy but was rejected because of poor health. Eliot fought his own war in a disastrously unhappy marriage. Drawing from his personal anxieties and anguish, he wrote *The Waste Land* while recovering from a nervous breakdown. As soon as he completed this "sprawling chaotic poem," he sent the manuscript to Pound, who heavily edited it and, in the final analysis, was almost as much the author as Eliot. Using a rich symbolism, Eliot reworked the legends of the search for the Holy Grail and the Fisher King and his incurable wound. He converted the spiritual emptiness following the war into a metaphor for the entire modern era.

Young writers revered *Ulysses* as Holy Writ and hung around Sylvia Beach's bookshop in the rue Odéon with the hope that Joyce might drop by, as he often did to borrow money. "Joyce is the greatest writer in the world," proclaimed Hemingway. These writers paid Eliot and Joyce the ultimate compliment of finding in *The Waste Land* and *Ulysses* themes for their own work. Jake Barnes is both a questing knight and impotent because of his wound. Dos Passos's *Manhattan Transfer* and *U.S.A.* and Faulkner's *The Sound and the Fury* owe much of their style and structure to *Ulysses*. In *The Bridge*, Hart Crane's cycle of poems, the protagonist wanders about New York City in the manner of Leopold Bloom's peregrinations through Dublin. And Jay Gatsby not only pursued the Holy Grail in the form of his lost love, Daisy, he found his own waste land in the Valley of Ashes—a landfill in Queens between Manhattan and West Egg—"where ashes grow like wheat into ridges and hills and grotesque gardens."

Unlike most of the expatriates, Fitzgerald was famous when he went to Europe. *This Side of Paradise,* two books of short stories, *Flappers and*

Philosophers and *Tales of the Jazz Age,* and another novel, *The Beautiful and Damned*—all published over a two-year period—made him the voice of the Jazz Age. He was luridly successful: his peak story fee from *The Saturday Evening Post* was $4,000, when a schoolteacher made $1,300 a year. Of all the writers of this frenzied era, Fitzgerald best fits its image. "Sometimes," he once said, "I don't know whether Zelda and I are real or whether we are characters in one of my novels."

For a brief period after the publication of *This Side of Paradise,* he was happier than he would ever be again. "Riding in a taxi one afternoon between very tall buildings under a mauve and rosy sky, I began to bawl because I had everything I wanted and knew I would never be so happy again," he wrote. He found himself mentioned in the same breath with Byron, Kipling, and Dreiser. He lingered in Fifth Avenue bookstores hoping to hear his book talked about.* To a large extent, Fitzgerald became famous because he told an older generation just how badly the young behaved. They drank and smoked and petted in the rumble seats of roadsters in reckless defiance of what was regarded as proper behavior. Readers felt a delicious shudder up and down their spines as one of his world-weary flappers brazenly confessed, "I've kissed dozens of men. I suppose I'll kiss dozens more."

Scott and Zelda wanted to be the toast of the town and in this they were spiritual twins. Sensation, romance, and thrills were necessary for both of them and they were forever egging each other into even more outrageous acts to attract attention. They seemed born to excite and destroy each other. Their sense of identicalness even led them sometimes to dress alike. They ventured into their new life almost innocently, hand in hand. "It was always tea time or late at night," said Zelda, and Scott observed, "We felt like children in a great bright unexplored barn."

Fitzgerald's blend of flippancy and glamour caught the mood of the moment and he became, in the words of a contemporary, "our darling, our genius, our fool." He was not the first idol of insurgent youth—that title probably belongs to Edna St. Vincent Millay—but he took on the role with zest. Even so, fame altered him surprisingly little and he accepted renown with irony. "Let's go down to the Plaza for lunch," he would say. "They'll swoon when they see me come in."

A montage of images swirls by: Scott and Zelda sitting glumly in a the-

---

* When Heywood Broun of the *New York Tribune* gibed that the book was a reprise of every college novel he had read, Fitzgerald invited him to lunch. Gently, he told the columnist that it was too bad he had become sour and allowed his life to slip away without accomplishing anything. Broun had just turned thirty.

ater during the comic parts of a play and laughing uproariously at the serious parts . . . Scott stripping in the sixth row of George White's Scandals and
being thrown out by a posse of ushers . . . Scott and Zelda holding hands
after a concert at Carnegie Hall and flying down 57th Street like a pair of
hawks . . . Scott doing headstands in the Biltmore lobby because he hadn't
been in the papers all week . . . the Fitzgeralds arriving at a party with Zelda
sitting on the roof of a taxi and Scott straddling the hood . . . Scott and
Zelda taking a midnight dip in the Pulitzer Fountain in front of the Plaza
with their clothes on . . . Zelda dancing the Charleston on tables at parties
while Scott got into drunken fights with waiters . . . The Fitzgeralds got
away with this and more because they were young and glamorous, and a
shocking unconventionality was still fun. A sense of turbulence and violence, an undertow of madness, lay just below the surface.

Fifth Avenue had become passé and Park Avenue was regarded as vul-
garly ostentatious, so fashionable society, successful writers, and famous
theater people blazed a trail to the elegant apartments on the East Side
around Sutton Place and Riverview Terrace. Festivities began about 6 P.M.
with a new social institution, the late afternoon cocktail party complete
with copious supplies of bootleg Scotch and gin. Guests might include
"young Hapsburgs, anxious to please; hawklike White Russian princesses;
insolent Hollywood stars; a darkly-sinister torch singer; a sprinkling of
docile intellectuals and dashing debutantes; a few petulant gigolos and a
large number of anonymous, agreeable people with vaguely familiar faces."
The announcement that "everybody's coming" was only too true because
the invited guests brought along their own guests, creating a crush. People
passed out in the bedrooms and the party continued until the booze was all
gone.

One evening, the Fitzgeralds embarked with a few friends on a round of
parties that began with cocktails and continued with a tour of nightclubs
that began on Broadway, swooped down to the Village, and then rocketed
uptown to Harlem. At five in the morning the revelers had breakfast at
Childs. Everyone wanted to go home and nurse their headaches, but
Fitzgerald was in no mood for home—home was where you dressed to go
out. He herded a few kindred spirits into a taxi and they rattled off downtown. The evening's gaiety ended with an inspection of the cadavers at the
city morgue.

Yet, for all his drinking and collegiate pranks, Fitzgerald was an astute
observer of his world. He registered every emotion, noticed every change
in manners and put it in his fiction. Zelda was both a torment and an inspi-

ration. He was proud of her good looks and not yet jealous of her ability to attract crowds of men. And her personality, her pranks, even her diary and letters provided him with raw material. "Plagiarism begins at home," she said. He took the facts of both their lives and made art out of it. In his second novel, *The Beautiful and Damned*, he wrote in words that were as much about himself and Zelda as his characters, "of all the things they possessed in common, the greatest of all was their almost uncanny pull at each other's hearts."

Fitzgerald's friends thought no greater catastrophe could have befallen him than winning his Southern belle, and they hoped the marriage would quickly break up. "He's going to leave Zelda," Edmund Wilson assured a mutual friend only a few weeks after the wedding, and he suspected that "she will seize the opportunity to run away with the elevator boy." They worried about her extravagance, her interference with his work, and her lack of understanding of the artistic standards he set for himself. She thought getting a story into *The Saturday Evening Post* was the height of literary success. "Scott was extravagant but not like her," said Max Perkins. "Money went through her hands like water; she wanted everything; she kept him writing for the magazines."

The Fitzgeralds' frenetic and punishingly expensive way of living left Scott constantly grubbing for more and more money. As Zelda observed, "It costs more to ride on the tops of taxis" than in them. From 1920 to 1924, Fitzgerald earned about $22,500 a year from his writing—perhaps $250,000 in modern values—and ended up broke. Once he went to the bank and asked the cashier, "How much money have I got?" The man looked into his big ledger and answered, "None."

In their attitude toward money, the Fitzgeralds followed the spirit of the times. "The Jazz Age . . . raced along under its own power, served by great filling stations full of money," Scott wrote. "Even when you were broke you didn't worry about money, because it was in such profusion around you." Money to the Fitzgeralds was merely a means to enjoy the good life, and they flung it around with the carelessness of eighteenth-century aristocrats. When a check came in from Harold Ober, his agent, Fitzgerald offhandedly handed Zelda a sheaf of bills for expenses and no one knew where the money went. A friend found a large wad of cash casually stuffed into a door pocket of their Rolls-Royce coupé and apparently forgotten. Fitzgerald began a lifetime habit of borrowing against future work from Ober and was usually in debt to him and to Scribners.

Although Fitzgerald professed to be uninfluenced by his shaky finances, there was always the nagging fear from his childhood of falling into poverty. Sometimes he panicked and there were penny-pinching episodes in which he resolved to be thrifty, but they passed as quickly as his promises to stop drinking. To keep the money coming in, he wrote *Saturday Evening Post* potboilers with what he called "the required jazz ending." Some were dashed off in little more than a few days—in fact he once wrote a seven-thousand-word story overnight. Even here he was incapable of turning out completely shoddy material. His early commercial stories, such as "Bernice Bobs Her Hair" and "The Offshore Pirate," introduced a new character to American fiction: the independent, determined young woman.

"He told me . . . how he wrote what he thought were good stories for the *Post,* and then changed them for submission, knowing exactly how he must make the twists that made them into salable magazine stories," Ernest Hemingway reported. "I had been shocked at this and I said I thought it was whoring. He said it was whoring but that he had to do it."*

Fitzgerald's reputation as a drinker and playboy inspired the myth that he didn't really care about his work. In reality, when doing a serious piece of writing, he doggedly went through draft after draft and revised constantly until the book or story was nearly on the press. *The Great Gatsby,* for example, was almost rewritten on the printer's proof. He was constantly searching for meaning and morality. But no matter what he wrote, it was always clear, lyrical, and colorful. When the opinion makers objected to the constant concern with money and status in his work, he replied: "But my God! it was my material, and it was all that I had to deal with."

In mid-1923, Fitzgerald wrote Perkins that he had an idea for a novel and wanted "to write something *new*—something extraordinary and beautiful and simple & intricately patterned." With the hope of settling down so he could write the book, he and Zelda rented a house in Great Neck (West Egg in *The Great Gatsby*), among the estates clustered on the North Shore of Long Island. But the couple's life was as erratic as it had been in New York. They gave large, drunken parties similar to those of Jay Gatsby and people came and went with nobody knowing who they were. And their drinking, no longer an amusing left-over-from-college affair, took a self-destructive turn. Fitzgerald frequently disappeared into Manhattan on benders.

Anita Loos, the author of *Gentlemen Prefer Blondes,* remembered being driven out to Great Neck by Fitzgerald. "I didn't know that he was tight. We had a wild ride. . . . I thought he was going to kill us both." Everything

* Hemingway had tried to sell stories to *The Saturday Evening Post* but they were rejected, so there is a certain amount of sour grapes to these comments.

ator that was the talk of the *plage*. Possibly, he shrugged it off at first because he was used to having men admire his wife. Zelda may have pursued the affair because with her husband living in his book she was bored; maybe she wanted to get her husband's attention by making him jealous.

Judging from the dramatic accounts from both sides, the incident was the turning point in their marriage. "I've been unhappy," Fitzgerald wrote Perkins in August. But in this same letter he proclaimed that his book, which he said would be finished in about a month, "is about the best American novel ever written." A few weeks later, Zelda took an overdose of sleeping pills, and then required a shot of morphine to pull her out of an attack of "nervous hysteria." Perhaps she was haunted by a line spoken by Judy Jones, the heroine of "Winter Dreams," one of her husband's best stories: "I'm more beautiful than anyone else, why can't I be happy?"

For some observers, this episode confirmed what had always been suspected: Zelda was psychologically unbalanced. "From the first moment I saw her, I knew she was mad," the novelist Rebecca West said of a visit to Great Neck the year before. Hemingway, who called Zelda a "cock teaser," also believed she was crazy. She, in turn, disliked him and thought he was gay—possibly because he resisted her advances. The Fitzgeralds' marriage became a desperate round of illnesses, battles, accusations, and—most painful of all—repeated attempts at starting over, after which the cycle began all over again. Years later, Fitzgerald wrote, "That September 1924 I knew something had happened that could not really be repaired."

Yet in the midst of this shambles, Fitzgerald's imagination, creativity, and nerve did not fail him. The new book, called *The Great Gatsby* when it was published in April 1925, fulfilled all his earlier promise. In telling the story of the rise and fall of Jimmy Gatz, otherwise known as Jay Gatsby, Fitzgerald created, in only fifty thousand words, a lasting portrait of the time. His theme was a universal one: the corruption of the American Dream by the American Nightmare. Theodore Dreiser's *An American Tragedy*, published that same year, echoed a similar theme but in a more massive, less elegant manner.

Scenes, passages, and lines from the book remain with the reader long after it has been put aside. Who can forget the image of Gatsby staring fixedly at the green light that shines—and promises—at the end of Daisy Buchanan's dock? Or that her voice "is full of money"? Or the all-seeing eyes of Dr. T. J. Eckenberry? And like Nick Carraway, the book's narrator, we hear the faraway music of Gatsby's lavish parties where "men and girls came and went like moths upon the whisperings and the champagne and the stars."

went well during cocktails, but Fitzgerald turned moody during dinner a
Miss Loos and Zelda ignored him, which made him angry.

Finally, he jumped up from the table and said, "I'm going to kill you
two." And he tried. He jerked off the tablecloth with everything on it
and then started throwing the candelabra and other big, heavy things at
us. Scott had locked all the doors, but the butler—he will always be a
hero to me—broke through a glass pane in one of the doors and came in
and held Scott. Then Zelda and I ran across to Ring Lardner's house.
Ring decided to go out looking for Scott. . . . [When Lardner found him]
Scott was kneeling in the road, eating dirt. "I'm a monster," he was saying. "I tried to kill those two darling girls and now I've got to eat dirt."

With the failure of *The Vegetable*, his first and only play, Fitzgerald had t
grind out more stories for the magazines to meet the bills and he put o
work on his new novel. Ring Lardner was Fitzgerald's only intimate i
Great Neck. Both had a mutual interest in drinking and drank slowly an
methodically and talked through the night over cases of Canadian ale o
stronger stuff. When daylight came, they went yawning and blinking an
stretching to bed. One morning, they drove over to the Doubleday estat
to perform a tipsy dance on the lawn, with the hope of attracting the atten
tion of the visiting Joseph Conrad, but were chased away by the caretakers

Lardner was a "disillusioned idealist," according to Fitzgerald. Despit
being a popular writer who earned $60,000 a year, he was prey to melan-
cholia and binge drinking. He deprecated his own work and regarded himself as a mere reporter. Fitzgerald, with the generosity he always showed to
writers he admired, helped him gather his stories into his first book, *How to
Write Short Stories*, and convinced Perkins to publish it.*

The time had come to move on again. In April 1924, the Fitzgeralds and
their three-year-old daughter, Scottie, went to the Riviera to live in a
pleasant villa at St. Raphael, which was set back in a cypress grove. That
summer, Fitzgerald was on the wagon and his novel was going well, so well
he didn't notice that Zelda was having a romance with a French naval avi-

* Fitzgerald brought Hemingway to Max Perkins's attention and not only arranged for
publication of *The Sun Also Rises*, but edited it. He lopped off the first two chapters, giving
the book its existing beginning. After Fitzgerald's literary and personal fortunes turned,
Hemingway repaid these favors by mocking him in both life and death. Some observers say
that as his own powers slipped away, Hemingway's attacks on Fitzgerald were motivated by
fear that Fitzgerald's posthumous reputation would exceed his own—which it has.

Fitzgerald hoped for another instant success like *This Side of Paradise*, and predicted sales of 75,000 copies. Although *Gatsby* was the great critical success he always wanted and he received letters of congratulation from T. S. Eliot, Gertrude Stein, Edith Wharton,* Willa Cather, and George Jean Nathan, among others, the book did not sell as well as he had hoped. When he died in 1940, Scribners still had some of the 23,000 copies of the first two printings in its warehouse. "The novel was never out of print," states Charles Scribner III. "It had simply stopped selling."†

No one had a greater influence upon American writers of the postwar generation than Sigmund Freud. The Viennese psychiatrist's theories about sexuality and the unconscious had already provoked considerable discussion in America before he visited the United States in the autumn of 1909 to present a series of lectures on psychoanalysis at Clark University in Worcester, Massachusetts. In five lectures delivered extemporaneously in German, Freud cannily emphasized those elements of his teachings that he thought would appeal to the "practical Americans" and stressed his system's optimism, practicality, and comparative simplicity. He was deeply moved when, in contrast to the years of contempt and ostracism he had experienced in Europe, Clark awarded him an honorary doctorate of laws. "This is the first official recognition of our efforts," Freud declared.

In all, Freud spent two weeks in the United States. He had a brief tour of New York City, took in his first movie, was overawed by Niagara Falls, and charmed by a porcupine. But America was not for him. It "is a gigantic mistake," he concluded. Freud was frustrated by his inability to speak English very well, American cooking upset his delicate stomach, and the dignity of the *Herr Professor Doktor* was affronted when the informal Americans called him by his first name. "America is useful for nothing else but to supply money," he announced.

Nevertheless, Freud's ideas had their greatest impact in the United States, and led to the revamping of virtually the entire cultural landscape.

---

* Wharton invited Fitzgerald to tea at her country place outside Paris. Becoming convinced that he had been summoned to be put down by her aristocratic friends, he got drunk on the way. Determined to shock the gathering, he told them that when he and Zelda first came to Paris they lived in a bordello. Wharton gazed benignly over her teacup as if waiting for the rest of the story.

"But Mr. Fitzgerald," she finally said, "you haven't told us what you did in the bordello."

Trumped, Fitzgerald slunk away in embarrassment.

† In 1998, the Modern Library issued a list of the one hundred best English-language novels of the twentieth century and *The Great Gatsby* ranked second only to *Ulysses*.

He became "the Darwin of the Mind" to the popular press and was credited with the creation of modern thinking in psychiatry, psychology, child
rearing, criminology, and sexual attitudes. Freudian doctrine spread rapidly
in its adopted homeland because it arrived in America at the right psychological moment. The nation was undergoing an upheaval in morality, and
Freud's teachings, with their emphasis on the importance of the subconscious as a guideline for the interpretation of human motivation, found a
ready audience among the moderns, who were leading the charge against
Victorianism. Freudian psychology was an escape hatch from such inhibit-
ing legacies of the past as sexual repression, unthinking patriotism, fundamentalist religion, and naive idealism.

Originally, psychoanalysis had only a small group of adherents in America—a few psychologists, a handful of neurologists who specialized in the
treatment of the nervous and mental disorders of the rich, and a larger
group of hospital psychiatrists who were going into private practice
because few institutional jobs were available. Most were in Boston, New
York, Baltimore, and Washington. Until then, physicians who treated what
would now be called emotional problems, especially among women, did so
within an older paradigm that mixed gynecology with advice. For example,
there was a well-known doctor in Greenwich Village who performed abor-
tions and also advised on marital problems. Medical practitioners still
largely relied upon a diagnosis of hysteria to explain women's depression
and anger.

Freud's chief drumbeater in America was Dr. Abraham A. Brill, who
more than anyone else was responsible for the ultimate acceptance of psychoanalysis in this country. A native of Austro-Hungary, he fled from an
overbearing father and arrived in New York's East Side ghetto as a lonely
and penniless youth. Brill was determined to become a physician and
worked his way through school with a series of poorly paid odd jobs. Several times, he was forced to drop out because of a lack of funds, but he
eventually achieved his goal. Later, he studied at Carl Jung's Clinic of Psychiatry in Zurich and was won over to Freudian theory. Brill was a founder
of the New York Psychoanalytic Society, and his English translations of
Freud's works, although severely criticized by some of the faithful, introduced the master to American audiences.

As a propagandist and popularizer, Brill preached the Freudian gospel
not only to intellectuals and opinion makers but to lay audiences as well.
In one brief period, he lectured on Freud before a group of social workers,
gave the New York Child Study Association the Freudian view of mastur-

bation, and then explained Freud to the Authors League, offering its members "a number of 'plots'" based on the case histories of his patients. Walter Lippmann brought Brill into Mabel Dodge's salon, where Freud's ideas had an immediate impact.

The *Forum*, a leading magazine of the day, introduced Freudian doctrine to general readers with an article on "The New Art of Interpreting Dreams"—that part of Freud's work that first attracted popular attention. Not long after, Freud's findings were expounded for a popular audience in a detective story, "The Dream Doctor," in which the key clue was the heroine's dream of a bull with the head of a former lover that turned into a snake. Lippmann wrote an unabashed panegyric to Freud in *The New Republic* in 1915. Articles appeared in *Century*, *McClure's*, and a half dozen other publications and Freudianism took root in popular culture.

World War I seemed to confirm Freud's theories about the irrational and brutal aspects of human nature, and wartime developments brought his work to public attention. Army intelligence tests used during the war plus the presence of a hundred psychologists on the surgeon general's staff helped make the nation psychology-conscious. Psychoanalytic theory also appeared effective in treating soldiers suffering from battle fatigue—then called shell shock—and restoring them to society. By the early 1920s, there were about five hundred Freudian and quasi-Freudian analysts in New York City and the center of psychiatry was shifting from Vienna to Park Avenue.

Psychoanalysis became popular, friends and foes agreed, because it was part of the liberating process, especially sexual liberation. "In his analyses of his patients' dreams and neuroses, [Freud] discovered what seemed to be an inherent conflict between the demands of human instinct, and the demands of society as a whole," wrote the social historian Robert M. Crunden. "The individual said, 'I want' and society, from its broader experience, said, 'You can't.'"

Popular writers produced a gallimaufry of articles and books with such titles as *Sex in Psychoanalysis*, *How to Psychoanalyze Yourself*, and the *Psychology of Golf*. Psychoanalysts were called in to testify in criminal trials such as the Loeb-Leopold case and journalists sought their opinions on social problems. *New Yorker* cartoons regularly featured bearded psychiatrists, patients, and couches. Newspaper and magazine readers became familiar with such concepts as the unconscious, sexuality, and repression, and people talked knowingly about the "libido," "defense mechanisms," and "fixation." Freud's name was offhandedly tossed about in *This Side of*

Paradise and *The Plastic Age*, another popular novel of the era. Psychiatry was also the center of gravity in Scott Fitzgerald's last completed novel, *Tender Is the Night*, written as Zelda descended into madness.

Sam Goldwyn, the producer, offered Freud $100,000 to write a "love story" for the movies. No one was better prepared than Freud, said Goldwyn, because of his mastery of "emotional motivations and suppressed desires."* Freud rejected the offer although he was acutely in need of money in the immediate postwar years. One quack, André Tridon, who wore open sandals and gilded his toenails for his "psychic teas" with women, superseded Freud's teachings with his own. He claimed in *Easy Lessons in Psychoanalysis* that the rice and old shoes thrown at a wedding were symbols of semen and female genitalia. Humorless, deeply conservative, and moralistic, Freud was not amused.

Freud's ideas—whether perfectly understood or not—were welcomed by American writers because they suggested new techniques for the exploration of human motivation. This attachment was not unexpected, because psychoanalysis is the most literary of the sciences—if it is a science—and Freud derived his labels for complexes from Greek mythology. Some of his disciples treated Shakespeare's characters as if they were actual people. Dr. Isadore Coriat blamed Shylock's vengeful wrath on "anal eroticism" and declared that Lady Macbeth had a repressed wish to have a child.

The audiences who flocked to see John Barrymore's production of *Hamlet* in 1922 were electrified not only by his genius but by his Freudian interpretation of the role. Freud had presented an Oedipal reading of Hamlet's character in *The Interpretation of Dreams*, and Barrymore utilized it. This Hamlet cannot kill Claudius because he wants to do what his uncle has done: kill his father and bed his mother. Blanche Yurka, the pretty actress who played Gertrude, was five years younger than Barrymore, and in their scenes together, they exuded a sexual tension that was palpable. Barrymore had extensive conversations with Dr. Brill as he prepared for his role.

Freud's greatest impact on literature was the stream-of-consciousness technique used by Joyce in *Ulysses* and by Faulkner in *The Sound and the Fury*. Karl Menninger, the Kansas psychiatrist and psychoanalyst, declared that Eugene O'Neill's dramas, with their obsessive characters and highly

---

* Goldwyn is also credited with saying, "Anyone seeing a psychiatrist should have his head examined."

charged language, introduced more people to psychoanalysis "than all the scientific books put together."

O'Neill's work plumbed the depths of human misery, reflecting his own tortured life. The son of James O'Neill, an actor who had become rich through his repeated appearances in a melodramatic *The Count of Monte Cristo*, and a morphine-addicted mother, O'Neill flirted with despair as long as he lived. Thrown out of Princeton after a freshman year largely spent drinking and chasing women, he prospected for gold in Honduras, became a newspaper reporter, an actor, and, most important for his later work, went to sea. All the while, O'Neill drank with a suicidal intensity. In 1912, he came down with tuberculosis and, with time on his hands as he recuperated in a sanatorium, systematically began to read the great dramatists. Strongly influenced by August Strindberg, he decided to write plays himself.

Bound East for Cardiff, O'Neill's first produced work, a one-act play presented in 1916 by the Provincetown Players on a stage hardly larger than a handkerchief, was based on his experience as a merchant seaman. In contrast to the trashy melodramas and the insipid musical comedies that ruled the American stage, it was starkly realistic. Several similar plays followed. As word of O'Neill's work spread, audiences flocked to the Village to sit on hard benches in a dim former stable to watch the birth of serious drama in the American theater.

In 1920, O'Neill moved uptown to Broadway with *The Emperor Jones*, the first American play to feature a black actor, Charles Gilpin. To the rising pounding of drums, the deposed dictator of a Caribbean country succumbs to fears that are, in reality, in his subconscious but appear physically present in the surrounding jungle. A mixture of German Expressionism and Freudian psychology dominated much of O'Neill's succeeding work, especially *Desire Under the Elms, Strange Interlude*, and *Mourning Becomes Electra*. All were sexually explicit dramatizations of mother-son attraction, incest, and murder.

Nevertheless, O'Neill defiantly refused to acknowledge any obligation to Freud. "I find fault with critics [who] read too damn much Freud into stuff that could very well have been written exactly as it is before psychoanalysis was ever heard of," he declared. Yet, *Electra*, the most Freudian of O'Neill's work, which centers on an Oedipal relationship, was begun after he had sought help from a psychoanalyst for his drinking and marital problems. The treatment appeared to be a success because, with the exception of a few lapses, O'Neill gave up alcohol. In all, he won four Pulitzer Prizes and is the only American playwright to be awarded the Nobel Prize for Literature. Toward the end of his troubled life, O'Neill distilled all his personal agony into the autobiographical *Long Day's Journey into Night*—"a play of old sorrow, written in tears and blood"—and the Mt. Everest of American drama.

"On a bright December morning in 1921," recalled poet Langston Hughes, "I came up out of the subway at 135th and Lenox into the beginnings of the Negro Renaissance." While young white writers found their Mecca in Paris, Harlem was the center of the cultural and intellectual life of black America during the Twenties. If you were black and wanted to write, you came to Harlem; if you were black and wanted to dance or sing, you came to Harlem; if you were black and wanted to effect social change, you came to Harlem. Harlem was more than a geographic location—it was the soul and heart of African-American culture.

Talented artists such as Hughes, fellow poets Countee Cullen and James Weldon Jones, novelists Claude McKay, Rudolph Fisher, Jean Toomer, Nella Larsen, Jessie Fauset, and Zora Neale Hurston, painter Aaron Douglas, and philosopher and first black Rhodes Scholar Alain Locke were only the best known of the hundreds of men and women who flocked to Harlem to join this vibrant colony. Like the white writers of the lost generation, black intellectuals considered themselves orphans—their people had been kidnapped from Africa and brought to an alien land—and they tried to create a culture that would be a source of pride and ultimate proof of their equality. Some, such as Toomer and Hurston, used the folk tales of the rural South as a foundation for their writing. Others, Larsen and McKay among them, wrote of the dilemma of the educated black cut off from his or her roots.

Harlem was in its glory in the late Twenties. The population of this city within a city had swelled to some 200,000 people, and the militant spirit of the "New Negro"—part of the legacy of Marcus Garvey—was in the air. Harlem was clean, it was prosperous, it was largely law-abiding. As a unique black city, it was shown off as an example of American democratic success. Harlem's residents ranged from dire poverty to substantial wealth, with the latter living in rows of handsome townhouses designed thirty years before by Stanford White for whites who never came, places known as Strivers Row and Sugar Hill.

The parties given by A'Leilia Walker, Harlem's wealthiest woman and daughter of Madame C. J. Walker, who had became rich from a hair culture business, rivaled in elegance and luxury those of white hostesses on Fifth

Avenue and Sutton Place. Langston Hughes crowned her "the joy-goddess of Harlem's 1920s." In fact, he later said that her death in 1931 marked the end of the Harlem Renaissance. At Mrs. Walker's parties, you met not only Harlem's social aristocracy but also its literary elite and members of the white intelligentsia. At the opposite end of the social scale was the rent party given by the tenant of a flat to raise the money to keep the landlord at bay. You brought your own liquor, paid a dollar to the host or hostess for admission, and joined the crowd. Sometimes there was music, sometimes not.

Whites flocked to Harlem jazz clubs and speakeasies such as the Cotton Club, the Savoy, Connie's Inn, and Small's Paradise for the music, excitement, alcohol, sex, and drugs. The Cotton Club, partly owned by the gangster Owney Madden, featured black talent but did not admit black customers.* At Small's, the waiters broke into a Charleston while carrying heavily laden trays. When these places closed at 2 A.M., the crowd moved on to Jungle Alley—Harlem's name for 133rd Street between Lenox and Seventh Avenues—home to dozens of all-night restaurants, cabarets, and nightclubs. The spirit of Harlem by night, exhilarating and sensuous, throbbing to the beat of drums and the wailing of saxophones, spread across the country, jumped the Atlantic, and became legend in London, Paris, and Berlin.

This explosion of cultural fireworks coincided with a trendy white interest in everything black. "It was the period when the Negro was in vogue," noted Hughes. *Survey Graphic,* a popular magazine, published a special issue devoted to the Harlem Renaissance, edited by Alain Locke. In the preface, he expressed a boundless optimism about the future: "We are witnessing the resurrection of a people." White patrons—satirically dubbed the "Niggerati" by Zora Hurston—such as critic and writer Carl Van Vechten championed black writers in the pages of *Vanity Fair* and helped get them published. Mencken opened *The Smart Set* and its successor, *The American Mercury,* to African-Americans. Between 1924 and 1933, he published fifty-four articles by and about blacks, despite his private prejudices. This dichotomy was most clearly exhibited in an article in the October 1927 issue of the *Mercury,* in which he proclaimed that America had

---

* Gangster ownership could under certain circumstances be a good thing for a nightclub. Duke Ellington and his band were scheduled to open at the Cotton Club on December 4, 1927, but the band had already agreed to appear that day at a theater in Philadelphia. Some mobsters made the theater owner "an offer he couldn't refuse" and Ellington opened as scheduled at the Cotton Club to begin a four-year stint that led to international fame through radio and records.

entered the "Coon Age." Even as he carelessly tossed off such demeaning words as "darkey" and "blackamoor," Mencken declared that much of what passed for American music, dance, cooking, language, church, and cabaret originated in black culture.

Eugene O'Neill examined, in *All God's Chillun Got Wings,* a marriage between a black man and white woman. He received death threats when he refused to change the final scene of the play in which the wife kisses the hand of her husband, played by the black actor Paul Robeson. Mencken printed the text in the *Mercury.* In 1927, *Porgy,* a play by Dorothy and DuBose Heyward about the black community in their native Charleston, was presented on Broadway and later became the basis of George Gershwin's folk opera, *Porgy and Bess.* That same year *Show Boat,* with its emphasis on race, alcoholism, and miscegenation, opened with a mixed cast and Jules Bledsoe singing "Old Man River." When the curtain fell on opening night, no one in the audience applauded; everybody was overcome by what they had seen. The reviews the next day proclaimed *Show Boat* the greatest musical in American theater history.

Paul Green's *In Abraham's Bosom,* a play about race relations in the rural South, won the Pulitzer Prize for drama in 1927. The most successful play with a black cast was *The Green Pastures,* which told the story of the Old Testament in terms of fable with Richard B. Harrison playing "de Lawd." Beginning in 1921, Eubie Blake and Noble Sissle's *Shuffle Along* led a succession of top-flight African-American musical reviews that introduced such black stars as Florence Mills, Bill "Bojangles" Robinson, Josephine Baker, and Ethel Waters to white audiences.

George S. Schuyler, a black writer who published numerous articles in white publications, presented a satirical account of the daily humiliation of being black in white America in *The Nation* of March 23, 1927:

Entering a restaurant . . . the customers look up, shocked and annoyed. Breaths are caught. The silence is ominous. What do I want. What would a person want in a restaurant? . . . I cannot help but enjoy all this. . . . Suppose I go to the theater. If it be in the liberal North or East, I approach the ticket window and ask for orchestra seats. . . . When seated I find that all the Negro audience is together. I indulge in a sardonic smile. . . . There is an empty seat [on the trolley] next to a rather dowdy female of the superior race. She is reading a tabloid . . . I take out my *New York Times.* She glances disdainfully at me . . . and moves as far away as possible. . . . Once I was offered a good job. . . . The position was secured by a friend over the telephone. The only slip was that my friend

neglected to mention that I was a Negro. When I walked into the palatial offices . . . there was much conferring and studied courtesy. I enjoyed
the whole thing hugely! Of course I didn't get the job. . . . Every night
the Negro is in danger. I walk down a dark street or cut across the park.
Suddenly, turning a corner, I come face to face with a white woman.
Will she get frightened and scream? I don't know.

The Harlem Renaissance's celebration of the urban culture of the black
masses did not sit well with the old black intelligentsia and members of the
new, upwardly mobile middle class. While they accepted a romanticized
version of black folklore and spirituals, they resented the emphasis by
Hughes and others on the rawness of black life. Similar attacks were made
against Van Vechten's novel *Nigger Heaven*, both because of its title and
subject matter, the way people lived in Harlem. In any event, the Great
Depression put an end to Harlem's Golden Age and its long descent into
poverty, drugs, and crime began. Some critics, Mencken among them,
lamented that no black writer had created a masterwork, but they forgot or
overlooked the fact that the Harlem Renaissance was a protest movement
as much as a literary movement. As such, it created a legacy of creativity
that served as a beacon to succeeding generations.

For all the later emphasis on the lost generation and literary modernism,
such writers as Hemingway, Fitzgerald, and Eliot were almost unknown to
ordinary American readers in the 1920s. Gene Stratton-Porter, Harold
Bell Wright, and Zane Grey were the most popular fiction writers of the
day. Their books appeared sixteen times on the national best-seller lists
between the end of the war and the Depression.* This trio may have been
outsold by Edgar Rice Burroughs's Tarzan books, the first of which was
published in 1914, but they were not taken seriously enough to be ranked.
Fitzgerald's *This Side of Paradise*, his most financially successful work,
which appeared in 1920, sold about fifty thousand copies; sales of Harold
Bell Wright's *The Re-Creation of Brian Kent*, published that same year,
approached a million copies.

Ordinary folk wanted escape from the present, and Porter, Wright, and
Grey supplied escapist material. Wright's books also had a strong religious
tone. They began appearing before the war and reflected the rural values
of the time. Plots and characters were one-dimensional—good always tri-

---

* Hemingway made the best-seller list for the first time in 1940 with the publication of
For Whom the Bell Tolls.

umphed, evil was confounded—and they featured sexless romance. These books appealed to "the kind of American whose eyes glazed and even dampened when they thought of the good old days when life was simple and generally lived in close proximity to nature," according to intellectual historian Roderick Nash.

Young, Harvard-educated Owen Wister, a friend of Theodore Roosevelt, introduced the western with *The Virginian* in 1902, and as the frontier faded into memory, Americans had an insatiable appetite for books about the West. Rex Beach, Emerson Hough, Peter B. Kyne, and James Oliver Curwood were familiar names to readers in the postwar years. All wrote books that were turned into movies; in fact, Beach's novel about the Alaskan gold rush, *The Spoilers*, was filmed repeatedly, with much attention lavished upon its classic fistfight.

Zane Grey, a dentist from Zanesville, Ohio, was the premier writer of westerns. Bored with his practice, he began writing novels and produced over eighty books. He created such staples of western fiction as the legendary lone gunfighter and the moralistic "Code of the West" in such books as *Lone Star Ranger* and *Riders of the Purple Sage*. Many Americans regarded him as the guardian of the nation's vanishing frontier heritage. "Never lay down your pen, Zane Grey," declared John Wanamaker, the department store tycoon. "You are distinctly and genuinely American."

In poetry, ordinary Americans, who had never heard of T. S. Eliot, preferred the homey rhymes of Edgar A. Guest, who had reversed the usual literary passage by going from Birmingham, England, to Detroit, Michigan. Robert A. Service, a minor-league Kipling who had made the trek to the Yukon, was another popular poet. He wrote about "strange doings in the land of the midnight sun" in "The Shooting of Dan McGrew" and the "The Cremation of Sam McGee"—much to the eternal delight of people who, after imbibing a few drinks, feel called upon to recite verse.

Bruce Barton's *The Man Nobody Knows* was the best-selling nonfiction book of the 1920s. Barton, a Congregational minister's son from Oak Park, the same Chicago suburb that produced Ernest Hemingway, portrayed Christ as a go-getting businessman.* He "picked up twelve men from the bottom ranks of business and forged them into an organization that conquered the world," according to Barton. Jesus was the most sought-after dinner guest in Jerusalem because of his vibrant personality, and his parables were "the most powerful advertisements of all time."

---

* Here, too, the 1920s showed the way to the future. A book named *Jesus, CEO* was published in 1995.

By and large, the nonfiction of the period was on a higher level. Charles and Mary Beard, the most influential historians of the day, stressed economic factors and promoted progressive principles in their widely read *The Rise of American Civilization*. Vernon L. Parrington presented some of the same themes in his massive study of the evolution of American culture, *Main Currents in American Thought*. Veteran progressive intellectuals such as Thorstein Veblen and John Dewey remained active and expounded on the need for "discipline" and experimentation in social policy.

Book sales and readership were given a spurt by the introduction of book clubs; the Book-of-the-Month Club began in 1926 and the Literary Guild the following year. The BOMC was the brainchild of Harry Scherman, who has been called "the greatest book salesman of all time." The increase in leisure and literacy had created a demand for books, but there were few bookstores in the United States. The circulation of Middletown's public library quadrupled while the population had doubled. Scherman, taking a leaf from Montgomery Ward and Sears Roebuck, decided to sell books by mail. The BOMC's selections had the imprimatur of a committee of distinguished literary lights, and the presence of these volumes in your living room testified to your cultural sensibilities. The first selection was a debunking biography of Anthony Comstock by Margaret Leech and Heywood Broun. Within a year, the club had over 100,000 members and was responsible for transforming book publishing from a cottage industry by helping create a mass market for books.

CHAPTER 11

"Whooping It Up for Genesis"

One evening in August 1915, a crowd gathered at a street corner in the small Ontario town of Mount Forest to watch a curious sight. A young woman with auburn hair and in a simple white dress was standing on a kitchen chair, motionless, silent, rigidly erect like a marble statue, with closed eyes and lifted arms, as if she were praying. A growing number of onlookers whispered, murmured, and speculated among themselves about what this meant. Suddenly, the woman's eyes snapped open. "People!" she shouted. "Come and follow me! Quick!" She jumped down from the chair and, with about fifty persons in tow, led them to a nearby storefront mission. When the last straggler was inside the shabby hall, her vibrant contralto voice commanded: "Shut the doors! Don't let anyone out!" Over the next forty minutes she presented a sermon that left her listeners exhausted.

Aimee Semple McPherson—soon to be billed as "the World's Most Pulchritudinous Evangelist"—had launched her remarkable career as Pentecostal preacher and saver of souls. Born on a nearby farm in 1890, Aimee Kennedy was still a teenager when she married a handsome, spellbinding evangelist named Robert Semple and accompanied him first to England and then to China as a missionary. When her husband died soon after their arrival in Hong Kong, the young widow returned with her child to Canada. She married a grocer named Harold McPherson, had another child, and left her husband, returning to the family farm.

Having heard the Lord's call following a near-death experience, Aimee advertised a revival meeting in Mount Forest. No one came. But God had told her to offer herself, and determined not to be foiled by man or the devil, she grabbed the chair and marched down Main Street to attract a crowd. The following night, word of her dynamic performance having spread, the mission was packed with a flock that overflowed into the street. By the end of the week, Aimee was preaching to as many as five hundred people a night, simple farmers and their wives eager "to give their hearts to the Lord"—and their "love offerings" to Sister Aimee.

Buoyed by this success, Aimee, her two children, and her mother, Minnie Kennedy, a onetime Salvation Army lassie, took to the road. She possessed only the barest essentials of the itinerant evangelist: an old car, a leaky tent, and a portable pulpit. "Jesus Is Coming Soon—Get Ready" was emblazoned on the side of the auto. Aimee drove, looked after the children, and helped raise the tent. Ma Kennedy served as business manager and supervised the collection.

Women preachers were a novelty, and the winsome Sister Aimee attracted attention. Over the next several years, she trekked through eastern Canada and the United States, traveling southward to Florida in winter and back north in summer. She preached and prayed for the healing of the sick in a hundred tank towns. "In summer and in winter, north or south," she recalled, "I worked by day and dreamed by night" of the day when she would have her own tabernacle. These were the years in which Aimee worked out the details of her Foursquare Gospel: salvation through Christ, the literal infallibility of the Bible, divine healing, and belief in the Second Coming. Aimee also became a practiced showman. Gradually, her audiences grew in size and their offerings became more generous. Her tent was replaced by hired lecture halls and civic auditoriums and the now well-dressed evangelist traveled by Pullman.

Over the next several years, Aimee barnstormed across the country and held revivals in Canada, New Zealand, and Australia. She distributed tracts from airplanes and preached in boxing arenas, where she had come to knock out the devil. All the while, she dreamed of the Zion of Southern California and saved every nickel for the temple she planned to erect in that land of milk and honey.

Revival meetings, a combination of crude theater and religious experience, were a familiar feature of life in rural America, and popular evangelists were treated like today's rock stars. In the eighteenth century, backwoods America was swept by a great religious awakening that was one of the precursors of the American Revolution. Up and down the Appalachian frontier, repentant sinners were overcome with religious ecstasy at camp meetings conducted by itinerant preachers in the light of flickering fires. Other revivals followed at periodic intervals.

Toward the end of the nineteenth century, Charles Darwin's theories of the origin of man triggered a new crisis of faith. The more liberal, sophisticated branches of Protestantism met the challenge by making adjustments in theology and downplaying the literalness of the Bible. They adopted the Social Gospel and tried to make the world better by fighting poverty, racism, and war.

Religion remained an important factor in American life, but its influence was declining. Although the number of Christian churches and Jewish temples rose from 210,000 in 1910 to 236,000 in 1926, the number of clergy declined along with their influence. Even worse, the faithful were less observant. The traditional Sabbath gave way to the Sunday drive in the country or baseball game or movie. "Three things may bind a member to his church: money contribution, attendance at services, and church work," the Lynds found in their study of Middletown. "Of these, the last is, according to the ministers, the least common."

Nevertheless, the old-time religion remained strong in the rural Baptist and Methodist strongholds of the South and West and among urban congregations made up of recent migrants from the countryside. What passed for reasonable doctrine in the pulpits of Episcopal and Unitarian churches was heresy to religious fundamentalists. Repelled by modernism, they were determined to maintain the centrality of religion in American life—a struggle that continues today. Appalled by the immoral movies coming out of Hollywood and the sight of women who wore short skirts and drank and smoked, the fundamentalists sought to purify American life and formed the core of Prohibition's defenders and the membership of the Ku Klux Klan. Insisting that the Bible be interpreted as fact, they expressed outrage at Darwinism and at any other challenge to the story of creation as related in the Bible. Humans had not evolved from lower orders of animals, the fundamentalists declared, but had been created by God in his own image as described in Genesis.

Revivalism again swept the country with Billy Sunday—the family name had once been Sontag—regarded as the king of the revivalists in terms of conversions and profits. Over a half century, he preached to 100 million people. The son of a Union soldier who had fallen sick and died, he grew up in an Iowa orphanage where he learned to play baseball. The boy became a star outfielder and base-stealer for the Chicago White Stockings (now the White Sox). Billy drank and chased women, until one day he "publicly accepted Christ as his Savior" after being moved by the come-to-Jesus hymns of a skid row mission. Refusing a $400-a-month contract offered by the White Stockings at a time when the average worker was lucky to earn that much in a year, he married and gave up baseball and liquor to become a traveling evangelist.

Sunday's sermons were full of fire and brimstone, and his two-fisted, bare-knuckles style of preaching appealed to blue-overalls audiences. He shadow-boxed with the devil, slid into bases ahead of a throw from Lucifer, and wound up like a pitcher about to unleash a fastball as he told audiences how David had hurled a stone that "soaked Goliath right between the lamps and he went down for the count." A minister who accepted evolution was in his view a "stinking skunk, a hypocrite and a liar," and as a leading prohibitionist he regarded the saloon as "the most damnable corrupt institution that ever wiggled out of hell."

Billy carried the banner of fundamentalism into Satan's own lair, holding mammoth revivals in New York, Chicago, Philadelphia, and other large cities. He was preceded by advance men who, borrowing from the circus and minstrel show, used preperformance parades to drum up crowds. He spoke in jerry-built wooden tabernacles with sawdust on the floor, and those who responded to his appeals to come to Christ were said to have "hit the sawdust trail." The tabernacles were left behind for the local ministers, who sponsored the revival and shared in the offerings of the saved. Tightly organized and run like a business, Sunday's crusades sold salvation with the ruthless efficiency of Henry Ford flogging Model Ts.

Billy Sunday was so famous that in 1914 he tied with Andrew Carnegie for eighth place in a national magazine poll to choose America's greatest man. John D. Rockefeller, a devout Baptist, called him "a rallying center around whom all people interested in good things may gather." Liberals complained, however, that his sermons contained a blend of political and cultural conservatism that played into the hands of big business and anti-union forces. "If I had my way with these ornery wild-eyed Socialists and IWWs, I would stand them up before a firing squad," said Billy. "America is not a country for a dissenter to live in." And he told his female listeners, "If some of you women would spend less on dope, pazzazza, and cold cream and get down on your knees and pray, God would make you prettier."

Sister Aimee offered a softer, less strident Christianity. At one of her meetings, she was annoyed when she heard an assistant shout to an indifferent bystander, "Brother, do you know you are on the way to perdition?" Even if it were true, she admonished, this was not the way to win souls for Christ. Aimee's religion was light on theology but heavy on hope and the helping hand. She substituted the Gospel of Love for the Gospel of Fear and delivered her followers from frightful visions of eternal damnation. She gave them flowers, music, singing, resounding trumpets, and sex appeal. "Who cares about the old Hell, friends?" she asked in a typical sermon. "We all know what Hell is . . . a terrible place no one wants to go. I

think the less we hear about Hell the better, don't you? Let's forget about
Hell. Lift up your hearts. What *we* are interested in, yes, Lord, is *Heaven*,
and how we get there!"

American messiahs, like the pioneers, have always looked westward,
and Aimee eventually made the trek to Los Angeles, already the center of
the movie business and various cults. Two days after her arrival, she held a
successful revival meeting and within a week was able to hire the largest
hall in town, which seated 3,500 people. "Heart-hungry multitudes came
and filled it to overflowing," she wrote. In 1921, Aimee set up shop in San
Diego, then known for its suicides and invalids. Between 1911 and 1927,
five hundred people killed themselves in the city, mostly, it was said,
because of despondency resulting from poor health. During one of Aimee's
open-air revivals in Balboa Park, a woman, said to be paralyzed since childhood, rose from her wheelchair in answer to Sister's call to come to Jesus
and took a few stumbling steps. A surge of hysteria gripped the audience as
other invalids pressed forward to her summoning embrace. "On they
came," she said, "hobbling up the steps with their crutches." A blind girl
said she could see, a deaf woman said she could hear.

Aimee never contended that she performed miracles or that she could
heal the sick. "I am not the healer," she said. "Jesus is the healer. I am only
a little office girl who opens the door and says, 'Come in.'" Once the word
spread that Aimee could cure the sick and lame, she was in the big time.
Her fame spread up and down the Pacific Coast and into the Midwest. In
the 1920s, an estimated 1.27 million new residents settled around teeming, sprawling Los Angeles, mostly transplanted Midwesterners, knowing
no one, puzzled by urban life and aching with loneliness. They found a
ready welcome in Sister Aimee's compassionate Church of the Foursquare
Gospel.

On January 1, 1923, amid the blare of golden trumpets, Aimee consecrated her $1.5 million stadium-sized Angelus Temple. Crushed seashells
mixed with concrete made the dome of the building glisten in the Southern California sunshine. At night, an electrically illuminated rotating cross
atop the temple could be seen for fifty miles. The main sanctuary seated
five thousand people and the building featured a powerful organ, the studios of KFSG, the third broadcasting station to go on the air in Los Angeles, a Bible school with thousands of students, a choir of one hundred, two
orchestras and a band, a lonely hearts club, a children's chapel, and a "Miracle Room" filled with discarded crutches, wheelchairs, and trusses left
behind by those cured by Aimee's ministrations. By placing her headquarters in a permanent tabernacle, she broke with the tradition of the travel-

ing revivalist exemplified by Billy Sunday, and the old tent show was soon relegated largely to the cultural backwaters of the South and Southwest.

Specially chartered streetcars unloaded thousands of believers who kept the temple's seats and the collection plates filled. The take totaled thousands of dollars a week—all cash. "Put your willing hand in your pocket, praise God, and bring out a five-dollar bill!" counseled Aimee when the collection was being taken. While she kept her eyes on heaven, tough and tight-fisted Ma Kennedy ran the business side of this multimillion-dollar enterprise. When the staff begged for a switchboard so they could make outgoing private telephone calls, she had pay phones installed in the lobby.

Billy Sunday turned fundamentalism into big business; Sister Aimee took a leaf from nearby Hollywood and made it into a branch of show business, complete with elaborate productions worthy of Cecil B. DeMille and King Vidor. Charlie Chaplin advised her on some of her sets and she obtained costumes, props, and scenery from the studios. She presided over services from a throne on a dais just below the organ loft, bathed in a creamy light and clad in flowing robes while carrying a small bouquet of flowers.

Sister Aimee urged sinners to come forward to the altar at the end of every sermon. "If you are unsaved come quickly to Jesus," she declared in a tender and compassionate voice. "Rise from your seats—make your way to Him." Lights were dimmed, the music became mournful and pleading as the solemn procession came down from the top gallery and the balcony and up the aisles toward her. Each convert was supported by a personal guide who had unexpectedly materialized at his or her side. And then Aimee would suddenly shout: "Ushers! Jump to it! Turn on the lights and clear a one-way street for Jesus!" The organ now boomed out and the temple rocked with excitement. Even a doubting newsman admitted that he had craned his neck to the entrance with the expectation of seeing Jesus.

In the space of only a few years, Aimee's empire spread well beyond the Angelus Temple. Acolytes prayed around the clock in response to the ten thousand "requests for prayer" received from around the world every month—each accompanied by an offering. She baptized some forty thousand people, established four hundred branch churches, or "lighthouses," and opened 178 missionary stations. The Foursquare City Sisters passed out food and clothing to the needy and nursed the sick while the men of the congregation provided jobs for the unemployed and ex-convicts. Aimee shrewdly assessed her audience. "I bring religious consolation to the great middle class leaving those below to the Salvation Army and those above to themselves."

Radio station KFSG carried her unforgettable voice to millions of worshippers rather than mere hundreds, establishing the pattern for today's television evangelists. The station was so powerful that it jumped across its assigned wave band and disrupted other stations. Reprimanded by Commerce Secretary Herbert Hoover, who was trying to bring order to the Babel of the airwaves, Aimee responded: "Please order your minions of Satan to leave my station alone. You cannot expect the Almighty to abide by your wave-length nonsense. When I offer my prayers to Him, I must fit into His wave-length reception."

Sister Aimee was in the top rank of Southern California's evangelists when, one day in May 1926, she went swimming off Venice Beach near Los Angles. Before going in, she sent her secretary on an errand; when the woman returned, Aimee had disappeared. She was presumed to have drowned. Thousands of nearly hysterical faithful swarmed to the scene to scan the horizon, sing hymns, and pray for her return. Fishermen dragged the area and divers searched in vain for her body. One diver died of exposure, a girl committed suicide, and a man flung himself into the sea, crying "I'm going after her!" and drowned. Front-page stories filled newspapers all over the country. "We know she is with Jesus," Ma Kennedy consoled a huge crowd of bereaved mourners at a twelve-hour memorial service at the Angelus Temple.

A month later, Aimee's followers hailed a miracle as she stumbled out of the desert near the Mexican border with a strange story. Sister claimed to have been kidnapped, tortured, drugged, and held for ransom in a shack in Mexico by "Steve," "Jake," and "Mexicali Rose." The kidnappers became careless, and she had escaped and walked thirteen hours to civilization— or so she said. Yet, as the faithful rejoiced that Sister had emerged from her Gethsemane, her return was surrounded by suspicious circumstances. Aimee showed no signs of the effects of torture, captivity, or a grueling hike in the hot desert sun, and while she was wearing only a pea-green bathing suit when she disappeared, she was fully clothed, including her corset, when found.

No trace of the kidnappers or their shack was discovered, and rumors spread that she had really gone into hiding to have an abortion or cosmetic surgery. Others suspected that Aimee had enjoyed a romantic fling with Kenneth Ormiston, a bald, wooden-legged radio technician at KFSG, who had been reported missing by his wife at the time of her disappearance. Witnesses said they saw Ormiston traveling with a woman who matched Aimee's description. The couple were also said to have hidden out in a love nest at Carmel up the Pacific Coast.

Asa Keyes, the Los Angeles district attorney, hauled Aimee before a grand jury and charged her with obstruction of justice when she stuck to the kidnapping story. Ormiston, while gallantly refusing to identify his companion, maintained it was not Aimee. This spectacular mixture of sex, mystery, and religion created the first celebrity media circus of the century, and an army of reporters from around the world pursued the story. The line between news and entertainment was blurred in a fashion that was to become increasingly familiar.

Aimee claimed that she was the innocent victim of a conspiracy by mobsters, who were trying to discredit her because she had shown so many prostitutes the way to a better life. The hellfire-and-brimstone fundamentalist clergy of Los Angeles, jealous of her success, bayed loudest for her conviction. The faithful responded with a $250,000 Fight-the-Devil Fund. And then, without explanation, the charges were dropped and Aimee returned to her throne. District Attorney Keyes was notoriously corrupt— indeed, he was later convicted of bribery in an oil swindle—and there was talk that large sums of money had changed hands to quash the case. Aimee's followers welcomed her back to her tabernacle. Nevertheless, rumors and ribald stories swirled about Sister Aimee for the rest of her life. Sinclair Lewis's gamy 1927 exposé of revivalist preachers, *Elmer Gantry*, which featured an Aimee-like evangelist among its characters, also did her no good. Loyal followers protested that the Gospel was being reversed— the Crucifixion was taking place after the Resurrection—but her star dimmed as new messiahs rose in the Southern California firmament.

Sister Aimee married for a third time in 1931—violating her own edict that divorced persons could not remarry and remain within the church— and was divorced again a few years later. A total of fifty-five lawsuits were entered against her for one reason or another, she fought with her mother over money, and members of her flock began to stray. Aimee continued to preach, but worn out and depressed, she died in 1944 at the age of fifty-four from an overdose of sleeping pills. She was buried in Forest Lawn Cemetery amid the movie stars she so much resembled. This time there was no resurrection. Sixty years later, the Church of the Foursquare Gospel still exists, and having reversed the setbacks of Aimee's last years, claims over two million members worldwide.

* * *

Henry Mencken was completely taken with Sister Aimee. He went to hear her several times while visiting Hollywood and enthusiastically claimed to have been baptized. "You have no idea of the peace that it has brought to my soul," he declared. Mencken's usual contact with religion was to lift Gideon Bibles from hotel rooms and send them to friends, signed "With the Compliments of the Author." His interest in Aimee seemed more carnal than spiritual. A discerning judge of feminine pulchritude, he wrote of "her shiny eyes, her mahogany hair, her eloquent hips and her lascivious voice" and nominated her for Miss America. "Her Sex Appeal is tremendous."

The Sage of Baltimore was at the height of his influence in the mid-1920s. *The Smart Set*, which he had co-edited with George Jean Nathan since 1914, was primarily a literary magazine. It was the first to publish James Joyce in America, and championed such realists as Frank Norris, Theodore Dreiser, and Sinclair Lewis. But Mencken's real interest was politics and social comment rather than literature. In January 1924, he and Nathan brought out a new publication, *The American Mercury*, which covered politics, social criticism, the arts, science, and medicine as well as literature.

Mencken's intention was "to combat, chiefly by ridicule, American piety, stupidity, tin-pot morality, [and] cheap chauvinism in all their forms." In the pages of the *Mercury* he railed against the stupidities of democracy, relished the bizarre, and pummeled the puritans and prohibitionists. Young and promising writers swarmed to him and Mencken published the writings of blacks, penitentiary inmates, prostitutes, and vagrants—anyone who had something interesting to say. "Uplift has damn nigh ruined the country," he wrote. "What we need is more sin."

The magazine was introduced at a happy time for new periodicals: *Reader's Digest* was founded in 1922 and *Time* in 1923, the latter the brainchild of Henry R. Luce and Briton Hadden, Yale classmates. Harold Ross brought out *The New Yorker* in 1925. The *Mercury*'s circulation mushroomed to over sixty thousand copies a month, a large number for a 50 cent magazine, and its arsenic green cover was a familiar sight on the nation's campuses and in editorial offices. No one with any pretense to intellectual standing could be without it. Mencken was idealized by sophisticated young people in revolt against everything their parents held sacred. He was soon the most denounced man in the country and, according to the *New York Times*, "the most powerful private citizen in the United States."

* * *

Henry Louis Mencken was born in Baltimore on September 12, 1880—a
local holiday called Defenders' Day*—into a solidly bourgeois German
family. "H. L. Mencken" came along eight years later. August Mencken, his
father and owner of a prosperous tobacco factory, gave the boy a small
printing press for Christmas, but all the r's were accidentally ruined. Harry,
as he was known to his family, henceforth printed his name as H. L.
Mencken.

"The printing press . . . left its mark, not only upon my hands, face and
clothing, but also on my psyche," Mencken recalled, and from then on his
ambition was to be a newspaperman. He read everything about journalism
he could find in the local public library, including the works of Stephen
Crane and swashbuckling Richard Harding Davis, and took a correspondence course on the subject. He also discovered *Huckleberry Finn*, an event
described as "the most stupendous in my life," and read furiously after that.
"I doubt that any human being in the world has ever read more than I did
between my twelfth and eighteenth years," he said. The boy attended a
German grammar school where he learned the language and was incul-
cated with German culture, and then went on to the Baltimore Polytech-
nic Institute.†

Upon graduation from high school at sixteen, first in his class, Mencken's
formal education ended. He wanted to get a job as a reporter but August
Mencken said no—he could either attend college and prepare for a professional career or go into the family tobacco factory. He chose the tobacco
business and dutifully stuck it out for more than two years. Within days of
his father's death in 1899, he turned up in the city room of the *Baltimore
Morning Herald*, and after hanging around for several nights, was given
a trial.

Taken on as a reporter at the munificent salary of $7 a week, he learned
the essentials of the newspaperman's trade: to be observant, to make certain he had the names in a story down accurately—including all the middle initials—and to be quick. There were two telephones in the *Herald*
office but most news was gathered by legwork. The young reporter, with his
sand-colored hair slicked down and parted in the middle, jug ears and

---

* The anniversary of the Battle of North Point, in which a British army was driven from
Baltimore during the War of 1812. Two days later, Francis Scott Key wrote "The Star-
Spangled Banner" during a land-sea attack on Fort McHenry in Baltimore Harbor.

†Mencken is not the only important literary figure to attend the school; Dashiell Hammett went there briefly, and like Mencken, did not go to college

china blue eyes, became a familiar figure in the police stations, waterfront saloons, and bawdy houses, where he liked to play the piano.*

Looking back nearly a half century later, Mencken told an interviewer:

> Most men that escape college have a regret that pursues them, but I must confess I am much too vain to have any such regrets. I think of what I was doing when the boys in my generation were in college listening to idiot lectures and cheering football games. . . . I was a young reporter on the street. . . . I believe that a young newspaper reporter in a big city at that time led a life that has never been matched on earth for romance and interest.

Something of a boy wonder, Mencken rose rapidly, moving up from police reporter to City Hall at nineteen, to star reporter assigned all the best stories at twenty, and at twenty-three, to city editor. Some times he filled in as drama or music critic. The *Herald* was no match for the *Baltimore Sun* in size of staff, circulation, and influence, but the latter sheet was staid and colorless and most of its reporters wrote like "bookkeepers," according to Mencken. To compete, he emphasized breezy writing and scoops as both a reporter and editor, even though he always believed scoops were usually bad, hastily reported stories.

On the morning of February 7, 1904, a Sunday, the youthful editor was sleeping off a long night at work followed by a session at a late-hours saloon, when he was awakened and told that a huge fire had broken out downtown. Mencken hastened to the office to put out an extra and for the next three days worked around the clock directing coverage, editing copy, and writing headlines. Feeding off the contents of a warehouse full of whiskey, the fire burned out a square mile of the heart of Baltimore before it was brought under control. When the *Herald* building went up in flames, Mencken hopped on a train and got the paper out on the presses of the *Washington Post*.

The *Herald* did not long survive its return to Baltimore and Mencken, who had by then become editor, leaped from the wreckage to the *Sun*, after turning down an offer from the *New York Times*. This relationship lasted

* In later years, after Mencken became friendly with Nicholas Longworth, the speaker of the House of Representatives and Theodore Roosevelt's son-in-law, Longworth confided that as a young man he, too, had played the piano in a sporting house in his native Cincinnati. From then on, they called each other "Professor." (Mencken, *Thirty-Five Years of Newspaper Work*, pp. 168–70.)

the rest of his life. He became Sunday editor, participated in the development of a new evening edition, and began writing a daily column called *The Free Lance*. A one-man wrecking crew, he was the terror of politicians, churchmen, businessmen, fanatics, and the respectable citizenry. His reputation as a foe of the established order achieved national status with his books, articles, and editorship of *The Smart Set* and, later, the *Mercury*. He was combative, rude, and rollicking and threw off ideas, opinions, and denunciations with the volatility of a human firecracker.

The Twenties were made to order for Mencken. Harding and Coolidge inspired him to new heights of ridicule and invective. The "numskull Gamaliel" was treated with comic contempt, and his successor was described as "a cheap and trashy fellow . . . a dreadful little cad." He despised the materialism of the Babbitts, whom he invariably referred to as *Boobus Americanus*, and had no confidence in the common man's ability to govern or even to think. He attacked the South as "the Sahara of the Bozart," and denounced fundamentalists and the Klan. "Heave an egg out of a Pullman and you will hit a fundamentalist almost everywhere in the United States," he declared. Most of all, he hated puritanism, "with its gross and nauseating hypocrisies."

His celebrated style had already emerged. Mencken admired Mark Twain's frontier-motivated exaggerations, and was influenced by Ambrose Bierce's cynicism, the malicious satire of George Bernard Shaw, and Friedrich Nietzsche's use of outlandish hyperbole. Wild exaggeration was used for effect, although it was always leavened with some truth. The elixir distilled from this mixture was all his own: pure, unadulterated, 100-proof, bottled-in-bond Mencken. To this, he added the knack of making each reader feel that he or she was having a laugh with the author, at everyone else's expense.

Imitators of Mencken's style are legion but no one has ever quite caught the good-natured ferocity, sparkle, and sheer joy of his prose. Criticism must be done boldly, he said, and to get a crowd, cruelly. Mencken saw himself as a social critic, but he was in reality a moralist, decrying the erosion of American values with a bitter humor. His best work still prompts belly laughs, even though the targets are now largely forgotten.

Mencken fired off opinions like scattershot:

On puritanism—"The haunting fear that someone, somewhere, may be happy."

On the South—"The bunghole of the United States, a cesspool of Baptists, a miasma of Methodism, snake-charmers, phony real-estate operators and syphilitic evangelists."

On conscience—"The inner voice which warns us that someone may be looking."

On justice—"Injustice is relatively easy to bear; what stings is justice."

On philosophy—"One horselaugh is worth ten thousand syllogisms."

On God—"God is the immemorial refuge of the incompetent, the helpless, the miserable."

From the pulpit and in the newspapers and lecture halls, Mencken was denounced as an ape, a dog, a weasel, a maggot, a ghoul, a jackal, a tadpole, a tiger, a howling hyena, a bilious buffoon, a cad, a British toady, a German spy, a cankerworm, a clever and bitter Jew, a mountebank, a radical, a dangerous Red, and a reactionary. "Shocking," said the *Brooklyn Eagle*. "A national menace," agreed the *Muskogee Times-Democrat*. Arkansas's Ku Klux Klan passed a resolution condemning "in the strongest language the vile mouthings of this prince of blackguards." And the Baltimore Chamber of Commerce added its voice to the protests on grounds that Mencken was bad for the city's business with the South. The target of all this billingsgate was delighted and collected the choicer bits of calumny into a self-promoting little book called *Menckeniana: A Schimpflexicon*.

Once, the joke was on him. Mencken was invited to speak at Goucher, a woman's college in Baltimore, and the confirmed bachelor addressed the students on "How to Catch a Husband." That evening, he was introduced to Sara Powell Haardt, an instructor in English and a short story writer. He was immediately smitten. Sara was gracious and charming and had a haunting, camelia-like beauty. She was from Montgomery, Alabama, and knew Zelda Fitzgerald. Mencken broke off his relations with other women, among them screen star Aileen Pringle, and following a lengthy courtship, he and Sara married in 1930. They had debated marriage for such a long time because he was eighteen years her senior and her health was delicate. Sara's doctor privately told Mencken she had probably no more than three years to live. Nevertheless, they had nearly five years together, a period he called the happiest of his life, and he missed her terribly after she died of meningitis. "I still think of Sara every day of my life, and almost every hour of the day," he confided to his diary on the fifth anniversary of her death.

Young rebels found their unspoken thoughts brilliantly expressed by Mencken. When he wrote of "a culture that . . . is in three layers—the plutocracy on top, a vast mass of undifferentiated human blanks bossed by demagogues at bottom, and a forlorn *intelligentsia* gasping out a precarious life in between," the aesthetes saw their position perfectly described. Yet no one was more surprised than Mencken himself to be regarded by these insurgents as one of them. For one thing, he had little sympathy for liberal or radical goals. Basically, his politics were libertarian and he believed with Jefferson that less government was the best government. This was later to make him a bitter enemy of the New Deal. In his own way, he was a demo-crat. The purpose of his denunciations was to show just how far the United States had strayed from the ideals of true freedom.

Nor was Mencken in sympathy with the skimpily dressed flapper and her baggy-trousered, raccoon-coated escort. In morals, he was a Victorian and angrily decried the loss of the values he thought necessary for a humane and civilized society. The new freedom flaunted by American women scandalized him as much as it did middle-class America. While he challenged old and established ways of thinking with exuberance and bold-ness, it was not to further any specific agenda, but to scold in his role as an eternal skeptic.

Yet for all his denunciations against the imbecilities and miseries of life in the United States, Mencken was fascinated by the "gaudy spectacle" set before him. He found the people, culture, language, literature, institutions, and politics of his native land endlessly intriguing, and he viewed them with an exasperated affection. Even his attacks on the South had a positive effect, because they were instrumental in bringing about a revival of Southern letters. He supported the editors of experimental magazines in Richmond, New Orleans, and "out in trackless, unexplored Arkansas." And he encouraged the group of novelists, poets, and critics centered around Vanderbilt University in Nashville, known as the "Fugitives" and the "Agrarians," to speak out against philistinism. A portion of W. J. Cash's classic *Mind of the South* appeared in the *Mercury* in October 1929.

"My literary theory, like my politics, is based upon one idea, to wit, the idea of freedom," Mencken declared. "I . . . can imagine no human right that is half as valuable as the simple right to pursue the truth at discretion and utter it where found." He vigorously opposed all attempts to silence free speech, even for those with whom he was in complete disagreement. He not only opposed the deportation of anarchist Emma Goldman but urged the government to allow her to return to the United States. The defense of free speech required eternal vigilance, Mencken noted, because "the American people really detest free speech. At the slightest alarm, they are ready and eager to put it down."

The Comstocks—the censors and book-banners—were always ready to emasculate any work of genius, he warned.* In Knoxville, Tennessee, a civic leader named Mary Boyce Temple advocated the suppression of *Rain*, a play based upon a story by Somerset Maugham that featured a prostitute. Temple said she had not seen the play or even read the story, but that was not important. Senator Reed Smoot of Utah demanded that such books as *Ulysses* be banned from entering the country. "I would rather a child of mine take opium than read one of these books," he declared. "I would rather keep out a thousand, than have one mistake made." James Branch Cabell's novel *Jurgen* was banned as pornographic even though it was written in an almost impenetrable style.

Small towns populated by "yokels" and the "booboisie" did not have a monopoly on prudery. In New York City, Mae West and the producers of her play *Sex* were arrested for putting on an indecent performance. West argued that sex was part of human life, but was sentenced to ten days in the workhouse—and she greatly enjoyed the notoriety. *The Captive*, a play about the breakup of a marriage engineered by the wife's lesbian lover, was closed by the police and the cast was arrested on obscenity charges. In 1927, the state legislature passed a law forbidding the presentation on stage of any work portraying "sex perversion." It remained in effect until 1967.

The hand of the censor fell most heavily upon motion pictures—and with the connivance of the film industry. From almost the beginning, moralists attacked the movies for licentiousness, low morals, and sexual laxity. Sex was a bankable commodity and the early moviemakers traded heavily in it. Taking advantage of the changing sexual attitudes following the war, they marketed such provocative titles as *Red Hot Romance*, *A Virgin Paradise*, and *Women Who Give*. Cecil B. DeMille spared no opportunity to exhibit bare female flesh in his biblical epics and Hunt Stromberg let it be known that he wanted "lots of tits" in *White Shadows in the South Seas*.

DeMille outdid the others in loading his films with sex, including *King of Kings*, ostensibly a biography of Christ. Rather than beginning with his birth in the manager, the camera zooms in on Mary Magdalene, who is wallowing near-naked in Babylonian-style splendor while pining away for her lover, Judas, who is wandering around with a troupe of beggars led by a carpenter named Jesus. "Ha!" says she to a servant: "Harness my zebras!"

---

* Anthony Comstock (1844–1915) was a crusader for "decency" in literature and painting. Unable to distinguish between art and pornography, he frequently attacked works of artistic and literary merit as "lewd."

Self-appointed guardians of public morality, such as the Women's Christian Temperance Union, the Federal Motion Picture Council, and the Catholic Church, called for government censorship. They noted that in 1915, the Supreme Court had ruled that making movies was a business, was thereby subject to prior restraint, and could not claim protection under the free speech clause of the First Amendment. Inasmuch as most of the movie moguls were Jews, there was an overtone of anti-Semitism in these demands for censorship; the men were charged with willfully corrupting the morals of Christians. In a tract entitled *Catechism of Motion Pictures in Inter-State Commerce*, the Reverend William S. Chase asked: "Shall no effective control be exercised over these Jews to prevent their showing such pictures as will bring them the greatest financial returns, irrespective of the moral injury they inflict upon the public?"

Hollywood was engulfed by a number of sordid sex scandals and there were rumors of riotous parties, widespread homosexuality, drinking, and narcotics addiction, all of which encouraged the clamor for censorship. In 1921, Roscoe "Fatty" Arbuckle, a popular film comedian, was charged with homicide in the death of a sometimes actress named Virginia Rappe, who died after a wild party in a San Francisco hotel. Her death was attributed to internal injuries and the press reported Arbuckle had raped her with a soda bottle. In actuality, her death resulted from a botched abortion. Arbuckle was acquitted after three stormy trials, but his career was ruined.

A year after, William Desmond Taylor, a prominent director, was shot to death, and two young stars, Mabel Normand and the teenage Mary Miles Minter, were romantically linked to him. The case was never solved.* Some reports tied Taylor to a Hollywood narcotics ring that included romantic star Wallace Reid, who died not long after from a morphine overdose.

The moguls were terrified that these and other scandals would inspire Congress to impose government censorship upon the industry. "Hollywood is a colony of . . . people where debauchery, riotous living, drunkenness, ribaldry, dissipation [and] free love seem to be conspicuous," thundered one U.S. senator. Following the example of organized baseball, which hired

---

* Director King Vidor launched his own private investigation of the case in 1967 and concluded that Taylor was shot by Charlotte Shelby, whose daughter, Mary Miles Minter, was having an affair with the director. She was purportedly afraid that Taylor would interfere with her influence over her daughter and her career. In an account of Vidor's inquiry, Sidney D. Kirkpatrick claimed Shelby paid as much as $750,000 in blackmail money to Asa Keyes, the corrupt Los Angeles district attorney, and others, to block an indictment. See Kirkpatrick, *A Cast of Killers*.

Judge Kenesaw Mountain Landis* to restore the game's image after the "Black Sox" scandal of 1919, they created the post of movie czar and gave it to Will Hays, former chairman of the Republican National Committee and postmaster general in President Harding's cabinet.

Hays, head of the newly organized Motion Picture Producers and Distributors of America at a yearly salary of $100,000, used his influence in Washington to block federal censorship and the formation of censorship boards in all but six states.† Hays inserted a "morals clause" in the contracts signed by movie stars that permitted the studios to cancel a contract for even the slightest hint of turpitude. Only Rin-Tin-Tin was said to be absolved from the clause. The studios also voluntarily agreed to submit all scripts to the Hays Office to ensure that they contained no questionable material. Hays's most brilliant ploy was to involve the groups urging censorship in the creation of the Production Code. Satisfied with the lengthy list of dos and don'ts, they dropped their demands for government controls. Barred from the screen were profanity, licentiousness, nudity, illegal drugs, sexual perversion, white slavery, miscegenation, venereal disease, childbirth, children's sex organs, ridicule of the clergy, and insults to nations, creeds, and races. For the next four decades, married couples in the movies always slept in twin beds, wore pajamas and nightgowns, and kept one foot on the floor when lying down together.

Mencken had his own run-in with the censors. In 1926, Boston's Watch and Ward Society banned the sale of the April issue of the *Mercury* on grounds that it contained a "filthy and degrading" article called "Hatrack" about a prairie-town prostitute. Watch and Ward was an alliance of traditional Boston bluenoses and puritanical Irish Catholics and was responsible for the banning of books by, among others, Aldous Huxley, John Dos Passos, and Sherwood Anderson.

The penalty for selling the banned magazine was a stiff fine or two years in jail, but Mencken decided to chance it in order to rally nationwide opposition to censorship. Having obtained a peddler's permit, he proceeded to Brimstone Corner, where the Park Street Church faces Boston Common. By prearrangement, he sold a copy of the outlawed magazine to an official of the Watch and Ward Society and was immediately arrested.

---

* Landis was named after the Battle of Kenesaw Mountain, outside Atlanta, where in 1864 his father, a Union soldier, had lost a leg.

† One of them was Mencken's own Maryland.

He bit into the 50-cent piece to see if it was sound as a large crowd of Harvard and Radcliffe students cheered. To Mencken's utter chagrin, the case against him was dismissed the next day by a magistrate who read the article and found nothing obscene. But the society persuaded the Post Office to bar the issue from the mails, and Mencken feared a permanent ban. An extensive—and expensive—legal fight followed before the issue was resolved in Mencken's favor.

There was a dark side to Mencken's work, however. Although he attacked bigotry in all its forms, his writing contained a strain of anti-Semitism, even though in his productive years most of his friends were Jews. Moreover, while he was a vital force in the Harlem Renaissance, his attitude toward blacks was a mixture of egalitarianism and patronizing superiority. Although he despised Hitler, he never publicly denounced him. In his posthumously published memoirs, Mencken gave his reason. When some leading American Jews insisted upon such a disavowal "categorically and at once," his response was typically and stubbornly Menckenian: "In the face of their attempt to browbeat me I could only refuse to write a line."*

Mencken, in common with followers of the more liberal religious creeds, regarded fundamentalist evangelicism with contempt, but he viewed one aspect of it with real alarm. Having written their views about alcohol into the U.S. Constitution, the fundamentalists were demanding legislation to

---

* Mencken's diary and two volumes of memoirs, published twenty-five years after his death, contained slurs against Jews and blacks, and prompted uninformed critics to charge that he was a Nazi or at the least a racist. He was neither. Basically, Mencken's private thinking reflected his German background and the general atmosphere of the Baltimore of his times, which was very much a Southern town where such sentiments were common. Besides, he was an equal-opportunity hater. He attacked the British, evangelical preachers, politicians, and feminists, and wrote even worse things about the "yokels" of Appalachia, whom he regarded as subhuman, than he ever did about the Jews or blacks. Nor is there any record that he ever committed a racist or anti-Semitic act or allowed such views to influence his critical judgment. Did he expect these thoughts to see the light of day? I think so, because he never wrote a word that was not intended for publication. Mencken probably relished the thought that well after he was dead, the publication of his private musings would again make him a controversial figure.

It is worth noting that on November 17, 1938—after Kristallnacht and long before anyone else cared—Mencken wrote a column in the *Sun* urging the government to relax the immigration laws to permit the Jews of Germany to come to America. "Why shouldn't the United States take in a couple of hundred thousands of them, or even all of them?" he

forbid the teaching of evolution in the public schools. "Read the Bible," counseled a Georgia assemblyman. "It teaches you how to act. Read the hymn book. It contains the finest poetry ever written. Read the almanac. It shows you how to figure out what the weather will be. There isn't another book that is necessary for anyone to read, and therefore I am opposed to all libraries."

To modernists, Darwinism was unvarnished scientific fact; if teachers were forbidden to teach evolution it would be tantamount to being forbidden to teach that the earth was round. They claimed the creationists questioned not only Darwinian theory, but the scientific method that makes contemporary civilization possible. With incredulity, they watched as lawmakers in fifteen states seriously considered the demands of the creationists. Kentucky failed to pass an anti-evolution law in 1922 by only a single vote. In March 1925, the Tennessee legislature, with the support of the Klan, approved the Butler Act, making it illegal for any public school teacher "to teach any theory that denies the story of the Divine Creation of man as taught in the Bible."

Not long after, a group of men gathered at a table in Robinson's Drugstore, the social center of Dayton, a town of some two thousand people in the foothills of the Cumberlands, to discuss these events. They included George Rappelyea, a transplanted New Yorker who managed the local branch of the Cumberland Coal and Iron Company, a couple of attorneys, and the superintendent of the Rhea County schools. Rappelyea, a free thinker, hated the fundamentalism espoused by most of the locals and was upset by the anti-evolution law. He told his companions he had seen an article in a Chattanooga paper in which the American Civil Liberties Union offered to defend any schoolteacher willing to be a legal guinea pig and contest the law. With a certain amount of guile, Rappelyea pointed out that if such a trial were held in Dayton, it would attract national attention and, even more important, tourist dollars and new businesses.

Who was to be the sacrificial lamb? Frank Robinson, owner of the drugstore and school board president, suggested John T. Scopes, a twenty-four-

---

asked. No one acted on the suggestion, although Mencken personally assisted several European Jews to come to America at considerable trouble and expense to himself. And the last thing he wrote before being silenced by a disabling stroke, a column published on November 9, 1948, was a vigorous condemnation of a ruling by the segregationist Baltimore Park Board forbidding whites and blacks from playing tennis together on city-owned courts. "It is high time," he declared, "that all such relics of Ku Kluxry be wiped out in Maryland."

year-old science instructor at the Dayton High School who doubled as athletic coach and substitute biology teacher. Unmarried, popular, and modest, he seemed ideal for the assignment. Scopes was summoned, perspiring from the tennis court.

"John, we've been arguing," said Rappleyea, "and I said that nobody could teach biology without teaching evolution."

"That's right," replied Scopes.

He went on to explain that evolution formed an integral part of the official textbook, Hunter's *Civic Biology*, used in the high school. He acknowledged having taught evolution in his biology class and after some hesitation agreed to be arrested. An exultant Rappelyea contacted the ACLU, and it assigned two well-known attorneys, Dudley Field Malone and Arthur Garfield Hayes, to the defense.

Out of this friendly conspiracy arranged over Coca-Colas emerged one of the most celebrated trials in American legal history. "The Monkey Trial," as Mencken labeled it, brought the struggle between traditionalism and modernism and between Main Street and the metropolis out into the open. He was involved in writing the script from almost the very beginning. In fact, Scopes later remarked that the entire episode "was Mencken's show." Mencken pounced upon the story early on and the *Baltimore Evening Sun*, his paper, posted $500 bail for Scopes. What would have normally been a simple misdemeanor trial lasting but a few hours was transformed into a major media event, and Scopes became all but an afterthought because of the high-profile players attracted to the case.

Newspaper stories about Scopes's arrest caught the attention of William Jennings Bryan, who offered his services to the prosecution. Bryan, who had made a fortune in the Florida real estate boom, saw the fight for Genesis as an opportunity to muster support for a fourth run at the presidency. Today, largely because of the Scopes trial, Bryan is regarded as a pompous know-nothing, but few American political leaders had greater success at that time in capturing the hearts and minds of ordinary people. A resolute champion of social justice at home, Bryan was an advocate of international understanding and peace abroad. He was the first major party presidential candidate to advocate such reforms as breaking up trusts, the direct election of U.S. senators, the graduated income tax, the regulation of banks and trusts, and votes for women. Unhappily, his political vision was compromised by self-righteousness and a simplistic worldview. For Bryan, the world was divided into Good and Evil and the horizons of his philosophy never extended beyond the simple Bible lessons of his childhood. He came to Dayton as the roundsman of the Lord and to defend old-time religion and a simpler America.

If the Great Commoner was to prosecute "the infidel Scopes," as he was dubbed by Mencken, who would defend him? Mencken decided that the ACLU lawyers, while able, were not well enough known to offset Bryan's fame, and earmarked Clarence Darrow for the task. Darrow had saved "thrill killers" Loeb and Leopold from the gallows the year before and was at the height of his celebrity. "Nobody gives a damn about that yap school-teacher," Mencken told him. "The thing to do is make a fool out of Bryan." Paradoxically, Darrow and Bryan had worked together for the same liberal causes and Darrow had supported Bryan for the presidency.

All roads led to Dayton and they were heavily traveled. Some two hundred–odd reporters, special correspondents, and wire service and newsreel teams descended upon the village that summer, Mencken and four colleagues from Baltimore among them. To his surprise, Dayton was a pleasant small town, the citizenry rather tolerant and already having second thoughts about playing host to this extravaganza. But it was also obvious to Mencken that it would be "no more possible in this Christian valley to get a jury unprejudiced against Scopes than it would be in Wall Street to get a jury unprejudiced against a Bolshevik."

Banners strewn across the streets gave Dayton a carnival atmosphere. Prophets down from the hills set up shop on every street corner and were "whooping it up for Genesis." Hot dog vendors, souvenir hawkers, peddlers with trays of toy monkeys, two rival real-life chimpanzees in cages, gospel singers, an organ grinder with a trained monkey, and a tent show movie on the life of Christ fought for attention. Lean mountain men sat on their haunches around the red-brick Rhea County Courthouse, chewing cuds of tobacco and conversing in monosyllables. To them, "Darwin was the Devil with seven tails and nine horns. . . . Scopes is the harlot of Babylon [and] Darrow is Beelzebub in person."

The trial finally began on the blistering hot morning of July 10, 1925, with Judge John T. Raulston presiding. A native of Fiery Gizzard, Tennessee, he had learned the Bible at his mother's knee and preached at revivals. He was up for election again the following year. The steaming courtroom was packed and the exploding flash powder set off by the news photographers added to the discomfort. Sweat rolled down foreheads and dampened shirts and dresses. A forest of palm-leaf fans beat vainly against the suffocating heat. This was the first national radio broadcast of a trial, with the words uttered in the courtroom sent to Chicago by wire and broadcast to the nation by the *Tribune*'s station, WGN.

"This is as brazen and bold an attempt to destroy liberty as was ever seen in the Middle Ages," Darrow proclaimed in his opening argument. Shoulders hunched and thumbs tucked into his suspenders, he held his audience in absolute silence. Bryan sat tight-lipped and unmoved through the first few days of the trial, allowing the local attorneys to present the prosecution's case. It consisted of several witnesses who testified that Scopes had indeed taught Darwinian theory in his biology class.

With Scopes's conviction all but certain, Darrow decided to put the anti-evolution law itself on trial. As in the Leopold-Loeb affair, his case turned on the testimony of experts: fifteen men of learning, including a clergyman, whom he had summoned to Dayton to testify to the validity of Darwinian theory and its compatibility with Christianity. He was examining the first, Dr. Maynard M. Metcalf, a Johns Hopkins University zoologist, when the prosecution objected and demanded the scientific witnesses be excluded. Silence fell over the courtroom as Bryan rose to speak for the first time. Scores of admirers leaned forward, anticipating that his magic voice and ringing phrases would rout the infidels.

Pointing to Metcalf, Bryan told the jury his degrees meant nothing. "I have more than he has. . . . Did he tell you where life began? Did he tell you that back of all there was a God? Not a word about it. Did he tell you how life began? Not a word and not one of them can tell you how life began. . . . They want to come in with their little padded-up evolution that commences with nothing and ends nowhere . . . to banish from the hearts of the people the Word of God as revealed."

Bryan's remarks, although vigorously applauded, were no Cross of Gold speech, but they served their purpose. Judge Raulston ruled for the prosecution and barred the testimony of the experts. The air seemed to have gone out of the defense case. Mencken, for one, thought so, and citing the work that had piled up on his desk, departed for Baltimore. But Darrow had one more card to play—to put Bryan on the witness stand and, by humiliating him, win in the court of public opinion. It would "show up fundamentalism [and] prevent bigots and ignoramuses from controlling the educational system of the United States."

The trial resumed on July 21, under the trees of the courthouse lawn because the crowds of spectators had caused the walls of the old building to crack and buckle. Soon after the proceedings opened, Darrow announced his intention to call Bryan as an expert on the Bible. Taken off guard, the prosecution lawyers leaped to their feet to object, but Bryan, convinced as always of the righteousness of his cause, consented to take the stand.

"Do you claim that everything in the Bible should be literally interpreted?" Darrow began.

"I believe everything in the Bible should be accepted as it is given there," Bryan replied easily.

And then his inquisitor made him look ridiculous. Yes, he believed that Joshua had made the sun stand still. Yes, he believed that God had made Eve from one of Adam's ribs. Yes, he believed Jonah had been swallowed by a great whale—or was it a great fish? Yes, he believed the world's languages derived from the Tower of Babel. Yes, he believed the Great Flood had actually occurred. Yes. Yes. Yes. Bryan slumped in the witness chair after an hour and a half of this, his face heavy with sweat, muttering over and over again, "Slurring the Bible . . . slurring the Bible . . ."

The image of Bryan seared into history by this exchange is that of a bigoted, ill-informed, hopelessly outdated old man. Sophisticates laughed and thought he had been disgraced, but his hold on true believers was unweakened. They praised him for defending the word of God against "the greatest atheist and agnostic in the United States." The trial was abruptly ended by Judge Raulston the next day without allowing Bryan to make a closing argument. Scopes was convicted by a jury that took only nine minutes to bring in a verdict. He was fined $100, which was paid by the *Evening Sun*.*

Bryan was undaunted by the ridicule heaped upon him. He not only regarded Dayton as a great victory, but saw it as the opening gun in a fight against modernism that was to climax in an anti-evolution amendment to the Constitution. He remained in town, editing for national publication the text of the closing speech he had not been able to give in the courtroom. Five days after the trial, Bryan led the congregation of a Methodist church in Sunday prayer and then dined grandly, as was his custom. Not long after, he went upstairs for a nap. When he did not reappear after several hours, his wife, Mary, felt a chill of foreboding and looked in upon him. He appeared to be sleeping, she later said, but "God had taken him."

Mencken celebrated his passing with a cruel mock eulogy that was more like an autopsy. Bryan fought his last fight, he wrote, "thirsting savagely for blood. All sense departed from him. He bit right and left, like a dog with

---

* In 1927, the Tennessee Supreme Court, probably embarrassed by the trial, upheld the anti-evolution law but reversed Scopes's conviction on a legal technicality. This prevented the ACLU from carrying an appeal of the conviction to the federal courts. The Butler Act remained on the books in Tennessee until 1967, when it was quietly removed.

rabies. He descended to demagogy so dreadful that his very associates at the trial table blushed. His one yearning was to keep his yokels heated up—to lead his forlorn mob of imbeciles against the foe. . . . He came into life a Galahad, in bright and shining armor. He passed out a pure mountebank."

"Well, we killed the son-of-a-bitch," he told a friend.

The Scopes trial, for all its farcical aspects, cast a long shadow. Far from having received a fatal blow at Dayton, the anti-evolutionists continued a fight that has stretched down to our own time. Evangelical preachers still thump the Bible and denounce the sins of modernism. Rather than preaching in tents and tabernacles, they now spread their message over television. Eighty years after Scopes, the battle between Darwinism and creationism continues to rage.

Several other states, emboldened by Tennessee, passed their own laws forbidding the teaching of Darwinism during the 1920s. In the years following World War II, the anti-evolution cause quietly gained new support as part of a conservative drift in American politics. Creationists argued that evolution was not true science because it could not be directly observed or measured. Such pressure resulted in 1968 in the first ruling by the U.S. Supreme Court on the issue. It threw out an Arkansas anti-evolution law, ruling that evolution can be taught in public schools because it is a science, but creationism cannot be taught because it is a religious concept that violates the separation of church and state.

In reaction, "equal time" bills, requiring that creationism be taught along with evolution in science classes, were considered in more than twenty states, but only two, Arkansas and Louisiana, actually approved such legislation. These laws were also struck down by the Supreme Court, which ruled in 1987 that state-mandated teaching of evolution and creationism side by side was unconstitutional, again because teaching creationism meant the state was sponsoring the teaching of religion.*

But the battle between evolutionists and creationists is far from over. In an effort to widen the appeal of creationism, some supporters have adopted a new alternative to evolution—"intelligent design"—to explain the creation of man. In contrast to the biblical literalness of the fundamentalists, proponents of intelligent design acknowledge that the earth is billions of years old and that organisms evolve over time. But they refuse to accept Darwin's theory of natural selection as the sole force of evolution, arguing that life is too complex, too rich, and too varied to be the result of

---

*Even in the new millennium, this debate goes on in several states.

a random accident. Only some intelligent designer, whether called God or something else, must be involved.

Critics view intelligent design as a sophisticated way of smuggling religious ideas about creation into the nation's classrooms. But supporters argue that the refusal to give it equal time in the nation's classrooms is wrong because it "undermines the pursuit of truth and the preservation of different points of view." In other actions, Kentucky has eliminated the word "evolution" from its school curriculum. Alabama and Oklahoma have ordered the teaching of evolution be coupled with disclaimers about the theory's uncertainty. In half a dozen other states, creationists have attempted to alter teaching standards.

"If the scientific community thinks they can sit back and say, 'Phew, we got that done,' that would be very presumptuous of them," said a creationist member of the Kansas Board of Education. "This issue is not going away."

CHAPTER 12

"Runnin' Wild"

Louise Brooks exemplified the youth and good looks worshipped by the Twenties. Strikingly beautiful, the girl with the sleek helmet of raven black hair was "cool and looked hot." Fair-skinned, long-legged, and slim, she came to New York from a small town in Kansas as a teenager for a brief but memorable fling as a Ziegfeld Follies dancer, model, and movie star. On film, she was luminous and her gaze was both inviting and enigmatic. "Exquisitely hard-boiled," in the words of *Photoplay* magazine, she was radiant, energetic, volatile, voluble, brazen, outspoken, rebellious, and set the standard for the flapper. Young women did their best not only to look like Louise Brooks but to act like her.

Pretty and impudent, the flapper was the symbol of the sexual revolution associated with the postwar era. She challenged prevailing notions about gender roles and defied the double standard. In essence, she demanded the same social freedoms for herself that men enjoyed. Flappers flouted conventionality, drank in speakeasies and the new nightclubs, doubled the nation's consumption of cigarettes by reaching "for a Lucky instead of a sweet," and flirted openly. Scott Fitzgerald described her as "lovely and expensive and about nineteen."

The flapper bobbed her peroxided or hennaed hair, wore bright red lipstick, and painted two circles of rouge on her face. She adorned her androgynous figure with flimsy dresses and short skirts, and wore a tight-fitting cloche hat, long strings of beads, flesh-colored hose rolled below her rouged knees, numerous bangles on her arms, and unbuckled galoshes. Sleeves disappeared and in summer the flapper sometimes dispensed with stockings. "Flapper Jane" was so ubiquitous that *New Republic* editor Bruce Bliven found space among the magazine's usual diet of politics and economics for an assessment:

She is frankly, heavily made up, not to imitate nature, but to an altogether artificial effect—pallor mortis, poisonously scarlet lips, richly ringed eyes—the latter looking not so much debauched (which is the intention) as diabetic. . . . [Flapper Jane's clothes] were estimated the other day by some statistician to weigh two pounds. Probably a libel; I doubt if they come to within half a pound of such bulk. Jane isn't wearing much this summer. If you'd like to know exactly, it is: one dress, one step-in, two stockings, two shoes.

The flapper was the antithesis of the Gibson Girl, the amply bosomed and rigidly corseted feminine ideal of her mother's day. The Gibson Girl wore her abundant hair piled up on her head, had the posture of a West Point cadet, in contrast to the flapper's "debutante slouch," and wore a neat shirtwaist tucked into a nearly floor-length straight skirt. As the embodiment of the female as the bearer of children and devoted homemaker, she was subservient to the appetites of men and was taught to please them rather than herself. Sex was regarded as the price women paid in exchange for the stability of marriage, and marriage was the price men paid for the easy availability of sex.

The term "flapper" originated in Britain and was applied to a girl who was an adolescent during the war and wore her galoshes open and flapping. Zelda Fitzgerald, the quintessential example of the breed, wrote that the flapper "flirted because it was fun to flirt and wore a one-piece bathing suit because she had a good figure, she covered her face with paint and powder because she didn't need it and she refused to be bored because she wasn't boring." Wits and jokesmiths had a field day. "We object," said the *Wheeling Intelligencer*, "to hearing a woman referred to as a 'skirt.' There is very little reason for such a name." The flapper's vogue was as brief as the life of a butterfly. Scott Fitzgerald said it was over by 1922, and although the Jazz Age continued, "the sequel was a children's party taken over by elders."

Although the flapper got all the publicity, the working girl was the norm. She enjoyed the benefits of the wartime experiences of a select group of upper-middle-class young women. Their jobs in the Red Cross, nursing, and other welfare work among the troops both at home and overseas relieved them of the usual restrictions of bourgeois society and gave them freedom of movement. Travel, informality, and the camaraderie of shared dangers eased relations between men and women, at least for brief periods and in special situations. Some of this easygoing familiarity carried over into the postwar period as large numbers of women left the security of their homes to enter the workplace, where they interacted with men, mostly for the first time.

Ten million women worked for wages during the 1920s—one in five wage earners in 1927 was a woman—but this was hardly a sign of equality or liberation, as it is sometimes portrayed. Often balancing a job, home, and children on low pay, working women had few, if any, opportunities to enjoy the independent and indulgent lifestyle portrayed in *Life*, *Vanity Fair*, and other popular magazines. Almost a third of working women, particularly blacks and the foreign born, were employed in the decidedly unglamorous field of domestic work.*

The increased presence of women in white-collar jobs changed the makeup of the female workforce, which had been primarily lower-class. Office and sales work was regarded as less demeaning than factory and domestic work, and middle-class girls and women flocked to these "lace collar" jobs. By 1930, the number of women in clerical jobs had surpassed the number of women working in factories. Government studies showed that women could be found in 537 of the 572 occupational categories listed in the census of 1920, but 86 percent of working women were clustered in female-designated occupations in which they made less money and had less status than men.

The typical working woman was single and under the age of twenty-five. Yet, one in four working women were married and presumably running a household, and their number was increasing three times faster than the rate of growth of the entire female workforce. A sign of the increased visibility of the working girl was her appearance in slick magazine fiction, advertisements, and the movies. The emphasis in these films and stories, however, was less on the job than on its possibilities for romance and attracting a husband.

For most women the reality was far grimmer. A job meant the drudgery of a low-level, low-paying position as a stenographer or a file clerk or a salesperson, and the work was usually monotonous and routine. There was a large wage differential between men and women in the same job: women earned little more than half of male salesmen's salaries. The National Industrial Conference Board reported that in December 1927, the average weekly wage for all males was $29.35; for women it was $17.36. Yet, a study by Columbia University Teachers College pointed out that it was "practi-

---

* Only the wealthiest families still had live-in servants in the Twenties; most domestic workers came in by the day for about $1 plus the cost of transportation, familiarly known as "carfare."

cally impossible for a girl to meet her daily needs as to clothing and keep her health up to par on less than $2,000" a year. To make ends meet, single women shared rooms, lived in residence clubs and boarding houses, scrimped, and hoped for dates with men who were generous with meals and entertainment.

Organized labor was slow, even reluctant, to accept working women. In 1927, according to the National Bureau of Economic Research, over three million women were eligible for union membership, but only 265,095 were actually organized. Most were in the garment trades and were members of the Amalgamated Clothing Workers Union. Some conservative union leaders thought a woman's place was in the home and were determined to keep her there. Women also tended to regard working as temporary and had no interest in joining a union. And many of the trades at which women worked, such as domestics, clerical workers, hairdressers, and teachers, were unorganized.

A cadre of female professionals stimulated much publicity as the exemplar of the New Woman, but the number of such fortunates was small because of the historic prejudice against women having careers. In 1910, it was estimated that 9 percent of working women were professionals. Over the next two decades, this rose to 14 percent. But the vast majority were in jobs usually reserved for women, such as teaching, nursing, and the new field of social work. Law schools made it difficult for women to enter and graduates faced numerous obstacles to engaging in practice. The number of female lawyers remained small, 3 percent of the feminine workforce. In medicine, men were doctors; women were nurses. The ranks of women physicians declined from 5 percent in 1920 to 4.4 percent ten years later. Women were thwarted by quotas from entering medical schools and by the refusal of hospitals to accept them as interns. Even in teaching, where eight out of ten teachers were women and they might be expected to achieve advancement, most of the administrative jobs were held by men.

But if job opportunities were limited for white women, African-American women bore the double burden of race and gender. Thousands had come North during the Great Migration to escape discrimination and sexual exploitation, and many had found jobs in industry during the war. Even here, discrimination prevailed, for, as the New York Age put it, black women were assigned tasks "which white woman would not do." Even these limited gains did not last as blacks were let go once the fighting ended. After the war, black women were overwhelmingly concentrated in domestic service, laundry, and farm work.

Those black women who succeeded in finding jobs in industry faced discrimination and harsh conditions. A Women's Bureau investigator found in 1922 that blacks working in Southern tobacco plants were barred from the manufacturing of cigars and cigarettes; that was white women's work. Instead, they were given seasonal jobs preparing the tobacco for the manufacturing process. "Tens of thousands of Negro women . . . are employed ten hours daily in old, unclean, malodorous buildings in which they are denied the most ordinary comforts of life," the investigator reported. They earned about $2 a week.

Well-educated black women enjoyed some opportunities. Social work was expanding and organizations such as the YWCA and the Urban League hired trained black professionals to serve their own communities. Teaching was another possibility, but jobs were scarce, particularly in the North. For example, in 1920 Chicago employed only 138 black female teachers. Nurses faced similar barriers and were paid significantly less than white practitioners. In both North and South, the races were rigidly segregated.

Working women demanded clothes that were simple and comfortable on the job. Although flapper wear was too extreme, petticoats were discarded and the sheath, often in basic black or beige, and a two-piece jersey outfit that was a knockoff of a Chanel design, were popular. Breasts were strapped down to attain a fashionable flatness. Some observers attributed the craze for slimness to the movies; most film stars were slender, so ordinary women thought they had to be thin. In an ironic twist, well-endowed women wore corsets to achieve the "natural" look. Even the Sears Roebuck catalog featured a sedate version of flapper wear for the women of Middle America.

Women no longer had time to make their own clothes. Mass production and merchandising—which created jobs for women in the garment and retail trades—made it more convenient to buy ready-made clothes that were available in a greater variety of materials, textures, and colors than those that could be run up at home. Modish designs that drew upon the fashions of New York society and *Vogue* magazine were offered at reasonable prices. Seven dress sizes would fit more than half the women in the country.

For conservatives, the rising hemline of women's skirts from the ankle to just a touch below the knee was an index of what they saw as a revolutionary change in morals and manners that they hated and feared. A disconcerted YWCA circulated a booklet called *Modesty Appeal* that implored women to show less skin. The state legislatures of Utah and Virginia tried to impose limits on rising hemlines and falling necklines, to no avail. A survey taken in 1927 of 1,300 working girls in Milwaukee revealed that fewer than seventy still wore corsets. Short skirts made silk stockings a necessity, for which typists earning 50 cents an hour paid $2 a pair.

Suddenly, women everywhere were wearing makeup, which had earlier been regarded as the mark of a "fast" woman. Seventy-three percent of women over eighteen used perfume, 90 percent face powder, 73 percent toilet water, and 50 percent rouge. Kissproof lipstick was the rage. Helena Rubinstein, Charles Revson, and Elizabeth Arden made fortunes by persuading American women they could capture their dream man if they used the right lipstick, mascara, or skin lotion. Palmolive soap promised the "beauty secret of Cleopatra hidden in every cake." New York, the hub of fashion, began the decade with 750 beauty salons, most catering to wealthy women. Within five years, three thousand such establishments were pampering working women as well as the rich. Nationwide, there were forty thousand beauty salons in 1930, and the cosmetic industry's earnings grew from $17 million a year to $200 million over the same period.

Young women no longer patterned themselves on their mothers; mothers imitated their daughters. The role models of the era were such rising movie stars as red-haired Clara Bow, Louise Brooks, and Colleen Moore, among others, who from the screen projected sexual attractiveness, energy, and independence. The virginal waif made famous by Mary Pickford and Lillian Gish was on the wane. Everyone talked about "It," a quality described by novelist Elinor Glyn as "animal magnetism" and "the open sesame to success in life and love," and associated in the public mind with the effervescent Bow. *The Rubáiyát of Omar Khayyám*, which sang of youth and seduction, sold millions of copies. "Many an American adult in the 1920s remembered as a landmark the day he read Omar's line: 'I myself am Heaven and hell.'"

Young people of college age made drinking fashionable. Formerly, any girl of good family would have been horrified if offered a drink, but by the second part of the decade, drinking was common among students at dances and football games. Hip flasks were part of party attire and the young man who couldn't offer his girl a silver flask and a drink was "a drip." Students were contemptuous of the self-righteous moralists they associated with Prohibition and accused them of invading the privacy of others. "To presume that one can define decency or legislate virtue is folly," said *The Daily Princetonian* in a typical statement.

Society was paying greater attention to the young than ever before. In every age, youth has a sense of destiny, of experiencing—rightly or wrongly—what no one else has ever experienced before, but this sentiment reached an unmatched intensity during the Twenties. For the first time—and in a prelude to the Sixties—the nation's youth rather than their elders set the standards for American society.

A major reason for the cult of youth was the increased size of the generation between sixteen and thirty years old. Adolescence was also recognized for the first time as a distinct period of life, the result of Freudian psychology and a recognition that the child was no longer merely an immediate economic asset to be exploited. The pressures of modern living were said to require a greater period of preparation before a young person was deemed ready to enter the workplace.

The state became what historian David M. Kennedy has called an "over-parent," and social reformers such as John Dewey looked to the schools to do what the family, neighborhood, shop, and farm had previously done: to socialize the young and train them to assume their responsibilities as citizens. In addition to providing education, the schools made certain children were healthy, instructed them in hygiene—touching gingerly on sex—tried to inculcate a taste for music and the arts, and introduced organized recreational activities and sports into their lives.

Larger numbers of people were in school in the 1920s than ever before. High school attendance more than doubled during the decade from 2.2 million to over 5 million, which meant that a majority of children of high school age were in school. Standardized intelligence tests administered to draftees during the war had disclosed a shockingly high percentage of men who appeared to be of substandard intelligence, and led to wide-ranging educational reform. Teaching standards were improved, the school year was lengthened, and the minimum legal dropout age was raised. In rural areas, the pace of reform was slow, however, especially in the South where the one-room schoolhouse persisted. Sometimes the school year was only three months long so children could work in the fields; often they were pulled out for good after the sixth grade. When black students finished elementary school, parents found there were no high schools open to their children. In Maryland, for example, there was only one such segregated institution for the entire state.

Ever-growing percentages of high school graduates went on to college, but many more went directly to work. Vocational training edged its way into the curriculum, under pressure from industry for practical courses in typing, bookkeeping, business English, carpentry, and auto mechanics.

However, one in every eight Americans between the ages of eighteen and twenty-three attended college in 1926, four or five times the number in any other developed nation. Not only did the number of students grow; so did the number of available courses. Stanford's offerings increased from 710 to 1,095, Howard's from 143 to 255, and Arizona State's from 105 to 284. American universities awarded 532 doctorates in 1920; a decade later almost four times as many were bestowed. Never before had young people enjoyed greater opportunities for advancement and fulfillment—and for greater defiance of traditional values.

Professional "viewers with alarm" were convinced that a sexual revolution had exploded in the Twenties. While it was believed that the war had turned traditional standards and morals upside down, the process of change had actually begun before the turn of the century. Sigmund Freud's lectures at Clark University in 1909 were only the most dramatic of a long series of importations of radically new ideas about sex from Europe. The explorations of sexuality by Havelock Ellis, Edward Carpenter, and Richard Krafft-Ebing were known in the United States before the war, and the Swedish feminist Ellen Kay was arguing that marriages denying women sexual satisfaction should be dissolved.

The more progressive sponsors of moralistic social purity campaigns against prostitution and venereal disease sometimes advocated more open discussion of sexual matters, on grounds that education would help the fight against these problems. Elements of the free love ethic of Greenwich Village bohemia, including a faint tolerance for premarital sex, the acknowledgment of female sexuality, and the acceptance of birth control, had infiltrated mainstream culture. As the magazine *Current Opinion* put it in 1913, the nation had "struck sex o'clock."

In reality, the supposed collapse of morals that so horrified alarmists during the Twenties was primarily a change in manners and in fashion. What was different from the past was that these changes took place within a short time, and were quickly disseminated to all parts of the country by the new arts of mass communications and advertising. Had they unfolded over a longer period rather than being compressed into a mere half dozen years, there probably would have been less shock.

Raymond Moley,* a professor of political science at Columbia who also taught at Barnard, later wrote that he knew hundreds of students and did not believe that

* Moley was later one of Franklin Roosevelt's "Brain Trust" of idea men and then a founder of *Newsweek*.

the general public morality differed from the years before. . . . Contrary to the impression conveyed by later reports, the 1920s were certainly not years of moral decline. Such reports are based upon lurid incidents . . . but perhaps because they were . . . unusual, they were more widely publicized. So far as drinking was concerned, there was much less than before the enactment of Prohibition. . . . Student morality was governed by long-standing middle-class standards.

Sheiks and Shebas superseded "calling" with "dating" in the rite of finding a mate. Calling meant visiting a girl in her home, dating meant going out rather than sitting stiffly in the parlor under the watchful eye of her parents or a chaperone. The Sheba's appeal was "the same as before but with more of it showing," said one writer. If the Sheba had a uniform, a variation on flapper-wear, so did the Sheik. The name—pronounced *sheek*—was a homage to Rudolph Valentino and his most romantic role. The Sheik parted his hair in the center, combed it straight back from the forehead, and slicked it down with brilliantine. He wore cinched, belted jackets and the new Van Heusen shirts with soft collars—the models in the ads resembled Scott Fitzgerald—and flannel trousers with wide legs called "Oxford Bags."

Couples now "necked" and "petted" in the rear seats of darkened movie houses and in the back seats of cars. No one was certain of the exact difference between necking and petting, for they both included groping and heavy breathing short of intercourse. In earlier times, the young hardly ever talked about sex; now, it was said, they talked about nothing else. Religious sanctions no longer had their earlier force in an increasingly secularized country.

The young people danced. The fox trot, the sexy tango popularized by Valentino—both requiring very close bodily contact—and, above all, the Charleston. For them jazz and wild dancing were symbolic, another badge of their rejection of traditional behavioral standards. Pigeon-toed dancers knocked their knees together and gyrated, according to scandalized critics, like drunken chickens. In Cincinnati in 1926, the Salvation Army sought an injunction barring the erection of a movie theater adjoining the Catherine Booth Home for Girls, on grounds that "jazz emanating from the theater would implant 'jazz emotions' in the babies born at the home."

The Charleston originated before the war but reached its heyday in 1924 after being featured in *Runnin' Wild*, an all-black Broadway musical review. Louise Brooks, during a stint as a dancer in a London nightclub, helped introduce the Charleston to eager Europeans. The dance received a boost when the popular young Prince of Wales took it up. Variations included the Varsity Drag, the Black Bottom, in which the dancers stuck out their rumps and shook them, and the Shimmy. "God help your child," sighed the *Ladies' Home Journal* as it let parents in on what their offspring were doing.*

Young people acted as if they had invented sex. Recording something so intimate as premarital intercourse is difficult, but the Kinsey Report of the 1950s indicated an increase in such activity during the Twenties. Women born after the turn of the century were twice as likely to have lost their virginity before they married as women of the previous generation. With the availability of contraception, the hazards of illicit intercourse were slighter than ever before, and the rate of illegitimate births remained fairly low. A 1928 study found approximately 25 percent of all married American men and women admitted to at least one adulterous affair.

Yet, despite all the talk of heightened sexual activity, peer pressure in Middle America against indiscriminate sex was strong, according to the Lynds. Usually, only committed couples went "all the way." Intercourse was generally confined to engaged couples as a prelude to marriage, although every campus and high school had its Jezebel. Most young people indulged in petting, and advice columns frequently printed anguished letters from girls bemoaning the fact that without petting they could not keep a boyfriend.

"What a gulf separates even two generations!" lamented a social commentator as he surveyed the state of American life in 1927.

> Mothers and daughters often understand each other's viewpoints so little it seems as though they [aren't] speaking the same language. . . . Changes are occurring throughout our whole social system. . . . Religion is no longer the unchanging rock of ages. . . . The family is becoming smaller. . . . Young people are marrying earlier and getting divorces more frequently. . . . More and more women are working for pay outside the home.

Feminists had preached that once the Nineteenth Amendment, which gave women the right to vote, was enacted in 1920, the moral tone of American politics would be elevated.† But votes for women had few con-

---

* In 1925, the floor of Boston's Pickwick Club buckled under the weight of a thousand people doing the Charleston, killing forty-four.

† Henry Mencken, always the contrarian, predicted sardonically that once women got the vote, adultery would replace boozing as the favorite pastime of politicians.

sequences. Millions of women voted, although not in the same proportion as men, mostly for Harding and Coolidge, just as their husbands did. By the end of the decade, several women had been elected to Congress and to state offices, but if there was any improvement in political morality it was indecipherable by the naked eye. As a result of the splintering of the women's movement over an equal rights amendment to the Constitution, the feminists operated on the political fringe during most of the 1920s.

The National Women's Party, led by Alice Paul, supported the ERA, which provided that "equality of rights under the law shall not be denied or abridged by the United States or by a State on account of sex." On the other hand, the League of Women Voters and a significant number of former suffragists regarded the ERA as a betrayal of all they had fought for, fearing it would nullify existing protective laws for women. Although state legislatures enacted child labor, health, and workmen's compensation legislation, the only major success scored by women on the national scene in the postwar period was the Sheppard-Turner Maternity Act of 1921. It provided matching federal-state funds for clinics to care for dependent mothers and infants—and even this modest program, opposed by conservatives, was phased out in 1929.

Young women honored the feminists for fighting past battles but were uncomfortable with their zealotry. Some feminists saw marriage as a trap designed to keep women in bondage, and sex as degrading. The younger generation thought the worst of the bitter trench war for equality was over and that it was hardly necessary to continue lobbing hand grenades at the opposite sex. The old admonitions of the militants—"Keep your maiden name," "Come out of the kitchen," and "Never darn a sock"—were seen as largely irrelevant. Women were beginning to view marriage as a partnership of equals, with the possibility of happiness and satisfaction. Newspapers gave considerable coverage to the decision of Abby Rockefeller, the daughter of John D. Rockefeller, Jr., to eliminate the word "obey" from her marriage vows. Not long after, the Episcopal Church dropped it from the wedding liturgy.

The 1920s saw the emergence of a national cult of "romantic love"—popularized by films, radio serials, and magazines—and women were not only demanding equality outside the home but in the bedroom as well. Hollywood produced such films as *Sinners in Silk*, *The Price She Paid*, and *Alimony* about "brilliant men, beautiful jazz babies, champagne baths, midnight revels, petting parties in the purple dawn, all ending in one terrific smashing climax that makes you gasp." Freud's ideas, which were spreading rapidly, undermined the view that sex was "dirty" or that a sexual appetite was unusual. Repression of the sex drive only produced guilt, anxiety, and mental illness, according to the Freudians. Behaviorism, a competing theory advanced by psychologist John B. Watson that was also popular, minimized the ability of men and women to consciously control their behavior.

Women now believed that sexual relations with their spouses were not simply a means of procreation, as their mothers had been taught, but the culmination of romantic love and a pleasurable experience in itself. "Sex-love and happiness in marriage . . . do not just happen," wrote Margaret Sanger, the birth control pioneer, in her 1926 book, *Happiness in Marriage*. "Eternal vigilance is the price of marital happiness . . . the nuptial relation must be kept romantic." For a dime, a woman could obtain a copy of *How I Kept My Husband*, a sex manual with a plain brown wrapper that gave instructions on sexual positions and oral sex. Thus, the real sexual revolution of the Twenties was not a revolution against marriage; it was a revolution within marriage.

The legitimacy of female sexuality was advanced by the increasing availability of birth control devices, especially the diaphragm. Yet, conventional morality, based upon the teachings of the Judeo-Christian religious tradition, insisted that procreation, not pleasure, was the sole legitimate function of sex. Self-styled protectors of public virtue, led by Anthony Comstock and his associates, called birth control "obscene, lewd, lascivious, filthy, and indecent." In 1873, they succeeded in having Congress ban contraceptives from interstate commerce and birth control information from the mails. Some states adopted measures making it illegal to use contraceptives.

The result was a two-tier system for birth control. While affluent and educated women practiced contraception, it was neither generally known nor used by the poor. Margaret Sanger reported that the advice commonly given Lower East Side women who wished to avoid having children was: "Have Jake sleep on the roof." In Middletown, reported the Lynds, all the wives of the businessmen interviewed practiced birth control, while less than half the working-class wives did so. They cited religious scruples, ignorance, and the resistance of husbands for not using contraception. Sanger made it her mission to extend knowledge of birth control to every woman. This struggle included repeated arrests and foreshadowed the current fight over abortion—with some of the same forces arrayed against each other.

* * *

For Sanger, this fight began in childhood. She was born Margaret Louise
Higgins on September 14, 1879,* in Corning, a factory town in upstate
New York, to Michael Hennessey Higgins, a rebellious, redheaded Irish
stonemason, and the devoutly Catholic Anne Purcell Higgins. Her father
squandered his talent and vision in too much talk and too much drink, and
his family was mired in poverty. Margaret, the sixth of eleven children, was
responsible for the care of her younger brothers and sisters because her
mother was overwhelmed by the size of her brood and by poor health. She
was forever worrying, cleaning and sewing in a failed attempt to bring order
to a chaotic household. Anne Higgins died at the age of fifty of tuberculosis and Margaret blamed the rigors of repeated childbearing for her premature death. Michael Higgins lived to be eighty, and his daughter took note
of the discrepancy in her parents' lifespans, implying that her mother was a
victim of her father's passions. To escape this grim heritage, the girl, then
seventeen, entered nursing school.

What Margaret saw there reinforced what she had seen in her own family. Like her mother, other poor women were giving birth to unwanted children whom they could neither nurture nor support. "So great was the
ignorance of women and girls concerning their own bodies that I decided
to specialize in women's diseases and took up gynecological and obstetrical
nursing," she wrote in her *Autobiography*. "A few years of this work brought
me to a shocking discovery—the knowledge of the ways of controlling
birth were accessible to the women of wealth while the working women
were deliberately kept in ignorance of this knowledge."

Margaret married a bright young architect and aspiring painter named
William Sanger and the couple settled in Hastings-on-Hudson, a Westchester County suburb of New York City, and had three children. Suburban life did not satisfy them. Bill Sanger decided in 1910 to give up his job
for the life of an artist in Greenwich Village. He became a rising star in
bohemia and ran for alderman on the Socialist Party ticket. Margaret was
friends with Emma Goldman, Mabel Dodge, John Reed, and Bill Haywood, was active in the Liberal Club, which met in a loft on MacDougal
Street, embraced the direct action doctrine of the anarchists, and took
part in demonstrations staged by the IWW.

Returning to work as a visiting nurse on the Lower East Side, Sanger
was angered by the double standard for birth control in this country. She
was especially saddened by the death from an attempted abortion of a
woman named Sadie Sachs whom she had nursed:

* In her *Autobiography*, she said she was born in 1883.

I looked out my window and down upon the dimly lighted city. Its pains and griefs crowded in upon me, a moving picture rolled before my eyes with photographic clearness; women writhing in travail to bring forth little babies; the babies naked and hungry, wrapped in newspapers to keep them from the cold; six-year-old children with pinched, pale, wrinkled faces, old in concentrated wretchedness, pushed into gray and fetid cellars, crouched on stone floors, their small scrawny hands scuttling through rags, making lamp shades, artificial flowers, white coffins, black coffins, coffins, coffins, interminably passing in never-ending succession. . . . As I stood there, the darkness faded . . . the sun came up and threw its reflection over the house tops. It was the dawn of a new day in my life also. . . . I was resolved to seek out the root of evil, to do something to change the destiny of mothers whose miseries were as vast as the sky.

Without much education, with little backing or funding, Sanger embarked on a crusade dedicated to the emancipation of women. In 1912, she began with a column on sex education in a Socialist daily paper, the *New York Call*, entitled *What Every Girl Should Know*. She quickly ran afoul of Anthony Comstock, who personally had the column suppressed by the postal authorities on grounds that it was obscene. The editors printed the column's head, "What Every Girl Should Know," and under it, "NOTHING! By Order of the Post Office Department."

No matter. In March 1914, Sanger was back with *The Woman Rebel*, a radical feminist monthly funded by Mabel Dodge that advocated every woman's right to a safe and reliable means of preventing pregnancy. "No woman can call herself free until she can choose conscientiously whether she will or will not be a mother," Sanger declared. Her motto, taken from the IWW, was: "No Gods. No Masters." Requests for birth control information poured in, not only from "rebel girls," but also from working-class women. The Comstocks descended on the magazine and Sanger was arrested for violating the postal obscenity laws. In all, she was arrested eight times during her career.

Unwilling to risk a lengthy jail term, Sanger jumped bail in October 1914, leaving her children with her husband, and fled to Europe. En route, she cabled friends to release 100,000 copies of *Family Limitation*, a sixteen-page pamphlet she had written that provided explicit instructions on the use of a variety of contraceptive methods. Bill Sanger was arrested by Comstock's undercover agents while handing them out and elected to go to jail for thirty days rather than pay a fine.

Sanger's sense of mission was strengthened by her exposure to the ideas of European radicals, and she was influenced by Havelock Ellis and his theories of female sexuality. Broadening her arguments, she now claimed that birth control would uncouple sex and procreation and provide women with both economic independence and erotic freedom. The generally available contraceptives—douches and suppositories—were inadequate, and she sought a more effective system. Sanger found what she was seeking on a visit to a Dutch birth control clinic, where midwives were distributing recently developed spring-loaded diaphragms and spermicidal jellies.

Now keen to focus media attention on the birth control issue, Sanger returned home to stand trial in the autumn of 1915. In her absence, there had been a shift in the public attitude toward birth control. The mass circulation magazines now considered it an issue at least worthy of serious, if limited, discussion, and public opinion was willing to entertain questions about existing standards. The makers of the disinfectant Lysol were even hinting in their ads that it could eliminate "calender fear"—or missed periods. When Sanger's only daughter, five-year-old Peggy, died shortly after her return, a sympathetic public persuaded the government to drop the charges against her.

Sanger, denied the public forum for which she had hoped, embarked on a nationwide tour. She was arrested several times and her confrontational style attracted even more attention. Despite ridicule, imprisonment, and strenuous opposition from organized medical and religious groups, especially the Catholic Church, she persisted in a campaign of civil disobedience, even smuggling forbidden diaphragms from Europe.

Sanger divorced her husband and, in keeping with her views on sexual liberation, had numerous affairs, with, among others, Havelock Ellis and H. G. Wells. Men adored her. Her "green eyes were flecked with amber, her hair a shiny auburn hue, her smile always warm and charming, her hands perpetually beckoning even to strangers," writes Ellen Chesler, one of her biographers. "She had a quick Irish wit, high spirits and radiant common sense." In 1922, she married an oil tycoon named Noah H. Slee, who became the main source of funds for the birth control movement, and even used the international operations of his oil refinery to bootleg contraceptives into the country.

The medical profession was wary of Sanger, not only because she was a mere nurse, but because she was a sexually liberated woman and an outspoken political maverick. As late as 1925, Dr. Morris Fishbein, editor of the *Journal of the American Medical Association*, asserted that there was no safe and effective method of birth control. Some physicians said birth control smacked of "murder and sexual perversion." Others feared that if it became widespread, the old-stock, white middle class would be swamped by the offspring of blacks and the rural and urban immigrant poor, a process they called "race suicide." A few physicians were willing to prescribe contraceptives for patients, but only if their health was involved. Sanger quickly pointed out the hypocrisy of this position.

America's first birth control clinic opened on October 16, 1916, in a storefront in an immigrant neighborhood in the Brownsville section of Brooklyn. Handbills in English, Yiddish, and Italian advertising the clinic were distributed beforehand. Women were already standing in line "halfway to the corner . . . at least one hundred and fifty, some in shawls, some hatless, their red hands clasping the cold, chapped smaller ones of their children" when the doors opened, Sanger later recalled. Nine days later, the clinic was raided by the New York police department's vice squad, a unit usually concerned with brothels and gambling dens, and Sanger and her staff were arrested. The courts rejected her First Amendment defense and, convicted of illegally disseminating birth control information, she spent thirty days in jail.

Sanger appealed her arrest and jailing and won a partial victory. Although her conviction was upheld, the court ruled that licensed physicians could legally prescribe contraceptives when the health of female patients was threatened. Sanger now faced a dilemma: whether to ally herself with the conservative, male-dominated medical profession and respectable middle class women, or to continue social agitation and her efforts to make contraception available to everyone.

Worried about government repression following American entry into World War I, Sanger divorced herself from her radical past.* She ceased her efforts to open clinics for poor and working women and organized the American Birth Control League to bring physicians and middle class women into the birth control movement. Sanger's support of legislation to give physicians exclusive authority to recommend contraception reduced opposition to birth control—even the AMA finally endorsed it—but the original principles of the movement were abandoned as birth control became a middle-class issue.†

* Sanger was under surveillance by government agents because of her radical activities and her support of Emma Goldman and Alexander Berkman, who were agitating against the draft.

† In 1936, the courts ruled that physicians were exempt from the laws banning the importation of birth control materials, although the ban on importing contraceptive devices for personal use was not lifted until 1971.

In 1927, when birth control had developed significant momentum, Sanger organized the first World Population Conference in Geneva. The meeting brought together medical professionals and social scientists who were concerned about worldwide overpopulation. "It has long been my desire to have the population question discussed from an international scientific standpoint," Sanger declared. But she was a prophet without honor. The distinguished scientists did not relish being associated with a woman whose formal credentials did not match their own, and her name was eliminated from the program. Nevertheless, so great was Sanger's desire to have the conference succeed, she swallowed her pride and stepped into the background.

In her eagerness to gather support, Sanger also embraced the eugenics movement, which sought to prevent the propagation of the genetically "unfit," meaning the mentally retarded and chronically criminal. Influenced by these ideas, many states had enacted compulsory sterilization laws that fell mainly on the impoverished and racial minorities. Upholding a Tennessee law, Justice Oliver Wendell Holmes, speaking for eight members of the Supreme Court, supported sterilization in the 1927 case of *Buck v. Bell* with the declaration that "three generations of imbeciles are enough." Justice Pierce Butler, the Court's sole Catholic, was the only dissenter.

Sanger's embrace of eugenics permanently tainted her reputation, because in the 1930s the movement had overtones of Nazism. Increasingly, she was viewed as too controversial for the cause she had launched and was eclipsed by younger professionals with more mainstream agendas. Moreover, as birth control became more acceptable, family planning came to the fore: wives and husbands now agreed on how many children they would have, how to space them, and how to plan for safe delivery and care of newborns. In 1939, the various groups organized by Sanger merged into what became the Planned Parenthood Federation of America.

Following World War II, Sanger again focused her attention on the international aspects of birth control and family planning. Growing alarm over the consequences of overpopulation, particularly in the Third World, prompted efforts to build an international birth control movement. Working with family planners in Europe and Asia, she helped found the International Planned Parenthood Foundation in 1952. She also helped provide funding for development of the first effective, anovulatory contraceptive—the birth control pill. In 1965, the Supreme Court, in *Griswold v. Connecticut,* struck down a law forbidding use of contraceptives, making birth control legal for married couples. A few months later,

Margaret Sanger, having lived to see her work supported by a federal government that once prosecuted her, died in a nursing home at the age of eighty-six. Today, her fight continues in the struggle over freedom of choice and the morality of genetic engineering.

The Twenties saw increasing national concern over the lack of stability in the American family and the weakening of the marriage bond. These worries were generated not only by the sexual revolution but also by the changing relationship between parents and children. For at least a century, the size of the family had been falling. With the exception of Catholics, two or three children became the norm among urban middle-class families. Rising living standards meant that children were no longer needed as productive hands. Other factors contributing to smaller family size included the ready availability of contraception, the fixation of women upon "staying young" by avoiding the physical strains of pregnancy, and the fact that both husbands and wives had jobs and worked outside the home.

The changing nature of marriage turned out to be a two-edged sword, for some men were unable or unprepared to adjust to the demands and attitudes of the new woman. The literature of the time reflects this growing male anxiety. When the departing Nora Helmer slammed the door of her home in Henrik Ibsen's *A Doll's House* to do her duty to herself, some thought the entire structure of Western marriage was shaken. The trend was also seen in D. H. Lawrence's novels, but even more so in such literary creations as the destructive Nina Leeds of Eugene O'Neill's *Strange Interlude* and Harriet Craig, the possessive tigress of George Kelly's *Craig's Wife*. Dorothy Canfield's popular novel *The Homemaker* depicted a woman who had failed as a mother but was successful in business, while her husband, kept at home by an accident, found in caring for his children the fulfillment he had missed in commerce.

The divorce rate soared, and the United States had the highest rate in the world, except possibly the Soviet Union. A sign of the times was the decision of the Nevada legislature in 1927 to halve from six months to three the residency period in the state for obtaining a divorce. This revision was quickly approved by the governor, "thus assuring that his state did not lose the revenue from one of its chief industries," observed the *Literary Digest*. Nevada was already the capital of the "quickie" divorce and had lowered its residency requirement to beat competition from Paris and Mexico. In 1931, this requirement was reduced to six weeks. Most states required a year.

Traditionally, the institution of marriage had been viewed as indissoluble. "What God hath joined together let no man put asunder," commanded the marriage ritual. But over the years, even as the percentage of Americans who married was increasing and their age was dropping—twenty-five for men and twenty-two for women—the taboo against divorce was disappearing. From 1914 to 1928, the annual ratio of divorce to marriage rose from about one in ten to one in every six. In 1914, the number of divorces topped 100,000 for the first time; over 205,000 couples were divorced in 1929.

Some experts blamed this development on the new woman's demands for equality in marriage, but historian Lynn Dumenil states that while this was certainly a contributing factor, there were other explanations. One was the growing secularization of society. This decline in religiosity led to a decrease in the number of marriages sanctified by religious authority. In Middletown, religiously sanctified weddings dropped from 85 percent of the total in 1890 to only 63 percent in 1923. As marriage itself became less sacred, there was an increase in divorce.

To help stem this rising tide, many states adopted waiting periods before a couple could marry, to make certain they did not rush blindly into matrimony. These attempts at limitation were not notably successful. When California approved a law requiring a three-day waiting period, eager couples flocked to neighboring Arizona and Nevada, where the law was less stringent. Elkton, in Maryland, where there was no waiting period, became the East Coast version of Gretna Green, complete with marrying parsons at the ready and wedding chapels open around the clock. The frequency of divorce and the speed with which marriages were dissolved became commonplace. "Anyone with $10 can get a divorce in ten minutes if it is not contested," a Middletown resident told the Lynds.

Even working-class families, where traditional religiosity and gender roles were strongly entrenched, resorted to divorce. There was also a discernible change in the grounds for separation. Adultery and abandonment had been the usual legal reasons for the breakup of a marriage; in the Twenties, "cruel treatment" superseded them. Cruelty covered a variety of marital maladjustments, and the increase in divorce on this charge indicated a growing flexibility in the reasons for ending a marriage, including problems in sexual relations. "Women never used to talk about such things," one woman told the Lynds. "Every woman used to think other women had to put up with what she did because that is the way men are. Now they are beginning to wonder."

CHAPTER 13

"Boy, Can You Get Stucco!"

With his bristling white mustache, spats, and gold-headed walking stick, Samuel Insull looked like a cartoon of a plutocrat in an old-fashioned Socialist tract. But there was nothing old-fashioned about Insull or his business methods. Coolidge Prosperity was powered by new forms of energy, and Insull—the "King of Kilowatts"—personified the dawning age of electricity and the boom times on Wall Street that accompanied it. Rich, powerful, and self-made, he was a pioneer not only in the distribution of electric power but also in financial innovation.

"The people—butchers, bakers, candlestick makers who invested their all in his stocks—fairly idolized Insull, and even titans viewed him with awe," according to Forrest McDonald, an admiring biographer. In 1931, however, he went from "Master of the Universe" to fugitive in a brief flick of an eye as his empire vaporized, taking the life savings of millions of shareholders with it.*

Insull, at the height of his influence in 1928, commanded a utilities empire valued at $3 billion, which produced one eighth of all the electricity and natural gas consumed in the United States.† Through the use of holding companies and interlocking boards, he pyramided small power companies into ever larger units. Eventually, he commanded twenty-seven pure holding companies with hundreds of operating subsidiaries in five hundred communities spread across thirty-two states. He also reigned over

---

* There is a historical pattern to such things. The warm glow of admiration investors and employees felt for Insull while his shares were going up and the charges of stock fraud and crooked accounting procedures that swirled about him after his collapse foreshadow the public outcry accompanying the spectacular rise and fall of Enron three quarters of a century later.

† The Enron bankruptcy at $49.8 billion is the largest business failure in history. Tex-

the transit systems of Minneapolis–St. Paul and Chicago and a broad range of other companies. Insull's empire was so complex that not even he knew its full extent. The Federal Trade Commission needed seven years to unravel it. "It's like the Hanging Gardens of Babylon," said a critic, "a pyramid structure, built in a weird design, worthy of a Nebuchadnezzar."

Insull's rise coincided with a second American industrial revolution in which electricity and petroleum replaced coal and the steam engine, catalysts of the original upheaval. Industrial growth in the twentieth century was spectacular and matched by a parallel demand for energy. Between 1900 and 1920, energy consumption grew by 250 percent, with petroleum's share of this market rising sevenfold.

The modern petroleum industry dates from January 1901, when a remarkable gusher exploded from a hole drilled 1,160 feet into a marshy hillock called Spindletop, just outside Beaumont, Texas. Until then, most of the nation's petroleum had come from wells in the Eastern states controlled by the Rockefeller interests. Within a year, the 138 wells drilled in the Spindletop field were producing more oil than the rest of the world combined. Spindletop, rather than a federal antitrust suit, broke the monopoly of Standard Oil. Wildcatters and companies such as Gulf and Texaco made rich strikes in Texas, California, Oklahoma, Louisiana, and Wyoming that reduced the Rockefellers' stranglehold. The skyrocketing demand for gasoline to meet the needs of the automobile was responsible for the oil boom, but petroleum also fueled the ever-turning generators that produced electricity for America's factories, offices, and homes.

From 1924 to 1929, the gross domestic product of the United States grew by 19 percent, rising from $85.2 billion to $101.4 billion. Even though the average workweek dropped to forty-four hours, output per man-hour in manufacturing grew by 72 percent in the ten years beginning in 1919. Investment in new plants and machinery rose from $11.1 billion annually to $20.7 billion. Electric power fueled these unprecedented gains in productivity. By 1929 electricity was running 70 percent of all the machines in use, compared to only 30 percent in 1914. Between 1920 and 1929, industrial and commercial use of electricity more than doubled, while residential use more than tripled. Insull promoted the "all-electric home" and about 16 million households had electricity. Of these, 80 percent had electric

---

aco's collapse in 1997 at $35.8 billion and the $33.8 billion failure of the Financial Corporation in 1988 are second and third (*CBS MarketWatch*, January 12, 2002). Insull's bankruptcy in 1931 involved $3 billion—or about $30 billion in current value—which would make it the fourth largest business collapse ever and probably more significant than the others because Insull controlled a larger part of the overall economy.

irons, 37 percent had vacuum cleaners, and 35 percent had clothes wash-
ers, fans, and toasters. Telephone use expanded by 70 percent.

Insull's rise was a page out of Horatio Alger. Born in London in 1859, he
was one of the eight children of parents with no knack for making money.
At fifteen he left school to get a job as an office boy in a firm of auctioneers
where he learned shorthand; within four years he was its chief stenographer. A rebel against the British class system that doomed boys like him to
"a life of alpaca jackets, penmanship and subordination," Insull was
devoted to self-improvement. He joined a literary society and, captivated
by a "screamingly funny" speech delivered to the group by P. T. Barnum,
became a lifelong admirer of fakes, freaks, and frauds. Some critics sourly
claimed Insull also absorbed Barnum's talent for ballyhoo.

Having lost his job, Insull answered an advertisement in the *Times* of
London for a secretary and was hired. It was a wonderful break for the
ambitious young man, because his new employer was the European representative of Thomas Edison. Insull worked hard, and some reports on elec-
trification in Europe that he wrote impressed Edison. In 1881, the inventor
invited him to come to the United States to serve as his private secretary.
Edison was the very epitome of the absentminded inventor and Insull
organized his office, took care of his mail, bought his clothes, and even
made certain he had his meals. He was tireless, ruthless, as reliable as the
tides and determined to rise.

Edison placed Insull in charge of the Edison Construction Company,
which built and sold generating stations to meet the new demand for electric power. Edison wanted to sell electricity as cheaply as possible and
thereby reap the profits of scale and volume. "We will make electric light so
cheap that only the rich will be able to afford candles," he proclaimed.
Insull put this plan into practice. The price of electric bulbs was cut from
$1 in 1888 to 44 cents in 1890 and to 40 cents in 1897.

Together, Edison and Insull created the General Electric Company,
which attracted the attention of J. P. Morgan, who bought Edison out for
$5 billion in cash. The inventor was happy to return to his workbench, so
Morgan offered Insull the presidency of the company, but the young man
was through working for others. In July 1892, he arrived in Chicago, where
with the help of a $250,000 loan from Marshall Field, the merchant
prince—"never pay cash when you can give a note" was Insull's motto—
he took over the Chicago Edison Company. The city had a population of a
million but only five thousand people had electric light. With the
Columbian Exposition, a world's fair, soon to open in Chicago, Insull saw
an opportunity and seized it.

A stiffly arrogant, red-faced man, he was in his office at 7:10 every morning. He expanded the company by aggressively cutting prices. The newly opened Great Northern Hotel was wooed with bargain rates and then Insull used this contract to advertise his company. He pioneered the idea that generating plants should operate twenty-four hours a day to cut costs. When politicians got in his way, he bought them. When labor leaders got in his way, he bought them, too. In his first forty-two months in Chicago Insull increased sales volume from an annual rate of 2.8 million kilowatts to 13.3 million.

Fifteen years later, when he merged Chicago Edison and Commonwealth Electric, his company was sixty times larger than when he had started, and he held a monopoly on electric power and gas in America's second city and its suburbs. Insull also brought electricity to farm areas, was a paternalistic if strict employer who hired blacks without prejudice, and gave his workers education allowances, medical care, pensions, and stock ownership.

Technological daring, bigger generators, and more extensive transmission lines were the keys to Insull's success. In 1912, he added financial legerdemain to his skills. That year, he organized his first holding company— Middle West Utilities—and from that point his empire rolled on like an avalanche. Insull did not invent the holding company, but along with the Van Sweringen brothers, Oris and Mantis, who were building a railroad empire at the same time, he was among its most ardent exponents. Unlike the merger movement of the turn of the century, when competing companies that produced the same or related products were combined into larger firms such as United States Steel and International Harvester, the new urge was to merge companies that were doing the same thing but in different communities. The trend was particularly strong in the utilities industry.

Leverage was the key to the holding company. Insull might set the capitalization of a newly captured operating company at $500 million, and issue $250 million in bonds, $150 million in nonvoting preferred stock, and $100 million in common stock, which alone had voting privileges. Thus, he had only to invest $50 million—usually borrowed—to buy half the common stock to control a firm capitalized at $500 million. A holding company might control ten identical operating companies worth $5 billion in combined assets. If each operating company paid a not unreasonable 7 percent profit annually—or $35 million—the gross profit earned by the holding company for all ten companies would be

$350 million a year on an investment of $500 million. Insull's touch was so golden that observers joked that had he run World War I, he would have made a profit.

The utility holding companies became the vogue all across the nation, they were pyramided atop one another as they fed the ever growing demand from investors for shares, and the value of their bonds was highly inflated. Between 1919 and 1928 some four thousand public utilities were folded into holding companies. Unlike operating companies, which made actual products or performed actual services, a holding company consisted of little more than the lawyer's office that housed its records. Some states, most notably Delaware, structured their laws to become legal havens for such operations. One building in Wilmington housed ten thousand corporations on a single floor. Holding companies that operated in more than one state were free from the control of state public utility commissions. The Insull Utilities Investment Fund shot up in value from $12 a share to $150 in the summer of 1929. Insull's own personal wealth was calculated at $150 million.

From Barnum, Insull had learned the techniques of publicity, and he created a security sales department to peddle stock to his customers and employees. Like his mentor, Edison, he loathed Wall Street and recognized that a huge, untapped pool of potential investors could be reached through mass-marketing techniques. Insull's employees had to buy and sell stock in his various enterprises to relatives, neighbors, and friends. Insull was the high-powered exponent of the doctrine of "customer ownership" of utilities, in which great corporations were "owned" by anonymous millions and operated by a managerial class.* A Chicago investment house linked to Insull sponsored Sunday radio talks by the "Old Family Counsellor," who urged listeners to buy the safest securities available—which, of course, were Insull's.

By the mid-1920s, Insull was a patron of the arts, a generous donor to charity, and a celebrity who made regular appearances on both the society and business pages of the daily newspapers. A generous contributor to political campaigns as well, he knew every president from William McKinley to Herbert Hoover and proclaimed them all colossal bores, with the exception of Theodore Roosevelt. He owned a 4,200 acre farm near Chicago with a home in which the bathtub was coated with $30,000 in

---

* Insull prefigured the modern "managerial revolution," in which large corporations are run not for the benefit of shareholders, consumers, or employees but for the gratification of the managers. They pay themselves enormous salaries and generous stock options and failure is cushioned by "golden parachutes."

gold leaf, and where the terraces looked out over lagoons stocked with goldfish and swans. The staff was so large the estate had its own post office. To the millions who used his electricity, owned his stock, and enjoyed his patronage, he was the symbol of dynamic capitalism.

Insull's name was synonymous with the Chicago Civic Opera and he even picked the programs. Mary Garden, the director, resigned in protest when he insisted on dropping her favorite French operas for German and Italian works because there were more Germans and Italians than French around Chicago. He built a new home for the opera on the ground floor of his forty-two-floor office tower. The social rebuffs Insull had suffered upon his arrival in town rankled, and when the new theater was unveiled, Chicago's dowagers were shocked to find there were no boxes where they could make an ostentatious show of themselves.

The bankers were hypnotized by Insull's operations. "The bankers would call up the way the grocer used to call up my momma, and try to push their money at us," recalled Insull's bookkeeper, James McEnroe. "We have some nice lettuce today, Mrs. McEnroe—we have some nice, fresh green money today, Mr. Insull. Isn't there something you could use—maybe $10,000,000." But as the *Wall Street Journal* later pointed out, Insull's companies had taken on an enormous amount of debt during the go-go years of the 1920s. If the profits of the operating companies ever fell, Insull's entire, jerry-built pyramid would collapse—as it did after the Crash.*

A get-rich-quick virus swept across the United States along with Coolidge Prosperity. "The propensity to swindle and be swindled run parallel to the propensity to speculate during a boom," explains economist Charles P. Kindleberger. Stock scams were so notorious that Chicago crime boss Al Capone complained, "It's a racket. Those stock market guys are crooked." The Iridium Gold and Platinum Company, which claimed to have found

---

* Insull fled the country and took refuge in Greece. At the request of the U.S. government, he was seized by Turkish authorities while cruising in Turkish waters on his yacht and extradited to America to stand trial for fraud and embezzlement. The politicians upon whom he had showered money took pains to distance themselves from him. He was tried three times and acquitted in each case. Unlike some modern managers, he had lost his fortune with the collapse of his operations. Insull went to live in France and in 1938, at the age of seventy-eight, he died from a massive heart attack in a Paris subway station. Someone apparently stole the stricken man's wallet, and the newspapers gloated over the fact that he had only 85 cents in his pocket when found.

gold and platinum nuggets in a Yonkers potato field, sold over 500,000 shares, mostly to Russian immigrants. Chicago promoters did a lively business selling stock in the League of Nations to the gullible. The wonderfully named Nova Adolphus Brown peddled shares in the Lexington Chocolate Company, which offered cod liver oil chocolate bars to people who wanted the nutritional benefits of cod liver oil without the taste. Birmingham Motors of Jamestown, New York, sold investors ownership in a company producing the world's first no-axle automobile. And the George Alot Company offered farmland in the Mississippi riverbed. The property was described as "unimproved except for running water."

Such promotions enjoyed success because optimistic Americans were convinced that with a combination of hustle and luck they could become wealthy, for God had intended Americans to be rich. It was an article of faith that the opportunities at hand were so wonderful that neither capital nor experience was necessary for success. The humblest investor could turn a few dollars into a fortune; the rawest promoter could build a business empire on a shoestring. The thing to do was to "get in on the ground floor." The precise moment when the bull began its rampage on Wall Street cannot be precisely established, but the stock market began an upward march in the mid-1920s that, except for a few momentary jolts, was not halted until 1929, when Easy Street became a dead end.

At the end of May 1924, the *New York Times* average price of twenty-five industrial stocks was 106. By December, the average had jumped to 134. A year later, it was 181. Volume nearly doubled to 462,722,000 shares during those years, showing the new volatility of the market. Attempts to corner the stock of the Piggly Wiggly stores and Stutz Motors emphasized the increasingly speculative practices of Wall Street.

The stock market was obviously attracting the interest of a wider segment of the public than the usual professionals. Bonds had been the investment of choice for most ordinary Americans because of their wartime experience with the Liberty Loans, but the action was switching to equities. Bonds purchased during the war were maturing and the money was pouring into new investments. Jesse L. Livermore, one of the Street's master speculators and a well-known bear, had a profound effect on the market when he went bullish, advising investors to "drop their wartime reasoning" and "adjust themselves to post-war conditions."

New organizations appeared to meet the needs of this crop of relatively unsophisticated investors. Charles E. Mitchell, head of the National City Bank, the nation's largest, led the way in turning conservative banks into one-stop financial department stores. A graduate of Amherst and a one-time salesman for Western Electric, he "sold bullishness on America and investment in general and succeeded to an unprecedented degree." Outlets were opened in fifty cities across the country, and they housed a combined bank branch, trust company, and securities office. National City had one of the largest sales organizations in the world.

One of the great fears of investors during the speculative boom of the 1920s was a shortage of common stocks, which was said to drive stock prices up. To meet this perceived need, National City became what Mitchell called one of the nation's largest "manufacturers" of securities. The bank underwrote or originated $10.7 billion worth of bonds in the 1920s, 21 percent of the total issued, more than any other bank. Young Ivy Leaguers like Nick Carraway of *The Great Gatsby* flocked to Wall Street to sell securities. Mitchell exhorted, bullied, and browbeat his salesmen to meet their quotas. Those who didn't were summarily fired. This close relationship between banking and securities sales would play an important role in the forthcoming Wall Street crash. Mitchell narrowly escaped jail, but he was fined $1 million for income tax evasion.

The skyscraper was the symbol of the era of prosperity, the cloud-cathedral of the Age of Success. Construction spending rose from $12.2 billion in 1919 to $17.4 billion in 1928. A housing boom sparked the industry in the early years of the decade, and when it faltered, commercial and industrial building picked up the slack. Skyscrapers were arrogant and proud physical manifestations of America's competitive culture. Few cities did not have at least one tower, and the skylines of the major cities had a distinctive profile based on the shape of the land on which the buildings were erected. In Chicago, where the skyscraper originated with the clean functionalism of Louis Sullivan, the lakefront was lined by a wall of tall buildings. Sullivan originated the phrase "form follows function," and function to him included not only utility but man's aspirations and ideals. But he died penniless and unrecognized in 1924 in a run-down Chicago rooming house, and Frank Lloyd Wright, his pupil, had no major commissions. Instead, the new skyscrapers were adorned with pseudo-gothic ornamentation and flying buttresses. In Manhattan, they formed a pyramid of Art Deco towers at the tip of the island.

Riveters kept up a fusillade of noise all over New York, and workmen dangled overhead like human spiders spinning webs of steel ever higher into space. By 1929, the city's skyline had taken on a semblance of its current appearance. Observed from the bay on a sunny morning, it seemed an island of glittering pinnacles. There were no fewer than seventy-eight buildings over twenty stories high, and nineteen reached forty stories or more. The Chrysler Building held temporary sway as the tallest, with its gigantic metal-tipped needle stabbing seventy-seven stories into the clouds. Towering hotels and enormous office buildings with the daytime populations of small cities mushroomed around Grand Central Terminal in Midtown. Regulations required tall buildings to have setbacks at certain floors to prevent them from completely blocking out the sunlight, giving some of the new structures a distinctive "wedding cake" profile.

Height conferred distinction and to attract tenants, developers advertised there was "nothing between us and the sun." These towers communicated the appearance of vibrant economic health, the architectural equivalent of flushed cheeks and sparkling eyes. Not everyone was enchanted with the prospect of more tall buildings, however. Thomas Edison warned that "disaster must overtake us" if skyscrapers continued to be built, because of the congestion they created in the hearts of America's cities. But most Americans were convinced that the continued growth of the central city was inevitable, even though people were already leaving its crowded, noxious, and noisy streets for nearby suburbs. Nevertheless, a busy downtown meant prosperity and even taller structures were projected. The Rockefellers leased a tract of land from Columbia University bounded by Fifth and Sixth Avenues between 48th and 59th streets, and planned to erect a fabulous business and entertainment center. Shortly after, it was announced that the grand old Waldorf-Astoria hotel* would be demolished to make way for the tallest building in the world—the 102-story Empire State Building, which would be surmounted by a mooring mast for dirigibles.

H. G. Wells, comparing the working classes of Europe and America in the Twenties, observed: "In the United States, the actual proletariat (defined as a degraded, propertyless class) must be a very small portion of the population." Hypnotized by the signs of boom, he completely misunderstood the actual situation of the American worker. The American craze for numbers and statistics cloaked the maldistribution of the nation's wealth. Even though real per capita income rose 37 percent during the 1920s, and the cost of living was stable and unemployment low—3.7 percent between 1923 and 1929—the benefits of the new prosperity were not equally distributed. The share of the farmer was disproportionately small. The share

* A new, forty-seven-story Waldorf was built in the block between Park and Lexington Avenues, between 49th and 50th Streets.

of labor, although slowly edging upward, barely kept pace with the essentials of a comfortable life—an auto, a radio, a telephone, a new kitchen or bathroom. Much of the profits resulting from gains in productivity were retained by the corporations rather than given to the workers as wages. They were reflected instead in earnings statements and dividend checks. Dividends rose from 4.3 percent of national income in 1920 to 7.2 percent in 1929, an increase far outstripping boosts in wages.

By 1929, according to the Bureau of Labor Statistics, a family of four required a yearly income of $2,500 to maintain "a decent standard of living." Nearly half of the 27 million families that filed income tax returns that year earned only $1,500 annually, and another six million families received less than $1,000—which meant that more than half of the nation's families were struggling in an era of supposed prosperity.* Yet, the number of Americans with incomes from $3,000 to $5,000 nearly tripled between 1927 and 1928. Those with incomes over $1 million almost doubled. In July 1929, the *Wall Street Journal* reported that there were "scores of men who are now worth more than $50,000,000."

Still, while industry was marching to the clang of the cash register and the beat of the assembly line, labor was marching in place. The AFL, headed by a colorless bureaucrat named William Green since the death of Samuel Gompers in 1924, showed no interest in organizing the vast number of unskilled workers. Nor did unions exist in the electrical equipment, textile, rubber, cement, auto, and chemical industries. Some employers resorted to strong-arm methods to keep their workers from organizing or going on strike. Union membership declined from 5.1 million in 1920 to 3.4 million in 1929, in a nonagricultural workforce of 30 million.

The unions were too impotent to protest the failure of wages to match productivity and the prevalence of the "yellow dog contract," in which workers agreed not to strike. Workers worried not only about the wage squeeze but also about the threat of losing their jobs through the introduction of new machinery and technology. And there was a palpable fear of being fired at the age of forty-five or fifty to be replaced by someone younger.

Some industrialists, such as John D. Rockefeller, Jr., talked about a "partnership" between industry and labor, but in the 1920s most firms fought unionization. Welfare capitalism was a weapon to rid themselves of

---

* An average working man with a family of five who earned about $1,500 a year spent his money as follows: $548 for food, $237 for clothes, $186 for rent, $74 for utilities, $74 for furnishings and household supplies, $306 for other expenses, while saving $79 for medical expenses or a rainy day.

unions. In lieu of the government-mandated social safety nets available in most Western European nations, large firms offered paternalistic programs to care for the health and safety of their workers, and pension funds for the retired, but only as long as their employees were passive. Such plans offered little real security because most workers were employed by small factories that could not afford pension programs or other benefits.

For farmers, these were lean years. Over the course of the 1920s, both the net income and real purchasing power of the producers of grains, live-stock, and cotton dropped by 25 percent from the boom times of the war years, and the total value of farm produce fell by half—from $21.4 billion in 1919 to $11 billion in 1929. Except during 1925 and 1929, it is esti-mated that as many as two thirds of the nation's farms operated at a loss. The beet fields, cranberry bogs, and other seasonal branches of agriculture were dependent upon child labor.* Tenancy increased from 38.1 percent of farms in 1920 to 42.4 percent in 1930. And the number of farms mort-gaged rose from 37.2 percent to 42 percent. Disgruntled farmers believed the minimal prices they received for their crops were purposely designed to subsidize the urban workforce, making up for reduced wages by providing low-cost food.

Eight million farm people lived within five miles of towns and cities and had access to schools and hospitals, but in mid-decade, 20 million still lived in isolation. Only 10 percent of farms had water piped into the houses and a mere 7 percent had electric light. The rest were lit by kerosene lamps. Lean years for the farmers were also lean years for those who served them. In the prosperous year of 1928, as many as 549 small-town banks went under; in 1929, another 640 collapsed—and this was before the Crash.

In the Marx Brothers comedy *Cocoanuts*, Groucho, playing the role of a slick Florida real estate salesman, rolled his eyes roguishly and announced to the audience, "Buy a lot! You can have any kind of house you want! You can get wood or brick or stucco—oh boy, can you get stucco!" And from 1922 to 1925, thousands of Americans went to Florida and got "stucco."

The Sunshine State underwent a boom in those years that had all the trappings of the Gold Rush of 1849, the Tulip Mania, and the South Sea Bubble. Suddenly, thousands of ordinary Americans, enticed by the

* In 1924, Congress sent to the states for ratification a proposed constitutional amend-ment that granted the federal government the power to regulate child labor. By a large mar-gin, the states failed to approve it. Most legislatures saw the proposal as a violation of the doctrine of states' rights.

prospect of getting rich quick, rushed to buy plots in developments that existed only on paper or were still alligator-infested mangrove swamps. For most, the idea was not to buy a place to live but to speculate in options to buy land—or "binders," as they were called locally, for 10 percent down— and then sell them to newcomers at an inflated price. Sometimes, the same front money was used to buy several binders so the little guy could feel like a tycoon.

Thousands of acres of orange groves were ripped up to make way for town sites. For three hundred miles, the whole strip of Florida coastline from Jacksonville to Miami, and on the Gulf Coast as well, was platted and staked out in fifty-foot lots. Everyone was convinced land values could go in only one direction—and that was up. Stories about the sudden fortunes supposedly made in Florida real estate glutted Northern newspapers: the coast guardsman who picked up ocean frontage for 25 cents an acre and sold it for a million; the ex-soldier who traded an old overcoat for ten seemingly worthless beach acres that turned out to be worth $25,000; the old woman who had bought a lot for $25 in 1896 and sold it for $150,000. The underlying theme of these tales was how amazingly easy it was for plain folks—tourists, vacationing elders, people with little in the way of money—to make their fortunes in Florida.

To drum up business, publicists trumpeted the discovery of pirate loot at one resort after another, from St. Augustine to Miami—"not little flakes of gold but buried treasure: doubloons, pieces of eight, gold bullion." Black-beard, Captain Kidd, Sir Henry Morgan, Jean Laffite—a veritable Who's Who of buccaneering—had apparently buried treasure in South Florida. Prospective investors were urged to buy now and recoup by digging for pirate gold on their own slice of beachfront paradise.

Only twenty-five years before, Miami had been little more than a remote crossroads junction on the fringe of the Everglades, with a malaria-ridden population of about sixty. By 1926, some 150,000 people were clog-ging the streets and boosters were talking of a population of a million in another ten years. The "Magic City" was growing faster than any place in the country, with the exception of Los Angeles. The two mushroom cities had much in common, enjoying balmy climates, tropical locations, and Spanish cultural traditions, which architects reproduced in red tile and bogus Andalusian buildings. And the two states benefited from sophisti-cated water use projects that, in the years before World War I, drained the Florida wetlands and irrigated the California wilderness, opening vast tracts of the interiors to development.

There were 25,000 real estate agents working in Miami in 1925 at the height of the boom. Property values soared from $63.8 million to $421 million between 1922 and 1926. Affluent visitors came by rail on the *Orange Blossom Special*, but most made the long trek by auto. Throughout the boom, lines of cars, ranging from Model Ts to limousines, headed south along the Dixie Highway, leaving behind the dreary cities of the North and the farms of the rural Midwest. Roadsides were dotted with tent colonies of tourists and fortune seekers.

Americans were enticed to Florida by massive advertising campaigns in newspapers, magazines, and on the radio. Developers opened sales offices in the North that targeted not only city people but small-town residents and farmers as well. Prospective buyers were given free transportation and room and board. Baby contests, alligator wrestling, and vaudeville acts were provided for their amusement. New developments seemed to be conjured out of nothing almost overnight, and slickers peddled life memberships in fake yacht clubs.

Observers explained the Florida phenomenon in a variety of ways. Exclusive resorts for the wealthy and socially elect such as Palm Beach and St. Augustine had already put the state in the public eye. Florida was relatively accessible by automobile and by train, and the winter climate was perfect for easy living. With the economy booming, middle-class Americans had, for the first time, money for winter vacations and second homes. Florida was attractive because Prohibition was hardly enforced there, and state income and inheritance taxes were unknown. Greed was also a factor, and the principle of the greater fool prevailed. Florida fever created, said John Kenneth Galbraith, "a world inhabited not by people who needed to be persuaded to believe but by people who wanted an excuse to believe."

The flamboyant Palm Beach architect Addison Mizner set the style. The son of California pioneers, Mizner had studied at the University of Salamanca in Spain, and then worked for the San Francisco architectural firm that created the California Mission style. Mizner's designs for the Everglades Club in Palm Beach and the massive beachfront villas he produced for nouveau riche millionaires established Mediterranean Revival as the appropriate style for Florida. Following his lead, developers offered a fevered dream of Spanish castles, Italian palazzos, Moorish arcades, and medieval cloisters. Most of the land was marshy, and imaginative developers transformed necessity into advantage by turning drainage ditches into Venetian canals complete with motorized gondolas, candy-striped mooring poles, and elaborate landings.

Carl Fisher, a onetime race car driver, manufacturer of automobile headlights, and creator of the Indianapolis Speedway, was dubbed by humorist

Will Rogers the "midwife" of the Florida boom. He had "rehearsed the mosquitoes till they would not bite you until after you bought." Fisher began in 1913 by building the first of three causeways across Biscayne Bay, from Miami to a narrow strip of offshore land that he dubbed Miami Beach, where he developed new hotels, homes, and other properties. Trees were planted, swamps were filled in to make more land, and the bay was sprinkled with artificial islands. Fisher held bathing beauty contests and deluged Northern papers with tantalizing photographs of pretty girls cavorting on the beach. He rented a giant billboard in New York's Times Square during the worst winter months to proclaim the day's balmy temperature in Miami Beach.

George Merrick did the same thing for Coral Gables, an elegant suburb he laid out on his family's orchards to the southwest of Miami. Beginning with 1,600 acres in 1921, he established a meticulously planned and beautifully landscaped community of wide avenues, red-tile roofs, white walls and spasms of wrought iron, the twenty-six-story, $10 million Biltmore Hotel, a country club, golf courses, and lagoons. A quarry that had provided stone for construction was transformed into a Venetian pool. Merrick rode the crest of the boom and within two years had expanded his holdings to ten thousand acres and had built five hundred houses, spending $3 million a year on promotion.

By late 1925, however, there were signs that the boom was sputtering; the supply of unsold lots was piling up as the supply of prospective purchasers dwindled. There were several reasons for the collapse of the bonanza. State officials in the North, worried about the drain of capital to Florida, erected bars against soliciting for customers within their borders. The Massachusetts Savings Bank League estimated that 100,000 depositors in that state had transferred funds to Florida. Reports of land swindles were appearing with regularity in Northern newspapers. Transportation bottlenecks on the railway and the roads to Florida were chronic, and railroad officials declared an embargo on all freight except for food.

Land buyers were scarce during the winter of 1926, a period that should have been the high season for promotion. As money dried up, developments were left half finished, binders went unpaid, and venture after venture went into receivership. "The Florida boom has collapsed," reported *The Nation* in July 1926. "The world's greatest poker game, played with building lots instead of chips, is over."

Nature provided a grim climax to the game, as in mid-September 1926 a hurricane slammed into the Miami area. In the deceptive lull of the eye of the storm, inexperienced visitors, believing the worst was over, poured out into the streets to inspect the damage. And then, the strong side of the killer wind struck at 135 miles an hour. Storm tides surged over the city, Lake Okeechobee overflowed, and snapped-off telephone poles crashed through masonry walls like missiles. Some four hundred people were killed, 6,300 were injured, and fifty thousand rendered homeless. Property damage topped $111 million.

As Miami dug itself out of the rubble, boosters promised that all traces of the damage would be repaired in time for the new season beginning in November, but there was only a trickle of visitors. Another hurricane two years later was even more devastating, killing as many as 1,800 people. Yet, even though Florida fever had run its course, the speculative fires of Coolidge Prosperity were hardly banked. In fact, ever-optimistic Americans pointed to the fact that the collapse of the Florida boom had merely ruffled the nation's economic feathers without doing serious damage as a sign of the boom's inherent strength. "Anyway," as one Florida "investor" put it, "it was worth it just to have been that rich for those few months."

Prosperity favored some sections of the nation more generously than others. The Middle Atlantic, the East North Central, and the Pacific states were winners. The South, with the temporary exception of Florida, New England, and the agricultural West North Central states were losers. New England suffered from the continuing loss of its textile mills to low-wage factories in the South, but there were other troubled industries: coal, shoes, shipbuilding, and railroad equipment. Massachusetts was one of the most depressed states in the nation—offering a grim and bitter vista of abandoned mills, shuttered shoe factories, and empty houses.

The coal industry was dealt a death blow by the competition from oil heating. By 1929, no fewer than 550,000 homes had oil heat. Mine closings cost 250,000 men their jobs between 1923 and 1929. Operators skimped on technology and safety devices to save money. Some mines, such as the Mellon-controlled Pittsburgh Coal Company, the largest producer in the nation, closed down in violation of their contract with the UMW and then reopened with nonunion workers, many of them blacks from the South. The miners went on strike to enforce the contract and violence flared on both sides. Company goons assaulted strikers and the unions used violence against scabs. Two dormitories housing black scabs were dynamited. A reporter for the *New York Daily News* wrote:

I have just returned from a visit to "Hell-in-Pennsylvania." I have seen horrible things there. . . . Many times it seemed impossible to think we were in modern, civilized America. We saw thousands of women and children, literally starving to death. We found hundreds of destitute families living in crudely constructed bare-board shacks. They had been evicted from their homes by the coal companies. We unearthed a system of despotic tyranny reminiscent of Czaristridden Siberia at the worst. . . . We unearthed evidence of terrorism and counterterrorism; of mob beatings and near lynchings, of dishonesty, graft, and heartlessness.

By 1927, southern Appalachia was the main textile-producing area in the nation. Textile towns stretched through the Piedmont between Washington and Atlanta like beads on a string: Lynchburg, Danville, Greensboro, High Point, Salisbury, Charlotte, Gastonia, Gaffney, Spartanburg, Greenville. Local boosters bragged there was a mill every mile. Nevertheless, there was trouble. Demand for cotton was shrinking because of competition from other fibers, notably rayon and silk. The downturn began in 1924, according to labor historian Irving Bernstein.

Southern mill owners, desperate to hold on to their share of the market, were ruthless in the demands they made upon their workers. Their power was not unlike that formerly held by the plantation owners over their slaves in the antebellum South. They owned the houses in which the workers lived and the stores in which they shopped, controlled the civil authorities of the mill towns, and selected the teachers in the schools and the preachers for the churches.

Most of the workers were hardscrabble mountain people from the hills and hollows of the Southeast where pellagra, respiratory diseases, and illiteracy were common. In some aspects, working in a mill was an improvement over subsistence farming. Millworkers had the stimulus of living in a town, had contact with their fellows, and earned some income, even it was pitifully small. Most company houses had running water, inside toilets, and electricity. The rent was $4 a month, deducted from a worker's pay, with coal extra. The working day began at 5 A.M. and lasted ten or eleven hours, six days a week. Night work was common and so was the labor of women and children over fourteen. Entire families worked in the same mill, with the parents supervising their children. Weekly pay rates for adults averaged about $12.83.

Periodically, to achieve maximum production and economy of scale, a "stretch-out" was ordered in which each mill hand was expected to tend an even larger number of looms than usual. The noise and vibration of the machines never stopped, the air was full of choking lint, and in the worst mills, "the floors were filthy, the toilets revolting and the drinking water contaminated with the residue of tobacco spit." Chronic fatigue and lack of safety devices on the machinery created a high potential for accidents, especially among children.

Paradoxically, labor organizers made little headway in the Southern mills despite such Dickensian conditions. The mill owners were rabidly anti-union and branded any attempt at unionization as Bolshevism. They controlled the local police and union organizers were usually run out of town. Following a directive from Moscow, the Communists had established unions to rival those of the AFL, and organized labor was weakened by internecine warfare between them. Nor were the workers themselves much interested in joining a union. They were clannish, parochial, and suspicious of outlanders. Nevertheless, there were signs of incipient revolt.

It began when 800 workers in Henderson, North Carolina, went on strike to demand that wage cuts be rescinded. An organizer for the AFL-affiliated United Textile Workers succeeded in signing up from 500 to 600 of the strikers. Reacting quickly, the mill owners evicted nine of the striking families from their company-owned homes as an example, and the walkout collapsed. But it revived in the Piedmont Revolt as strikes spread from Elizabethtown, Gastonia, and Marion, in North Carolina, to Danville, in Virginia. With the Communists participating in some of the strikes, the mill owners contended the walkouts were part of a radical plot to take over America.

Gastonia was the leading textile center of the South, with more than 570 mills within a hundred-mile radius of the town center. Loray was the largest mill in the area with 3,500 employees. Trouble began when the local manager was ordered to slash expenses by $500,000 to meet losses resulting from competition and overproduction. Wages were cut by 20 percent, a stretch-out was ordered, and all the better-paid hands were fired and replaced by low-wage employees. By early 1929, the workforce had been reduced to 2,200, and there was widespread anger and resentment in every quarter of the mill.

"North Carolina is the key to the South," said a spokesman for the Communist-led National Textile Workers Union. "Gaston County is the key to North Carolina and the Loray Mill is the key to Gaston County." Fred E. Beal, a New England–born radical and onetime Wobbly who had walked the picket line of the great Lawrence strike of 1912 with Big Bill Haywood, began building an underground organization in the mill. On

March 30, 1929, he brought the union into the open with a mass meeting attended by more than one thousand workers, who voted for a strike. Both shifts walked off the job almost to a man.

In the beginning the strike was labor-issue-oriented with goals such as a minimum standard wage of $20 a week, elimination of the stretch-out, a forty-hour, five-day week, and equal pay for women and children. These demands were immediately rejected by the company, and political agendas emerged on both sides. The National Guard was called out and the *Gastonia Gazette* ran a full-page ad proclaiming that the strike was aimed at "overthrowing this Government and destroying property and to kill, kill, kill."

Seizing an opportunity to win international publicity, representatives of the Young Communist League, the Workers' International Relief, the International Labor Defense, and the *Daily Worker* rushed to Gastonia. What the simple and phlegmatic Loray mill hands made of all the talk of Marxism and the proletariat that followed is not recorded. But within a few weeks, after their final paychecks were spent and union welfare proven inadequate, some workers drifted back to the mill. Even so, management quickly struck back. A mob of armed and masked men utterly demolished the National Textile Workers headquarters while a detachment of guardsmen ignored the melee. The company evicted sixty-two strikers and their families from their homes and the strike appeared all but broken.

The NTW established a tent city on a vacant lot to serve as its headquarters and as housing for the evicted families. Morale was sustained by Ella May Wiggins, the union's troubadour, who lived in the camp and composed and sang ballads about the struggle. Fearing another attack, union leaders established an armed guard. On the night of June 7, 1929, Gastonia police chief O. F. Aderholt and four policemen entered the camp without a warrant and were confronted by the guards. Shooting broke out, and Aderholt was killed and the other officers wounded.

Vigilantes demolished the tent colony in the wake of the shooting, sending men, women, and children fleeing into the night with only the clothes on their backs. Beal and fifteen others, including three women, were arrested and charged with conspiracy to commit murder. A mistrial was declared when the prosecution dramatically unveiled a bloodstained dummy in the courtroom, made up to look like the murdered Aderholt. The lawyers got the idea from a movie called *The Trial of Mary Dugan*. More violence followed. Two Communists were kidnapped and flogged by a mob of night riders. Ella May Wiggins was killed while riding with a truckload of unionists, when it was fired upon in broad daylight. No one was ever charged with her murder.

By the time a second trial was convened in September 1929, tempers had cooled enough for nine of the defendants to have been freed and charges against the remaining seven, including Beal, reduced to second-degree murder. But the Communists were more interested in martyrs than justice. To the horror of the defendants, a witness from the Young Communist League proclaimed revolution from the stand and denounced religion. The jury took less than an hour to return a verdict of guilty. Beal and three others received sentences of seventeen to twenty years; two got twelve to fourteen years, and the last man got seven years. The strike had already spluttered out. On bail while pending appeal, they all fled to the Soviet Union, and were paraded about as martyrs to capitalist injustice.*

The strikes in Monroe and Danville were equally hopeless. Following several explosive encounters, they ended with workers being fired from their jobs and their families evicted from company housing. The Piedmont uprising was ill-timed because the wave of walkouts occurred in the midst of a depression in the textile industry, and all the economic big guns were in the hands of the employers. Moreover, the AFL failed to provide adequate support and leadership. Yet there were some improvements in working conditions: the workweek in Gastonia was reduced to fifty-five hours with the same take-home pay; at Marion wages were raised 5 percent; and night work for women and children was abolished in mills across the South. And, as Irving Bernstein wrote, "the strikes left a nuclei of workmen, though bitter in defeat, determined to do battle again for their unions when the time was ripe."

It was one of the strangest processions in the history of the nation's capital. Hordes of Ku Klux Klansmen, estimated at 25,000 strong, paraded in the sweltering heat of August 9, 1925, along Pennsylvania Avenue from the Capitol to the Washington Monument. Marching sixteen abreast, the "Knights" wore full regalia but with faces unmasked, and carried American flags and banners emblazoned with mystic symbols. Crowds lined the streets, but there was no violence. In the shadow of the towering shaft of the Washington Monument, speakers downplayed the usual anti-black, anti-Semitic, anti-Catholic rhetoric and denied the charges of "hate, malice or prejudice" leveled against the Klan. They claimed the organization stood for "love for all." As night fell, the Klansmen and their families

---

* Fred Beal became disillusioned with the "workers' paradise" and returned to the United States in 1933 to serve his sentence. "I would rather be an American prisoner than a free man in Russia," he declared. He was released in 1942. Four of Beal's fellow defendants remained in Russia, one died there, and one returned home.

marched across the Potomac to a fairgrounds in Arlington, where a huge flaming cross was set afire that could be seen on the other side of the river in the capital.

Klan leaders hailed this as the greatest day in its history, and claimed a membership of five million. In reality, the Invisible Empire was breaking up beneath their feet. Only two years later, membership fell to 350,000, and Klansmen who paraded in Northern cities were jeered and mocked by hostile crowds.

Race relations in the United States had hardly improved, but by mid-decade, the postwar tensions responsible for the Klan's mushrooming growth had largely abated. The number of lynchings declined in the 1920s, from eighty-six in 1919 to nine in 1929. Some analysts theorized that racial unrest and lynchings must therefore be products of economic distress, and as the economy improved such tensions would decrease. Movies, automobiles, and radio filled the spare time of Americans and fraternal organizations had lost their appeal. As the nation relaxed, there were fewer calls for stridency. Moreover, the Klan had won one of its greatest goals, the passage of the National Origins Act of 1924, which closed down immigration to the United States.

Numerous scandals also did much to discredit the Klan leadership. A Klan chieftain in Buffalo, the Reverend Charles C. Penfold, was arrested in an auto in "an improper position" with a woman who was not his wife. In Youngstown, Ohio, Evan Watkins, a "driving force" in the local Klavern, was "exposed as a charlatan" and fled. Imperial Wizard Hiram Wesley Evans expelled a number of prominent Denver Klansmen who had been arrested in vice raids. But the scandal that did more than anything to kill the Klan involved David Stephenson, the powerful Grand Dragon of Indiana.

Stephenson had been feuding with Evans over the share of funds to be sent from Indiana to Atlanta. "The present Imperial Wizard is an ignorant, uncouth individual who eats his peas with a knife," declared Stephenson. "He has neither courage nor culture. He cannot talk intelligently. His speeches are written by hired intelligence." Evans retaliated by expelling him from the Klan. Undaunted, Stephenson organized an independent Klan in Indiana and other Northern states. He also had higher ambitions. Senator Samuel M. Ralston was in poor health, and Stephenson expected Indiana governor Ed Jackson, who had been elected with Klan backing, to name him to the seat when Ralston resigned. Already, he was eying the Republican presidential nomination in 1928, and claimed he would sweep the South.

Stephenson had a history of sexual attacks on women and was arrested for being drunk in public, but experienced little difficulty in covering up these scandals. In March 1925, he finally went too far and kidnapped and raped a former schoolteacher named Madge Oberholtzer. She had bite marks all over her body, and her breasts were so badly chewed they bled. The unfortunate woman swallowed a handful of bichloride of mercury tablets in an unsuccessful attempt at suicide, and although she was vomiting blood, Stephenson refused to obtain medical assistance for her. Oberholtzer died, and medical experts testified her death was due as much to the infection resulting from the bites as to the poison. With prompt attention, they said, she would have survived. Stephenson was convicted of murder and sentenced to life in prison.

The man who had once declared "I am the law" confidently awaited a pardon from Governor Jackson, but he was ignored by the men whom he had put in power. In revenge, Stephenson revealed his secrets, and a congressman, the mayor of Indianapolis, and the sheriff of Marion Country went to jail, while the governor barely escaped a similar fate. A generation of Indiana politicians thought Stephenson's case too hot to handle and he remained behind bars for thirty years. Upon his release, he disappeared into the obscurity from which he had emerged.

These incidents and others made a joke of the pretensions of the Klan to guard the nation's moral purity. Even Calvin Coolidge, who had remained silent about the Klan during the 1924 campaign, now spoke out against it. "Progress," the president told an American Legion convention, "depends very largely on the encouragement of variety. . . . Divine Providence has not bestowed upon any race a monopoly of patriotism and character. . . . Whether one traces his Americanism back three centuries to the *Mayflower*, or three years to the steerage . . . we are all now in the same boat."

With the Klan all but out of the way, and with Prohibition regarded as an untouchable third rail, the 1926 congressional election turned on prosperity. The ruling Republicans hoped good times would help them maintain their substantial margins in both houses of Congress. "Our present state of prosperity has been greatly promoted by three causes," Coolidge said, "one of which is economy, resulting in reduction and reform in national taxation. Another is the elimination of many kinds of waste. The third is the general raising of standards of living."

Historically, the party in power usually loses congressional seats in off-year elections, and despite Coolidge's personal popularity, 1926 was no exception. The Republicans lost ten seats in the House and seven in the

Senate. While they maintained a good working majority in the House, 237 to 195, their majority in the Senate was reduced to only three. Party leaders had to go hat in hand to the radical farm bloc to obtain their votes to organize the Senate, and it was a certainty that the vexing demands for farm relief would come up again. In spite of this setback, Coolidge was optimistic about the state of the union in his annual message to Congress on December 7, 1926. "I find it impossible to characterize it other than one of great peace and prosperity."

CHAPTER 14

Seven Against the Wall

New Yorkers adored Jimmy Walker. An Irish charmer from the side-walks of Greenwich Village, he was the ideal mayor for the metropolis during the Jazz Age. Nearing fifty when he became mayor in 1925, James J. Walker, as he was formally known, looked thirty-five. Short, dapper, and cocky, he carried himself with a jaunty air and dressed with a Broadway flair. Whenever he arrived at dinners, rallies, and parades—and at night-clubs where he squired a pretty musical comedy actress named Betty Compton—the band struck up "Will You Love Me in December As You Do in May?," a hit song of 1908 for which he had written the lyrics.

A swift man with a wisecrack and one-liner, Walker made numerous contributions to political commentary:

No girl was ever ruined by a book.
A reformer is a guy who rides through a sewer in a glass-bottomed boat.
There are two places where politicians end up, the farm or the bread-line. I am a farmer—at the moment.
I'd rather be a lamppost in New York than mayor of Chicago.

Under Walker's easy hand, the city of seven million was wide open and everything had its price. New Yorkers were in full rebellion against Prohibition and there was a high level of corruption to keep illegal liquor and beer flowing. Grover Whalen, Walker's affable and urbane police commissioner, put the number of speakeasies at about thirty thousand—most probably known to his cops, who took payoffs for allowing them to remain open. Izzy Einstein, the Prohibition agent, put the number at 100,000. Corruption and municipal finagling were profitable on a scale not seen since the heyday of the Tweed Ring—and numerous city officials were accomplished grafters with their loot secreted away in "little tin boxes." At one end of the spectrum, a Tammany wheelhorse got away with half of a $16 million sewer contract; policemen fixed tickets in the streets at the other.

Although Walker professed to be a man of the people, he liked millionaires and they reciprocated his affection in grand style. A prominent businessman named Jules Mastbaum spent $25,000 renovating the mayor's boyhood home on St. Luke's Place, as a gift. When Mastbaum died, Paul Block, a publisher, succeeded him as benefactor. Later, it was discovered that Mastbaum was the bag man for a deal that involved a $26,000 payoff to Walker for a public transit franchise. And Block, who was involved with a firm that sold wall tiles to contractors building the city's subways, opened a Wall Street brokerage account with the mayor, from which Walker received $246,692.72 in cash without having invested a penny. He called it "a benifiance."

Yet, in spite of all the rumors of payoffs and corruption, Walker easily won reelection in 1928 over Fiorello La Guardia, who echoed the themes of reform and progressivism. Most subway straphangers didn't mind Walker's offhanded attitude toward his job because, seventy years before Bill Clinton, they saw him as a charming rogue. He made the city seem glamorous and romantic, and to the rest of the nation he symbolized the splendor, vivacity, and wickedness of the metropolis.

Bootlegging was big business during the 1920s and operated parallel with the boom on Wall Street. Although the consumption of alcoholic beverages dropped in the early years of Prohibition, from 1923 onward the demand for illicit booze and beer exploded with the coming of Coolidge Prosperity. In Detroit, for example, bootlegging was the city's second largest industry after autos. Prohibition created a new class of tycoons that rivaled their predecessors, the great nineteenth-century robber barons, in wealth, power, business acumen—and ferocity.

The fundamental reason for the failure of Prohibition was that an ever increasing number of otherwise good American citizens refused to obey the law. Bootleggers—from the corner grocer selling pints of bathtub gin out the side door, to such giants of the profession as Al Capone—met a public demand. "I violate the Prohibition law, sure," Capone groused one day. "Who doesn't? The only difference is that I take more chances than the man who drinks a cocktail before dinner and a flock of highballs after it. But he's just as much a violator as I am."

Efforts to strictly enforce Prohibition only contributed to its rejection by many Americans. Juries refused to convict offenders; in San Francisco charges were dismissed in one case after the jury drank up the evidence. And the high-handed attitude of enforcement agents created contempt for the law.* The life sentence given a Detroit mother of ten for a fourth offense of selling two pints of liquor, the jailing of a janitor who had made some home brew for an American Legion social, and the killing of a house-wife by a deputy sheriff sniffing out liquor all helped sour public opinion on Prohibition enforcement. Out of this grew a willingness to tolerate lawless-ness and the corruption of law enforcement agencies and government offi-cials. "Prosecuting criminals today is like trying to catch a 1927 automobile with an ox-team," wrote one authority on crime in America.

Prohibition did not create organized crime; criminal syndicates already flourished in the big cities. It did, however, provide them the opportunity to expand. Gangsters, taking a leaf from big business, saw the advantage of rationalizing competition, dividing territories, and consolidating resources. Financed by the immense profits from bootlegging, these criminal groups infiltrated every aspect of American society. Arnold Rothstein, the man who allegedly fixed the 1919 World Series, is reputed to have tried to organize a national crime syndicate based on cooperation of all the leading gangs, with the argument that the internecine warfare among the Italian, Irish, and Jewish mobs was bad for business. He created a central buying office to procure alcohol from Canada, the West Indies, England, and Scotland.

When Rothstein was killed in 1928 in the Park Central Hotel over a gambling debt, his protégé, Salvatore Lucania—known as Lucky Luciano—became the pivotal New York crime boss. Luciano was one of the new breed of gangsters who made alliances based on common interests that leaped over ethnic boundaries. Although he was a Sicilian, his right-hand man was a Calabrian named Francesco Castiglia, a.k.a. Frank Costello. At his other hand was Meyer Lansky, a Jew, who ran the financial side of the business. Frank Erickson, another of Rothstein's men, oversaw a network of off-track betting parlors and the numbers racket, which catered to gam-blers—most of them black—who had only a few pennies to wager.

Enforcement of the Volstead Act was difficult because the United States had 18,700 miles of border, land and sea, to patrol, and the outside world was eager to meet the American demand for booze. Herbert Hoover estimated that it would take a quarter of a million men to make America completely dry, and the taxpayers were unwilling to pay the price. Still,

---

*Just as it has in the case of narcotics in our time.

Prohibition, which he described as "noble in motive," had its defenders, especially in the rural Midwest and South.* As a popular doggerel of the day put it:

> Prohibition is an awful flop,
>   We like it.
> It can't stop what it's meant to stop,
>   We like it.
> It's filled our land with vice and crime,
> It's left a trail of graft and slime,
> It don't prohibit worth a dime,
> Nevertheless, we're for it.

"Hello, Sucker!"

You've just paid a $25 cover charge to enter a basement joint in Midtown Manhattan where Chinese lanterns and velvet hang from the ceiling. Drinks are $5 and a bottle of dubious champagne is $35. The place is called the El Fey Club or the Three Hundred Club or the Club Intime or Texas Guinan's or any of a half dozen other names. The name and the location are not important because both will probably change by tomorrow night. What is important is that Mary Louise Cecilia Guinan—a name she hardly ever used—is there to greet you with her brash and sardonic welcome: "Hello, Sucker!"

If Jimmy Walker was the "Night Mayor" of New York, Texas Guinan was the self-styled "Queen of the Night." As fast as Prohibition agents closed down and padlocked her illegal clubs, Guinan and her backer, Larry Fay, a prominent bootlegger who was arrested forty-nine times, moved on to another location. She wore a necklace of miniature padlocks, symbols of the times she was arrested and her clubs closed. None of the charges ever stuck and she was always soon out again. New clubs opened and closed and reopened with dizzying rapidity.

Patterns of entertainment changed with Prohibition, and the "new" people with money wanted to flaunt their wealth where it could be seen. In her clubs, Texas Guinan blended Social Register names, Broadway and Hollywood stars, showgirls, top-drawer racketeers, and a few intellectuals into what would become café society. Her guests might include Lord and

---

* Most writers say Hoover called Prohibition a "noble experiment." What he actually said was that it was a "social and economic experiment, noble in motive." (Fausold, *The Presidency of Herbert Hoover*, pp. 26–27.)

Lady Mountbatten, Mayor Walker and Betty Compton, William J. Fallon, the reigning criminal lawyer of the day, Harry K. Thaw, who had killed Stanford White, Mae West, William Beebe, the scientist, and Aimee Semple McPherson.

Bold, blond, and brassy, Texas Guinan was born in Waco, Texas, and had been a circus rider, a chorus girl, a vaudeville trouper, and a rootin' tootin' cowgirl in a series of minor Hollywood westerns. She usually arrived about midnight, bellowed her famous greeting, and set about rescuing the world from the sin of dullness. If you were "a big butter and egg man"—her term for a wealthy out-of-towner—or a prominent politician, gangster, or celebrity, you received personal attention. She traded insults with the guests, emceed the show, and shamelessly urged the customers to buy more drinks. From the ridiculous cover charge to the outrageous price for drinks and indifferent food, everybody knew they were being taken for a ride, but Guinan's openness about it made them feel they were in on the joke.

Texas playfully mussed the hair and undid the ties of eminent men, and made suggestive remarks. She might jump up on the piano and sing a torch song or lead the crowd in a sing-along. She cracked jokes on subjects in the news. Or she would clear the dance floor so energetic young dancers such as George Raft, Ruby Keeler, and Ruby Stevens (later known as Barbara Stanwyck) could show off their stuff. Next up were the singing and dancing Guinan Girls, teenage hopefuls for the Ziegfeld Follies and Earl Carroll's Vanities, who strutted about wearing almost nothing. "Give the little girls a great big hand!" Guinan would command after their performance. Cigarette girls in skimpy attire worked the tables. Bald and stuffy business tycoons were cajoled into playing leapfrog with chorus girls. "I had a helluva time," said a patron who blew $1,300 in one evening at Texas Guinan's for a party of four. "It was worth it."

Some nightclubs provided unscheduled entertainment. One evening, several gangsters were celebrating at the Club Abbey, on West 54th Street, among them Charles "Chink" Sherman, who made some disparaging remarks about Arthur Flegenheimer, better know as Dutch Schultz. The lights went out and there were bursts of gunfire. Girls screamed, tables were upset, and bottles smashed. When the lights went on again, Sherman had been badly wounded. The Hotsy Totsy Club on Broadway was also the scene of spontaneous gaiety. Two gunmen were killed and another wounded in a shoot-out with Jack "Legs" Diamond, a notorious racketeer and one of the proprietors. The witnesses contracted amnesia and Diamond walked away scot-free.

Such diversions were unwelcome in most nightclubs. The only explosions heard at the Silver Slipper were the zany antics of the comedy team of Clayton, Jackson, and Durante, who specialized in wrecking pianos. Helen Morgan, the sultry star of *Show Boat*, made patrons weep as she sang "Bill" and other melancholy songs while perched on a piano at the Embassy Club. The fey Beatrice Lillie—formally Lady Peel—appeared at the exclusive Sutton Club on the East Side. Libby Holman sang the blues in a deep-throated, husky voice at the Lido. Adele and Fred Astaire danced at the Trocadero. Paul Whiteman and his band supplied the music and Follies stars entertained at Ziegfeld's Midnight Frolic above the New Amsterdam Theater. Belle Livingston, a one-time chorus girl, operated an urban "country club" on East 58th Street where the girls played miniature golf and table tennis in the nude.

Yet, the popular concept of the "Roaring Twenties" as a time when everyone danced the Charleston until dawn in speakeasies and swigged hooch out of silver hip flasks is pure myth. "The number of patrons of speakeasies and bootleggers was infinitesimal compared with the total population," noted Raymond Moley, of Columbia University. Besides, liquor in the clubs was not cheap. Not many people could afford to pay 75 cents for a shot of Scotch or bourbon of questionable antecedents. Drink, said Thorstein Veblen, was a sign "of the superior status of those who are able to afford the indulgence." Speakeasies and the cocktail hour were unknown to a majority of Americans. Ordinary folk drank home brew in the privacy of their homes.

Large-scale rum-running and bootlegging operations yielded enormous profits and were run like large businesses. Prohibition is estimated to have put $2 billion a year—$20 billion in current value—in the pockets of the bootleggers. The enormous investment of capital and manpower required to operate such enterprises placed them beyond the realm of the common small-time crook. Fleets of powerful speedboats and heavily guarded trucks were dispatched to move illegal liquor from ships riding insolently just outside the three-mile limit on both coasts—Rum Row as it was called—or across the border from Canada and from domestic breweries and distilleries. Once in hand, it was moved under guard to drops or warehouses, usually large garages with concealed sub-basements and elevators capable of receiving a fully loaded ten-ton truck and quickly dropping it from view.

Syndicates operated their own printing plants to run up fake labels and glassworks that reproduced the bottles used by foreign distillers. They ran cutting plants and employed bookkeeping staffs, as well as trustworthy payoff men to bribe the coast guard and police. Gunmen guarded these shipments from hijacking by rivals and were employed as "salesmen" to convince speakeasy operators to carry the "goods" offered by their employer. Lawyers and bondsmen had to be available at all times, in the event of unforeseen arrests. This new generation of tycoons bought the cooperation of the politicians, and the arrangement was mutually advantageous.

Some of those involved showed a genius for business organization and made fortunes. Every major American city had its own underworld gang that peddled beer and booze and carved out territories for its distribution. Big Bill Dwyer was a longshoreman on the Brooklyn docks in 1920 and, three years later, was the largest importer of whiskey in the nation. Waxey Gordon—né Irving Wexler—began his career as a pickpocket on the Lower East Side but, by the mid-1920s, owned a pair of skyscraper hotels, a brewery in New Jersey, and had an interest in a large distillery in upstate New York. Dutch Schultz controlled the beer business in upper Manhattan and the Bronx. In Detroit, the Purple Gang, a loose coalition of Jewish groups, liquidated the competition. In Boston, Charles Solomon assumed the role of boss; in Philadelphia, there was Max "Boo Boo" Hoff; in Denver, Joseph Roma; in Cleveland, the Mayfield Road Mob. None had the power and influence of Chicago's Al Capone.

One day in the autumn of 1928, Frank J. Loesch, a prosperous corporation lawyer and president of the Chicago Crime Commission, went to the Hotel Lexington, Al Capone's headquarters in the Loop, on a bizarre mission. He had personally named the mobster as Public Enemy No. 1 and was pledged to his destruction, yet he had come to beg Capone to guarantee the citizens of the nation's second city a free and honest election. No one but Capone could do that, according to biographer John Kobler. Not the governor of Illinois, Len Small, who had narrowly escaped conviction for embezzlement. Not three-time mayor "Big Bill" Thompson, who had promised, to the delight of his Irish constituents, "to punch King George in the snoot" if the unwary monarch ever ventured into town. Not State's Attorney Robert Crowe, who had failed to make a single racketeering case stick. And certainly not the police. "I own the police," Capone once declared.

"It did not take me long after I had been made president of the Crime Commission to discover that Al Capone ran the city," Loesch later recalled. "His hand reached into every department of the city and county government."

Run by brigands, Chicago was wide open and took on all the aspects of a seventeenth-century buccaneers' paradise. During the fourteen years of Prohibition, 703 men were killed in the beer wars that raged among the city's mobsters. Drunken driving cases were up 476 percent and deaths from alcoholism by 600 percent. Petty criminals exploited the breakdown of authority, and car theft, holdups, bank robberies, and burglaries were common. Sixty percent of the police were estimated to be actively involved in the liquor trade, not merely taking bribes, but making and selling the stuff. The stench of malt, fermenting mash, and alcohol distillate hung like a cloud over entire neighborhoods.

No city was more under the thumb of one man than Chicago during Capone's reign, and he lived as regally as a Caesar in ancient Rome. So, when the Republican primary in April 1928 exploded into a wave of bombings, beatings, and murders, mostly the work of Capone's hoodlums to ensure the renomination of Thompson, Loesch went hat in hand to the mobster to seek assurances that the violence would not be renewed in the November general election. Bodyguards with ominous bulges beneath their tight coats ushered Loesch up to Capone's fourth-floor suite, the nerve center of his multimillion-dollar racketeering empire.

With the assistance of his Russian-born financial manager, Jake "Greasy Thumb" Guzik, Capone ran a vast criminal enterprise that included breweries, distilleries, speakeasies, nightclubs, brothels, gambling houses, and horse and dog racing tracks. Padlocked sacks of cash lay scattered about, awaiting deposit in banks under a myriad of false names. Secret doors and passages enabled Capone to arrive and leave without being seen. To guard his realm against interlopers, he kept an army of a thousand "sluggers" and gunmen on his payroll who had accounted for some 250 murders over the past seven years. Lawyers, judges, policemen, politicians, and at least one newspaper reporter were all on the pad.* He rode about his realm in a $30,000 armor-plated Cadillac with a secret gun locker and a police siren.

The take was enormous. Federal authorities estimated that ten thousand speakeasies operated in Chicago—others thought the correct number was double that. If they each bought six barrels of beer a week at $55, Capone and his allies realized a weekly gross of $3.5 million from the sale of beer alone. Each speakeasy also bought an average of two cases of liquor a

---

* Jake Lingle, a police reporter for the Chicago *Tribune*, who was killed in a mob hit in 1930.

week at $90 a case, or another $1.8 million. The beer cost $4 a barrel to produce; the liquor about $20 a case. To this must be added the profits from gambling and prostitution.

Only twenty-nine and at the height of his power, Capone held a near monopoly on bootlegging, gambling, prostitution, and labor racketeering in the Chicago area. In a blaze of Thompson submachine-gun fire, shotgun blasts, and bomb explosions, he had become the overlord of Chicago crime, and had forced the surviving independent barons to end their internecine war and accept his rule.

Capone had a flabby but menacing face with a flattish nose, thick lips, and a roll of flesh at the back of his neck. "Mountains of pasta and Niagaras of Chianti had deposited layers of fat" on his bulky figure, "but the muscle beneath the fat was rock-hard, and in anger [he] could inflict fearful punishment," according to Kobler. A snappy dresser, he wore monogrammed silk shirts and made-to-measure suits, with the right-hand pocket reinforced to hold a pistol, his famous silver fedora, and pearl gray spats. On his middle finger he flashed a $50,000 blue-white, eleven-carat diamond. Capone's most distinguishing features were a long scar that ran across his left cheek from ear to jowl, another across the jaw, and a third behind the left ear—souvenirs of a youthful indiscretion. Sensitive about these wounds, he tried to cover them with thick coats of powder and always showed his undisfigured profile to photographers. The press dubbed him "Scarface," but no one dared use the name in his presence; he preferred that associates call him "Snorky"—slang for elegant.

Loesch found Capone in an expansive mood, enjoying a fine cigar and sitting at a large mahogany desk. On the wall behind him, the attorney noted, hung framed pictures of George Washington and Abraham Lincoln and the text of the Gettysburg Address. Quickly explaining his mission, Loesch asked, "Will you help me by keeping your damned cutthroats and hoodlums from interfering with the polling booths?"

"All right," said Capone. "I'll have the cops send over squad cars the night before the election and jug all the hoodlums and keep 'em in the cooler until the polls close."

Capone was as good as his word, reported Loesch. The night before the election, the police swarmed all over Chicago with unaccustomed zeal, arresting and jailing known criminals, and on Election Day seventy police cars cruised the streets. "It turned out to be the squarest and most successful election in forty years," Loesch recalled. "There was not one complaint, not one election fraud and no threat of trouble all day."

* * *

Why did Capone do it? He had a good sense of public relations and had learned that such magnanimous gestures could win him quick, easy admiration. Besides, Thompson was likely to win anyway. And, it was a startling display of the enormous power that he wielded in Prohibition-era Chicago. "I'm no Italian," Capone would angrily protest when the press reported that he was an immigrant from Sicily or Naples. "I was born in Brooklyn." The date was January 17, 1899, and the place a cold-water flat in the slums that festered around the Brooklyn Navy Yard. He was the fourth of nine children of Gabriele and Teresa Capone, poor immigrants from Naples. The elder Capone was a barber by trade but worked in a grocery store until he could save enough money to open his own shop. He was hardworking and respected in the Italian community and became an American citizen in 1906. Young Alphonse and his siblings showed no criminal tendencies. "The children and the parents were close; there was no apparent mental disability, no traumatic events that sent the boys hurtling into a life of crime," writes Laurence Bergreen, a Capone biographer. "They displayed no special genius for crime, or anything else, for that matter."

The poverty-stricken Italians who poured into the United States after 1880, largely from the south and Sicily, were clannish and suspicious of outsiders. For centuries, they had been exploited by both foreign invaders and rapacious domestic masters alike, and they mistrusted all forms of authority. Politicians and the police were to them part of a system created to protect the rich and enslave the poor—beliefs that they brought with them to America. Loyalty to family and community transcended everything else.

Older Italian immigrants accepted the prejudice and discrimination directed against them with a shrug, but the younger generation fought back. Following the example of the Irish and the Jews who had adopted crime as a left-handed endeavor to pull themselves up out of poverty, they organized gangs to protect their turf and exact tribute. The methods of the predatory Italian secret societies such as the Neapolitan Camorra, the Carbonari, and the Mafia were adapted to the American scene. Nevertheless, at no time did these criminals represent more than a minute fraction of the hardworking Italian population resident in the United States.

Shortly after Al's birth, his father moved the family to better lodgings in an apartment over his barber shop on Park Avenue in Brooklyn. The area, in the shadow of the newly completed Williamsburg Bridge, was mixed Italian, Irish, and German, and although life was rough, it was never stagnant. Bands of children played stickball, dodged traffic, and brawled in the streets. Fruit and vegetable carts lined the curbs and provided a splash of color.

Al Capone started school at the age of five and did better than average. The educational system was rigid and dogmatic, more interested in imposing discipline than learning, and the teachers thought nothing of striking recalcitrants. Most immigrant children left school as soon as they were old enough to go to work. Al had a solid record of Bs but in the sixth grade it began to deteriorate. The lure of the street gangs was probably too great. These were not the vicious urban gangs of a later day, but groups of tough, scrappy neighborhood boys who hung together on street corners seeking adventure and experience. Al belonged to several gangs, finally becoming a member of the Five Points Juniors. One of his closest buddies was Lucky Luciano and they became lifelong friends. At fourteen, Capone got into an argument with a teacher and when she hit him, he struck back. He was expelled from school, effectively ending his formal education.

Not far from the Capone home was a small, unobtrusive building, the headquarters of Johnny Torrio, one of New York's more successful gangsters. The cool and soft-spoken Torrio was a different breed of mobster, a pioneer in the transformation of crude racketeering into efficient criminal enterprise. Rather than battling rivals for turf, he formed alliances and expanded his business as fresh opportunities emerged. Physically small and always quietly dressed, Torrio believed brains and ingenuity were more important than brawn. He neither smoked nor drank, claimed to have never murdered anyone, and said he didn't even carry a gun.

Torrio was a role model for young Al Capone and the other Italian street kids of the area, and they earned pocket money by running errands for him. Over time, Torrio, seventeen years older than Capone, came to trust him more than the others. Despite these associations, there was no evidence that the youth was headed for a life of crime. He still lived at home and after leaving school went to work to help support his family. Affable and soft of speech, he was already a classy dresser and a good dancer. He held ordinary jobs, first in a munitions plant during the war, and then as a paper cutter in a bindery. "You didn't hear stories about Al Capone practicing with guns," writes Bergreen. "You heard that each night he went home to his mother."

Not long after Capone turned eighteen, he was hired by Frankie Yale (formerly Ioele) to be bartender and bouncer at a bar he owned on Coney Island called the Harvard Inn. In contrast to Johnny Torrio, who had recommended Al for the job, Yale specialized in contract murder and extortion and was believed to have killed a dozen men. Later, he became national head of the Unione Siciliane, or the Italo-American National Union, which began as a fraternal society to advance the interests of Sicilian immigrants but developed into a criminal organization.

Capone was popular with the customers at the Harvard Inn, but one night, as he waiting on a young couple, he was taken with the beauty of the girl. "Honey, you have a nice ass and I mean that as a compliment," he leaned over and told her. Her escort, who turned out to be her brother, was angered by the insult to his sister and in the brawl that followed, cut Capone three times on the cheek and neck and fled. Capone later claimed to have gotten the scars while serving in the U.S. Army in France.

Capone became a father and husband, in that order, in December 1919. He married a pretty blond Irish girl named Mae Coughlin, two years older than himself, when their son, Albert Francis Capone, was three and a half weeks old. Johnny Torrio, who had largely shifted operations to Chicago, was his godfather, and every year on the boy's birthday gave him a $5,000 bond. Sonny, as he was known, was born partially deaf and wore a hearing aid from early childhood. Over the years, Capone had a string of mistresses—one of whom gave him syphilis—but he was faithful to Mae in his own way.* In 1919, his career took a fateful turn when Torrio summoned him to Chicago.

Al Capone's first jobs in Chicago were humble—bodyguard, chauffeur, and manager of a speakeasy called the Four Deuces, which was a front for a brothel. Obviously embarrassed by his position, Capone had business cards printed up identifying himself as a "second-hand furniture dealer."

Torrio had come to Chicago to manage the criminal enterprises of his uncle, James "Big Jim" Colosimo, the boss of the city's underworld. Big Jim operated the Colosimo Cafe on South Wabash Avenue, the town's hottest nightspot, where the band alternated between the new music known as jazz and opera medleys. Mobsters, college boys, journalists, politicians, and the social elite all rubbed shoulders at Big Jim's. Colosimo's real speciality was the flesh trade, and together with his wife, Victoria Moresco, a highly successful madam, he ran a string of whorehouses that brought in $50,000 a month. Johnny Torrio worked quietly behind the scenes and was bub-

---

* Like AIDS in our time, syphilis was rampant in the United States in the World War I years. About 10 percent of the men summoned for the draft were found to be infected. Like Capone, many of those infected thought they had been cured, but the disease has a tendency to return with devastating effect as long as twenty years after the original infection and "cure."

bling with ideas for expanding and modernizing the business to take into account the coming of Prohibition.

Unfortunately, Big Jim's mind was diverted by Dale Winters, a pretty café singer, and Torrio thought he was not paying proper attention to business. Colosimo divorced Victoria after settling with her for $50,000 and married Dale. "It's your funeral, Jim," shrugged Torrio. And it was. Not long after, Big Jim was found sprawled on the floor of his club with two bullets in the head. No one was ever charged with the murder, but the police believed Torrio had imported Frankie Yale from New York and paid him $10,000 for the hit. Colosimo received the first of the great Chicago gangster funerals. Five thousand mourners attended the gaudy rites, including three judges, two congressman, eight aldermen, and the leading singers of the Chicago Opera Company.

Torrio seized control of the empire he had built for Colosimo, and made Capone a partner. Al brought two older brothers to Chicago, Salvatore, now known as Frank, and Ralph, and gave then jobs in the organization. Unlike most bootleggers, Torrio did not stoop to selling the vile stuff that passed for beer in most localities during Prohibition; he entered into alliances with the heretofore legal brewers who were eager to keep their breweries going and sold real beer. And he organized the rackets so the contending barons, Dion O'Banion, the Druggans, the Gennas, the West Side O'Donnells, the Saltis mob, and other factions, all had pieces of the action.

Those who violated the peace imposed by Torrio were summarily dealt with. A minor criminal named Joe Howard, mistaking Torrio's mild manner for weakness, hijacked a shipment of his beer. The next day, as Howard was standing at a cigar counter in a saloon near the Four Deuces, two men came in. "Hi, Al," a grinning Howard said to one of the men and stuck out his hand. The other fellow also put out his hand, but there was a pistol in it. He fired six times and Howard died with the grin still on his face. Witnesses identified Al Capone as the killer, but they soon had second thoughts and recanted.

Torrio made repeated visits to Italy and left control of the syndicate largely in Capone's hands. Capone expanded the business, but in 1923, the voters of Chicago underwent a brief spasm of reformist fervor. Big Bill Thompson was voted out of the mayor's office and replaced by Judge William "Decent" Devers, who ordered the police to crack down on the Torrio-Capone gang. Capone decided to focus operations on the working-class suburb of Cicero. The entire city government was either cowed or bought in wholesale lots. The only opposition came from Robert St. John, the crusading young editor of the *Cicero Tribune*. Capone tried to buy him off and when that failed, had him beaten up. When St. John got out of the hospital, he found his bill had been paid by Capone. St. John persisted in defying the mobsters, but soon found himself out of a job; Capone had bought the paper.* He lorded over Cicero, making his headquarters in the fortresslike Hawthorne Inn, which had heavy doors and steel shutters on the windows.

The peace among thieves engineered by Torrio soon started coming apart. Bad blood developed between the Genna brothers, Torrio-Capone allies, and Dion O'Banion, the leader of the Northside Irish mob. O'Banion had the face of a choir boy—which he had once been—and loved flowers so much he ran a florist shop on North State Street, but he had the cold eyes of a psychopathic killer. "The hell with them Sicilians," he declared. Torrio was worried about O'Banion's unreliable conduct and when he was double-crossed by the Irishman on a deal, the latter's fate was sealed.

Two days after the death from cancer of Mike Merlo, the head of the Chicago branch of the Unione Siciliane, on November 10, 1924, O'Banion was in his shop preparing flowers for the funeral when three men arrived to pick up a wreath they had ordered. He greeted them and prepared to shake hands, but one of the men pulled him off balance while the others pumped six bullets into him. The gunmen were said to be Frankie Yale, John Scalise, and Albert Anselmi, two gorillalike assassins from Sicily, but no one was ever charged with the killing. O'Banion was given a handsome send-off that included twenty-six carloads of flowers, including a basket of roses with a card: *From Al.*

Although the police professed not to know who had killed Dion O'Banion, his ally, Hymie Weiss, knew exactly who was responsible and along with another former O'Banion associate, George "Bugs" Moran, vowed revenge. Weiss's real name was Earl Wojciechowski. Everybody assumed he was a Jew, but he was a devout Catholic. Weiss launched several attempts to assassinate Torrio and Capone, and succeeded, in January 1925, in seriously wounding the former.

"Sure, I know all four men," Torrio told a reporter who had asked if he knew who had shot him, "but I'll never tell their names." Having had enough, he retired to Italy, leaving control of his empire of breweries, brothels, speakeasies, and gambling houses to Capone. At the age of twenty-seven and after only five years in Chicago, Scarface Al was now a

---

* St. John later became a prominent radio commentator.

contender for the role of the city's top crime boss, but he had a perilous situation on his hands.

War broke out over Torrio's legacy with numerous killings on both sides. Chicago took on its legendary reputation as a place where the streets were public shooting galleries and the average citizen wore a bulletproof vest to walk his dog. Mixing tigerish ferocity with efforts to maintain Torrio's policy of pacification, Capone offered peace and had his rivals gunned down if they refused to accept it. Hymie Weiss not only rejected his overtures but machine-gunned the Hawthorne Inn, in an unsuccessful effort to kill him.* Not long after, on October 11, 1926, Weiss and several companions were shot to death in broad daylight, outside his headquarters in Dion O'Banion's old flower shop, at the ripe old age of twenty-eight. He left an estate of $1.3 million.

"Hymie Weiss is dead because he was a bull-head," Capone told the press. "Forty times I tried to arrange things so that we'd have peace in Chicago and life would be worth living. . . . There was, and there is, plenty of business for all, and competition needn't be a matter of murder." The surviving members of Weiss's gang agreed, and a peace parley was held at the Hotel Sherman a week after his death. Chicago was again divvied up, an amnesty was declared, and past killings were forgiven. Al Capone emerged from the conference as the supreme ruler of the Chicago underworld.

Peace among the gangs—which lasted only temporarily—coincided with the return of Big Bill Thompson to the mayor's office. Capone moved back to Chicago, taking over regal quarters in the Hotel Lexington. His fame had spread beyond the city and to Europe. Whenever his name was mentioned, people's eyes brightened knowingly, they formed machine guns with their fingers and cried "rat-a-tat-tat."

The Medill School of Journalism at Northwestern University polled its students on whom they considered the "ten outstanding personages of the world," and Alphonse Capone was among them. His smiling face appeared on the cover of *Time*. When an Italian aviator who was making an around-the-world flight landed his seaplane on Lake Michigan, Capone was among those chosen by the city fathers to welcome him to Chicago. Visiting celebrities sought him out and fawned over him. The U.S. attorney's

---

* Capone, who liked to assume the guise of Robin Hood, paid $5,000 for an eye operation for a local woman, an innocent bystander, injured in the attack and also for the repair of the surrounding shops that were damaged in the raid.

office estimated that Capone was taking in approximately $105 million a year—or more than $1 billion today. The breakdown was as follows:

Bootlegging	$60 million
Gambling	$25 million
Vice	$10 million
Other rackets	$10 million

Following the example of Johnny Torrio, Capone forged a large, heterogeneous, yet disciplined criminal organization. Jake Guzik stood at his right hand as business manager. Frank "the Enforcer" Nitti moved from gunman to treasurer and was Capone's link to the Unione Siciliane. Brother Ralph, who had acquired the name "Bottles" for his skill at persuading saloon keepers to stock Capone merchandise, was in charge of liquor sales.* He entered alliances with the Jews of Detroit's murderous Purple Gang and the Northside Irish. Laurence Bergreen says that Capone dominated his colleagues not by threatening or bullying "but by appealing to the inner man, his wants, his aspirations. . . . By making them feel valued, they gave unstintingly of their loyalty, and loyalty was what Capone needed and demanded; in the violent circles through which he moved it was the only protection from sudden death."

But even as Capone was consolidating his power, a tiny cloud was forming on the horizon. In May 1927, the U.S. Supreme Court ruled that a bootlegger named Manny Sullivan had to report his illegal earnings and pay taxes on them. The justices rejected the argument of Sullivan's lawyers that reporting and paying taxes on an illegal enterprise would be self-incrimination. Following the ruling, the Internal Revenue Service began to dig into Capone's life style and to compare it with his tax returns. In a parallel move, George E. Q. Johnson, the newly appointed U.S. attorney in Chicago, also targeted Capone and his associates.

Ben Hecht's fond name for Chicago in the Twenties was "the Jazz Baby," and the nightclubs, speakeasies, and dance halls of the "toddling town" provided bountiful employment for musicians who produced the city's own hard-driving style of music. Jazz developed under the thumbs of the gangs that operated the nightclubs, and the mobsters were an appreciative audience. When they liked something, they scattered large bills among the musicians. "Jazz has got guts," one gunman said. Al Capone himself

---

* Brother Frank was killed in a shoot-out with the Chicago police.

became a jazz impresario with the opening of the Cotton Club in Cicero, which featured some of the best jazzmen of the day. "Scarface got along well with musicians," remembered Earl Hines. "He liked to come into a club with his henchmen and have the band play his requests. He was free with one-hundred-dollar tips."

Chicago had been introduced to New Orleans jazz during the war years, but the city's golden age of jazz began in 1919 with the arrival in town of Joe "King" Oliver, the noted cornetist. Two years later, he organized the Creole Jazz Band, which opened in the smokey, down-at-the-heels Dreamland Cafe at 35th and State in the Tenderloin. State Street, said Langston Hughes, was "a teeming Negro street with crowded theaters, restaurants and cabarets" where the raucous new music was heard.

Oliver sent for his protégé, twenty-year-old Louis Armstrong, in 1922. Like most early jazz musicians, Armstrong was from a poor family, and after a catch-as-catch-can existence was sent to reform school at the age of twelve for firing a pistol in the air on New Year's Eve. There, he learned to play the cornet. Released two years later, the boy peddled newspapers, worked as a stevedore on the docks, and sold coal from a cart. Too poor to own an instrument of his own, he listened at the doorways and windows to the bands in the Storyville dives and observed the various styles of the musicians. King Oliver was his favorite and the older man acted as a father to him. He gave Armstrong his first real cornet and instructed him on the instrument. By 1917, Armstrong was playing in the honky-tonks. Already, he was showing the technical brilliance, the joy and spontaneity, that was to make him the greatest of all jazz musicians.

Armstrong was a complete provincial when he arrived in Chicago. "All the musicians called him Little Louis, and he weighed 226 pounds," recalled Lil Hardin, piano player and arranger for the Creole Jazz Band. But Little Louis's amazing playing immediately attracted attention. He possessed a gift for melodic invention that was new and startling and which no one else could match.

In 1925, the easygoing Armstrong married Hardin, who urged him to be more ambitious and to go out on his own. Beginning in November of that year, he began recording the Armstrong Hot Five and Hot Seven series of records with pickup studio bands. Included are such classics as "Muskrat Ramble," "Struttin' with Some Barbecue," "West End Blues," and "Cornet Chop Suey." His work influenced a generation of musicians and vocalists. Blues also began reaching a wider audience in those years. Big Bessie Smith recorded the "St. Louis Blues" with Armstrong, and her records became popular with some whites as well as blacks. Alberta Hunter, another great blues singer, also appeared in Chicago and introduced W. C. Handy's "Loveless Love" to appreciative listeners.

White youths—Eddie Condon, Muggsy Spanier, Pee Wee Russell, Bix Beiderbecke, Mezz Mezzrow, Jimmy McPartland, and others—haunted places like the Lincoln Gardens on the South Side to listen in awe to Armstrong and other black musicians, and then tried to make similar sounds leavened with some touches of their own. Bud Freeman remembered that the doorman of the Gardens, who weighed 350 pounds, always greeted them with the same words: "I see you boys are here for your music lessons tonight."

"We did our best to copy the colored music we'd heard," said Paul Mares. "We did our best, but naturally we couldn't play colored style." Chicago jazz, growing out of another environment and set of experiences than black New Orleans, reflected the intensity of the town and was different from the buoyant and swinging music of the Crescent City. It had a driving, gritty rhythm, a harsh and brutal excitement—the sounds of Chicago itself. The trumpet replaced the cornet and the saxophone took over from the trombone as the ensemble playing of New Orleans jazzmen gave way to a more open, hot solo jazz, in which every man seemed to be out for himself.

Life could be hazardous for a musician in Jazz Age Chicago. The rule was that no matter what happened you continued playing. Muggsy Spanier saw two men shot one night in a club where he was working, and continued blowing his trumpet while bathed in perspiration. Later, he couldn't remember what tune he had played even though he kept playing it over and over again. A party of Capone mobsters commandeered the Friar's Inn, a basement joint in the Loop, and ordered all the other customers out. One eyed Jimmy Lannigan's bass for some time before pulling out a pistol and neatly drilling it. The instrument flew apart in Lannigan's hands, but the band kept on playing for dear life. Having satisfied a whim, the gunman asked how much a replacement bass would cost. He was told $850—the actual cost was $225—and nonchalantly peeled the bills off his roll.

The hot, wild sound produced by the jazz musicians was a symbol of their lifestyle. Bootleg booze, women, and dope were all hazards of the job. Bix Beiderbecke, the master cornetist who was first attracted to jazz by hearing Louis Armstrong play on a passing riverboat, destroyed himself with liquor at the age of twenty-eight. "I think one of the reasons he drank so much was that he was a perfectionist and wanted to do more with music than any man possibly could," observed Jimmy McPartland. Nevertheless, as clarinetist and bandleader Artie Shaw noted, "While there were some musicians who did a fair amount of boozing and whoring around and marijuana smoking, there was also a hell of a lot of damn good honest jazz being played."

On the morning of February 14, 1929—St. Valentine's Day—a large black touring car of the type used by Chicago detectives pulled up to a nondescript garage at 2122 North Clark Street. Bugs Moran's North Side gang used the place to receive and store bootleg liquor and beer. Five men got out, three in police uniforms and two in civilian hats and coats. Soon after, the neighbors heard a clatter followed by two dull thuds. They also observed the departure of the five men. The men in civilian clothes came out with their hands raised while the "policemen" covered them with drawn guns. "They were walking slow, easy-like," said one of the witnesses. "I thought an arrest had been made." Everyone got back into the black auto and drove away.

Worried by the howling of a dog, another neighbor ventured into the garage and quickly ran out, pale and sick. "They're all dead!" he shouted. The police were summoned and found seven men lying against a wall in pools of blood and mangled flesh, six of them dead and one dying. They were members of the Moran gang and had been lined up and machinegunned; two had been finished off by shotgun blasts to the head. Frank Gusenberg, the dying man who had been wounded fourteen times, was urged by a policeman to tell who had shot him. "Nobody shot me," he whispered, faithful to the end to the code of silence. By a lucky chance, Moran, the target of the massacre, escaped death because he had arrived just as the "police" car drove up. Suspecting a raid, he fled. "Only Capone kills like that," said the shaken gang leader.

Capone himself was at his palatial and heavily guarded Miami Beach estate, where he liked to pose as a genial, self-made millionaire. In fact, he was being questioned by the local district attorney in another matter, at the exact time the execution took place. "I've been accused of every death except the casualty list of the World War," he declared with a shrug. Despite Capone's denials of being the brains behind the St. Valentine's Day Massacre, no one else had more to gain from the murders. Everyone *knew* Scarface Al was responsible and he was endowed with a certain grisly glamour.

As reconstructed by the police, the incident began when Moran, restive under Capone's control of the rackets, hijacked some beer trucks belonging to Capone and the Purple Gang. An informer sent by Capone told Moran of another shipment of beer that was due, and the Northsiders were trapped in a cleverly arranged ambush as they plotted a new hijacking. The police disguise was used so the victims would surrender their arms without suspicion. Capone was called before a grand jury investigating the crime, but no one was ever charged with the mass killing.

By then, he had more pressing problems; evidence was mounting that three of his Sicilian colleagues—John Scalise, Albert Anselmi, and Giuseppe Giunta—were showing signs of turning traitor. Scalise, in fact, was suspected of planning to assassinate Capone and seize power. Capone decided to deal directly with the problem. On May 7, 1929, the trio were invited to be guests of honor at a party at a roadhouse in Hammond, Indiana, not far from Chicago. The ancient tradition of hospitality before execution was duly observed, according to John Kobler. When the meal was over, the guests of honor leaned back in their chairs, sated and smiling. But as silence fell over the room their smiles faded.

> Capone leaned toward them. The words dropped from his mouth like stones. So they thought he didn't know? They imagined they could hide the offense he could never forgive—disloyalty? . . . Capone's bodyguards fell upon them, lashing them to their chairs with wire and gagging them. Capone got up, holding a baseball bat. Slowly, he walked the length of the table and halted behind the first guest of honor. With both hands he lifted the bat and slammed it down full force. Slowly, methodically, he struck again and again. . . . He moved to the next man, and when he had reduced him to mangled flesh and bone, to the third. One of the bodyguards then . . . shot each man in the back of the head.

The St. Valentine's Day Massacre brought Capone to the attention of Herbert Hoover, who became president a few weeks later. "I directed that all of the Federal agencies concentrate upon Mr. Capone and his allies," he wrote. And whenever he saw Treasury Secretary Andrew Mellon, the president pointedly asked: "Have you got this fellow Capone yet? I want that man in jail." Mellon authorized a two-pronged campaign against Capone and the key members of his organization.

A twenty-six-year-old Prohibition agent named Eliot Ness organized a handpicked team of a dozen or so incorruptible young agents like himself, and launched a vigorous search-and-destroy operation against Capone's bootlegging empire. Having obtained information through widespread telephone taps, Ness used a truck with a snowplow fitted to the front to ram through the armored front doors of Capone's breweries and storage warehouses. Speakeasies turned to other suppliers because Capone's deliveries were now erratic, and his revenues fell off sharply. Ness, who had a finely tuned sense of public relations, allowed the press to cover these raids. The reporters dubbed his team the Untouchables and made heroes of them.

Capone was eventually brought down not by Ness's flamboyant frontier-style tactics but by the painstaking digging of IRS auditors. Over a two-and-a-half-year period, they worked their way through mountains of records to determine the full extent of the mob chieftain's holdings—and the amount of unpaid federal income taxes due. As 1930 drew to a close, Capone embarked on a public relations campaign of his own to rehabilitate his image by opening the first soup kitchen that served free meals to Chicago's unemployed, as the nation slipped into the Great Depression.

On June 5, 1931, George Johnson, the federal prosecutor, announced that a grand jury had indicted Capone on twenty-two counts of income tax evasion involving over $200,000 in unpaid taxes. Capone faced a possible thirty-four years in jail if convicted on all counts. A week later, Capone and sixty-eight associates were also charged with some five thousand violations of the Volstead Act, some extending back to 1922, that had been dredged up by the Untouchables. The income tax cases took precedence over the Prohibition violations and were set down for trial first. To the surprise of Chicagoans, Capone offered to plead guilty to the income tax charges in exchange for a prison term of between two and five years. Obviously, he believed he would serve his time in comfort and would be able to run his organization from behind bars. To even greater public shock, the prosecutors accepted this offer.

Why did the government, after all its efforts to get Capone, agree to such a light sentence? Johnson explained that the prosecutors were not at all certain the charges could be made to stick because of questions about the statute of limitations. The plan went awry when Judge James Wilkerson refused to go along and made it clear that if the mobster copped a plea, he would sentence him to the full jail term required by the law. Upset by this turn of events, Capone withdrew his plea and a trial was scheduled for October 1931.

Fifteen detectives escorted Scarface Al into the Federal Court Building in Chicago for trial, but he was feeling confident. The fix was in. The organization had obtained the names of prospective jurors and, by a mixture of bribery and threats, had suborned enough to ensure an acquittal for its leader. Once again, however, Judge Wilkerson had a surprise for

Capone. Aware of the rumors of jury tampering, he ordered the entire panel exchanged for another made up mostly of men from rural areas outside Chicago, who had not been reached by Capone's men.

The jury found Capone guilty of income tax evasion on October 17, 1931, after nine hours of deliberation. Wilkerson sentenced him to eleven years in prison plus a fine of $50,000 and court costs of $30,000—the stiffest penalty yet meted out to a tax evader. "Capone tried to smile," reported the *New York Times*, "but the smile was bitter."

Capone was sent first to the federal penitentiary at Atlanta and then to the rigorous new maximum security prison at Alcatraz in San Francisco Bay. When he was released in January 1939, he was a shadow of his former self: syphilis had eaten away his brain. "Al," said Jake Guzik, "is as nutty as a fruitcake." Frank Costello and Lucky Luciano had already seized control of the rackets. They were businessmen-gangsters who took the mob semi-legitimate—moving from bootlegging and high-interest "juice" loans to the ownership of Las Vegas casinos, the sale of narcotics, and the looting of the treasuries of major labor unions such as the Teamsters and those in the Hollywood studios. In doing so, they shattered the credibility of the American labor movement.

Al Capone had feared dying in the streets, but he passed away in bed in Miami Beach in 1947 at the age of forty-eight, in the presence of his mother, his wife, and his son. A week before, Andrew Volstead, the father of Prohibition, had died at the age of eighty-seven. To the end, he was unshaken in his conviction that a ban on alcohol would improve the morals of the American people.

CHAPTER 15

"You Ain't Heard Nothin' Yet!"

"So long," said Charles A. Lindbergh offhandedly on the misty morning of May 20, 1927, as if he were leaving on a vacation trip to the beach.

Settling himself in the tight cockpit of his silvery, single-engine monoplane, the *Spirit of Louis*, Lindbergh ordered the chocks pulled away from the wheels. As he advanced the throttle, the engine roared and the plane lurched forward.

Long Island's Roosevelt Field was muddy, and the fuel-laden craft threw up sod and chewed up runway faster and faster, reluctant to become airborne. A handful of onlookers groaned inwardly as it fast approached a line of telephone wires that marked the end of the field.

Suddenly, the plane made a sluggish leap into the air, but fell back to more groans. Again, it sailed into the air—this time to claw its way above the wires by a few scant feet. Now, a soft glow penetrated the mist, the first sign of sun breaking through. Lindbergh headed northeast toward Paris—approximately 3,600 miles away—at a little more than a hundred miles an hour. The flight was the greatest sensation of 1927—a year of startling sensations in nearly every aspect of American life.

The daring twenty-five-year-old mail pilot was inspired by a $25,000 prize offered in 1919 by Raymond Orteig, a French-born New York hotel owner, for the first successful nonstop flight by a heavier-than-air craft between New York and Paris. The Atlantic had been crossed several times, but no one had yet managed to fly the vast distance between the two cities—or tried to do it alone.

The first transatlantic flight was made in May 1919 by the NC-4, a huge U.S. Navy flying boat. Powered by four engines producing a total of 1,600 horsepower and with a wingspan only four feet short of a Boeing 707, the craft flew from Newfoundland to the Azores with a crew of six, and then leapfrogged on to Plymouth, England.* A month later, a pair of Royal Air Force officers, John Alcock and A. W. Brown, flew a converted twin-engine bomber from Newfoundland to a bog in Ireland. And in July 1919, the British dirigible R-34 crossed from Scotland to New York with a crew of thirty-five.

Numerous aviation records tumbled during the postwar years. In 1921, Edward Stinson and Lloyd Bertaud established a new record for sustained flight by remaining aloft for twenty-six hours and nineteen minutes. That same year, J. A. McReady, a U.S. Army pilot, set a world altitude record by reaching 37,000 feet, eclipsing the previous mark of 33,114 feet. In 1924 a pair of army floatplanes hopscotched around the world, covering 27,523 miles in fifteen days. And in 1926, Commander Richard E. Byrd of the U.S. Navy and civilian pilot Floyd Bennett claimed to have made the first flight across the North Pole. Nevertheless, the Orteig Prize was unclaimed because no airplane had the reliability and range to cover the required distance. The nonstop record, established in 1923, was 2,500 miles, set on a flight from San Diego to New York.

World War I had given aviation a jump start, but government interest fell off in the postwar years. Unlike European nations, which subsidized commercial aviation and airline passenger service after the war, Washington did little to encourage civilians to build and operate commercial aircraft. In fact, the market was glutted with surplus Curtiss JN4s, or Jennys, and De Havilland DH-4s hastily disposed of by the government. It was still the era of leather flying helmets and goggles, thick flying suits, and fur-lined boots, and while many Americans were eager to go for thrill rides with barnstorming pilots, they had little interest in scheduled air travel. They were captivated by the romance of aviation rather than by its commercial prospects.

American passenger airlines grew out of the Post Office air mail service.† These operations began in 1918 with daily flights between New York and Washington, and were gradually extended until regular day and night service was established in 1924 between New York and San Francisco via Chicago and Cheyenne. The postage was set at 24 cents for a one-ounce letter, which was reduced to 5 cents in 1928. Originally, the Post Office operated its own planes, hired its own pilots, and established a network of routes, flight paths, and airfields. In 1923, it contracted out air mail deliv-

---

* Two other flying boats, NC-1 and NC-3, were forced down in the Atlantic without loss of life.

† Six years after the start of the U.S. Postal Air Service only ten of the original forty pilots were still alive.

ery to private companies, which were encouraged to carry passengers to subsidize their operations. The first regular passenger service, based on the air mail system, was established between Boston and New York, but the planes were primitive. The Boeing B-40, an early airliner, was a biplane that carried only two passengers inside the cabin while the pilot sat in an open cockpit.

Commerce Secretary Herbert Hoover believed that the federal government should do more to stimulate commercial aviation. He thought government subsidies were the key to the expansion of civil aviation, just as they were in the previous century for the railroads and transocean steamship companies. At his urging, Congress, in 1926, enacted the Air Commerce Act, which vested regulatory powers over commercial aviation in the Commerce Department. Cities were encouraged to build airports and establish a network of radio beacons, lights, emergency landing fields, and weather reporting stations. Subsidies for these projects were justified on the grounds that the airlines provided speedy delivery of the mail, and a backlog of aircraft and personnel for national defense. In 1929, Hoover reported that there were "25,000 miles of government-approved airways" with "regular flights of over 25,000,000 miles per annum."

Military and naval aviation were also undergoing change. The flight of the NC-4 heightened the U.S. Navy's interest in the airplane. The development of fleet aviation, said the service's General Board, was "of paramount importance and must be undertaken immediately if the United States is to take its proper place as a naval power." But how was this to be accomplished? Sharp infighting developed between the battleship admirals, who saw aircraft as useful only for shell-spotting and reconnaissance, and the advocates of the aircraft carrier, who foresaw a wider role for the airplane in naval operations.

Naval and military strategists tend to think in terms of the last war. They were worried about an expansionist Japan, and most believed that if war came between Japan and the United States, it would climax in a great clash between battleships, in which the big gun would be the decisive weapon. But some strategists, including Admiral William S. Sims, the president of the Naval War College at Newport, Rhode Island, saw the traditional role of the battleship being usurped by the carrier. Two decades before the debut of the Fast Carrier Task Force, Sims included carriers in the school's war games. In future wars, he declared, the fleet with the stronger carrier force "will sweep the enemy fleet clean of its airplanes and proceed to bomb the battleships and torpedo them with torpedo planes."

Carrier advocates had a surprising—if temporary—ally in Brigadier General William Mitchell, chief of the Army Air Service in Europe during the war. Billy Mitchell had returned home with a vision of an independent air force, similar to Britain's newly created Royal Air Force, equal in stature to the army and navy—and with equal claim on the national budget. Letting fly a scattershot of claims that were picked up by an admiring press, he announced that the airplane had made both of these services obsolete. "Air power has completely superseded sea power and land power as our first line of defense," Mitchell declared in a statement designed to raise the hackles of the admirals and generals. He zeroed in on the battleship, claiming it was "as obsolete as knights in armor after gunpowder was invented."

Much of Mitchell's argument was not as revolutionary as it sounded— after all, Admiral Sims and others were saying the same thing. Like most zealots, he resorted to exaggeration to attract public attention to his cause. "A superior air power will dominate all sea areas where they act from land bases," Mitchell said, summarizing his basic philosophy, "and no seacraft, whether carrying aircraft or not, is able to contest their aerial supremacy." World War II, of course, proved Mitchell wrong. Nevertheless, fearing popular acceptance of Mitchell's claim that bombers had made the battleship obsolete, the navy arranged for a series of tests to determine the amount of punishment that could be absorbed by such vessels.

The most spectacular test took place in July 1921, when the old German battleship *Ostfriesland,* a 22,500-ton survivor of Jutland, was towed out beyond the Virginia Capes for use as a target. Much to the satisfaction of the navy, she survived two days of intensive bombing attacks. On the third day, Mitchell led a formation of seven twin-engine Martin bombers to a final attack. Each carried a specially designed two-thousand-pound bomb. The first was a near miss. Six more bombs rained down on the *Ostfriesland* in quick succession, and amid a series of direct hits and near misses, her bow rose from the sea like a stricken thing. Assistant Secretary of War Benedict Crowell reported that some naval officers had tears in their eyes as they watched the vessel capsize and sink.

Officially, the navy was less impressed. It pointed out that the ship was anchored and a sitting duck, the bombers knew her exact position, the visibility and weather were good, she could not return antiaircraft fire, and had no fighter cover or damage control parties to work on her between raids. Three years later, the uncompleted battleship *Washington,* which had been ordered scrapped under the Washington disarmament treaty, survived bombing and internal and underwater explosions designed to stimulate the effect of bomb and torpedo hits, and had to be finished off by the fourteen-inch guns of the battleship *Texas*.

The immediate response to the sinking of the *Ostfriesland* was not support for Billy Mitchell's independent air force but advancement for the cause of naval aviation. The Bureau of Aeronautics was created in 1921, the first new bureau since the Civil War. The partially completed 33,000-ton battle cruisers *Lexington* and *Saratoga*, scheduled for scrapping under the terms of the Washington treaty, were converted into aircraft carriers and commissioned in 1927. The 14,500-ton *Ranger*, the navy's first ship designed and built as a carrier, was authorized that same year.

With prospects for an independent air force fading, Mitchell, in desperation, became even more intemperate in his remarks. He was passed over for promotion to chief of the army's air service and was repeatedly warned by superiors to remain silent. The last straw came in 1925, when Mitchell charged in a six-thousand-word statement to the press that the fatal loss of the navy dirigible *Shenandoah* during a storm was the result of "incompetence [and] criminal negligence" by the War and Navy Departments. Mitchell was court-martialed and suspended from military service for five years. The U.S. Air Force was created following World War II, but as a friend told Mitchell, "in all great reforms some fanatic has got to be crucified for the public good before people believe in his doctrines."

The newspapers dubbed Charles Lindbergh the "Flying Fool" and the "Flying Kid," but there was nothing foolish about his decision to fly the Atlantic. Like everything else he did, the flight was meticulously planned. The product of a dysfunctional family, Lindbergh rebelled against disorganization and conflict; much of his life was a search for order. He exercised tight control over himself and everyone about him.

He was born in Detroit on February 4, 1902, the son of Charles August—known as C.A.—and Evangeline Land Lindbergh. C.A. was a successful lawyer and real estate operator in Little Falls, Minnesota, and was considered the handsomest man in town, while his wife was a member of a prominent Detroit family. The boy was named Charles Augustus; C.A. never supplied an explanation for the extra syllable in his son's middle name. Young Charles's early years were spent on a farm outside Little Falls that overlooked the Mississippi River, but life was punctuated by constant bickering between his parents. Evangeline was critical of her husband, and Little Falls bored her. C.A. also had money problems as the nation suffered financial difficulties, and Evangeline was forced to trim back her rather lavish spending, which further angered her. The one thing that kept the Lindberghs together was their affection for "the boy."

C.A. always had socialistic ideas, which were brought to the fore by the financial upheaval. One of his great interests was the creation of an insurance cooperative for farmers free of the huge insurance companies of the East. He also denounced the "Money Trust"—the Morgan interests, the National City Bank, and the investment house of Kuhn Loeb—which he claimed had a stranglehold on the nation. In 1906, he was elected to Congress as a Republican and served for five terms. In Washington, he pressed his financial views and successfully fought for a congressional investigation of the Money Trust that brought J. Pierpont Morgan himself to the witness table.

In the beginning, the family lived together, but the arguments between C.A. and his wife never ceased. She accused him of having an affair with a stenographer and, holding a pistol to his head, threatened to shoot him. "O.K., Evangeline," he said wearily, "if you must do it, do it." She threw down the weapon and ran from the room in tears. The Lindberghs separated but did not divorce because it would have ruined C.A.'s political career; both maintained quarters in Washington. Charles lived with his mother in a series of boarding houses, but spent time with his father, performing such tasks in his office as running errands and stamping envelopes. He was also rotated to Detroit and Little Falls, which meant he was always being taken out of one school and put into another.

In Washington, he attended Sidwell Friends School. The name, he observed in later years, was a misnomer as far as he was concerned. "I did not find much friendship among the children there. I did not understand them, nor they me." They made fun of his name, calling him "Limburger" or simply "the Cheese." Lindbergh had no close friends and was an outsider everywhere. His hobbies were those of the solitary child—reading, collecting stamps, and toy soldiers.

A high point of Lindbergh's childhood was a visit arranged by his father in 1912 to Fort Meyer, just outside Washington, for a test by the army of new aircraft. A half dozen primitive planes were on display. "One took off and raced a motor car around the oval track in front of us," Lindbergh later recalled. "You could see its pilot clearly, out in front—pants' legs flapping and cap visor pointing backward to streamline in the wind." From that moment on, "I wanted to fly myself."

* * *

"You are living in an extraordinary time," C.A. told his son after the outbreak of World War I. "Great changes are coming." In 1916, convinced the
bankers and industrialists were trying to inveigle the United States into the
struggle to protect their investments in an Allied victory, he gave up his
safe seat in Congress to seek the Republican nomination for senator. Fourteen-year-old Charles, the only member of the family who could drive, was
pressed into service to chauffeur his father about the back roads of Minnesota as he campaigned for votes. C.A. lost the nomination to Frank B.
Kellogg, a St. Paul lawyer who later became secretary of state under
Coolidge.

Nevertheless, C.A.'s term was not over until March 1917, and he was
among the handful of congressmen—a "little group of willful men," in
President Wilson's angry words—to vote against a bill authorizing the arm-
ing of American merchant ships to repel attacks by German U-boats. War
was coming, Lindbergh warned, and only the Money Trust would benefit.
A month later, a new Congress declared war on Germany. The following
year, in the midst of the war, C.A. ran for the Republican nomination for
governor with the support of farm and labor groups. "It is impossible,
according to the big press, to be a true American unless you are pro-
British," he declared. "If you are really for America first, last, and all the
time . . . you are classed as pro-German by the big press which are supported by the speculators"—words that would resonate in Charles Lindbergh's life two decades later. Mobs booed C.A., he was pelted with eggs,
threatened with tar and feathering and lynching, and lost by an overwhelming margin.

Food was needed for the war effort and the younger Lindbergh managed
the family farm at Little Falls, for which he received academic credit during his senior year in high school and graduated in June 1918 at the age of
sixteen. Years later, no one could recall ever seeing him at a social function
in town or looking at a girl. He read everything he could find about
wartime flying and resolved that if the conflict lasted long enough, he
would become a pilot. The war ended before the year was out, and Lindbergh, at loose ends, enrolled as an engineering student at the University
of Wisconsin. Evangeline went with him to Madison where they shared an
apartment near the campus.

Charles was unsuccessful both socially and scholastically at Wisconsin.
Although he had inherited his parents' good looks and was already over six
feet tall, he was painfully shy around strangers and covered it with a studied aloofness. If he had any dates, they were unrecorded. His one triumph

was to become a member of the university's champion rifle team, for he was a dead shot with both rifle and pistol. Poorly prepared academically because of his Gypsy-like childhood, he flunked out of college after three semesters, just before his twentieth birthday.

The young man decided to follow up his interest in aviation and enrolled in a flying school in Lincoln, Nebraska, after promising his father he would return to college later. Flying was the first thing in his life that really interested Lindbergh, and he dropped his mask of diffidence. "I shall never forget flying the first time over the farm in Minnesota where I grew up," he later recalled, and "the new and seeming god-like perspective it gave to me." He was a natural flier but never officially soloed because he was unable to post the cash bond required by the school for the use of a plane without an instructor. Young Lindbergh joined a band of itinerant aviators who barnstormed around the Midwest, trying to make a living by wing walking, parachute jumping, and performing other stunts at county fairs.

Although his father was dubious about the future of aviation and short of cash, he helped him buy a plane of his own, a surplus Jenny, for $500. Lindbergh set himself up in business, taking people up for five-minute flights for $5 and doing some instructing. Some weeks he barely made expenses. Once he flew the minister in an aerial wedding while another pilot carried the bride and groom. And he took up a passenger who wanted to urinate on his home town.

To get more flying time and be paid for it, Lindbergh—who already had about 350 hours in the air—became an army aviation cadet. While practicing dog-fighting a few weeks before the end of training, his plane collided in midair with that of another student pilot. Both parachuted safely to the ground and within an hour, they were back in the air. Lindbergh won his wings in 1925, first in his class, and was commissioned a second lieutenant, but the army was short of funds and he was placed on reserve status. His father had died the year before of a brain tumor and there was no more talk of returning to college. Flying was now the young man's life.

"Slim" Lindbergh signed on as a pilot for the Robertson Aircraft Company, which had a contract to fly the St. Louis to Chicago mail route, for a salary of $450 a month. Flying in the fog and at night on instruments was dangerous. "Our route was not lighted at first and the intermediate airports were small and often in poor condition," he wrote. "Our weather reports were unreliable and we developed the policy of taking off with the mail whenever local conditions permitted. We went as far as we could and if the visibility became too bad we landed and entrained the mail." Lindbergh and his two fellow pilots flew old DH-4s, known as "Flaming Coffins" for their tendency to burn upon crashing. Bad weather and engine failure caused him to bail out three more times: he was the first pilot to make four emergency parachute jumps to save his life.

On these long and lonely flights, Lindbergh began to think about the Orteig Prize for a nonstop flight to Paris. Talk of flying the Atlantic was again in the air because improvements in the quality of aircraft and engines made success more likely. Several top-notch aviators announced their intention of accepting the challenge, and they were preparing a variety of two- and three-engine craft manned by crews of two to four. Although he had never flown over a large body of water or for longer than five hundred miles, Lindbergh decided to make the flight in a single-engine plane and to fly alone.

This startling decision was not based on bravado, but was carefully thought out. Extra engines took up weight that could better be used for fuel, he reasoned, and a single-engine plane would meet less resistance from head winds. And if he flew alone, he would not have to worry about the bruised egos of a crew. In spite of his shyness, Lindbergh convinced William B. Robertson, his employer, and several other St. Louis businessmen to bankroll the project. With $15,000 in hand, including $2,000 of his own savings, he ordered a specially modified version of a monoplane, built by the Ryan Aeronautical Company in San Diego, that was equipped with a 220-horsepower Wright Whirlwind engine.

Lindbergh required that the cockpit be placed behind the engine and main fuel tank rather than between them, because he did not want to be crushed in case of a crash. This meant he could not see directly forward from the cockpit. He dispensed with most usual equipment to reduce weight. There was no radio, no special instruments for night flying, no navigational aids—and, to save twenty pounds, not even a parachute. If he came down at sea, it would be useless anyway, Lindbergh reasoned, but he did carry a small rubber raft. He was not heroic, but methodical. In three months time, the craft, named the *Spirit of St. Louis* in honor of Lindbergh's backers, was ready.

One by one, his rivals had fallen by the wayside. René Fonck, France's leading wartime ace, crashed his trimotor Sikorsky on takeoff. Noel Davis and Stanton H. Wooster, who were sponsored by the American Legion, were killed in Virginia. The big Fokker carrying Richard Byrd, the polar explorer, and a crew of three, was damaged during a test flight. Two Frenchmen, Charles Nungesser, another wartime ace, and François Coli, took off from Paris headed for New York, but were never seen again.

Charles D. Chamberlain, who planned to carry a passenger-observer, also in a single-engine plane, had a takeoff accident.

Uneasy about public attention, Lindbergh tried to avoid notice. He took off unannounced from San Diego on May 10, 1927, and crossed the country in a flying time of twenty-one hours, forty-five minutes, a record for a coast-to-coast flight. His arrival on Long Island was the first moment newsmen realized that he was in the race. The press was immediately taken with the handsome and modest air mail pilot and ground out reams of copy about him. Lindbergh wanted to leave for Paris immediately but the weather was dismal. On the evening of May 19, he went to New York City with a group of friends for dinner and a show. A chance call to the Weather Bureau brought a prediction of clearing conditions over the Atlantic, and Lindbergh raced back to Long Island. Following an unsuccessful effort to get a few hours sleep, he had his plane wheeled out early the next morning.

The world held its breath after Lindbergh took off for Paris. People looked up from the newspaper and radio accounts of the sordid Snyder-Gray murder trial to follow the progress of the gallant young aviator, but there was no news for the first thirty hours. Forty thousand spectators stood bare-headed at Yankee Stadium on the night of May 20 for a moment of silent prayer for Lindbergh, before a boxing match between Jack Sharkey and Joe Humphreys. "No attempt at jokes today," wrote Will Rogers. A "slim, tall, bashful, smiling American boy is somewhere over the middle of the Atlantic Ocean, where no lone human being has ever ventured before." In France, where there was general mourning for Nungesser and Coli, the authorities ordered a powerful beacon at Cherbourg kept burning day and night in hope that Lindbergh would see it.

The flight was a nightmare. Over Nova Scotia, Lindbergh ran into fog, heavy rain, and turbulence. When he tried to climb above the poor weather, ice formed on the wings of his plane and dragged it down toward the ocean. The air turned warm over the Gulf Stream and the danger of icing subsided, but the fog persisted. Seventeen hours out—and almost forty hours since he had last slept—Lindbergh was struggling to stay awake. "It seems almost impossible to go on longer," he wrote, as he tried to prop open his eyes with his fingers. "All I want in life is to throw myself down flat, stretch out—and sleep." To keep from dozing off, he dropped close enough to the ocean for the spray to splash his face through the open cockpit windows.

At twenty-two hours, he began hallucinating. The fuselage behind him

seemed filled with phantoms—"vaguely outlined forms, transparent, moving, riding weightless with me in the plane"—but these spirits were benign.
And then he saw land where there should be no land unless he was far off-
course. It was a mirage, a rolling fog bank. Finally, twenty-six hours after
leaving Long Island, he spotted a gull, a harbinger of land. He forced himself to eat one of the five sandwiches he had brought and to take a swig of
water from a canteen. And then, Lindbergh saw beautiful, deep green
fields below him—Ireland!

> I first saw the lights of Paris a little before ten P.M. . . . and a few min-
> utes later I was circling the Eiffel Tower at an altitude of four thousand
> feet. The lights of Le Bourget were plainly visible, but appeared very
> close to Paris. I had understood that the field was farther from the city,
> so continued out . . . to the county for four or five miles. . . . Then I
> returned and spiraled down closer to the lights. Presently I could
> make out long lines of hangars and the roads appeared to be jammed
> with cars. I flew low over the field once, then circled about into the
> wind and landed. After the plane stopped rolling I turned it around
> and started to taxi back to the lights. The entire field ahead, however,
> was covered with thousands of people all running toward my ship.

In this typically restrained fashion, Lindbergh described the climax of
his epoch-making flight. He had been aloft for thirty-three and a half hours
and had covered 3,614 miles, a greater distance than anyone had ever
flown nonstop before. Although he had expected only a handful of people
to greet him, he was overwhelmed by a rip tide of some 150,000 excited
Frenchmen. "The movement of humanity swept over soldiers and policemen and there was the wild sight of thousands of men and women rushing
madly across a half a mile of the not even ground," reported the *New York
Times*.

No event of the Twenties was more widely hailed than Lindbergh's flight
across the Atlantic, and he became the unchallenged hero of the decade, a
role that surprised him. For days, all other news disappeared from the front
pages of the nation's newspapers, and people talked of little else. When the
Lone Eagle returned to New York on the cruiser *Memphis*, which was dispatched by President Coolidge to bring him and his plane home, four million people flooded the streets to give him the first of the city's famous
ticker tape parades. He was made a colonel in the Air Service Reserve and
was awarded the Congressional Medal of Honor. Souvenir hunters stole
his laundry when he sent it out, and people kept his checks rather than

cashing them. In 1927, he was *Time's* first Man of the Year, and dozens of reporters trailed him everywhere—much to his disgust. Lindbergh "is our Prince and our President combined," observed Will Rogers.*

Many Americans feared that the excesses of the Jazz Age had tainted the moral fiber and character of the nation's youth. Lindbergh and his accomplishment were seen as living proof of the fundamental soundness of American society, despite the transforming effects of population growth, urbanization, and economic expansion. Courage, self-reliance, and dignity still meant something. Lindbergh also reinforced the faith of Americans in the myth of the self-made man who achieves wealth and renown by pulling himself up by his bootstraps. He had succeeded where more experienced fliers with heavy backing had failed—even as numerous commentators argued that, because of the growing complexity of modern life, such success was impossible. Lindbergh had proved them wrong. Along with Henry Ford and Thomas Edison, he had mastered modern technology, yet was successful without formal education and through his own efforts.

In Paris, Lindbergh had lunched privately with Louis Bleriot, who, only eighteen years before, was the first man to fly the English Channel. "You are the prophet of a new era," declared the Frenchman.† Lindbergh's flight revived flagging public interest in commercial aviation, and once the initial hullabaloo died down, he became technical adviser to several airlines and personally surveyed routes in the United States and Latin America. He was one of the organizers of Transcontinental Air Transport—later TWA—and it was called "the Lindbergh Line."

Other new airlines included United Aircraft and Transportation, which became United Air Lines; the Aircraft Corporation, which developed into American Airlines; and North Atlantic Air, which was the predecessor of Eastern Airlines. By 1930, these lines and others were operating aircraft that carried between twelve and fifteen passengers on each flight, and were flying about 73 million passenger miles a year. The need for refueling stops and service hubs contributed to the development of Atlanta, St. Louis, and Fort Worth. Small fields blossomed on the fringes of towns all over the country, reminding some observers of the stage depots of the previous century.

---

* The nearest thing in our time to the tidal wave of worship that engulfed Lindbergh is the outpouring honoring the courage and devotion to duty of the New York City firefighters who entered the flaming World Trade Center towers on September 11, 2001.

† A month after Lindbergh's flight Charles Chamberlain and his passenger, Charles A. Levine, flew to Berlin, an even greater distance than that flown by Lindbergh. Two years later, Commander Byrd flew over the South Pole. In May 1932, Amelia Earhart became the first woman to fly the Atlantic alone.

Two years after his flight to Paris, Lindbergh married Anne Morrow, whom he had met in Mexico, where her father, Dwight Morrow, Calvin Coolidge's classmate at Amherst and a Morgan partner, was U.S. ambassador. She was twenty-one, a quiet, shy girl a year out of Smith, with a gift for poetic writing. Their first child, Charles Jr., was born in June 1930. Lindbergh's search for order seemed to be ending in success. But there were shadows. Before the wedding, there were reports of an attempt to kidnap Anne's sister, and the media continued to hound the Lindberghs.

Charles Lindbergh arrived on the scene as a culture of celebrity was taking root in America—a culture encouraged by the flashy new tabloid newspapers that were revolutionizing American journalism. Scandal, sex, and crime were the lifeblood of the tabloids—or half size—newspapers designed for subway straphangers. The *New York Daily News* was the first and most successful with a daily circulation of over a million copies. William Randolph Hearst's *Daily Mirror* and the *Graphic*—known as the *Pornographic*—imitated their rival with varying degrees of success. The taboos of genteel journalism had already been broken by the yellow journalism of Hearst and Joseph Pulitzer at the turn of the century, but the tabloids went even further in presenting journalism as entertainment, gossip as news, the trivial and salacious as the drama of life—a trend that sent quality journalism into full retreat and has since taken over television.

The number of newspapers in the United States declined by two thousand from 1914 to 1929, primarily because of their cannibalization by such press barons as Frank A. Munsey. Munsey also cheapened the papers he continued to print. By 1927, chains controlled 230 major newspapers and wire services, and syndicates exposed readers around the country to the same standardized material. New York City lost six papers, Chicago lost five out of seven morning papers, and Detroit was reduced from three morning papers to one despite a fivefold increase in population. The *New York World* estimated in 1928 that there were a thousand small American cities in which one paper held a monopoly. Yet the number of newspaper readers increased—probably as a result of the tabloids.*

The *Daily News* was the creation of Captain Joseph Medill Patterson—like his cousin Colonel Robert R. McCormick, publisher of the Chicago *Tribune*, he adopted the British practice of carrying his military title into civilian life. Near the end of World War I, Patterson, a wounded veteran of

---

* The *World* itself was one of the casualties. The tabloids cut into its circulation and the Pulitzer family killed off the paper on February 27, 1931.

the Rainbow Division, visited the British press baron Lord Northcliffe, publisher of the London tabloid *Daily Mirror,* who suggested there was a market for a similar paper in America. Patterson was the family maverick, a political reformer and Socialist who had denounced America's idle rich in a muckraking novel. Before launching the new paper, he sought the opinions and attitudes of ordinary Americans by dressing as a tramp, pan-handling, and living in a Bowery flophouse.

The *Daily News* made its appearance in June 1919, and caught on after a shaky start. Headlines were often startling and amusing, the writing sharp and pungent, and there were plenty of photographs of scantily clad women, fires, and murder victims. Even people who could not read could look at the pictures. The paper was as close as most Americans came to the myth of the Roaring Twenties. Patterson's greatest coup was a ghoulish, blurrily enlarged front-page shot of murderess Ruth Snyder in the electric chair—a picture taken by a witness with a miniature camera strapped to his ankle.

Patterson made his readers identify with the paper. Tipsters received 50 cents for each call whether the information panned out or not; they got $2 or $5 for tips that led to stories. By 1927, the paper was paying out $1,000 weekly for news tips. He was also a genius at creating circulation-building gimmicks. Readers were paid $1 each for "Bright Sayings from Children" and "My Most Embarrassing Moment," and he sponsored a lottery in which the prize reached $20,000 before the government halted it. But the mainstay of the tabloids was a steady diet of gilt-edged divorces, Holly-wood scandals, gangland killings, sports, domestic slaughter, comic strips, natural disasters, and sexual hijinks.

Walter Winchell, the Broadway columnist of the *Graphic* and later the *Daily Mirror,* set the tone. Even though he was a grammar school dropout, Winchell was one of the principal architects of modern American culture. He created the idea of celebrity as we now know it—a fame conferred by ballyhoo, or a synthetic reputation rather than one earned by achievement or distinction. He prepared the way for *People* magazine, Matt Drudge, and television "reality" shows.

Winchell's readers were served a fizzy cocktail of gossip, crime, opinion, and populist politics, laced with a few dollops of hard news. His ear for flashy slang and mastery of gossip—whether it was true or not—won him an avid following. Politicians courted Winchell, socialites and actors fawned over him and feared him. Writing like a man impatiently honking his car horn in a traffic jam, he created such terms as "blessed event" and "phffft." H. L. Mencken and Ernest Hemingway admired his breezy send-up of the American language. Winchell created a glamorous Great White Way where the lights never dimmed, the crowds never thinned, and the revelry never stopped. He understood that envy was the bitter subtext of gossip. Having been let in on the supposed foibles and secrets of celebrities, his audience could feel superior to them.

Praise from Winchell made careers and reputations in and out of show business. To be placed on his "Drop Dead List" of enemies was the kiss of death. He consorted with mobsters yet did much to establish the crime-fighting reputation of J. Edgar Hoover and the FBI. His stock tips started runs on Wall Street. Wary of personal relationships, Winchell was a creature of the night. Most of his evenings were passed at his favorite haunt, a permanently reserved table in the Cub Room of the Stork Club, which began as an upmarket speakeasy, where he held court surrounded by fawning celebrities, showgirls, and press agents. Lonely, restless, and unwilling to face the void of an empty private life, he prowled the dark canyons of the city, chasing police radio calls until sunrise.*

The tabloids feasted upon one big story after another. The various Fatty Arbuckle trials filled their columns for weeks. A frantic but unsuccessful seventeen-day effort in 1925 to rescue Floyd Collins, a young cave explorer who was trapped in a Kentucky cavern, momentarily hypnotized the nation. The death of Rudolph Valentino in August of that year inspired tabloid editors and Hollywood public relations men to new heights. The line of sobbing women and girls outside New York's Frank E. Campbell Funeral Home, where the body lay in state, stretched for eight

---

* At the height of Winchell's fame during the late 1930s and early 1940s, some 50 million people, or two thirds of American adults, huddled about their radios for his Sunday broadcasts or read his daily newspaper column, which through syndication had two thousand outlets. Franklin Roosevelt was a willing ally when Winchell decided to translate his authority in the world of celebrity gossip to a broader stage. Grateful to be legitimized by the president, Winchell repaid him by rallying support for Roosevelt's policies at home and abroad. Winchell's influence was at its height during World War II, but Roosevelt's death marked the beginning of his downfall. He had no president, no cause, not even café society, to champion. Harry Truman had no use for him and television killed off the night life so central to his column.

His influence dwindling, Winchell disintegrated into paranoia and rage. He was drawn into the orbit of Red-baiting Senator Joseph R. McCarthy, and was vicious in his denunciations of alleged subversives. Only a few years after the height of his fame, Winchell had gone phffft. He had lost his column and radio show. All his old haunts—the Mirror, the Stork Club, the Roney Plaza Hotel in Miami Beach—had closed. "The silence of the phones in his suite was awful," observed one of his few remaining friends. Having celebrated the cult of celebrity, he died in 1972 by the unforgiving rules he had helped to invent, alone and forgotten.

blocks, and several women committed suicide in their grief. There were signs that Valentino had been slipping at the box office but the hoopla made his latest film, *The Son of the Sheik,* into a big hit. Later, it was learned that the genuine shock over Valentino's death had been purposely magnified by studio publicists, and some of the mourners had been hired.

The Hall-Mills murder trial of 1926, which occurred after a prominent minister and a female choir leader were found shot to death in a lonely rural lane, inspired the transmittal of 12 million words over the wires from the courthouse in Somerville, New Jersey—more than any other news event in history until then. The defendants were found innocent. Even the *New York Times* was caught up in the frenzy and outstripped the tabloids in its coverage.

Revivalist Billy Sunday, novelist Mary Roberts Rinehart, and popular historian Will Durant were among the hundred correspondents from all over the world mobilized by the tabloids to cover the Snyder-Gray murder trial. The public was fascinated because the central figures were the epitome of Babbittry. Ruth Snyder was a chilly-looking blond Long Island housewife with a yearning for the bright lights who persuaded her married lover, corset salesman Henry Judd Gray, to murder her husband. The case, said Damon Runyon of Hearst's *New York American,* "probably makes many a peaceful, home-loving Long Islander of the Albert Snyder type shiver in his pajamas as he prepares for bed."

Ruth tricked her husband, art editor of *Motor Boating* magazine, into signing a double-indemnity insurance policy with a $96,000 payoff for violent death, and then hounded Gray into killing him.* She told her lover that she had already tried several times on her own and failed. "With some veiled threats and intensive love-making she reached the point where she got me in such a whirl that I didn't know where I was at," Gray confessed. On the night of the crime, Ruth secreted him in the house and went to a bridge party with her husband, where she persuaded him to have several drinks. They returned home late and went to bed.

After Snyder was asleep, Ruth went to the room where Gray was waiting and they embraced. It was 3 A.M. "She took me by the hand," he related. "She opened the door. I followed her." Gray struck the sleeping man on the head with a sash weight, but Snyder was full of fight. "He got me by the necktie and a struggle ensued in which I was getting the worse, because I was being choked." In panic, Gray cried out, "Mommie, Mommie! For

---

* The Snyder-Gray case was the inspiration for James Cain's novel *Double Indemnity,* and the classic film noir made from it with a script by Raymond Chandler and Billy Wilder.

God's sake help me!" Ruth coolly picked up the sash weight and knocked he husband unconscious. She and Gray finished their victim off with chloroform and by strangling him with a loop of picture wire. Ruth told police Snyder had been killed by burglars, but she and Gray were an inept set of murderers and were quickly arrested. They turned on each other, blaming the other for the killing, but both died in the electric chair. Aimee Semple McPherson, writing in the *Graphic*, said the case should teach young men to say over and over again: "I want a wife like Mother—not a Red Hot Cutie."

The Twenties produced more sports heroes than any previous era. Babe Ruth and his big bat dominated baseball. In tennis, Bill Tilden represented the United States on the Davis Cup team every season from 1920 to 1930, and Helen Wills triumphed at Wimbledon. Johnny Weissmuller went from swimming champion to movie Tarzan. The great golfers Bobby Jones, Walter Hagen, and Gene Sarazen controlled the play not only on American courses but on the greens of Britain as well. Red Grange, the "Galloping Ghost" of the University of Illinois, was picked for three successive All-American college football teams and then turned professional. At Notre Dame, Knute Rockne broke the WASP control of college football and coached a team of immigrants' sons to three national championships. Jack Dempsey and Gene Tunney battled for the heavyweight boxing championship in the "Fight of the Century" before 150,000 spectators, who paid $2.6 million for their seats.

Freed from the Puritan ethic that equated play with sin and floating on the high tide of prosperity, Americans developed an insatiable hunger for amusement and diversion to fill their newly available leisure time and to help them escape from routine. "Not far from one quarter of the entire national income of America is expended for play and recreation," noted Stuart Chase. Two hundred million dollars a year was spent on sporting goods. Golf, heretofore a rich man's game, captured the popular imagination and by 1928, eighty-nine cities had municipal golf courses. More than $2 billion was invested in country clubs and golf courses and 100,000 workers were employed in maintaining the greens. Amused Europeans noted that Americans played with the same intensity with which they worked and wondered what kind of fun they could be getting out of it.

Spectator sports were part of the new mass society created by movies, advertising, the tabloids, and radio. All helped convince a nation divided by race, class, and ethnicity that it had a common identity. Huge football stadiums and baseball parks were built in many cities, and the number of

Americans attending games doubled during the Twenties. Professional football made its debut in September 1920 with the organization of the American Football Association, and within a few years, 65,000 spectators were turning out at the Polo Grounds to see Red Grange in action.

Newspapers expanded their sports pages to meet the demand for coverage. Throwing aside objectivity, sportswriters were cheerleaders and endowed the bronzed heroes of the playing fields with the virtues of gods. Sports was both big business and show business. Before World War I, college football had been primarily of interest to the students and aging graduates of Dear Old Ivy. Now, because of the well-publicized victories of their teams, colleges and universities had legions of subway alumni who had never seen the campus and probably had never gone beyond grade school. Nevertheless, they were as vested in the team of their choice as any graduate. Notre Dame and leading schools in the Ivy League, the Big Ten, and California netted an estimated half million dollars a season. Fifty-five of the nation's seventy concrete arenas—seven of which held more than seventy thousand spectators—were built after 1920.

Even in those years some people protested that college football was the tail that wagged the dog on too many campuses. Former president Taft grumbled that "the stadium overshadows . . . the classroom . . . athletics have a dollar sign in front of them." Professors lamented the pressures to keep academically marginal students eligible to play. As early as 1928, Heywood Broun suggested that collegiate football become professional to reconcile the tension between academic and athletic excellence, a clear-cut solution to a problem that has metastasized as basketball has exceeded football in popularity on many campuses.

Baseball had fallen on evil times after the fixed World Series of 1919 and attendance was dropping off, but the game was saved by a spindle-legged, rubber-faced graduate of a Baltimore reform school named George Herman Ruth, Jr. Simply stated, Babe Ruth could hit a ball harder, higher, and farther than anyone else. Over the course of his career, he hit 714 home runs, and in 1927 produced more homers than *all* the other teams in the American League combined. But the Babe's influence extended far beyond the record books. He made baseball exciting. Until Ruth's coming, it was a low-scoring game in which batters aimed for singles, not home runs. Ruth blew the game open. Whenever he stepped up to the plate, the crowd waited in awful suspense for him to blast the ball over the fence.

The Babe's life off the diamond was as colorful as his performance on it. He consumed huge meals, had a limitless capacity for booze, dressed flamboyantly, and was usually accompanied by one or more ladies of easy virtue. He drove a white roadster, mostly at high speed, scattering pedestrians right and left like bowling pins. Ruth survived several wrecks, and after each he quickly bought another high-powered car—usually for cash, because he always carried large wads of bills with him. One year, someone complained Ruth was making more than President Hoover. "I know," replied the Babe, "but I had a better year."

Ruth's gargantuan appetites were probably an outgrowth of a childhood of deprivation and denial. The son of a Baltimore saloon keeper, he was born in 1895 and was unloved by his family.* The boy ran free on the nearby waterfront and was considered incorrigible. At the age of eight, his parents consigned him to the care of the Xaverian Brothers, who ran St. Mary's Industrial School, a grim place surrounded by high stone walls on the outskirts of the city. He hardly ever had visitors. Louis Armstrong learned to play the cornet in a similar institution, and Babe Ruth learned to play baseball at St. Mary's. The minor league Baltimore Orioles gave him a tryout as a pitcher in 1914 and immediately signed him. Jack Dunn, the owner of the Orioles, had recruited other youngsters, and the boy became known as one of Dunn's "babes"—hence his nickname.

Within a few months he proved so talented that he was sold to the Boston Red Sox and went on to become the best left-hander in baseball. But his days as a pitcher were numbered because he was too good with a bat, and he became an outfielder. Five years later, Ruth was sold to the New York Yankees for the then astonishing sum of $100,000 and a $300,000 loan. In spring training in Tampa that year, he hit a ball that traveled nearly six hundred feet from home plate.

The Yankees had never won a league championship before, but with the Babe wielding his mighty bat and backed up by a Murderers Row that included Lou Gehrig, Bob Meusel, and Tony Lazzeri, they won seven pennants and four World Series from 1920 to 1933. In his first year, Ruth hit fifty-four home runs—nearly double the previous record—and a million fans paid to see him do it. The following year he boosted his total to fifty-nine and in 1927 he hit sixty. Newly constructed Yankee Stadium was known as "The House That Ruth Built."

Near the end of his career, Ruth hit the legendary called shot that many regard as one of baseball's greatest moments. The Babe came to bat in the fifth inning of the third game of the 1932 World Series against the Chicago

---

* The senior Ruth's saloon was located in what is now the outfield of Camden Yards, current home of the Baltimore Orioles.

Cubs. He took two called strikes as the Cubs bench rode him as it had done all through the series. In response, Ruth pointed to the center field fence, apparently predicting where he intended to hit the next ball. Taking a tremendous swing, he sent it soaring over the wall at that point for the longest home run in the history of Wrigley Field.

Like Babe Ruth, William Harrison "Jack" Dempsey came up the hard way. The ninth of thirteen children of a luckless miner, he grew up in Manassa, a Colorado mining camp, which later provided him with the name "Man-assa Mauler." He left home at sixteen and drifted about the country, work-ing sometimes as a miner and sometimes riding the rails. A young tough with steel fists and an iron jaw, he fought for small purses in saloons, win-ner take all. Most were only a cut above barroom brawls. Fighting first under the name Kid Blackie and then his own, the swarthy, beetle-browed Dempsey moved on to win eighty professional fights.

Dempsey was renowned for his ferocity in the ring. He won most of his fights by quick knockouts in the early minutes of the match. "Going for a quick knockout was just common sense," he later explained. "I had a little motto about getting rid of my opponents. 'The sooner the safer.'" At Toledo in 1919, Dempsey fought the hulking Jess Willard, who had taken the heavyweight championship from Jack Jackson four years before. Willard outweighed Dempsey by fifty pounds, but playing David to Willard's Goliath, Dempsey fractured Willard's cheekbone in thirteen places with a single punch.

Boxing had come a long way in the decade. Until after the war, prize-fighting was banned in several states as brutal, and it was illegal to even import fight films into some jurisdictions. The fight game was dominated by gangsters and gamblers and matches were often fixed. The transforma-tion of boxing into an accepted sport was largely the work of George "Tex" Rickard. Rickard had mined for gold and operated saloons and gambling halls in Alaska, the Yukon, and Nevada, where he staged some prizefights. He discovered Dempsey and, with a genius for showmanship, made him one of the greatest box office attractions of the time.

Dempsey was fast, shifty, hard-hitting—weaving in and out and striking with short, rapid, savage punches—a killer in the ring. For a time, he was unpopular. He was unjustly accused of having dodged the draft during the war and of encasing his fists with plaster of paris before putting on boxing gloves. In 1921, he destroyed Georges Carpentier, a Frenchman who held the European heavyweight championship, in four rounds. Dempsey's fight with the Argentine Luis Firpo in 1923 was one of the most savage on record. Firpo was floored seven times in the first round by Dempsey, who stood over him and knocked him down each time he got up. Yet, the "Wild Bull of the Pampas" rose once more and, with a wild swing, knocked the champion through the ropes into the laps of the newsmen covering the fight. They helped him back into the ring before the count of ten—which was against the rules—and Dempsey put Firpo away in the next round.

Taking up a career as an actor, Dempsey cavorted with Broadway and Hollywood stars—in fact, he married one—and neglected training. When he fought Gene Tunney in 1926 for the first time, he had lost his fighting edge and dropped his title to Tunney. Tall, blond, and handsome, James J. Tunney was the opposite of Dempsey in almost respect. A product of an Irish-American working-class family in Greenwich Village, he had quit school as a boy to go to work. He fought in amateur bouts while working as a teamster and had turned professional before the war, in which he served in the marines. While overseas, he won the light-heavyweight championship of the AEF.

Tunney, unlike Dempsey, was a defensive fighter. He parried blows rather than attacking the other fellow, and wore down stronger fighters before moving in for the kill. These tactics left him unscarred after sixty fights. Tunney was not popular with fight fans, however. He was openly contemptuous of his chosen profession, was a "highbrow" who was seen reading books, and mixed with high society rather than the raffish characters associated with the fight game. Following his first fight with Dempsey, he announced that instead of going out to celebrate, he was returning to his hotel room for a nice cup of tea.

Tex Rickard billed the rematch between Tunney and Dempsey at Soldier Field in Chicago on September 22, 1927, as the "Fight of the Century." Twenty-seven special trains brought in boxing fans from all over the country. Twelve hundred reporters were on hand, as well as Douglas Fairbanks, John Barrymore, Florenz Ziegfeld, financier Bernard Baruch, steel tycoon Charles M. Schwab, six governors, and a clutch of royalty. The fight was broadcast to an audience estimated at 50 million people, with Graham MacNamee, the best-known announcer of the day, at the microphone. In those pre-television days, a pair of boxers reenacted the fight at the 71st Regiment Armory at Park Avenue and 34th Street in Manhattan for an audience, as MacNamee's broadcast was piped in. Inmates at Sing Sing were allowed to stay up past the normal lights-out to hear the fight.

The fight was very close for the first six rounds, with the officials giving

Tunney a slight edge. Let MacNamee describe the the fateful seventh round:

> Dempsey drives a hard left under the heart, Jack pounded the back of Tunney's head with four rights. Gene put a terrific right—hardest blow of the fight—Gene beginning to wake up—like a couple of wild animals—Gene's body red—hits Dempsey a terrific right to the body—Jack is groggy—Jack lands hard left—Tunney seems almost wobbling . . . some of the blows Dempsey hits make this ring tremble—Tunney is down—down from a barrage.

MacNamee's account of what happened next was hidden by the cheers, screams, and catcalls of the crowd. Dempsey was standing over his downed foe rather than going to a neutral corner, as specified in the new rules. Instead of immediately beginning the count, Referee Dave Barry pushed Dempsey to a neutral corner. "I couldn't move," Dempsey said later in explanation. "I just couldn't. I wanted him to get up. I wanted to kill the son of a bitch."

Barry began his count, but Tunney had shaken off the effects of Dempsey's punch and was up at the count of eight. No one listening on radio was certain what was happening, and seven radio listeners reportedly died of heart failure during the round. Tunney went on to outbox the frustrated and angry Dempsey for the next three rounds—even knocking him down in the eighth—and retained the title on points by a large margin, despite Dempsey's protests over the "long count."

Tunney and Dempsey each earned about $900,000 from the night's work and both soon retired. Perhaps out of sympathy for a man seemingly deprived unfairly of victory by the long count, Dempsey, who opened a Broadway restaurant, was transformed into a folk hero. Tunney was even more unpopular than before. He defended his title only once before marrying a Connecticut socialite and becoming a business executive. In April 1928, he appeared before a Yale literature class to lecture on Shakespeare. The Bard of Avon was "a sport," Tunney noted. "Harvard, I trust, will counter by asking Babe Ruth to tell the boys at Cambridge just what Milton meant to him," observed Heywood Broun.

With all the other attractions available by mid-decade, movie theater owners were having trouble filling the seats in the newly opened palaces. The average admission for a first-run movie was about 60 cents, putting the cost of a night's entertainment out of the reach of many families.

Instead, they stayed home and listened to the radio, which cost nothing. To attract patrons, theaters offered such extra attractions as John Philip Sousa and his band or Gertrude Ederle, the Channel swimmer, performing in a tank. Obviously, some new sensation was needed to bring audiences back to the movies.

Hollywood found its answer in the talkies. Several methods of making the movies talk were under development. Lee de Forest perfected a method of recording sound on the edge of a film strip and by 1923 had produced several short films with synchronized sound, including one of Calvin Coolidge making a speech on the economy. Two years later, the Western Electric laboratories of Bell Telephone announced a system called Vitaphone that included a disc revolving on a turntable linked to a projector.

Most Hollywood moguls were reluctant to switch to the revolutionary new medium for numerous reasons: the new equipment for both the studios and movie theaters carried a heavy cost; some silent stars had voices or accents that were unacceptable for sound; production and artistic standards would suffer because the camera would have to be rooted to a single spot so the actors could be recorded by a stationary microphone. The ease and fluidity developed by D. W. Griffith and others that had made films an art would be lost. In the end, Warner Brothers took the plunge into Vitaphone because the studio was in dire financial straits and had to take greater risks than the others if it was to remain in business.

The first feature movie with a sound track was *Don Juan*, starring John Barrymore, Mary Astor, and Myrna Loy. This film, which opened in 1926, had no spoken dialogue, but did have a musical background recorded by the New York Philharmonic Orchestra and such sound effects as the clanging of swords.

Oddly enough, in view of the tacit agreement among the Jewish Hollywood moguls to shy away from Jewish themes—"don't ruffle the *goyim*" was their motto—the vehicle chosen for the first use of synchronized sound dialogue was *The Jazz Singer*, the tale of a Jewish entertainer's estrangement from the faith of his fathers. For the star of the show, Al Jolson, the son of a Baltimore cantor-rabbi who became successful as a blackface singer, the story was almost autobiographical.

Only a handful of sequences—including one in which Jolson sang his signature song "Mammy"—were in sound, but the movie was a tremendous hit. *The Jazz Singer* was the top-grossing film of the year although only five hundred theaters in the whole country were wired for sound. Early sound films were crude: the crumpling of a newspaper sounded like an earthquake and the patter of raindrops sounded like thunder. Sibilants were turned into lisps. In one film, a female actress said: "Why do you perthith in perthecuting me? I am innocenth." Nevertheless, sound films were soon being made in all languages.

Al Jolson had the last word. In ad-libbed remarks at the opening of *The Jazz Singer*, he told the audience: "You ain't heard nothin' yet!"

CHAPTER 16

"The Final Triumph over Poverty"

Shortly before noon on the drizzly morning of August 2, 1927, the thirty or so reporters covering the vacationing Calvin Coolidge filed into a high school classroom in Rapid City, South Dakota, that was being used as a press office. The White House in Washington was undergoing renovation and the Coolidges had been vacationing at a lodge in the nearby Black Hills since mid-June. The president was already in the room. Some of the newsmen noted that Coolidge had been sworn in as president exactly five years ago to the day.

"The line forms on the left," Coolidge said as soon as the door was closed. As each man filed past him, Coolidge handed him a slip of paper that had twelve words neatly typed on it: "I do not chose to run for President in nineteen twenty-eight."

Shocked, the reporters clamored for comment. "Mr. President, can't you give us something more on this?" they pleaded.

"There will be nothing more from this office today," Coolidge curtly replied, and his steel trap of a mouth snapped shut. The newsmen raced to the telephones to inform the outside world of the momentous news. Wall Street took a dip upon first hearing the report but quickly recovered.

Senator Arthur Capper of Kansas, who had lunch with the president that afternoon, noted his delight in having put one over on the press. The announcement had been so closely held that it was a shock even to Grace Coolidge. Most Americans were just as surprised. As usual in American politics, discussion of the 1928 presidential campaign had begun a year before, and many voters thought Coolidge would run—and wished he would. Except for the farmers, who were angry over his vetoes of the McNary-Haugen crop-subsidy bill, he was the patron saint of the New Era with its prosperity and tranquillity at home and overseas. His administration was free of scandal and he was in the prime of life; in 1928 he would be only fifty-six years old. "As to Mr. Coolidge's wanting another term, that is too obvious to argue," columnist Frank R. Kent had assured the readers of the *Baltimore Sun*. "No president ever liked the White House better than he. No president wanted to hold on to it more."

Numerous reasons have been advanced for Coolidge's decision to refuse certain reelection. Did he sense what lay around the corner? Mrs. Coolidge was later quoted as telling friends that "Poppa says there's a depression coming." But that indicates a prescience that Coolidge had never shown. More likely, he no longer found the presidency a novelty and had grown tired of the job. Never energetic, he was worried about his health and that of his wife, who did not flourish in Washington's erratic climate. Moreover, he was deeply depressed by the death of their youngest son and, more recently, that of his father. With the country on a sound footing, he may have felt he could safely retire from the scene.

Some political leaders thought Coolidge's declaration a ploy designed to overcome any latent anti-third-term sentiment among the voters, but Coolidge was adamant despite pleas that he change his mind. Several possibilities for the Republican presidential nomination were already being mentioned: Senator Charles Curtis of Kansas, the majority leader, the always available William Borah, Vice President Dawes, former governor Frank Lowden of Illinois, who had been a favorite in 1920, and Charles Evans Hughes, the nominee in 1916. Herbert Hoover stood above them all.

Yet, for all his accomplishments and popularity with the public, Hoover had to work for the nomination. Republican conservatives such as Andrew Mellon were reluctant to support him. They thought him too progressive and refused to forgive his admiration of Woodrow Wilson and support for the League of Nations. The nation's banking and industrial elites believed Hoover unsound on certain issues. He opposed injunctions in labor disputes, favored government spending on public works in times of economic distress, and thought inheritance taxes should be raised to break up large fortunes. Wall Street was also worried that Hoover would curb the inflation of credit that was the lifeblood of stock market speculation.

Republican insiders also pointed out that the only office to which Hoover had ever been elected was treasurer of his class at Stanford University, and he had not even announced that he was a Republican until 1920. They knew he had a contempt for politicians. Big, bluff, hearty men, they were fond of a joke and a drink; Hoover was sober and somber. Admirers called him "America's handy man," but critics sneered at him as

"Wonder Boy." "That man has offered me unsolicited advice for six years, all of it bad," Coolidge sourly commented when privately asked about Hoover's qualifications for the presidency. But Hoover's ambitions were unbanked. Agnes Meyer, wife of a Hoover confidant, financier Eugene Meyer, wrote in her diary that he "was consumed with ambition. . . . The man's will-to-power is almost a mania."

Even as Coolidge made his announcement, Hoover was on center stage, fighting the after-effects of the Great Mississippi Flood of 1927 and dominating the headlines in his familiar roles of engineer, humanitarian, and administrator.

In the early months of 1927, the Mississippi River Valley had been deluged by heavy rains, and the river was rising. A large snowmelt in the Rockies added to the threat. On every gauge over the thousand miles from Cairo, Illinois, to New Orleans, the river had reached flood stage early. At Baton Rouge, it crested at forty-seven feet, a new record. Backwater streams and tributaries to the Mississippi were overflowing, inundating thousands of acres and making hundreds homeless. Water poured out of the White River into the Mississippi; water poured out of the Ohio, water poured out of the Arkansas.

Flooding had always been the implacable systole and diastole of America's heartland. Every spring the Mississippi boiled over its natural floodplain and then receded, leaving deposits of rich alluvial soil at the juncture of the Mississippi and Yazoo Rivers. The Delta was one of the most fertile areas in the world and the seat of a vast, semifeudal cotton empire, in which wealthy whites owned most of the land while black and poor white sharecroppers and tenant farmers worked it.

To protect this domain, the U.S. Army Corps of Engineers had built a network of levees. Although independent engineers urged the construction of spillways to reduce the buildup of water contained by the levees in flood time, the Corps insisted that a levees-only policy could tame the river. Now, the water was ominously piling up between the embankments, dark and angry, thrashing about like an imprisoned snake. Without spillways, it had no place to go.

Whites and blacks anxiously eyed the levees and wondered if they would hold. Earth tremors, electrical storms, tornadoes, and unseasonably cold weather added to the misery. For hundreds of miles up and down both sides of the river, gangs worked in the driving rain, buttressing the levees with thousands of sandbags. Some thought of Bessie Smith's "Backwater Blues":

Backwater blues done cause me to pack my things and go . . .
Cause my house done fall down and I cain't live there no mo'.

Without warning, the break everyone feared occurred near Greenville, Mississippi, on the morning of April 21, 1927—the seventeenth anniversary of the death of Mark Twain. The water cascaded through the crevasse and a great, chocolate brown sea soon covered the fields. Cottonwoods were uprooted and houses, deep-driven fence posts, and livestock were carried away as if they were fallen leaves. As the water rose inside their houses, people took to the rooftops and prayed for rescue. Others clung to trees or maintained a precarious existence atop still unbroken levees. As many as a thousand people died, and 700,000 were destitute. Property damage totaled $1 billion, and the devastation covered an area as large as New England. The carcasses of thousands of dead mules, horses, cows, and hogs were hung up on the logjams, raising the specter of an epidemic.

"For thirty-six hours the Delta was in turmoil, in movement, in terror," wrote Will Percy, a member of one of the great landholding families. "Then the waters covered everything, the turmoil ceased, and a great quiet settled down. Over everything was silence, deadlier because of the strange cold sound of the currents gnawing at foundations, hissing against walls, creaming and clawing over everything. . . . Out on the water there was unimaginable silence. . . . There was not the bark of a dog, the lowing of a cow, the neighing of a horse."

In New Orleans, there was panic. While the newspapers purposely played down the threat, the men who really ran the city, the bankers and business leaders, feared the levee protecting the town would not hold. To relieve pressure upon it, they convinced the governor to authorize the dynamiting of the levee downriver, flooding out thousands of poor rural people. New Orleans's elite promised them indemnification for the sacrifice of their homes and property.

Six state governors beseeched Calvin Coolidge for help, for government assistance, for at least a presidential visit to inspect the disaster area. To all, he turned a deaf ear. "I urgently request and insist that you make a personal visit at this time," wired Mississippi's governor. Still, Coolidge refused. Newspapers all over the country demanded that he go to the flooded area to show concern and restore morale. Finally forced to act, Coolidge appointed Herbert Hoover, the American official with the most experience in dealing with massive relief efforts, as chairman of a newly organized Mississippi Flood Committee, and gave him wartime powers to deal with the crisis.

*　*　*

Hoover immediately established headquarters in Memphis, overlooking the still surging river. To get a closer look at the disaster, he repeatedly circled the flood area from Cairo to New Orleans by Pullman car. The flood, he said, was "the greatest peace-time calamity in the history of the nation." The work was divided into three stages—rescue, refugee care, economic rehabilitation—and Hoover took personal charge.

Six hundred boats, sixty government airplanes, hundreds of Red Cross nurses, thousands of national guardsmen, and even more thousands of volunteers were mobilized. At the height of the rescue effort, some 35,000 people worked under Hoover's direction. He put together $50 million in Red Cross and private assistance and distributed it with such efficiency that overhead accounted for only 1 percent. In the second phase of the operation, some 350,000 people were moved into 150 tent cities in seven states—an instant urbanization of a largely rural population. Hoover also persuaded the Rockefeller Foundation to finance a hundred community health units, the first seen in some areas. On April 30, he made a radio appeal on behalf of a Red Cross fund drive that was one of the first speeches made over a nationwide hookup.

Small boats manned by one or two men—double-ended, flat-bottomed bateaux, motorboats, even rowboats—edged out in the great sea searching for survivors, plucking families from levees and the rooftops of floating houses. Local bootleggers volunteered their fastest and best craft. Rescue operations soon became systemized. Large mother ships, usually paddle wheel steamers, pushed barges holding as many as 1,500 people along the river, while smaller boats searched for survivors in what only a few days before had been back country. Planes circled overhead and acted as spotters.

Once, a steamer stopped to rescue some two hundred black sharecroppers huddled on top of a levee, but the two armed white men for whom they worked would not allow them to board out of fear that if their workforce left, it would not return. A white doctor climbed down the gangplank to the levee, but the men refused to allow him to land. "I came here by the authority of the American Red Cross and the God of all creation!" he declared. "If either of you has guts enough to pull the gun you carry please start now or get out of my way." He pushed past them and ushered the refugees on board the steamer.

Rigid racial segregation prevailed at the refugee camps, which were run under local direction and custom. Whites were sheltered in neatly planned tent cities, with each family having its own tent and each person having a cot, and food and clothing were adequate. Religious services were held several times a week by the Church of Christ at some camps, and the residents developed a sense of community. "I love this place," said a white refugee. "It's just like a camp meeting." Northern observers noted that poor whites often enjoyed better food and medical care in the camps than they received under normal conditions.

For blacks, however, conditions were less ideal. Several families occupied the same tent, and cots were available for only the aged and infirm. Everyone else slept on the ground. In violation of Red Cross rules, county relief officials gave food, clothing, and other necessities to the planters for distribution to their tenants. Some distributed the supplies at no cost; others charged for them. Since the tenants had no money, they fell even more into debt to the plantation. The camps also became virtual prisons for blacks. National guardsmen prevented them from leaving until they were "retrieved" by plantation owners. Pellagra and venereal disease were rampant. "There was no laughter, no music, no Negro light-heartedness, in the black camps," observed *The Crisis*, the journal of the NAACP.

Reports poured in to Hoover of mistreatment of blacks, forced labor at gunpoint, brutality, and conditions reminiscent of slavery. A scandal was the last thing he wanted, because he saw a successful campaign against the ravages of the flood as the key to winning the Republican presidential nomination in 1928, if Coolidge did not run. Moreover, although blacks had little clout in national elections, they were a presence at Republican presidential conventions and could not be simply disregarded.

In response to these concerns, Hoover appointed a Colored Advisory Committee, composed of sixteen prominent black men and women, mostly of conservative bent. The group was headed by Dr. Robert Russa Moton, who had succeeded Booker T. Washington at Tuskegee and had inherited his mantle as the white man's favorite black. Whites were largely ignorant of the increasing radicalization of black Americans, and were surprised when the Moton Commission issued a scathing report of abuses in the black refugee camps. Hoover accepted the report and a subsequent one and tried to see that its recommendations were carried out, despite continued strong resistance from local officials.

As always, Hoover was already looking beyond the moment to the reconstruction of the flooded zone. The Delta, although known as an alluvial empire, was one of the most poverty-stricken areas in the world. Why not help the rural poor, especially blacks, to buy the land they worked? Hoover considered a nonprofit "resettlement corporation" to lend leftover relief funds to finance such purchases. Former tenants and sharecroppers would be supplied with seed, animals, equipment, and technical assistance and offered incentives to diversify crops and end their boom-and-bust reliance on cotton. Hoover estimated that an initial capital of only $4.5 million would allow seven thousand farmers to buy their land.

The plan was kept a secret, but Moton and some other black leaders knew enough to convince them to eagerly support Hoover for the Republican presidential nomination. It turned out to be only a tantalizing dream, because the Red Cross refused to make the unexpended funds available. When Hoover became president he revived the proposal, but it became a casualty of the Depression.

The federal government did nothing to help the stricken states. The treasury had a record $635 million surplus in 1927, but would not create a loan-guarantee program for the displaced farmers. The War Department even insisted that the Red Cross reimburse it for the old army blankets it supplied the refugees. Forty years before, Grover Cleveland had vetoed a $10,000 emergency appropriation for drought victims in Texas on grounds that the government had "no warrant . . . to indulge a benevolent and charitable sentiment through the appropriation of public funds"—and the same philosophy prevailed.

There were demands from the devastated area for government flood relief, but Congress was out of session, and Coolidge refused to summon it back to Washington to appropriate such funds. "Fortunately there are still some things that can be done without the wisdom of Congress and the all-fathering Federal Government," said an approving New York Times. On the other hand, the Paducah News-Democrat bluntly stated: "Either [Coolidge] has the coldest heart in America or the dullest imagination, and we are ready to believe he has both." In the end, the only organized program of rehabilitation was a group of "reconstruction corporations" established by Hoover to provide credit to flooded-out farmers—and even these, in keeping with Hoover's emphasis on voluntarism and cooperativism, were underwritten by private sources, not the government.

There was extensive fallout from the flood. The dynamiting of the levee below New Orleans exploded the Corps of Engineers' levees-only policy. The Mississippi Flood Control Bill of 1928, which Hoover helped craft, contained provisions for a spillway to protect New Orleans and flood and storage basins to drain off floodwaters. And when the city's elite reneged on their promises to indemnify residents below the city for flooding their homes, the angry outcry led to the election of the populist Huey Long as governor of Louisiana in 1928. He called for the redistribution of wealth, to the alarm of the old guard. "We'll show 'em who's boss," Long told his cheering supporters after the election. "You fellers stick by me. . . . We're just getting started."

Finally, after three months, Hoover declared the crisis at an end. "The people of the valley are settling their own problems of rehabilitation without a great deal of outside help," he declared. "It is upon such independence and self-government that is based the greatness of the United States." To the country, Hoover emerged from the flood as a hero, reclaiming the title of Great Humanitarian he had earned through his European relief efforts—just in time to launch his campaign for the Republican presidential nomination.

When Coolidge returned from his Black Hills vacation, he found world peace the first order of business. One of the great myths of the Twenties is that the United States was isolationist during the Coolidge years. In truth, however, Americans were willing to have contacts with the outside world—as long as it was on their terms. Historian Joan Hoff Wilson observes that the nation pursued a policy of "independent internationalism" rather than isolation. Where the United States lacked power, as in Asia, it acted haltingly; in the Western Hemisphere, where it possessed power, it acted vigorously. In Europe, the successive Republican administrations of the 1920s worked to rehabilitate Germany, relieve France's strategic anxieties, resolve controversies over war debts, and ensure international tranquillity through collective security.

Like Harding, Coolidge wanted no official links to the League of Nations, but by 1925, American diplomats were quietly attending League functions. Again like his predecessor, Coolidge supported adherence to the World Court; in 1926, the Senate approved American membership. But there were so many restrictions that the other members refused to accept the United States.

Relations between the United States and Japan soured following the passage of the Johnson Act of 1924, which barred Japanese immigration to the United States. Japan fell increasingly under the domination of a military clique, and the nation launched a massive naval building program. Although the Washington Naval Conference had placed limitations on the number of battleships and aircraft carriers in the world's navies, there were no restrictions on cruisers, destroyers, and submarines, and the arms race switched to these types of vessels.

Economy was the watchword of the Coolidge administration, and the U.S. Navy not only could not match the Japanese, but was unable to build up to the strength allotted by the Washington treaty. When the Japanese began constructing a dozen large cruisers, Congress, paying heed at last to repeated warnings that the United States was being outclassed in the Pacific, appropriated funds for eight such vessels. Obviously hoping to entice Coolidge into approving the new ships, the navy announced that the first would be named the *Northampton* after the president's hometown. Coolidge did not rise to the bait, and only two ships were built.

Instead, Coolidge encouraged an attempt to impose treaty limitations on cruisers. The basic idea was to check the growth of rival navies while the growth of the U.S. Navy was restrained through budgetary restrictions. The Geneva Conference, which resulted from Coolidge's efforts, was attended by the United States, Britain, and Japan but foundered because each nation had its own defensive needs. Obstructionist tactics by lobbyists for the international arms industry also contributed to the failure to reach an agreement.

An important by-product of the failed Geneva Conference was reinforcement of the belief of American peace activists that the only way to ensure peace was not to limit arms but to outlaw war itself. In the years since the end of World War I, several small but vociferous groups had advocated such action. One of the leaders of this movement was James T. Shotwell, a Columbia University professor and trustee of the Carnegie Endowment for International Peace. Shotwell, while visiting France in the spring of 1927, presented his ideas to Foreign Minister Aristide Briand. Back in 1919, the United States and Britain had assured the security-conscious French that they would guarantee France's territorial integrity against a revived German militarism, but nothing had come of it after the Senate refused to ratify the Versailles Treaty.

Briand seized upon Shotwell's proposal as a substitute for the lapsed guarantee and announced on April 6, 1927, the tenth anniversary of American entry into the war, that France was prepared to enter into a bilateral agreement with the United States that would outlaw war. Briand's suggestion met a cool reception from Secretary of State Frank B. Kellogg, but Shotwell; Senator Borah, the chairman of the Senate Foreign Relations Committee; peace groups; and the liberal press pressured the Coolidge administration to follow up on the French initiative.

The Pact of Paris, as the Kellogg-Briand agreement was formally known, was signed by fifteen nations on August 27, 1928, amid the splendors of the Quai d'Orsay Palace. Eventually, sixty-two nations were signatories to the treaty and it was approved by the Senate by a vote of eighty-five to one. Today, the Kellogg-Briand treaty is dismissed as having been about as effective as Prohibition, but even then, peace advocates were not so naive as to think that it guaranteed a peaceful world. The treaty was seen as merely the first step on the long road to international peace. Frank Kellogg was awarded the Nobel Peace Prize.*

By the mid-1920s, American officials were directing the financial affairs of half the twenty Latin American republics, and marines were in and out of Haiti, Honduras, the Dominican Republic, and Nicaragua. American strategists had an especially keen interest in the latter because of its proximity to the Panama Canal. To end the periodic fighting between rival political factions that had adopted the labels "Conservative" and "Liberal" although their main motives were spoils, not ideology, Nicaragua was virtually ruled by American marines from 1912 to 1925. By then, the country appeared to be solvent, stable, and secure and the marines were withdrawn, leaving a Conservative regime in power with the support of the American-trained National Guard.

Once again, the Liberals revolted and established a rival regime, which had the support of Mexico. Some two thousand marines were landed the next year to protect the Conservative government. Secretary Kellogg, to justify the intervention, warned that Russian agents operating from Mexico were plotting to take over Central America. No evidence was produced to support Kellogg's charge, but it served as an example for dealing with emergencies in Guatemala and the Dominican Republic forty years later. Anti-imperialists and Democrats were highly critical of the intervention, but Coolidge rigorously defended it: "We are not making war on Nicaragua," he declared, "any more than a policeman on the street is making war on passersby."

With opposition to the intervention mounting, Coolidge sent Henry L. Stimson, who had served as secretary of war in the Taft administration, to Nicaragua to work out a solution to the civil war. The struggle had reached a stalemate, and both sides agreed to accept the result of a presidential election in 1928, to be supervised by the Americans. The Liberals won, but one of their leaders, Augusto César Sandino, fought on, with the intention of expelling the Americans from Nicaragua. Over the next six years, he conducted a guerrilla campaign that tied up some five thousand American marines and *guardistas*.

Sandino set the pattern for future guerrilla movements all over the

---

* Following World War II, when the German and Japanese war leaders were brought to the bar of international justice, the prosecution was justified on grounds that they had violated the Kellogg-Briand treaty when they led their nations into aggressive war. As far as is known, this was the only time the Kellogg-Briand treaty was ever invoked.

world. Avoiding mass formations, his forces moved in small groups under the cover of dense foliage, and lived off the land. Following an attack, his men dispersed. Usually, he struck from ambush, and then only when the odds favored him; otherwise he avoided combat. These became the tactics of the People's Liberation Army in China, the National Liberation Front in Algeria, Fidel Castro in Cuba, and the Vietminh and Vietcong in Vietnam. In 1934, after the U.S. Marines were withdrawn, Sandino agreed to a truce with the Nicaraguan government but was murdered by the National Guard. Not long after, the country came under the control of the corrupt and brutal General Anastasio Somoza, who established a U.S.-backed family dictatorship in Nicaragua that lasted until 1979. The leftist rebels who ousted the Somozas called themselves Sandinistas.

As the 1928 election approached, the Democrats had no illusions about their chances of victory. Not only had James Cox and John Davis been soundly trounced in 1920 and 1924, but the Republicans had also controlled both houses of Congress since 1918. With the exception of Woodrow Wilson, whose two victories were due to flukes, Grover Cleveland was the only Democrat elected president since the Civil War. A major reason was because the Democratic Party was dangerously schizophrenic. No one was certain as to what it stood for. "I'm not a member of an organized political party," joked Will Rogers. "I'm a Democrat." The Republicans were the party of big business and prosperity, while the Democrats were an ill-matched pack of mutually antagonistic factions with little in common. The party's two major constituencies—the Irish Catholic urban masses and the white rural Southerners—detested each other.

The national conventions that year were anticlimactic, for both parties had settled on their nominees well before they met. Herbert Hoover quickly disposed of his rivals for the Republican nomination. And the Democrats, having no desire to repeat the bloodbath of 1924, were ready to nominate Al Smith, despite warnings that he would not carry the Solid South because he was a Roman Catholic, a creature of Tammany Hall, and an unwavering wet. Smith was too important a political figure to ignore, and party leaders feared that if he were again denied the nomination, urban voters would desert.

The Republican convention opened on June 12, 1928, in Kansas City. Hoover—touted as "the minister of mercy to the hungry and poor"—won the nomination on the first ballot with 837 out of 1,089 votes. The vice presidential nomination went to Senator Charles Curtis, as a sop to the farmers because he had voted for McNary-Haugen.

The Republican platform sang the praises of Coolidge Prosperity, which had filled the workingman's dinner pail—and gas tank—and vowed to continue it along with the protective tariff, sound money, and "Republican efficiency" in government. Labor was offered the prospect of fewer injunctions in strikes and temperance forces were promised continued enforcement of Prohibition. Hoover favored cooperatives for farmers rather than government subsidy programs. "Bring on the Tammany Tiger!" roared the delegates as they headed for home.

Few Democrats even seemed interested in the nomination in view of Coolidge Prosperity. The death of William Jennings Bryan had left the Prohibition forces without a national leader. William McAdoo, never fully able to shake the taint of scandal that clung to him, withdrew from the race. Senator Tom Walsh of Montana, who had done more than anyone to unravel Teapot Dome, was an attractive candidate, but he, too, was a Catholic and fared poorly in the primaries. This left the nomination to Smith, who was serving his fourth two-year term as progressive governor of New York. The convention, which met in Houston on June 26, was racially segregated: chicken wire fences separated blacks and whites.

Franklin Roosevelt again placed Smith's name in nomination, but in a speech designed for the millions of listeners tuned in by radio rather than the fifteen thousand delegates and spectators. Roosevelt revealed his early mastery of the new medium. America needs "a new leader," he declared. "One who has the will to win—who not only deserves success but commands it. Victory is his habit—the Happy Warrior, Alfred E. Smith!"

In vivid contrast to 1924, Smith was nominated on the first ballot after only a single fistfight on the floor. Senator Joseph T. Robinson of Arkansas was chosen as his running mate to placate the drys, rural voters, and Protestants. In their platform, the Democrats promised "an honest effort" to enforce Prohibition—a plank that Smith would have been wise to accept, but he came out flatly for repeal. They also trotted out the ghost of the Harding scandals, advocated collective bargaining and an end to labor injunctions, a tariff less tinctured with favoritism, nonintervention in Latin America, and farm subsidies. Thus, irony of ironies, Al Smith, the cigar-puffing, derby-wearing epitome of the city politico, became the paladin of America's embattled farmers.

Nevertheless, there was only a surface gloss of unity at Houston. Ominously, anti-Smith holdouts stubbornly refused to make his nomination unanimous, and he received no votes in the delegations from four of the former Confederate states. Bishop James Cannon, Jr., leader of the Southern Methodist Church, wasted little time in declaring that "no subject of the Pope" would be allowed to enter the White House. And several Southern party leaders let it be known that even though Smith was the nominee, they were still Democrats—but would be "very still" during the campaign.

"I come of Quaker stock."

So said Herbert Clark Hoover on the eve of becoming president, and his Quaker upbringing was probably the most significant aspect of his background. Although he strayed from formal Quakerism—he was no pacifist, drank socially, went to the theater, read secular books, and played roulette—the Quaker doctrines of hard work, self-reliance, thrift, and temperance were deeply ingrained in his personality. Even more important to his makeup was the emphasis on individual effort conveyed by the creed. In 1922, he published a slim volume entitled *American Individualism* in which he professed his "abiding faith in the intelligence, the initiative, the character, the courage, and the divine touch in the individual." Society and government owed the people only three things: "liberty, justice, and equality of opportunity," he declared. Hoover's version of individualism was not a ruthless Darwinism, however, but based upon coordination of capital, government, and labor—a reflection of the community effort embodied in the Quaker tradition.

The first Quaker president and the first from west of the Mississippi, Hoover was born on August 11, 1874, in West Branch, Iowa.* A somber Quaker settlement of some three hundred people, the town was only a few years removed from the frontier. There were no brick buildings or porches or cupolas; Quakers frowned on such architectural gewgaws. Waving prairie grass extended as far as the eye could see, and smoke from distant settlements looked as if it came from a ship's hull down below the horizon.

The Hoovers—the name was originally Huber—had come to Pennsylvania from Germany in 1738, become Quakers like their neighbors, and steadily pushed westward. Jesse Clark Hoover, the future president's father, was West Branch's blacksmith and made and sold farm implements in a shop that prospered. He was also an inveterate tinkerer who turned out various labor-saving devices designed to ease the drudgery of farm life. In 1870, Jesse married Huldah Minthorn, a member of another Quaker family. She had more education than most Quaker women on the Middle Border, having attended classes at the University of Iowa, and she was a schoolteacher. They set up housekeeping in a one-story, two-room

* There is some question about the actual date of Hoover's birthday. Some biographers give it as August 10, but Hoover said it was August 11.

cottage across the lane from the blacksmith shop and had three children: Theodore, known as Tad; Herbert, known as Bertie; and Mary, called May.

Life in West Branch was governed by strict Quaker practice. Absolute silence reigned at the First and Fourth Day meetings until a brother or sister was moved by the "Inner Light" to speak. Jesse was reserved in religious expression, but Huldah was known as an impassioned speaker at meeting. Bertie learned to sit quietly for hours without squirming, daring only "to count his toes. . . . All this might not have been recreation, but it was strong training in patience," he later recalled.

Thrift, individualism, conscience, plain living—that was the Quaker way. The children had their chores: helping plant corn, hoeing the garden, learning to milk the cows, sawing wood. Life had its lighter side, as Hoover recalled when he was an old man. In winter, the children went flying on their homemade sleds down Cook's Hill and out onto the frozen Wapsinonoc River. In warm weather, they fished for catfish, swam, and played baseball; in autumn they hunted for pigeon with bow and arrow—Quakers did not keep guns. Bertie was quiet, shy, inarticulate, and thought a long time before speaking. He was good at arithmetic and wanted to be a locomotive engineer.

The boy was six when his father died of a heart attack at the age of thirty-three. Huldah kept her brood together, taking in sewing to augment her income, but three years later she succumbed to pneumonia. The three Hoover children, now orphans, were parceled out among relatives, and their inheritance, a few hundred dollars each, was placed in the hands of a trustee. Bertie went to live with an uncle, and the estate paid $6 a month for his board. Even then, he was self-sufficient. In summer, he cleaned the barn and helped out at threshing time, so his board was reduced to $4. Hoover never talked about his feelings following the death of his mother, but a biographer observes that while his uncle was kind, "no one could replace his parents. Sometimes during the night, the boy would lie awake yearning for his mother."

At ten, Bertie was shipped off to Oregon to live with another uncle, Dr. John Minthorn, whose son had recently died. He was put to work caring for the doctor's team when he was not in school, splitting wood, and helping out generally. When the boy was fifteen, his uncle moved to Salem to run a Quaker land settlement office, and Bertie became office boy and then assistant bookkeeper at $15 to $20 a month. At night, he took classes at a business school. The boy was eternally grateful to a spinster lady who introduced him to the novels of Scott and Dickens. *David Copperfield* lived on in the quiet orphan lad's imagination as the most important book he ever read.

One day an engineer came to the office and idly began chatting with Bertie about his work. The youth was impressed by the idea that engineers build, create, and construct. He began to hang around the local foundry and sawmill to observe their operations, and decided to become a mining engineer. Although Dr. Minthorn expected him to attend a Quaker college, perhaps Earlham or Haverford, Bertie sent away to various engineering schools for catalogs. In 1891, when he was sixteen, newly opened Stanford University, which had an engineering program, announced that it was accepting applicants for its first class tuition-free, and Portland was one of the places where entrance examinations were to be held.

Although he had not graduated from high school, Bertie decided to give the test a try. He did well in mathematics but flunked all the other examinations because of his lack of formal preparation. Dr. Joseph Swain, the mathematics professor who conducted the tests and who was also a Quaker, saw something in the youth, however. He suggested that Bertie go down to Palo Alto for the summer for special tutoring and then take the examination again. This time he passed and was admitted to Stanford's "pioneer class" of 559 students with a "condition" in English. "For the rest of his life he struggled with his prose," writes Richard Hofstadter.

Hoover had $160 in savings, two suits, and a bicycle. To make ends meet, he got a job for $5 a week as a typist in a school office, waited on tables, picked up laundry, and delivered newspapers. "The crowning of his personality was shyness," recalled Will Irwin, a classmate and later a prominent author. Tall and lanky—he was a gawky six feet—Bert Hoover walked with his eyes fixed upon the ground and a lock of his mousy hair always dangling over his forehead. "I would that I had the words to say what is in my heart," he often said.

Yet, he could be gregarious and, as his list of campus activities attests, his four years at Stanford were happy and productive. Hoover impressed his professors in the Department of Geology and Mining, and they found laborer's jobs for him with the U.S. Geological Survey in the Ozarks and Sierras during the summers. Failing to make the baseball team, he took on the thankless task of manager. Stanford started a football team and he managed that, too. He was elected treasurer of the junior class and then of the entire student body—his only contact with electoral politics until 1928. In this post, Bert worked to build a baseball diamond, grandstand, and running track, and balanced the accounts before graduating in 1895.

"We have a young lady taking Geology as a speciality now," Hoover confided in a letter to a friend in his senior year, "a very nice lady too." She was Lou Henry, a tall California girl whose banker father had moved from Iowa to the old mission town of Monterey. He had wanted a son and had taught her to ride, hunt, and fish. When asked who would marry a woman geologist, she replied: "I want a man who loves the mountains, the rocks, and the ocean like my father does." She found him in Bert Hoover. She was gay and liked parties and, for her, he made the ultimate sacrifice: he learned to dance. By the time he left Stanford, they had an "understanding."

Hoover graduated with $40 in his pocket and, wishing to remain near Lou Henry, looked for a job in the California gold fields. But the country was in the grip of a depression and there were few jobs. Finally, he caught on as an ordinary miner, working with pick and shovel and pushing an ore cart at the Reward Mine in Nevada City, earning $2.50 a day for a ten-hour day, seven days a week. This was the area written about by Mark Twain and Bret Harte a half century before. "So you want to learn mining," said the shift boss. "There's only one way, get in there and dig." Business continued to slide, however, and he was laid off after a few months.

While hanging around the assay office in Nevada City looking for work, Hoover spotted Louis Janin, a prominent mining engineer employed by the Rothschild interests, whom he had met casually, and asked him for a job. The only opening he had, said Janin, was for a typist in his office in San Francisco. Hoover took it and made himself so useful that he was appointed assistant manager of a mine at Steeple Rock in New Mexico. It was a rough introduction for a young mining engineer. The miners were mostly Mexican and carried guns and brawled in the streets and cheap barrooms. Hoover went down into the mine, slept on the desert floor, ate wherever he could. "You need a nose for gold," he had been told. "It can't be learned sticking your nose in a book."

In 1897, the British mining firm of Bewick, Moreing and Company asked Janin to recommend an engineer to inspect and evaluate gold mines in Western Australia for potential purchase, and he suggested Hoover. To appear older, the twenty-three-year-old engineer grew a beard on the voyage across the Pacific. Coolgardie, where he was first employed, offered a diet of "red dust, black flies and white heat." At midnight the temperature stood at a hundred degrees. Hoover traveled deep into the Outback by camel to inspect various mines and suggested that the firm purchase the Sons of Gwalia mine, which they did for a half million dollars on little more than his recommendation. He was made manager and the mine produced $55 million worth of gold.

Bewick next sent him to China at a salary of $20,000 a year, and he stopped off in Monterey long enough to marry Lou Henry. An Episcopalian by birth, she had resolved to become a Quaker, but there was no Friends meeting house there. The couple were married by a Roman Catholic priest, a family acquaintance who acted in his civil capacity. They spent their honeymoon on a ship bound for the Orient.

In China, they began their "adventuring years." Hoover doubled as the Chinese government's resident chief engineer in the northern provinces, while prospecting for coal and minerals for his firm. Lou set about learning Chinese—she had a gift for languages—while her husband dealt with the intrigues of the corrupt court of the boy emperor, Kwang Hsu. Now all of twenty-five, Hoover negotiated with Chinese officials and searched for coal deposits. The all-encompassing poverty bothered his Quaker sensibilities and he thought a different system of government would improve conditions. He traveled under escort of a hundred cavalrymen; to do otherwise, explained Chinese aides, meant a loss of face. He explored Tibet, the Gobi Desert, Manchuria, and Mongolia and discovered an anthracite field larger than all the world's then known reserves.

In 1900, China was swept by the revolt of the Boxers—the "righteous, harmonious fists"—who, with the support of the sinister Empress Dowager Tzu Hsi, sought to expel foreigners and foreign influence from the country by fire and sword. The Hoovers took shelter in the international settlement at Tientsin (now Tianjin), which was defended by about a thousand Western troops, but the city was besieged by 25,000 Boxers. Hoover helped build barricades out of sacks of sugar, rice, peanuts, and grain and directed relief efforts. Mrs. Hoover packed a Mauser pistol and worked in the hospital. Keeping close to the sheltering walls of buildings to avoid artillery shells and frequent stray bullets, Hoover inspected the barricades each day and performed his other chores on a bicycle. In microcosm, the episode resembled his work in Europe during World War I. The siege lasted a month. Hoover later said he never heard any sound more beautiful than the bugles of the Welch Fusiliers, as a relief column reached Tientsin. The couple sent a one-word cable to Lou Hoover's father in Monterey: "Safe."

Hoover was twenty-seven in 1901 and a much sought after engineer-businessman when Bewick, Moreing offered him a partnership with a base in London. Donning seven-league boots, he explored for gold, lead, zinc, copper, and tin in India, New Zealand, Hawaii, Egypt, Korea, Ceylon, and

Russia. He crossed the Pacific ten times and the Atlantic twenty-five times. The Hoovers had two sons, Herbert Jr. and Allan, both born in London. The family went everywhere with him, and by the time young Herbert was three, he had circled the globe several times. Mrs. Hoover's training as a geologist allowed her to help her husband in his work. Together, they translated the classic Latin mining text, Agricola's *De Re Metallica*, into English, a task that took fifteen years. Hoover also published a textbook, *Principles of Mining*, which was used in college courses for many years.

In 1908, he went out on his own, opening a consulting business with offices in New York, San Francisco, London, St. Petersburg, and Paris. The only sign on the door was "Herbert C. Hoover." By the time he turned forty, he had a $4 million fortune and was thinking about a job in public service. It was the Quaker way. A man with a comfortable living had an obligation to do something for mankind. Politically, he identified with the vigorous progressivism of Theodore Roosevelt and donated $1,000 to the Rough Rider's insurgent campaign in 1912. Hoover's public career lasted forty years, and whenever he held government jobs with fixed salaries, he endorsed the checks over to charity.

Hoover was in London when war broke out in August 1914, and the U.S. embassy, besieged by hordes of Americans stranded in Europe by the cancellation of their ships, asked him, as the head of a small charitable committee that aided Americans abroad, to help out. Using his own funds and business contacts, he made arrangements and provided money for some 120,000 American tourists to live on for the six weeks required before enough ships were found and organized to evacuate them.

Once this task was accomplished, Hoover was asked to head a relief program for Belgium, which had been overrun by German troops during the opening weeks of the war. The Belgians, who had resisted the German occupation, were harshly treated. Without any government support—and in the face of obstructions by the British and Germans—Hoover organized the Committee for the Relief of Belgium, raised $1 billion, and purchased and distributed food, clothing, and medicine that kept ten million people from starving. It was the first humanitarian effort intended to relieve distress on a grand scale, and it brought him widespread praise and publicity as a man who knew how to get things done. Among his hardworking staff, who called him "the Chief," he inspired respect and loyalty, if not affection. There was a feeling that Hoover was too much of a machine. While he was personally kind, he gave people the impression he was too busy to engage in small talk or to slap them on the back and tell them they had done a great job.

The day after the United States entered the conflict, President Wilson cabled Hoover, asking him to return home to run the U.S. Food Administration and to organize the nation's food resources for war. To "Hooverize" rapidly became shorthand for saving food and fats, and Americans became familiar with "meatless" and "wheatless" days of the week. Hoover called for patriotism, sacrifice, hard work, and, most important, voluntarism and cooperation—the key elements of his philosophy. His sense of organization and efficiency became legendary.

Once the war was over, he returned to a shattered Europe to deal with the threat of starvation and pestilence. Shiploads of food, medicine, and clothing were rushed to European cities, and Hoover's agents, who operated from Belgium to Azerbaijan, fed millions of hungry people and provided medicine and treatment for the sick. He worked every day for eleven months. Although he detested Communism, Hoover's relief efforts extended into the Soviet Union. "You have saved from death three and one-half million children [and] five and one-half million adults," Maxim Gorki, the Russian writer, told him.

"Mr. Hoover is the only man who emerged from the ordeal of Paris [the peace conference] with an enhanced reputation," observed John Maynard Keynes. "This complex personality, with his habitual air of weary titan . . . his eyes steadily fixed on the true and essential facts of the European situation, imported into the Councils of Paris . . . precisely that atmosphere of reality, knowledge, magnanimity and disinterestedness, which if found in other quarters would have given us a good Peace."

"We in America today are nearer to the final triumph over poverty than ever before in the history of any land," Herbert Hoover said in formally accepting the Republican presidential nomination on August 11, 1928—his fifty-fourth birthday. Seventy-five thousand people crowded into the Stanford football stadium, and his speech was broadcast to a radio audience of 30 million Americans. Yet Hoover was anything but ebullient at this moment of triumph. One hand jammed into his pants pocket and his head bowed over his text, he delivered words that were to haunt him for the remainder of his long life:

The poorhouse is vanishing from among us. We have not yet reached the goal, but given a chance to go forward with the policies of the last eight years, we shall soon with the help of God be in sight of the day when poverty will be banished from this nation.

As if to confirm Hoover's statement, the bull market had in early 1928 begun a historic climb into the stratosphere. "The mass escape into make-believe, so much a part of the true speculative orgy, started in earnest," observed John Kenneth Galbraith. Beginning on March 1, 1928, the New York Times stock average rose from 177.43 to a record high of 199.53 on May 14. Volume during this run exceeded four million shares a day no fewer than twenty-two times and twice flirted with five million. Prior to this surge, volume had exceeded three million shares only eight times; in 1928 it did so 159 times. Predictions of five-million-share days no longer seemed a fantasy. Radio Corporation of America jumped eighteen points in a single day, although it paid no dividends. General Motors crossed the psychologically important figure of 150. Soon, the stock ticker, unable to cope with the volume of transactions, was running two hours late. Even such a staid stock as New York Central rose seven and a half points to its highest level since 1901. "Two chickens in every pot and two cars in every garage," was the Republican campaign slogan.

To keep up with the demand for stocks, giant investment trusts, an early version of the mutual fund, were created to pump out even more shares. Goldman, Sachs created the Shenandoah Company, which sold $102 million in stock in one day. Next, Goldman spawned the $127 million Blue Ridge Corporation. Their number had quadrupled by 1928, as optimism spawned financial euphoria.

Hoover hardly mentioned Smith during the campaign. Shy, far from articulate, hating the indignities of politicking, he confined the bulk of his campaign to six major addresses, written by himself. They were delivered in a dry, metallic voice, more lectures than political speeches. Smith, on the other hand, was dynamic and down-to-earth. He made wide use of radio to reach the voters—it was the first campaign in which the new medium played a vital role—but radio betrayed him. His New York accent, complete with pronunciations like "foist," "poisonally," "raddeo," and "horspital"—not to speak of "dese" and "dem" and "dose"—grated on the ears of Middle America and reminded them of his background and why they feared him.

Smith compounded his problem by consulting only with his New York–centric inner circle. He chose John J. Raskob, a wet, a Catholic, until recently a Republican, and a General Motors millionaire, to head the campaign, further antagonizing prohibitionist, Protestant, and rural America. Smith had no understanding of life beyond his home state. His universe "begins at Coney Island and ends at Buffalo," said Henry Mencken.

Like most self-made men, Smith was basically a conservative and there was little to distinguish him from Hoover. Rather than attacking the selective nature of prosperity and assailing his opponent as "the rich man's candidate," he offered little more than me-too-ism by trying to convince the voters that he could manage prosperity as well as Hoover. For the first time in history, a Democratic presidential candidate backed a protective tariff. He tried to appeal to the corporate barons mustered by Raskob, but business was solidly for the Republican nominee.

With little in the way of issues to divide the candidates, Smith himself, and his Catholicism, Tammany, anti-Prohibition, and urban ties became the central issue of the campaign. Hoover called upon his partisans for tolerance, but it was too much to expect in a presidential election. Catholics accounted for about 16 percent of the population,* and only about a third of the remaining 84 percent of Americans attended Protestant churches and Jewish synagogues, but these figures belied the religious intolerance of the age.

Mabel Walker Willebrandt, the assistant attorney general charged with the enforcement of Prohibition, ranted before a group of Methodist ministers in Ohio about the evils of Catholicism. "The Catholic so-called religion should not secure a dominant influence over the nation's life," wrote William Allen White in his *Emporia Gazette*. Rumors circulated that Smith slept with nuns, was a drunk, and that his election meant the pope would be installed in the White House. "Watch the trains! The Pope may arrive perhaps on the northbound train tomorrow!" proclaimed a Klansman to a crowd in North Manchester, Iowa. Fifteen thousand people met the next day's northbound train. Smith was welcomed to Billings, Montana, by a huge flaming cross on a hillside.

Smith used an open letter from a prominent Anglican layman, calling upon him to say what he would do as president if a conflict arose between the Constitution and the doctrines of the Roman Catholic Church, to try to allay fears about his creed. "I have been a devoted Catholic since childhood," he declared, "and I recognize no power in the institution of my church to interfere with the operations of the Constitution of the United States or the enforcement of the law of the land."

Worried about losing New York and its forty-five electoral votes, Smith and his advisers tried to persuade Franklin Roosevelt to run for governor. Bored by a campaign largely run by "the General Motors publicity and advertising staff," Roosevelt went to his retreat at Warm Springs, Georgia,

---

* When John F. Kennedy ran for president in 1960, Catholics accounted for about 23 percent of the population.

in the hope of finding a cure for his paralyzed legs. A torrent of letters, telegrams, and telephone calls poured in, emphasizing that as a Protestant with upstate connections and an unblemished reputation, only he could save the state for Smith. Roosevelt was convinced that Smith had no chance and thought the entire Democratic ticket would be dragged down with him, but reluctantly agreed to make the run.

The Democratic debacle on November 6, 1928, was even more of a disaster than expected. States that had been Democratic since well before the Civil War went Republican. Unlit cigar drooping in his mouth, Smith watched glumly as Hoover's tally mounted to 21,392,000 popular votes—68 percent of the total cast—and 444 electoral votes, to his own 15,016,000 and 87.* It was the worst defeat suffered by any major candidate in the country's history. Hoover won all but eight states, cracked the Solid South by winning Virginia, North Carolina, Florida, and Texas, and lost Alabama by only seven thousand votes, which may have come from ballot box stuffing. To Smith's shock, he was even beaten in New York by 100,000 votes, while Franklin Roosevelt carried the state by only 25,464 votes, out of 4.25 million cast. "Well," Smith is supposed to have remarked, "the time just hasn't come yet when a man can say his beads in the White House."

Hoover's coattails were long enough to increase the Republican edge in the House to one hundred seats and to seventeen in the Senate. The number of Americans who cast ballots almost doubled over 1920, due in part to a greater turnout of women voters in the South than ever before, which probably caused the Republican sweep in the area. For the most part, blacks remained loyal to the party of Lincoln and voted for Hoover. The AFL withheld its endorsement from both candidates, but William Green voted for Hoover. So did Charles Lindbergh, who cast a ballot for the first time. Babe Ruth voted for Al Smith.

Yet, in the final analysis, reports of the death of the Democratic Party were exaggerated. Smith won more popular votes than any previous Democratic candidate in history. The Democrats made inroads into 122 traditionally Republican counties and the twelve largest cities, which had been Republican since 1896. Smith captured St. Louis, Cleveland, San Francisco, and New Haven, and picked up votes in such traditional Republican bastions as Philadelphia, Pittsburgh, Chicago, Detroit, and

---

* Norman Thomas, making the first of his numerous runs as the Socialist candidate, won 267,420 popular votes.

Omaha. Although Smith had lost the Solid South, he had cracked the solid Northeast for his party—heralding a political shakeup that would make the Democratic Party the party of urban America.

Wall Street celebrated Herbert Hoover's triumph with a "victory boom" in which the market leaders climbed as much as fifteen points. On November 16, a record 6.6 million shares traded hands—well above the previous high. For all of 1928, security values increased by $11 billion. Radio Corporation of America went from 85 to 420; Du Pont from 310 to 525; Montgomery Ward from 117 to 440; Wright Aeronautics from 60 to 289.

CHAPTER 17

"Wall Street Lays an Egg"

Groucho Marx went to his broker's branch office in Great Neck out on Long Island every morning after breakfast, to follow the ticker and gloat over his good fortune. Although he was tight with a dollar, Groucho had sunk the bulk of a $240,000 nest egg into Goldman, Sachs at the suggestion of his fellow comedian Eddie Cantor. He also put money into United Corporation, following a tip from an elevator operator, and passed it on to his brother Harpo, who invested heavily in the stock. "What an easy racket," Groucho chortled one day. "RCA went up seven points this morning. I . . . made myself seven thousand dollars."

Groucho was not alone. Throughout the summer of 1929, brokerage houses were crowded with customers hypnotized by an endless procession of numbers that hurried past their eyes on lighted screens. An ever larger percentage of them were women, perhaps as many as 35 percent. On Labor Day, astrologist Evangeline Adams, who had a sizable following because of her success in predicting the gyrations of the stock market, issued a new forecast. Taking note of the alignment of the planets and other pertinent data, she told a reporter for WJZ radio: "The Dow Jones could climb to Heaven." Adams seemed to be right. On September 3, 1929, the first trading day after the holiday, the Dow reached a record high of 386.10—a peak not seen again until November 1954.

"How high can stocks go?" everyone asked. The market rose, not by slow steady steps, but by great vaulting leaps. Sunshine Charley Mitchell, head of the National City Bank, announced that the market "is like a weather-vane pointing into a gale of prosperity." Alfred Sloan of General Motors said, "Personally, I believe it is going to be a very good year—I don't see how it could be otherwise." Irving Fisher, a highly regarded Yale economist and market guru, claimed that "stocks have reached what looks like a permanently high plateau." A seat on the Stock Exchange cost $625,000, and the number of brokerage houses and branches had increased from five hundred in 1919 to 1,192.

Nevertheless, it is easy to overstate popular involvement in the stock market in 1929. Most Americans knew nothing about investment trusts, brokers' loans, or pools, and were as likely to speculate in stocks as they were to play roulette at Monte Carlo. Paul Bologna, a Wall Street shoeshine man, had a margin account in City Bank and the household servants of a leading banker had their own ticker, but the picture of thousands of small stockholders throwing their life's savings into the market is a false one. This legend was created by Frederick Lewis Allen's popular chronicle of the era, *Only Yesterday*, which grossly distorted the actual level of market participation.

Only about 1.5 million people out of a total population of 120 million had brokerage accounts in 1929, and fewer than half of these were speculators, according to a Senate study.* But as John Kenneth Galbraith points out, the striking thing about the stock boom of 1929 "was not the massiveness of the participation. Rather it was the way it became central to the culture." It included a substantial share of the nation's professional and business leadership, and they set the popular perception.

To those who were involved in the euphoric "New Era," the old laws of economics seemed to have been repealed, and what went up did not necessarily have to come down. "Never before . . . have so many become so wondrously, so effortlessly and so quickly rich," according to Galbraith. As in the bubble of the 1990s, stocks were manipulated. In the 1990s, analysts touted profitless Internet stocks whose shares traded at astronomical prices so their firms could win underwriting deals for the sale of new stocks, from which they earned lucrative fees. In the 1920s, insiders organized pools to drive up the price of stock by heavy buying. Once a stock reached the desired level, the pool dumped its shares—leaving the small fry holding the bag as the price dived.

Much of this speculative buying was on margin, with the purchaser putting up as little as 5 percent of the value of his shares, while his broker advanced the rest by borrowing from the banks. This meant a speculator put up $5 to buy $100 in shares. In 1929, the top 1 percent of the people owned 44.2 percent of household wealth; at the other end of the scale, 87 percent of the people owned only 8 percent of the wealth.

* In contrast, about 49 percent of American households owned stock in 1998, usually through mutual funds in which their retirement savings were invested.

* * *

Herbert Hoover captured the mood of the nation in his inaugural speech. "I have no fears for the future of our country," he told the sodden crowd gathered in a cold rain before the Capitol on March 4, 1929. "It is bright with hope." Huddled under their umbrellas, the spectators looked from the platform like a field of giant black mushrooms. As they left the White House for the last time, Calvin Coolidge told his wife: "Well, Grace, it always rains on moving day."

In a highly symbolic gesture, Hoover ordered a telephone placed on the desk of the president as soon as he moved into the White House. There had never been one there before. Previous chief executives thought it undignified to speak from the Oval Office on the telephone. On the rare occasions when they used the instrument, they went to a special adjoining room. The telephone on his desk made it clear that the new president intended to take command and control of the government; the lackadaisical Coolidge years were over. Hoover also employed five secretaries, while all other presidents had made do with only one. An elaborate buzzer system was installed to summon them to his side as needed, and it was always ringing.

No one seemed better equipped to lead the march toward perpetual prosperity than the Quaker engineer-businessman. Along with Charles Lindbergh, Hoover was seen both as the harbinger of a new technological age and a symbol of the old self-sufficient rural past. "There has been an almost unprecedented display of conviction on the part of the investing public that with Hoover at the throttle the signal is full speed ahead," reported the New York Herald Tribune following the inauguration. Hoover himself was the only one with doubts. "I have no dread of the ordinary work of the presidency," he told the editor of the Christian Science Monitor. "What I do fear is the result of the exaggerated idea the people have conceived of me."

Over the next eight months, Hoover fired up the long dormant engine of progressive reform. Congress was called into special session to deal with the farm problem and the tariff. He ordered the publication of the names of all those who received large tax refunds, despite the protests of Treasury Secretary Mellon, publicly divulged the names of political backers of judicial appointees, allowed the press to quote him directly, placed legal bars against leasing the naval oil reserves to prevent another Teapot Dome, permitted picketing of the White House, resolved a threatened railway strike, freed the remaining political prisoners, entertained a black congressman's wife at the White House, increased funding for all-black

Howard University, which enabled its School of Law to be accredited, and sacked rabble-rousing Assistant Attorney General Mabel Willebrandt. In June, he announced a budget surplus of $110 million and proposed a tax cut of one fifth on higher incomes, one third on middle incomes, and two thirds on lower incomes.

Hundreds of experts and scholars were called to attend conferences and worked on studies of Prohibition,* recent economic and social trends, housing, public land policy, education, and child welfare. The White House stables were closed and the presidential yacht was retired. The Agricultural Marketing Act, which Hoover rammed through Congress, provided a $500 million revolving fund for making loans to expand farm cooperatives, and helped stabilize prices and production by buying surpluses. He was less successful with the tariff, and congressional log rolling prevented immediate action.

Progress was also made in handling the international debt problem. Under a plan negotiated by Owen D. Young, the head of General Electric, Germany's reparations were reduced to $9 billion. A "good neighbor" policy was announced for Latin America, and the withdrawal of the marines from the Caribbean and Central America began. There were discussions of the possibility of recognition of the Soviet Union and independence for the Philippines. Mark Sullivan had voted for Al Smith, but he now cast an admiring eye at the new president:

> Hoover is making enemies right and left—especially right. High-tariff barons, jingoes, brass-hats, big navyites, Prohibition fanatics, patronage hounds, and in general those who dread change—for each of these multifarious enemies he rises higher in the estimation of us small fry.

Wall Street was not the only thing going up that summer. Dr. Robert H. Goddard, a physicist at Clark University, had been experimenting with rockets intended to reach high altitudes. Some of Goddard's devices, thin metal cylinders propelled by a volatile mix of liquid oxygen and gasoline, exploded on takeoff, and he was ridiculed by the press as "a mad scien-

---

* Privately, Hoover thought Prohibition unenforceable, and there are reports that he was thinking about a constitutional convention to consider its future. Although Mrs. Hoover was a temperance supporter, Hoover had maintained a fine wine cellar when they lived in London. There are reports that when he was commerce secretary, he stopped off for two cocktails every evening after work at the Belgian embassy, which was foreign territory. (Burner, *Herbert Hoover*, p. 218.)

tist."* Nevertheless, his work attracted the attention of Charles Lindbergh in the summer of 1928, and the pilot sought out the professor. Impressed by what he saw, Lindbergh persuaded the Guggenheim family to finance Goddard's experiments at a new testing range at Roswell, New Mexico.

The first antibiotics were discovered at about the same time. A London bacteriologist named Dr. Alexander Fleming, who was conducting experiments at St. Mary's Hospital with *Staphylococcus* bacteria, left some of the stuff in a petri dish and went away for a holiday. When he returned to his laboratory, he noticed that the bacteria had been contaminated by a mold growth that prevented it from spreading. Fleming's chance finding led to the development of penicillin.

Also in the summer of 1929, a teenager named Richard Milhous Nixon ran a wheel of chance at the Slippery Gulch Rodeo in Prescott, Arizona, which was a front for backroom poker and crap games. John D. Rockefeller III graduated from Princeton with the title "Most Likely to Succeed." Thomas Wolfe published his first novel, *Look Homeward, Angel*, which was quarried by Scribners editor Max Perkins out of a mountain of manuscripts. A Texan named Bill Williams won a $500 bet by pushing a peanut up Pikes Peak with his nose; it took him twenty-two days. In-flight movies were shown on an airliner for the first time. And a Louisville housewife, Mildred Daniel, won a $200 prize offered by a radio station to the person who listened for the longest period without falling asleep. She kept at it for 106 hours until hospitalized for a combination of delirium and exhaustion.

Yet, despite the continuation of the era of wonderful nonsense, cracks in the nation's economic foundation were evident to those who looked closely. Of course, the farmers had been in trouble for years, and though there had been a slight pop in wheat prices, now they were falling again. Coal mining and textiles were chronically sick industries, construction had turned gloomy, wages and purchasing power lagged, unemployment was creeping upward, and production was falling. Unsold radios filled the store shelves, and cars were piling up in the dealers' garages. Auto sales appeared to be reaching the saturation point, because most new cars were being bought as replacements rather than by first-time purchasers. Bank failures—mostly small institutions—averaged two a day. Industrial pro-

---

* The *New York Times* debunked Goddard's theory that a rocket could function in a vacuum, and said he lacked the "knowledge ladled out daily in our high schools." Forty-three years after Goddard's first rocket launch in 1926, on the day Apollo 11 headed for the moon in July 1969, the *Times* issued an apology.

duction peaked in June 1929, when the Federal Reserve index hit 126. By October, it had fallen to 117.

Some smart operators already thought the game was up. Roger Babson, a well-known prognosticator, warned that "sooner or later a crash is coming" that will send the Dow plunging "60 to 80 points." Veteran *New York Times* market analyst Alexander D. Noyes issued repeated warnings. Insiders such as Joseph P. Kennedy, Bernard Baruch, Owen Young, and Paul Warburg of Kuhn Loeb were getting out of the market. In August 1929, Baruch began selling his stocks and buying gold, but when the market continued to climb, he doubted the wisdom of his decision. On the way to his office on Wall Street one day, he was stopped by a panhandler who offered him a tip on the market in exchange for a coin. That was enough to convince the master speculator it was time to get out. Baruch also passed the word on to Will Rogers. "You're sitting on a volcano," he told his friend. "Get away as far as you can."

Alfred H. Wiggin, chairman of the Chase Bank, secretly began selling his institution's shares short, a bit of foresight that would net him wide opprobrium—and $4 million in profits—when the market collapsed. Through various manipulations, he avoided taxes on the transaction. A scandal in London added to the unease. A financial finagler named Charles Hatry was charged with fraud, and some British investors were forced to liquidate their holdings in New York to cover their losses. Rising interest rates in England, intended to stem a drain of gold, also hastened the siphoning off of British investments from the American market.

As early as 1925, President Hoover, then secretary of commerce, was concerned about the "growing tide of speculation." Upon several occasions, he urged his friend and neighbor, Adolph Miller of the Federal Reserve Board, to convince the other members to restrict credit and make funds tighter for brokers and speculators. But Benjamin Strong, governor of the New York Federal Reserve Bank and the dominant personality in a system of mostly mediocrities, favored low interest rates for reasons of international finance. Winston Churchill, the chancellor of the exchequer, who was not renowned for economic acumen, had in 1925 returned Britain to the gold standard at the old prewar rate of $4.86, more out of imperial pride than for financial reasons. As a result, British goods became too expensive, trade collapsed, and investors fled to America. Strong, a believer in the global market, agreed to buoy up the British economy by making the United States less attractive to flight capital by keeping interest rates low. In doing so, the Fed overstimulated the market.

In the months and years that followed, Hoover's uneasiness turned to premonition and then to alarm at the possibility of total disaster. But Hoover's attempts to restore a semblance of sanity to the stock market were frustrated by Coolidge and Mellon. Upon assuming the presidency, he tried to persuade the Fed to restrain speculation and appealed to the nation's bankers to restrict credit. Richard Whitney, the debonair vice president of the Stock Exchange, was summoned to Washington to discuss the problem. Whitney, who later went to jail for stock fraud, promised much and did little. New York governor Franklin Roosevelt was urged to propose legislation tightening up Wall Street, but the request was ignored.

In August 1929, the Fed raised its discount rate—the interest at which it lends money to member banks—from 5 to 6 percent. But Charley Mitchell undercut the move by announcing that City Bank would make $25 million available for brokers' loans, even though he was a member of the New York Federal Reserve Board. "The only trouble with capitalism is capitalists," Hoover acidly observed. "They're too damn greedy." Expecting the worst, he instructed his own financial agent to liquidate his personal holdings, but made no public announcement—although it would have given more weight to his warnings of trouble ahead.

The long gathering storm finally broke on October 24, 1929—a date that lives in history as Black Thursday. Following heavy selling the day before, stocks opened sharply lower. Some were skidding precipitously as the opening bell was still reverberating across the floor of the Exchange. Prices fell so swiftly that the ticker was hours behind. Ripping off collars and ties, red-faced brokers and clerks bellowed at each other in a vain attempt to be heard above the din. "A kind of madness" had seized control of the exchange, reported one witness. Brokers were pinned against the trading counters by a frenzied throng that waved unfilled sell orders in their faces.

"Margin!" demanded the brokers. "More margin!"

Investors unable to come up with fresh cash were sold out, pouring more shares into the bottomless pit. Montgomery Ward plunged from 83 to 50 ... Radio (which had split) from 68 ¾ to 44 ½ ... U.S. Steel from 205 ½ to 193 ½. An observer thought people's expressions showed "not so much suffering as a spirit of horrified incredulity." In one of history's ironies, Winston Churchill, who had helped precipitate the disaster, watched from the visitors gallery.

Special police details were sent to the financial district to keep order. A workman appeared atop a building near the Stock Exchange to make repairs, and the crowd, assuming he was a would-be suicide, impatiently waited for him to jump. Wild rumors spread across the country: stocks were selling for nothing; the Chicago and Boston exchanges had closed; at least eleven speculators had committed suicide.

The big bankers rode to the rescue early in the afternoon. Having formed a pool to support the market, they sent Richard Whitney to the floor to buy stocks. He put in a bid for ten thousand shares of U.S. Steel at 205 and placed orders for other stocks. The market steadied and prices began to revive. Montgomery Ward rallied to 74 and U.S. Steel to 206. The lords of finance had stopped the panic, and some experts professed to see some good in the shakeout. John Maynard Keynes thought the money formerly used for speculation would now flow into productive enterprise. "The fundamental business of the country—that is the production of goods and services—is on a sound and prosperous basis," President Hoover assured the nation.

Evangeline Adams's studio over Carnegie Hall was crowded that night with worried clients. The movement of the planets was creating "spheres of influence over susceptible groups, who in turn will continue to influence the market," Adams said. She forecast that the Friday and Saturday sessions would see a rise in stock prices. And then she called her broker and told him to sell everything. Prices rose slightly on Friday, but turned lower during the short Saturday session and again on Monday.

On Tuesday—October 29, 1929—the bottom fell out. Huge blocks of shares were thrown on the market "as if they were so much junk," for whatever they would bring. The institutions were selling now, not the small stockholders. The sell orders came in like a tidal wave, and buyers could not be found for even high-quality stocks. A bright messenger boy jokingly bid a dollar a share for a block of White Sewing Machine Company shares—which had opened at 11—and got it. The investment trusts that had attracted the small investors were horribly battered. Goldman, Sachs Trading Corporation opened at 60 and fell to 35; Blue Ridge plummeted from 10 to 3. Blue-chip stocks did no better. Telephone and General Electric each lost 28 points; Westinghouse dropped 19 points and Allied Chemical 35. Cries of "Sell at the market!" and "Sell at any price!" filled the air. The Federal Reserve Board met for six hours in Washington but adjourned without taking any action.

Values melted before the eyes of investors as they slumped deeper into their chairs in the brokers' offices. Some were tearful; others sat stony-eyed. The dream of opulence—home, car, furs, jewelry—had vanished. Big fish and minnows, insiders and outsiders, speculators and prudent investors were cleaned out before the worst day in Wall Street's history finally came to an end. In a few frantic hours, stocks had shed some $10 billion in value—or twice the amount of currency in circulation—and such an implosion was not seen again until the Nasdaq collapse in 2000. This time the bankers did not come to the rescue, creating the suspicion that they had merely stabilized the market long enough to get out themselves. The Dow lost 30 percent of its value in the five days since Black Thursday. The next day, *Variety*, the show business paper, headlined: "Wall Street Lays an Egg."

The ghastly slide continued for two weeks. Pat Bologna salvaged less than a third of his money; Groucho Marx lost his entire $240,000 nest egg; "I would have lost more but that was all the money I had," he declared. Harpo was also wiped out. "My holdings . . . were probably worth a medium-size bag of jelly beans."

Few people envisioned that the collapse of the stock market would lead to the Great Depression. In fact, the rest of the country was hardly affected by the "little flurry" on Wall Street, as Franklin Roosevelt called it. By mid-November, press accounts of the state of the stock market had dropped off the front pages. In the months immediately after the panic, the economy seemed to be in good shape. Steel production rose and so did orders for new autos. The word "crash" has misled later generations. There was no overnight plunge from glittering prosperity to a grim world of closed factories, shuttered shops, and breadlines. The onset of the Depression was more like the slow leak in an automobile tire than a sudden blowout.

President Hoover, along with many other leading Americans, regarded the frenzied events on Wall Street as just retribution for the small group of plungers and gamblers, and expected the stock market to rebound just as it always had. Previous experience indicated a crisis of relatively short duration and a resumption of growth once the economy had shaken itself out. American Can and U.S. Steel raised their dividends. Raskob announced that he and his friends were buying stocks at their current bargain levels. Ninety-year-old John D. Rockefeller issued an encouraging statement: "Believing that fundamental conditions in the country are sound . . . my son and I have for some days been purchasing sound common stocks." "Sure," cracked Eddie Cantor, "who else has any money left?"

Rugged individualists like Andrew Mellon, safe with his own millions, told Hoover that the upheaval in the market "will purge the rottenness out of the system. High costs of living and high living will come down. People will work harder." The only remedy was to "liquidate labor, liquidate stocks, liquidate the farmers, liquidate real estate." But Hoover was not ready to send the people of the United States through the wringer. To prevent distress and "maintain social order and industrial peace," he issued optimistic statements and summoned business and labor leaders to the White House. From business he extracted the promise to trim profits before wages were cut or factories closed, while the unions agreed to forgo wage increases. It was voluntarism and cooperativism—Hoover's twin beacons—in action. It was the American way, no handouts, no favoritism, everyone working together for the common good.

Telegrams were sent to the governors of all the states and to the mayors of the largest cities, urging them to undertake the "energetic but prudent" construction of public works to show their confidence in the economy and to take up the slack in employment.

"Prosperity is just around the corner," said Vice President Charles Curtis in a statement usually attributed to Hoover. But in the spring of 1930, the tide started running in the other direction. The economy slowly drifted downward, first into a slump, then into a recession, and finally into a full-fledged depression. Factories and businesses cut wages and followed up with layoffs and plant closings, which led to a decline in consumer spending, which created a vicious circle of more closings. Farm prices continued to fall. Banks, many in small towns, closed, taking their depositors' savings with them. As if the economic crisis was not enough, drought burned up the farmlands of the South and Midwest, and there was an infantile paralysis epidemic. The seven good years of prosperity from 1922 to 1929 were being followed by the "Years of the Locust."

With money short, people entertained at home. The sale of playing cards took a spurt after the first international bridge tourney, in which Ely Culbertson led the American team to victory over the British. On May 15, 1930, the first four nurse-stewardesses took to the air on United Airlines's Oakland to Cheyenne flight. Four more took over in Cheyenne and carried on until the plane reached Chicago. Besides ministering to the passengers, they helped clean the aircraft, push it out of its hangar, and carry the luggage.

The Soviet government, short of cash, sold twenty-one paintings from the Hermitage Palace to Andrew Mellon for $7 million. Al Smith, now head of the company that operated the Empire State Building, brooded over his grievances in a nearly empty building. The Continental Banking Company introduced Wonder Bread, the first bread packaged already sliced. The Lone Ranger made his debut on WXYZ in Detroit as Rossini's *William Tell Overture* pounded in the background. Women no longer had the filmy, diaphanous look associated with the flapper. Hemlines were dropping to the lower calf, breasts and waists reappeared, and the once mandatory bob seemed to grow out overnight.

For a brief moment in 1931, economic conditions took a turn for the better, and it looked as if Herbert Hoover had been right. The crisis was merely a temporary aberration that would work itself out if market forces were allowed free rein. Production, payrolls, and the price of shares all began to rise. The tempo of construction increased, and some of the unemployed returned to work. The worst appeared to be over. When a delegation of businessmen came to the White House to discuss government assistance, Hoover assured them: "Gentlemen, you have come . . . too late. The Depression is over."

And then the storm, which had so tauntingly veered away, roared back in full fury—this time rolling in from across the Atlantic and engulfing the American banking system. The European nations, dependent upon a brisk trade with the United States as well as American loans and credits, had been hard hit by the liquidity crisis after the crash. The beggar-my-neighbor Hawley-Smoot Tariff, enacted by the Republican Congress in 1930, all but blocked foreign goods from coming into the United States, causing disruption in Europe, which retaliated against American goods and agricultural products. The Creditanstalt, Austria's largest bank, failed, sending out ever-widening ripples of panic and despair. European investors dumped their American stocks and bonds, creditors stopped payments on their American loans, and American exports to Europe dropped precipitously. Fearing the collapse of the European financial system, Hoover, in an act of consummate statesmanship, ordered a one-year moratorium on payments of the war debt. But it was already too late.

In Hoover's words, "a nightmare" followed. With Britain in the lead, every important industrial nation except France and the United States went off the gold standard. American banks, already shaky due to the weakness of the domestic bonds and mortgages in their portfolios, tumbled over the brink as the price of foreign bonds, in which they had invested, plummeted. In September 1931, 305 banks closed; in October the tally reached 522. Hoover was convinced that "blows from abroad" had frustrated his efforts to end the crisis just as he was beginning to succeed.

The statistical dimensions of the Great Depression are quickly sketched. At its worst, unemployment ranged upward to as many as 17 million people—well over a quarter of the workforce. In Cleveland, the level of unemployment was 50 percent, in Akron 60 percent, and in Toledo 80 percent. Farm prices dropped 60 percent from the already depressed levels of 1929. Share values on the Stock Exchange slumped from $87 billion before the crash to $19 billion in 1933. Onetime high fliers such as Alleghany Corporation now sold for 3⅝; General Electric for 9⅜; General Motors for 7¾; and U.S. Steel for 21½. National income fell to almost half what it had been. Industrial stagnation was accompanied by a fever of bank failures, and as many as two thousand banks closed their doors. In some cash-strapped cities, teachers and municipal workers received scrip in lieu of cash, which they redeemed at selected stores.

But statistics do not provide a living impression of what the Depression was like to ordinary Americans. There was the fruitless, never-ending search for work . . . the relentless dwindling of savings . . . the ceaseless scrimping that made life an agony . . . the sale of whatever possessions that could be sold . . . the overwhelming feeling of shame, inadequacy, and lost pride. America's anguish was everywhere. It was in the sad eyes of women as love and laughter vanished from their lives . . . it was in the face of a Baltimore grocer who watched as the store fixtures for which he could no longer pay were carted away . . . it was in the cries of immigrant women who came to the banks to withdraw their money and, when they found them closed, pounded on the doors for hours.

Once prosperous suburban families lived on stale bread. Near famine stalked the coal fields of West Virginia and Kentucky. Breadlines were familiar sights in the nation's cities and stretched for blocks. Salvation Army soup kitchens were crowded with men and women. As many as a million men and boys—and some women—rode the rails headed anywhere, as long as it was somewhere else. A writer saw a crowd of fifty men, women, and children fighting over a barrel of garbage outside a Chicago restaurant. People scavenged for lumps of coal beside the railroad tracks. Amtorg, the Russian trading agency, received 100,000 applications for jobs in Russia. Men in suits and ties peddled pins and needles and spools of thread and sold apples on street corners. Women peddled themselves. John Maynard Keynes was asked if there had ever before been anything like this and replied that indeed there had. It had lasted four hundred years and was called the Dark Ages.

Racism was exacerbated by hard times. Black joblessness was four to six times worse than among whites. Even menial jobs such as garbage collection and street cleaning, which had largely been held by blacks, were taken over by whites. Unemployed whites in Atlanta formed an organization called the Black Shirts whose slogan was: "No Jobs For Niggers Until Every

White Man Has a Job." Nine black youths falsely accused of raping a pair of white women on a freight train passing through Alabama were convicted by an all-white jury and sentenced to the electric chair, despite overwhelming proof of their innocence. The Supreme Court reversed the convictions, but five of the Scottsboro Boys were again found guilty, although not of capital charges, and the last did not emerge from prison until 1950.

American writers were already looking back upon the Twenties with regret for wasted time. Scott Fitzgerald captured the mood of this new era in his story "Babylon Revisited." Like Fitzgerald, many American writers wanted to forget the Twenties and "jump back a whole generation and trust in character again as the eternally valuable element."

Most of the expatriates returned home when the money that had sustained them abroad ran out. Paris, Majorca, Capri, and the Riviera were empty of Americans. Harold Stearns, whose departure for Paris in 1922 had caused so much comment, returned unnoticed and rediscovered America. The former expatriates talked about Paris and how good it had been to sit in a sidewalk café sipping wine and letting the world go by, said Malcolm Cowley, "but nobody had time to listen, and soon, the exiles, too, were caught up in the new life, adopting political doctrines and . . . marching in demonstrations."

One evening, Henry Mencken and his wife, Sara, accepted an invitation to visit the Fitzgeralds at the home they were renting outside Baltimore, where Zelda was being treated at the Sheppard Pratt Hospital for a nervous breakdown. Neither man had weathered the crash very well. Fitzgerald had published nothing except *Saturday Evening Post* stories since *The Great Gatsby* in 1925, and the magazine had not only reduced his fees as an economy measure but complained about the quality of his work. His book royalties had fallen to about $50 a year. He was working on what was to be his own favorite among his novels, *Tender Is the Night*, based upon Zelda's struggle with madness. At the same time, he tried to take care of his daughter, Scottie, and to deal with a mountain of debt, his notoriety as a drunk, and his despair over a schizophrenic wife. Mencken found that politics was not a laughing matter after 1929 and had stepped down as editor of the *Mercury*. It was no longer enough in the proletarian 1930s to merely carp at national absurdities; a positive faith was now required, and many of his followers had moved leftward toward a rather naive Marxism.

Mencken described the visit to the Fitzgeralds as "a somewhat weird evening. . . . Zelda is palpably only half sane . . . Scott himself also begins to show signs of a disordered mind. . . . Their house was a ramshackle old barn in a deep woods, and the whole place has a spookish air." The role of the hostess was taken by Scottie, who was then about ten.

> The courses came on in the wrong order [wrote Mencken] with the soup last. . . . Fitz was too drunk to notice, but to Sara and me the meal was painful indeed. Zelda did all the talking, and what she had to say was only half rational. As soon as dinner was over, we prepared to go home, but Zelda insisted that we stay to see her drawings. . . . She ran up stairs for the drawings and came down with a large armful. Laying them on the floor of the living room she sprawled on her belly to show them to us. They were mostly in color, and most of them were only too painfully psychopathic. But we had to linger over them for an hour or two, and when we escaped at last we were shivering. Fitz, meanwhile, had kept on drinking, and was by now so drunk he could hardly stand up.

The peaceful, idealistic world that Americans hoped would emerge from the various treaties and conferences of the 1920s faded under the pressure of the economic crisis. Hoover's debt moratorium failed to produce financial stability, and economists and political leaders urged him to cancel the war debt. The United States refused and several nations defaulted. A World Disarmament Conference in Geneva in 1932 rejected the Quaker president's proposal for a 30 percent cut in land and naval forces. Mussolini's Fascist regime in Italy was growing increasingly nationalistic, and Japan, reeling from an economic crisis of its own, invaded Manchuria in defiance of League of Nations sanctions, beginning a policy of expansion. And on January 30, 1933—Franklin Roosevelt's fifty-first birthday—Adolf Hitler was hailed by cheering throngs as he become chancellor of Germany.

As disaster followed disaster, President Hoover, the world's greatest expert on assisting ruined nations, waited for the economic machinery to make its own adjustments. As an engineer, he saw society in the abstract, as the organization of matter and energy. Once something was clear and tidy in his mind, it should conform to the blueprint. Most nights, he got little more than three hours sleep, and his eyes were red-rimmed from work and worry. But he was unable to dramatize his fight against the Depression in a way to kindle the popular imagination or rally the nation's morale. Gloom enshrouded him. "I would that I had the words to say what is in my heart," he had lamented as a young man—and he still found it impossible to bare his soul in public. "If you put a rose in Hoover's hand it would wilt," said sculptor Gutzon Borglum.

In past economic upheavals, workmen who had lost their jobs due to blind operation of the system could cultivate a patch of garden until conditions improved, or could begin again on the frontier. Now, they were truly helpless, for the United States was the only major industrial nation without some form of national unemployment insurance. Only eleven states provided old age pensions.* Private charities were overwhelmed by the magnitude of the problem and were running out of money. Unable to cope with the disaster facing them, the unemployed turned in desperation to the federal government for help.

Hoover was not unmindful of the misery stalking the land and was personally generous with contributions to charity. But the man who had saved the starving people of Europe never left the White House to inspect the soup kitchens or to look into the faces of the apple sellers. In fact, Hoover was not convinced the apple sellers were really a sign of distress.† He opposed direct relief for the unemployed, regarding it as a handout. "If we start appropriations of this character we [will] have not only impaired something infinitely valuable in the life of the American people but have struck at the roots of self-government," he declared. History had proved not only the efficiency but also the morality of American individualism. Nothing was to be gained by government interference in the domestic economy. In the words of Herbert Feis, a State Department economic adviser, "Hoover could not grasp or would not face the grim realities which called for deviations from principles and practices that he deemed essential to American greatness and freedom."

But the apostle of American individualism was forced to move closer to state socialism than any previous peacetime president. Rejecting the demands of fiscal conservatives for a balanced budget, Hoover increased spending on public works to $434 million—an enormous sum at the time. The Federal Farm Board bought and stored the agricultural surplus to help stabilize farm prices. The Federal Reserve Board expanded the supply of

* In 1931, there were 3.8 million single-parent families headed by a woman, and only 19,280 of these families received some form of state aid. The average monthly payment varied from $69.31 in Massachusetts to $4.33 in Arkansas.

† Hoover maintained that the apple growers' associations, stuck with a surplus, shrewdly appraised the sympathy of the public for the unemployed, and established a system of selling apples on street corners that allowed them to get a higher price for their fruit. "Many persons left their jobs for the more profitable one of selling apples," he wrote. (*Memoirs*, Vol. III, p. 195.)

credit. The Reconstruction Finance Corporation, the most significant of Hoover's recovery measures, channeled $2 billion to banks, railroads, and insurance companies teetering on the brink of collapse. But these measures required time and a vast outlay of money to have any effect, and Hoover was unwilling to make these sacrifices. The Farm Board, for example, lacked sufficient funds to soak up the surplus. When economic conditions worsened, Hoover became less willing to increase government spending, worrying instead about avoiding a deficit.

Americans were puzzled—and then deeply angered—that a president who handed out relief to corporations could ignore the misery of people grubbing in garbage cans for food. No leader who permitted such a policy could maintain the confidence of his people. The Democrats won great gains in the 1930 off-year elections, including control of both houses of Congress. Hoover saw his name transformed into a symbol of derision: encampments of shacks erected by the homeless on the edges of the great cities were "Hoovervilles," broken-down automobiles pulled by mules were "Hoover wagons," and empty pockets turned inside out were "Hoover flags." He was the butt of a hundred bitter jokes. When he dedicated a monument and a twenty-one-gun salute boomed out, an old man was supposed to have said: "By gum, twenty-one chances and they missed him."

From all points of the compass, exuberant Democrats streamed into Chicago in the last days of June 1932, confident that they were about to choose the next president of the United States. Any doubts had been allayed by the Republicans, who had just glumly renominated Herbert Hoover in the same city, at a convention that reminded some observers of a funeral. Nine candidates vied for the Democratic nomination, with Franklin Roosevelt the front-runner. But the clusters of delegates who gathered in the lobby of the Congress Hotel, slapping backs, trading rumors, and launching conspiracies, were not at all certain that Roosevelt could overcome the two-thirds rule that had toppled so many previous favorites.

The two-term New York governor—he had been reelected in 1930 by a million-vote margin—was perhaps the most advanced of the forty-eight state chief executives in dealing with the Depression. Fresh ideas were provided by a talented team of academic advisers, called the "Brain Trust." Although, like Hoover, he was unable to free himself from obeisance to the totem of balanced budgets, Roosevelt had established a program of state-sponsored relief financed by an income tax increase. He called for diversion of Reconstruction Finance Corporation funds to loans to small businessmen, farmers, and homeowners facing foreclosure. He demanded "bold, persistent experimentation" to solve the nation's problems. At the same time, he berated Hoover for resorting to deficit spending.

For many Americans, however, the center of attention was not Chicago but the tiny town of Hopewell, New Jersey, where on the night of March 1, 1932, the twenty-month-old son of Anne and Charles Lindbergh was kidnapped from his crib. A note advised the traumatized young couple that the baby would be returned safely when a $50,000 ransom was paid. The public was fascinated by the case and newspaper sales increased 20 percent. President Hoover pledged the assistance of federal authorities, and Al Capone offered a $10,000 reward from his jail cell. No trace of the child was found until two months after his disappearance, when his body was discovered in a shallow grave near the Lindbergh home.*

Roosevelt and his political managers—the ever-faithful Louis Howe and James J. Farley—won the support of both rural and urban Democrats by astutely avoiding such divisive cultural issues as Prohibition and religion. Instead, they emphasized the economic grievances that all Democrats had against Hoover and the Republicans. By the time the convention was gaveled to order, Roosevelt had won primaries and caucuses in thirty-four states and six territories, most in the South and West. Al Smith had the support of many of the big-city machines; William Randolph Hearst, who controlled the California delegation, backed Texas's favorite son, John Nance Garner, the speaker of the house; some conservatives thought Maryland governor Albert C. Ritchie had a chance, while liberals hoped Newton D. Baker, Wilson's secretary of war and a champion of the League of Nations, would emerge from a deadlocked convention as the dark horse. Walter Lippmann, a Baker supporter, portrayed Roosevelt as a charming but slippery master of the art of carrying water on both shoulders. "Franklin Roosevelt is no crusader," he wrote in a much quoted column. "He is no tribune of the people. He is no enemy of entrenched privilege. He is a pleasant man, who, without any important qualifications for the office, would very much like to be president."†

Roosevelt remained behind in the Governor's Mansion in Albany while Howe and Farley conducted operations on the scene in Chicago. The vice

---

* Bruno Richard Hauptmann, a German-born carpenter, was arrested in 1934 and convicted of the crime based largely on circumstantial evidence and was executed after one of the Trials of the Century. In recent years, there has been some doubt that Hauptmann operated alone.

† Speaking of this column in later years, Lippmann said: "That I will maintain to my dying day was true of Franklin Roosevelt in 1932." (Steel, *Walter Lippmann and the American Century*, p. 292.)

presidential nomination was dangled before Ritchie, Garner, and Governor Harry Byrd of Virginia, in exchange for their support. Joe Kennedy telephoned Hearst with the warning that unless he released California's votes to Roosevelt the convention would deadlock as in 1924, and nominate Baker. Farley sounded out Representative Sam Rayburn of Texas, one of Garner's closest friends. Both Hearst and Rayburn said they wanted to see the outcome of the early balloting before making a move.

The actual balloting began at 4:28 in the morning of July 1, 1932. The Chicago stadium was rancid with the smell of sweat and stale cigars, and pop bottles, old newspapers, and sandwich wrappings littered the floor. Some of the delegates, worn out by three days of heat and oratory, pushed chairs together and slept. Farley sat on the platform, furiously jotting down the vote of each state. The galleries, packed with supporters of Al Smith, jeered each mention of Roosevelt's name.

Roosevelt led on the first three ballots, but was eighty-seven votes short of a two-thirds majority when the convention adjourned at 9:15 A.M. Unwashed and unshaven, the disheveled delegates staggered out of the stadium, blinking in the bright sunshine. Many were convinced that Roosevelt had passed his peak. Rumors circulated that Newton Baker would be the compromise candidate when they convened again that evening.

For the Roosevelt forces, the next few hours were crucial. A weary Farley returned to the Congress Hotel to find Howe, who suffered from asthma, gasping on the floor of his room with a pair of electric fans playing over him. He got down on the floor to whisper in Howe's ear that Texas was Roosevelt's best hope, and Howe assented to a deal. Garner was again promised the vice presidency in exchange for the delegation's votes, and Rayburn accepted. Hearst also agreed to release the California delegation. That night, early in the fourth ballot, William McAdoo appeared on the platform to explain his state's vote. "California came here to nominate a President," he declared, as a tremendous roar almost drowned out his voice. "California casts forty-four votes for Roosevelt!"

Breaking with tradition, Roosevelt immediately boarded a waiting plane and flew to Chicago to accept the nomination in person, without waiting for the usual formal notice. A trivial matter in itself, it was a sign of things to come. As an organ ground out the lilting rhythm of "Happy Days Are Here Again!" he stood at the rostrum, his brilliant smile and the cock of his chin symbolic of confidence. "Let us now and here highly resolve to resume the country's uninterrupted march along the path of progress, real justice, of real equality for all of our citizens great and small," Roosevelt told the cheering delegates. "I pledge you, I pledge myself to a new deal for the American people."

For the first years of the Depression, most Americans were too stunned or too confused to protest conditions, but as the crisis deepened, the specter of class warfare loomed. Huey Long frightened the rich with a bellicose crusade to "Share Our Wealth." A spellbinding radio priest named Charles E. Coughlin poured out a mixture of undigested religio-economic doctrine and populism that smacked of fascism. Out on the high plains, bands of grim-faced, taciturn men thwarted attempts to auction off foreclosed farms by frightening off other bidders at gunpoint, bidding on the property for only a dollar, and returning it to the original owner. Iowa farmers poured unsalable milk out on the highways, and the skies of the Dakotas, Iowa, and Kansas were dark with the acrid smoke of burning grain that had no market. "Unless something is done for the American farmer we'll have revolution in the countryside," warned Edward A. O'Neal, president of the American Farm Federation. The governors of Nebraska and Minnesota signed bills declaring a moratorium on farm foreclosures.

In Detroit, where in 1931 the number of cars produced had dropped a million from the 1925 level, the workforce was cut in half—and most people with jobs were working part-time. Known radicals and men with union ideas were fired. Utilities were cut off in the homes of the jobless. An abortive strike at the Briggs body plant revealed that men were working fourteen hours a day for 10 cents an hour. Apple sellers reappeared on city streets. Large crowds milled about factory gates hoping for a few hours work. On March 7, 1932, a Communist-led demonstration of three thousand jobless autoworkers marched on Ford's River Rouge plant, where more than two thirds of the workers had been laid off. Guards and goons from the company's "Service Department" met them with tear gas; the marchers replied with a barrage of rocks and frozen mud. The Ford fire department turned hoses of freezing water on the men and the guards opened fire. Four demonstrators were killed and several wounded.

Thousands of World War I veterans—dubbed the Bonus Army— descended upon Washington demanding the immediate payment of the soldier's bonus promised for 1945. By the summer of 1932 it had grown to twenty thousand men, some living in half-demolished buildings on Pennsylvania Avenue, most encamped in shacks and tents on the Anacostia flats, south of the Capitol. The encampment reminded John Dos Passos of a wartime army camp, with bugle calls and mess lines. "There's the same goulash of faces and dialects . . . but we were all youngsters then," he wrote. By and large the veterans were well-behaved.

When the Senate overwhelmingly rejected a proposal for immediate payment of the bonus, most of the demonstrators accepted Congress's offer of free railroad tickets. A few thousand remained behind, however. Where had they to go? Official Washington became uneasy. The gates of the White House were chained and the nearby streets were blocked off. On July 28, 1932, the police were ordered to evacuate the squatters from the Pennsylvania Avenue buildings. There was a scuffle, rocks were thrown, and the police opened fire. In the tumult, two veterans were killed and several policemen were injured. Panic-stricken local officials pleaded for help from the army. Hoover ordered Patrick Hurley, the secretary of war, to move against the squatters. Resplendent in full uniform and medals, General Douglas A. MacArthur, the chief of staff, assisted by an aide, Major Dwight Eisenhower, took personal charge of the operation.

As some eight hundred soldiers—cavalry under the command of Major George S. Patton, infantry with bayonets fixed, and a handful of light tanks—approached the disputed area, they were greeted by cheers from the veterans and several thousand spectators. Suddenly, there was chaos. Cavalrymen rode into the crowd with drawn sabers, infantrymen hurled tear gas bombs, and men, women, and children were choked and trampled. Scattering veterans and spectators alike, the troops crossed the bridge to the Anacostia flats, where some veterans had already set their shacks afire, and completed the destruction. Throughout the night, the sky glowed with flames—and the Bonus Army was in full retreat in all directions. "A challenge to the authority of the United States Government has been met, swiftly and firmly," Hoover declared.

The presidential campaign itself was anticlimactic. Roosevelt traveled some thirteen thousand miles, making sixteen addresses and sixty-seven minor speeches, as well as countless informal talks from the rear platform of his train. He was shocked by what he saw. No smoke poured from factory chimneys in the nation's industrial heartland, and farmers were idle. "I have looked into the faces of thousands of Americans," he told Anne O'Hare McCormick of the *Times*. "They have the frightened look of lost children." But those who sought a consistent pattern of future policy in Roosevelt's speeches looked in vain. The reporters who covered him were certain he favored repeal of Prohibition but were not sure where he stood on anything else.

Upon examination, his proposals were often vague and sometimes contradictory. In Columbus, Ohio, he proposed wide-ranging banking and Stock Exchange reforms that cheered trust busters, but he also promised less interference in American life from a "prying bureaucracy." In Topeka, he outlined a farm program stitched together from the offerings of twenty-five contributors. In Pittsburgh, he pledged a 25 percent cut in government expenditures.* While Hoover continued to insist upon the international origins of the upheaval, Roosevelt portrayed it as a domestic and Republican crisis with domestic solutions.

Most Americans may have been in doubt about Roosevelt's intentions, but not Herbert Hoover. He perceived in the Democratic candidate's blithe promises the danger of revolutionary change. The philosophy espoused by his opponent "was the same philosophy of government which had poisoned all Europe . . . the fumes of the witch's cauldron which boiled in Russia." Despairing of victory, lacking Roosevelt's ease of manner and eloquence, he campaigned doggedly, goaded by what he regarded as his rival's potential for mischief. To the burdens of the presidency he added the drafting of his own speeches, turgid affairs delivered in a droning voice. Warnings against the threat of radicalism, justifications of past actions, and optimistic predictions of recovery were all jumbled together. Sometimes he was greeted by cheers; more often the crowds were sullen and sometimes threatening. "Hang him! Hang him!" cried a mob in Detroit. Hoover was a victim of the primitive impulse to personify misfortune in the person of an individual—the scapegoat for the Depression.

Roosevelt voted early on the morning of November 8 at Hyde Park, near his Hudson River estate, and came down to New York City, where surrounded by family and friends he awaited the outcome. He jumped out in front in the early returns and was never behind. He gleefully took the telephone calls himself as his field commander reported. "You mean I'm getting votes in rock-ribbed Pennsylvania?" he laughed, after learning that it appeared the Keystone State might go Democratic for the first time in sixty years. Sam Rosenman noted that two men in dark suits slipped into the room and took up positions near the governor. They were Secret Service agents—and for the rest of his life Roosevelt would always be under their surveillance. He swept to victory by 22,800,000 popular votes to

---

* The budget-balancing promise of the Pittsburgh speech became an embarrassment for FDR, as government spending under the New Deal far exceeded revenues. He decided to speak again in Pittsburgh during the 1936 campaign and instructed Sam Rosenman, his speechwriter, to provide an explanation of his statement of four years before. "Mr. President," said Rosenman, "the only thing you can say about that 1932 speech is to deny categorically that you ever made it."

15,750,000. The margin was even greater in the Electoral College—472 to 57—with Hoover carrying only six states, all but two in New England. The Democrats also won both houses of Congress and for the first time broke the Republican stranglehold on the black vote.

Later that night, as his son James helped him into bed, the president-elect was subdued and thoughtful. As James bent over to kiss his father good night, Roosevelt looked up at him and said: "You know, Jimmy, all my life I have been afraid of only one thing—fire. Tonight I think I'm afraid of something else."

"What is it, Pa?"

"I'm afraid that I may not have the strength to do this job."

And he asked his son to pray for him.

Epilogue

Inauguration Day—March 4, 1933

The day dawned dour and cheerless, matching the mood of the nation. Tugging at the flags and bunting hanging from buildings and lampposts, the raw wind chilled the spectators, who had been gathering since early morning to see Franklin Roosevelt installed as thirty-second president of the United States. A cold rain had fallen and sleet clung to the trees. Some people stomped their feet to keep warm. Others warded off the cold by standing on torn and grimy newspapers that told of a country gripped by one of the most serious crises in its history.

Herbert Hoover had spent his last night in office helplessly watching the paralyzation of the nation's financial system. To stave off runs on the banks that were still operating, governor after governor had ordered them to close. The final blow had fallen at 4 A.M., when Herbert H. Lehman directed New York's banks not to open that morning. "We are at the end of our rope," the weary president had murmured to an aide. "There is nothing more that we can do."

Shortly before eleven o'clock, the open automobile carrying the president-elect swept up to the North Portico. Because of his disability, Roosevelt did not call on Hoover but awaited him in the car. The facade of the old mansion had not been painted for some time as an economy measure, and he noted that some of the columns were peeling badly.

Hoover sat motionless, eyes lowered, on the ride down Pennsylvania Avenue to the Capitol. Roosevelt struggled to make conversation with his somber predecessor. Even though he was a master of small talk, he finally gave up and began to acknowledge the scattered applause from the spectators pressing against the rope lines. The tension in the air was palpable. Some observers believed a revolution was impending and feared this would be the last inauguration. Troops were being held in readiness if trouble developed. "What are those things that look like little cages?" someone asked. "Machine guns," replied a woman with a nervous giggle.

The incoming and outgoing presidents, upon arriving at the Capitol, went their separate ways. Hoover was escorted to the ornate President's

Room, just off the Senate Chamber, where, puffing on a cigar, he signed or vetoed last-minute bills. A delegation of senators escorted Roosevelt to the Senate Chamber for the swearing in of John Garner as vice president. And then, paralyzed legs locked in heavy braces and leaning on the arm of his eldest son, Roosevelt laboriously made his way down a maroon-carpeted ramp to the rostrum. Hoover followed him to a seat in the front row after pausing, hat in hand as if lost in thought, at the top of the Capitol stairs to look out over the crowd that filled the plaza between the Capitol and the Library of Congress. Chief Justice Charles Evans Hughes, white-bearded and black-robed and looking like a giant bird, came forward to administer the oath of office. Roosevelt placed his left hand on the old Dutch Bible that recorded more than two centuries of family births and deaths and lay open to St. Paul's Epistle to the Corinthians: *And now abideth faith, hope, charity, these three; but the greatest of these is charity*.

Sixty million Americans huddled anxiously about their radios in homes, in shops, in hotel lobbies, and in speakeasies, seeking guidance and hope from their new president. From the start, they were galvanized by the confident and vibrant voice that proclaimed "the only thing we have to fear is fear itself."

"This Nation asks for action, and action now," Roosevelt declared, as a sense of excitement crackled through the audience. "We must act and act quickly," he continued, and then outlined his plans for overcoming the sense of drift gripping the country. Public works projects would be launched to put the jobless to work, farm prices stimulated, funds made available to stem the tide of foreclosures, banking and credit would be subjected to strict supervision to prevent speculation, a sound currency guaranteed, and government spending curbed.

Roosevelt said that Congress would be immediately summoned into special session to approve the measures needed to get the "stricken nation" moving again. And if Congress failed to move rapidly on these measures, he raised the specter of dictatorship. "I shall ask the Congress for the one remaining instrument to meet the crisis—broad Executive power to wage war against the emergency, as great as the power that would be given to me if we were in fact invaded by a foreign foe." The American people "want direct, vigorous action. They have asked for discipline and direction under leadership," he grimly concluded. "They have made me the present instrument of their wishes. In the spirit of the gift I take it."

The crowd roared its approval. The new president tossed back his head in a soon to be familiar gesture, and his face brightened with an incandescent smile. As he entered his car to lead the inaugural parade back to the White House, Roosevelt responded to the cheers by clasping his hands over his head in the gladiator's gesture of triumph.

The 1920s were over. America stood on the brink of a new world.

Notes

PROLOGUE

The basic source for this section is Mizener, *The Far Side of Paradise*, and Turnbull, *Scott Fitzgerald*; for the Summit and Fitzgerald's life there see Page and Koblas, *F. Scott Fitzgerald in Minnesota*; "Dear God" is in Turnbull, *op. cit.*, p. 17; "pleasantest country club" is in Fitzgerald, *This Side of Paradise*; "I want to be" is in Mizener, *op. cit.*, p. 35; "Flirt smiled from" is in *ibid.*, p. 58; Eisenhower as company commander is in Turnbull, *op. cit.*, p. 80; Hemingway in hospital is in Hemingway, *Men at War*, p. xiv; "buckets full of arms" is in Carr, *Dos Passos* p. 148; "I lived" is in Fitzgerald, *The Crack-Up*; "the prettiest girl" is in Cowley's introduction to *The Stories of F. Scott Fitzgerald*; Mencken's description of Fitzgerald is in *My Life As Author and Editor* pp. 256–57; Fitzgerald's memories of New York are in *The Crack-Up*; "roaring, weeping" is in Fitzgerald, *This Side of Paradise*; "Since I last" is in *The Letters of F. Scott Fitzgerald*, pp. 324–25; "glorious yellow hair" is in *This Side of Paradise*, p. 149.

CHAPTER 1: "THE PERSONAL INSTRUMENT OF GOD"

The basic source for Wilson's life is Heckscher, *Woodrow Wilson*; for Edith Wilson see Levin, *Edith and Woodrow*; for Wilson's departure for Paris see Dos Passos, *Mr. Wilson's War*, pp. 442–45; Wilson leaping into the air is in Starling, *Starling of the White House*, p. 62; for a succinct account of Wilson's first terms see Link, *Woodrow Wilson and the Progressive Era*; for Wilson and the blacks see Franklin and Moss, *From Slavery to Freedom*, p. 324; Pound's comment is in Pound, *Patria Mia*; "Whether in literature" is in Stansell, *American Moderns*, p. 12; for a history of the IWW see Dubofsky, *We Shall Be All*; "You carry" is in Smith, *When the Cheering Stopped*, p. 32; for Theodore Roosevelt and his relations with Wilson see Miller, *Theodore Roosevelt*, pp. 555–56 and 563; "like a divine-right monarch" is in Paterson, *American Foreign Policy*, p. 293; Truman's comment is in editor's preface to Smith, *op. cit.*, p. x; for the intervention in Russia see Kennan, *The Decision to Intervene*; for the Armistice Day battle see Dos Passos, *op. cit*; for the details of the peace conference see Bailey, *Woodrow Wilson and the Lost Peace* and *Woodrow Wilson and the Great Betrayal*, and Heckscher, *op. cit.*, pp. 495–562; for Eleanor and Franklin Roosevelt see Eleanor Roosevelt, *This Is My Story*; pp. 288–93; "I feel as if" is in Paterson, *op. cit.*, p. 286. Lodge's comment is *ibid.*, p. 287 (caption); "If I didn't feel" is in *Felix Frankfurter Reminisces*, p. 161; Keynes' comment is in *The Economic Consequences of the Peace*; for the fight over the treaty see Bailey, *Woodrow Wilson and the Great Betrayal* and *Woodrow Wilson and the Lost Peace* and Heckscher, *op. cit.*, pp. 581–610; for Prince Konoye see Kennedy, *Freedom from Fear*, p. 7; for the conversation between Watson and Lodge see Watson, *As I Knew Them*; Wilson's comment on Harding is in Bailey, *A Diplomatic History*, p. 671; Lippmann's comments are in Heckscher, *op. cit.*, p. 589; for Wilson's speaking tour see Smith, *op. cit.*, Hoover's view is in Burner, *Herbert*

Hoover, p. 115; pp. 57–81, Starling, *op. cit.*, Heckscher, *op. cit.*, pp. 595–610, and Edith Wilson, *My Memoir*; for Wilson's illness see Smith, *op. cit.*, pp. 85–128 Wilson, *op. cit.*, Heckscher, *op. cit.*, pp. 611–21, and Levin, *op. cit.*; for Grayson's private memo see Levin, *op. cit.*, p. 13; for Washington during Wilson's illness see Lowry, *Washington Close-ups*; "is bad as it can be" is in Noggle, *Into the Twenties*, p. 122; "We have no president" is in Murray, *The Red Scare*, p. 201; "we've been praying" is in Wilson, *op. cit.*, p. 299; "For my sake" is in *ibid.*, p. 297; "We can always" is in Dos Passos, *op. cit.*, p. 496; Lodge's comment is in Smith, *op. cit.*, p. 142.

CHAPTER 2: "TO THE RED DAWN!"

Klingaman's *1919* is an excellent survey of that troubled year; also see Noggle, *Into the Twenties*; for the attempt to kill Palmer, see *Washington Evening Star* and *Washington Post*, June 3, 4, and 5, 1919, and Longworth, *Crowded Hours*; for FDR's reaction to the bombing see James Roosevelt, *Affectionately, FDR*, pp. 56–57; the most complete account of the Red Scare is Murray, *The Red Scare*; for organization of the General Intelligence Division see Lowenthal, *The Federal Bureau of Investigation*, pp. 84–92; Niblack's warning is in Dorwart, *Conflict of Duty*, pp. 12–13; for a discussion of anti-radical activities during World War I see Jensen, *The Price of Vigilance*; for postwar economic conditions see Soule, *Prosperity Decade*, pp. 81–95; the failures of Wilsonian demobilization are in Noggle, *op. cit.*, Chapters 2–5; for Debs see Ginger, *The Bending Cross*; the May Day riots are in Murray, *op. cit.*, pp. 76–77; for the schism on the left see Draper, *The Roots of American Communism*; for postwar labor conditions see Soule, *op. cit.*, pp. 187–90; for the 1919 strikes see Lingaman, *op. cit.*; for the Seattle strike see Murray, *op. cit.*, pp. 60–67, and Friedham, *The Seattle General Strike*; for the Boston police strike see Russell, *A City in Terror*; for the steel strike see Murray, *op. cit.*, pp. 135–52, and Brody, *Labor in Crisis*; for the coal strike see *ibid.*, pp. 153–63; Randolph Bourne on the New Women is in Stansell, *American Moderns*, p. 231; for the Great Migration see Franklin and Moss, *From Slavery to Freedom*, pp. 339–45; Jelly Roll Morton is in Barry, *Rising Tide*, p. 215; for the revival of the Klan see Chalmers, *Hooded Americanism*; for the East St. Louis riot see Rudwick, *Race Riot in East St. Louis*; Du Bois is in Noggle, *op. cit.*, p. 41; for the postwar race riots see Franklin and Moss, *op. cit.*, pp. 346–54; "eleven of whom" is in *ibid.*, p. 348; for the Washington riot see Abernathy, "Washington Race War"; the Duluth lynching is in Dray, *At the Hands of Persons Unknown*; the most complete account of the Chicago riot is Tuttle, *Race Riot*; my discussion of the Berger case is based upon my unpublished seminar paper written in 1949; for Centralia see Murray, *op. cit.*, pp. 182–89, and Dubofsky, *op. cit.*, pp. 455–56; for the Palmer Raids see Murray, *op. cit.*, pp. 212–17, and Draper, *op. cit.*, pp. 202–4; for Goldman's gesture see Stansell, *op. cit.*, p. 326; Lippmann's comment is in Steel, *Walter Lippmann*, p. 167; for Palmer's decline and fall see Murray, *op. cit.*, pp. 239–62; Mencken's comment is in Mencken's *The Editor, the Bluenose and the Prostitute*, p. 170; Borah is in Noggle, *op. cit.*, p. 108; for a study of the Sacco and Vanzetti case see Russell, *Tragedy in Dedham*; Porter's comment is in *The Atlantic*; for the Wall Street bomb see Brooks, *Once in Golconda*, pp. 1–20; for Keynes's comment see *The Economic Consequences of the Peace*, pp. 296–97.

CHAPTER 3: "WE'RE ALL REAL PROUD OF WURR'N"

For a description of Marion, Ohio, in the summer of 1920, see an unsigned article in the *New York World*, June 20, 1920, and Sullivan, *The Twenties*, pp. 86–89; "To understand Harding" is in Sullivan, "The Stump and the Porch," *Collier's*, October 9, 1920; "Usually he seated" is in Pollard, *The Presidents and the Press*, p. 699; for a discussion of Harding and the small-town mentality see Sinclair, *The Available Man*, pp. 3–12; for population shifts see Hicks, *Republican Ascendancy*, p. 4; White's "The Other Side of Main Street" is in *Collier's*, July 30, 1921; for biographical detail on Harding see Russell, *The Shadow of Blooming Grove*, "As I neared" is in *ibid*. p. 47; for background on Mrs. Harding see Anthony, *Florence Harding*; for Amos Kling and Harding see Russell, *op. cit.*, p. 85; "easy-goingness" is in Sullivan, *The Twenties*, pp. 96–97; child and toothbrush is in Russell, *op. cit.*, p. 401; for Harding's health see Ferrell, *The Strange Deaths of President Harding*, pp. 1–2; Harding and the Masons is in Russell, *op. cit.*, pp. 139 and 407; Harding's reading is in *ibid.*, p. 120; Daugherty's first meeting with Harding and background on Daugherty are in Sullivan, *The Twenties*, pp. 16–19; for Harding been reasonably honest see Murray, *op. cit.*, p. 10; for Harding and Carrie Phillips see Anthony, *op. cit.*, pp. 82–95; no decorations on Phillips store is in Russell, *op. cit.*, p. 401; "conciliation and harmony" is in Murray, *op. cit.*, p. 11; for Madame Marcia Champney see Champney, "When an Astrologer Ruled the White House," *Liberty*, April 9 and June 11, 1938; "stopped with the Senate" is in Sullivan, *The Twenties*, p. 29; for Ponzi see Sobel, *The Great Bull Market*, pp. 17–21; for Harding's view of his nomination possibilities see Murray, *op. cit.*, p, 23; "I don't expect" is in Russell, *op. cit.*, pp. 341–42; "I cannot see why" is in Sinclair, *op. cit.*, p. 151; Mencken on the 1920 Democratic convention is in "Heathen Days," *The Days of H. L. Mencken*, p. 176; Cox and Roosevelt's visit to Wilson is in Miller, *F. D. R.*, p. 172; Penrose's comment on Harding's campaign is in Sinclair, *op. cit.*, p. 160; Lippmann is in Steel, *Walter Lippmann*, p. 169; "It is not only possible" is in Smith, *When the Cheering Stopped*, p. 159; for the Chancellor affair see Russell, *op. cit.*, pp. 403–5; Penrose's comment is in Sinclair, *op. cit.*, p. 171.

CHAPTER 4: "GEE, HOW THE MONEY ROLLS IN!"

For Harding's inaugural, see Smith, *When the Cheering Stopped*, pp. 172–78, Russell, *The Shadow of Blooming Grove*, pp, 1–16, and Wilson, *My Memoir*, pp. 316–19; Mrs. Harding's lips moving is in Anthony, *Florence Harding*, p. 260; Mencken's comments are in Mencken, *A Carnival of Buncombe*, p. 39, and Manchester, *Disturber of the Peace*, p. 117; for the details of Harding's presidency see Murray, *The Harding Era*, and Trani and Wilson, *The Presidency of Warren G. Harding*; "God, I can't be" is in Sinclair, *The Available Man* p. 190; for the Hardings in the White House see Russell, *op. cit.*, pp. 437–38, and Murray, *op. cit.*, pp. 113–14; for Wilson on Debs see Ginger, *The Bending Cross*, p. 405; for Debs and Harding see *ibid.*, pp. 413–15; for economic conditions in 1921 see Murray, *op. cit.*, 83; for comments to Butler see Murray, *op. cit.*, p. 418; "John, I can't" is in Werner and Starr, *Teapot Dome*, p. 38; "I don't know anything" is in Russell, *op. cit.*, p. 452; for Hoover see Burner, *Herbert Hoover*; Morgan's thanks is in Sinclair, *op. cit.*, p. 200; Mellon's tax cuts are discussed in Trani and Wilson, *op. cit.*, pp. 70–71; for the tariff see Trani *ibid.*, and Wilson, *op. cit.*, pp. 73–74; for the 1921 Immigration Act see Goldberg, *Discontented America*, "I want to see" is in Sinclair, *op. cit.*, pp. 231–35; for the Tulsa race riot see Ellsworth, *Death in Promised Land*; "Now you can shoot" is in Franklin and Moss, *From Slavery to Freedom*, p. 352; for Harding's foreign policy see Trani and Wilson, *op. cit.*, Chapter 6; for the Washington arms conference see Miller, *The U.S. Navy*, pp. 193–97; for Franklin Roosevelt's ordeal see Miller, *F.D.R.*, pp. 182–87; for Harding's White House see Russell, *op. cit.*, p. 447; Starling's comment is in *Starling of the White House*, p. 167; Forbes's story is in Murray, *op. cit.*, p. 447; for Mrs. Harding in the White House see Anthony, *op. cit.*, p. 352; "invented by demons" is in *New York Herald Tribune*, February 28, 1921; Nan Britton is in Anthony, *op. cit.*, p. 282; "This law will be obeyed" is in Allsop, *The Bootleggers and Their Era*, p. 31; Jane Addams's comment is in Addams, *The Second Twenty Years at Hull-House*, pp. 240–41; for Ralph McGill see McGill, *The South and the Southerner*, p. 86; "the unrivalled embodiment" is in Dumenil, *The Modern Temper*, p. 155; Chicago chemistry is in *ibid.*, p. 35; twelve people died is in Sullivan, *The Twenties* p. 571; for Izzy and Moe see Asbury, "The Noble Experiment of Izzy and Moe," in Leighton, ed., *The Aspirin Age*, pp. 34–49.

CHAPTER 5: "MY GOD, THIS IS A HELL OF A JOB!"

For an overview of the Harding scandals see Miller, *Stealing from America*, Chapters 15–16; "You yellow rat" is in Adams, *The Incredible Era*; the Forbes affair is covered in Russell, *The Shadow of Blooming Grove*, pp. 554–58; Adams, *op. cit.*, Chapter 22 and Sullivan, *The Twenties*, pp. 229–41; for Teapot Dome see Werner and Starr, *Teapot Dome*, and Noggle, *Teapot Dome*; one bootlegger claimed is in Trani and Wilson, *The Presidency of Warren G. Harding*, p. 280; Alien Property Bureau case is in Adams, *op. cit.*, pp. 323–24; for Jess Smith see Sullivan, *op. cit.*, pp. 232–37, and Werner and Starr, *op. cit.*, pp. 95–100; for Gaston Means see Hoyt, *Spectacular Rogue*; "Harding of the arterios" is in Anthony, *Florence Harding*, p. 410; the most complete account of the Rosewood incident is Jones, *A Documented History*; for strikes see Goldberg, *Discontented America*, pp. 73–76, and Hicks, *Republican Ascendancy*, pp. 68–73; for Marcus Garvey see Franklin, and Moss *From Slavery to Freedom*, pp. 357–60; "I was determined" is in *Current History*, September 1923; "The president has aged" is in Ferrell, *The Strange Deaths of President Harding*, p. 3; "You must take back" is in Champney, "When an Astrologer Ruled the White House," *Liberty*, April 9 and June 11, 1938; for Harding's speeches on the transcontinental trip see Murray, *The Harding Era*, pp. 443–45; "My God" is in White, *op. cit.*, p. 619; Dill's comment is in Anthony, *op. cit.*; Hoover's comment is in Hoover, *Memoirs*, Vol. II, p. 49; "I hope" is in Russell, *op. cit.*, p. 588; for the Seattle speech see Russell,

CHAPTER 6: "I THOUGHT I COULD SWING IT"

Mencken's story is in Mencken, *A Carnival of Buncombe*, p. 134; for Coolidge's coming to power see Calvin Coolidge, *Autobiography*; Sobel, *Coolidge*, pp. 230–33, and McCoy, *Calvin Coolidge*; "been weaned on a pickle" is in Longworth, *Crowded Hours*, p. 337; "tired of watching" is in Daniels, *The Time Between the Wars*, p. 118; "I thought I could swing it," is in Ferrell, *The Presidency of Calvin Coolidge*, p. 39; Sullivan's joke is in *ibid.*, p. 40; "In a week" is in Murray, *The 103rd Ballot*, p. 224; Alice Longworth's visit is in McCoy, *op. cit.*, p. 157; for Coolidge's biography see *ibid.*, and Sobel, *op. cit.*; "In politics, one must" is in McCoy, *op. cit.*, p. 8; for the details of Coolidge's administration see Ferrell, *op. cit.*; "The chief business" is in *ibid.*, p. 61; Steffens is in Abels, *In the Time of Silent Cal*, p. 43; "In public life" is in Calvin Coolidge, *op. cit.*, p. 20; Coolidge's press conferences are in Quint and Ferrell, eds., *The Talkative President*; the warning against shorthand is in *ibid.*, p. 26; Coolidge and radio is in Sobel, *op. cit.*, p. 301; "a natural talent" is in Mencken, *op. cit.*, p. 131; "Why can't they" is in Abels, *op. cit.*, p. 243; "Look at the record" is in DeGregorio, *The Book of Presidents*, p. 460; conversation with Couzens is in in Barnard, *Independent Man*, p. 178; "Mr. Mellon himself" is in Parrish, *Anxious Decades*, pp. 54–55; "Any law" is in Sobel, *op. cit.*, p. 280; "Mr. Coolidge's genius" is in, *ibid.*, pp. 4–5; "Isn't it past" is in McCoy, *op. cit.*, p. 159; "was a perfect helpmate" is in *ibid.*, p. 32; Coolidge on Borah is in Abels, *op. cit.*, p.

36; "If you keep" is in Russell, *In the Shadow of Blooming Grove*, p. 334; Starling's story is in *ibid.*, pp. 341–42; Ike Hoover's comment is in Hoover, *Forty-two Years in the White House*.

CHAPTER 7: "MY COUNTRY 'TIS OF ME"

For the Kokomo Klan rally see Coughlan, "Konklave in Kokomo," in Leighton, ed., *The Aspirin Age*, and Harrison, "Gentlemen from Indiana," *Atlantic Monthly*, May 1928; for the history of the Klan see Chalmers, *Hooded Americanism*, and Goldberg, *Discontented America*, Chapter 6; Evans's statement is in Evans, "The Klan's Fight for Americanism," *North American Review*, March 1926; for figures on Jews on college faculties see Dinnerstein, *Antisemitism in America*, pp. 87–88; for Nevins's comment on Ford see Nevins and Hill, *Ford: Expansion and Challenge, 1915–1933*, p. 321; for brief profiles of Grant and Stoddard see *Dictionary of American Biography*; for a study of the melting pot versus restrictions see Gerstle, *American Crucible*, Chapter 3; for the Johnson Act see Goldberg, *op. cit.*, pp. 159–66, and Ferrell, *op. cit.*, pp. 113–17; "constantly demonstrate" is in *New York Times*, March 11, 2001; Lippman's statement is in Steel, *Walter Lippman and the American Century*, pp. 24–248; "My dog" is in Ferrell, *The Presidency of Calvin Coolidge*, p. 114; for Coolidge and race see *ibid.*, pp. 107–12, and Sobel, *Coolidge*, pp. 249–50; the beginnings of prosperity are in Soule, *Prosperity Decade*, pp. 107–25; for advertising see Slosson, *The Great Crusade*, pp. 365–271, and Lears, *Fables of Abundance*; for euphemisms see "That Which We Call a Rose" in *New Republic*, January 9, 1929; for public relations see Furnas, *Great Times*, pp. 502–5.

CHAPTER 8: "COOLIDGE OR CHAOS"

"Moses, what do you think" is in Miller, *F.D.R.*, p. 199; "Have something you want to say" is in Eleanor Roosevelt, *This Is My Story*, p. 352; the basic source for the Leopold-Loeb case is Higdon, *Crime of the Century*; the best source for the 1924 campaign is Murray, *The 103rd Ballot*; for Coolidge's handling of Pinchot and Ford, see Ferrell, *The Presidency of Calvin Coolidge*, pp. 51–52; "remain a hero" is in Mencken, *A Carnival of Buncombe*, p. 70; Muscle Shoals is in Lacey, *Ford*, pp. 211–14; the best account of the Democratic convention of 1924 is Murray's *The 103rd Ballot* and I have followed it; for F.D.R. see James Roosevelt, *My Parents*, pp. 92–93; Mencken on La Follette is in *Carnival of Buncombe*, p. 116; "If scandals break out" is in Sobel, *Coolidge*, p. 304; "We Democrats" is in Miller, *op. cit.*, p. 207; "I don't anticipate" is in Goodfellow, *Calvin Coolidge*, p. 372.

CHAPTER 9: "WE LOVED EVERY RATTLE"

Cather's comment is in *Not Under Forty*, unnumbered prefatory page; the "average man" is in Hollingworth, "The Average Man," *Literary Digest*, May 28, 1927; "Why on earth" is in *ibid*, p. 251; number of cars in U.S. in 1924 is in *Statistical Abstract* (1925), p. 364; bacterial infection is in Green, *The Uncertainty of Everyday Life*, p. 32; number of accidents is in *Statistical Abstract* (1925), p. 369; suburban growth is in Glabb in Braemen et al., *Change and Continuity*, p. 404; an estimated $1 of every $5 is in Abels, *op. cit.*, p. 109; comment of Middletown union leader is in Lynds, *op. cit.*, p. 256n; "I'll go without" is in *ibid.*, p. 256; for Henry Ford's biography and the history of his company, I have used, Lacey, *Ford*, Sward, *The Legend of Henry Ford*, and Nevins and Hill, *Ford*, Vols. I and II; "Mr. Ford the automobileer" is in Dos Passos, *U.S.A.*, pp. 806–7; White's recollection is in "Farewell My Lovely," in White, *Second Tree from the Corner*, pp. 36–37; "Ford employees are not" is in Abels, *op. cit.*,

p. 118; "It will cost" is in Parrish, *Anxious Decades*, p. 45; for the history of General Motors and a biography of Durant see Madsen, *The Deal Maker*; for retail conglomerations see Clark, "Big Business Now Sweeps Retail Trade," *New York Times*, July 28, 1928; "He never thought" is in Madsen, *op cit.*, p. 2; for financing of cars in Middletown see Lynds, *op. cit.*, p. 255; for Sloan's strategies see Sloan, *My Years with General Motors*, pp. ; for Chrysler's biography see *Dictionary of American Biography*; Eisenhower's trip is in Ferrell, *The Presidency of Calvin Coolidge op. cit.*, p. 98; for highway construction see Paxson, "The American Highway Movement, 1916–1935," in *The American Historical Review*, 1945, and Flink, *The Car Culture*; for the beginning of the motel see *ibid.*, pp. 358–63; for the history of the movies see Sklar, *Movie Made America*, and Griffith, *The Movies*; for the Jewish moguls see Gabler, *An Empire of Their Own*; Griffith "carried the ideas" is in Abels, *op. cit.*, p. 184; "When she comes home" is in Klein, *Rainbow's End*, p. 114; for Mencken on Valentino see *A Mencken Chrestomathy*, pp. 281–84; for the death of Rin-Tin-Tin see Bassinger, *Silent Stars*; "All I need" is in Chaplin, *Autobiography*; "a poet, a dreamer" is in *ibid.*

CHAPTER 10: "A LOST GENERATION"

For Stearns see Mencken, *My Life As Author and Editor*, pp. 395–97, Stearns, *The Street I Know*, pp. 193–206, and Stearns, *Civilization in the United States*; Lachaise's comment is in Nash, *The Nervous Generation*; "I'm going to Paris" is in Cowley, *Exile's Return*; p. 79; for Hemingway's life in Paris see Donaldson, *Hemingway vs. Fitzgerald*; "You are all" is in Hemingway, *A Moveable Feast*, pp. 25–31; Dos Passos is from his Introduction to the Modern Library edition of *Three Soldiers*; Stearns's observation is in Douglas, *Terrible Honesty*, pp. 108–9; for gay life in Paris, see Lynn, *Hemingway*, pp. 318–20; Benét is in Nash, *op. cit.*, p. 74; for the influence of Eliot and Joyce see Cowley, *op. cit.*, p. 16; for Fitzgerald's life see Turnbull, *Scott Fitzgerald*, and Mizener, *The Far Side of Paradise*; "Sometimes" is in Cowley, *op. cit.*, p. 30; "Riding in a taxi" is in Mizener, *op. cit.*, 118; "It was always" is in Cowley, *A Second Flowering*, p. 24; "Our darling" is in *ibid.*, p. 109, as is "Let's go"; for the description of café society see Morris, *Incredible New York*, p. 298; "Scott was extravagant" is in Mizener, *op. cit.*, p. 122; Fitzgerald's earnings are in *ibid.*, pp. 179 and 126; "The Jazz Age" is in Cowley, *Second Flowering*, p. 25; cash found in car is in Turnbull, *op. cit.*, p. 141; Hemingway's comment is in Hemingway, *A Moveable Feast*, p. 155; "to write something" is in Turnbull, *op. cit.*, p 146; Anita Loos's story is in Latham, *Crazy Sundays*, p. 3; for Zelda's affair with the French airman see Mizener, *op. cit.*, and Turnbull, *op. cit.*; "From the first moment" is in Turnbull, *op. cit.*; "That September" is in Mizener, *op. cit.*, p. 164; for Freud's visit to America see Jones, *The Life and Works of Sigmund Freud*, pp. 266–68; for the history of Freudian theory in America see Hale, *Freud and the Americans*, Vols. I and II; Freudians in Greenwich Village is discussed in Stansell, *American Moderns*, p. 302; for Freud and the movies see Douglas, *op. cit.*, p. 123; for Barrymore see *ibid.*, p. 125; for Menninger see Hale, *op. cit.*, Vol. II, p. 77; for O'Neill see the Gelbs' *O'Neill*; O'Neill and Freud is in *ibid.*, pp. 595–97; for the Harlem Renaissance see Huggins, *The Harlem Renaissance*; for A'Leila Walker see Bundles, *On Her Own Ground*; for the popular novel see Nash, *op. cit.*, pp. 137–42; "the kind of American" is in *ibid.*, p. 138; for the development of the Book-of-the-Month Club see Furnas, *Great Times*, pp. 489–94; for the Middletown library see Lynds, *Middletown*, p. 237.

CHAPTER 11: "WHOOPING IT UP FOR GENESIS"

The basic sources on Aimee Semple McPherson are Epstein, *Sister Aimee*, and McWilliams, "Sunlight in My Soul"; statistics on churchgoing are in Klein, *Rainbow's End*, p. 104;

"Three things" is in Lynds, *Middletown*, p. 356; for Billy Sunday see his obituary in *New York Times*, November 7, 1935, and McLoughlin, *Billy Sunday Was His Name*; the best Mencken biographies are Manchester, *Disturber of the Peace*, and Hobson, *Mencken: A Life*; "You have no idea" is in Manchester, *op. cit.*, p. 228; nominated Aimee for Miss America is in Kemler, *The Irreverent Mr. Mencken*, p. 227; "The printing press" is in Mencken, *Happy Days*, p. 212; "Most men" is in a recorded interview at the Library of Congress on June 30, 1948; "I still think of Sara" is in *The Diary of H. L. Mencken*, pp. 139–40; "the American people" is in *ibid.*, p. 357; Smoot's statement is in Manchester, *op. cit.*, p. 117; "lots of tits" is in Leff and Simons, *The Dame in the Kimono*, p. 6; "Read the Bible" is in de Camp, *The Great Monkey Trial*, p. 35; "Nobody gives a damn" is in Manchester, *op. cit.*, p. 164; the account of the Scopes trial is based upon *ibid.*, and de Camp, *op. cit.*; "Well, we killed" is in Manchester, *op. cit.*, p. 185; "This issue is" is in *Washington Post*, February 15, 2001.

CHAPTER 12: "RUNNIN' WILD"

"Exquisitely hard-boiled" is in *Photoplay*, April 1926; "Flapper Jane" is in *New Republic*, September 9, 1925; "flirted because" is in Mizener, *The Far Side of Paradise*, p. 76; "We object" is in Sullivan, *The Twenties*, p. 562; "A coonskin coat" is in *New Yorker*, January 2, 1926; data on working women is in Hager, "Occupations and Earnings of Women in Industry"; wage differences between the sexes is in Leinwand, 1927, p. 51; female union membership is in *ibid.*, p. 53; for women professionals and black women see Dumenil, *The Modern Temper*; girls not wearing corsets is in *Collier's*, July 28, 1927; for cosmetics and hairstyles see "How the World Is Perfumed" in *Literary Digest*, April 9, 1927, and Slosson, *The Great Crusade*; p. 155; for the *Rubáiyát* see Sullivan, *The War Begins*, p. 182; drinking among students is in Fass, *The Damned and the Beautiful*, p. 311; for Bourne and the youth movement see Stansell, *American Moderns*, pp. 92–95; for school attendance see Slosson, *op. cit.*, pp. 320–24; increase in the number of university courses, see Green, *The Uncertainty of Everyday Life*, p. 127; a 1928 study is in *ibid.*, p. 133; for wider discussion of sex see Kennedy, *Birth Control in America*, pp. 8–15; Moley's comments are in Abels, *In the Time of Silent Cal*, p. 85; "jazz emotions" is in Ogren, *The Jazz Revolution*, p. 3; illegitimate births is in Slosson, *op. cit.*, p. 149; "What a gulf" is in Leinwand, *op. cit.*, p. 175; to eliminate the word "obey" is in Abels, *op. cit.*, p. 86; for biographical detail on Sanger see her sometimes unreliable *An Autobiography*, also Kennedy, *op. cit.*, and Chesler, *Woman of Valor*; death of Sadie Sachs is in Sanger, *op. cit.*, p. 92; Nevada divorce decision is in *Literary Digest*, April 9, 1927; Dumenil's views are in Dumenil, *op. cit.*, p. 130; for couples flocking to Arizona and Nevada see *New York Times*, December 17, 1927; "Anyone with $10" is in Lynds, *op. cit.*, 121; "Women never used" is in *ibid.*, p. 123.

CHAPTER 13: "BOY, CAN YOU GET STUCCO!"

For Samuel Insull see Forrest McDonald's biography and Klein, *Rainbow's End*, pp. 153–54, for a shorter account; "It's like" is in Parrish, *Anxious Decades*, p. 36; for the growth of the petroleum industry see Olien and Olien, *Easy Money*, Chapter 2; for GNP growth see Klein, *op. cit.*, pp. 24 and 28; for growth in use of electricity see Slosson, *The Great Crusade*, p 136; "a life of alpaca" is in a profile of Insull in Dos Passos, *U.S.A.*, p. 1211; for new trends in mergers see Galbraith, *The Great Crash*, pp. 48–50; Kindleberger's comment is in Kindleberger, *Manias, Panics and Crashes*, p. 81; Capone's complaint is is Olien and Olien, *op. cit.*, p. 11; for the various frauds see *ibid.*, pp. 1–2; for speculation in the stock market see Klein, *op. cit.*, p. 99; Charles Mitchell's operations are discussed in Geisst, *Wall Street*, p. 163, and

Klein, *op. cit.*, pp. 51–60; for the history of the skyscraper see Burchard and Bush-Brown, *The Architecture of America*, pp. 256–63; Edison's comments are in *Popular Science Monthly*, March 1927; Welles's comment is in Leinwand, *1927* working family expenses are in Slosson, *op. cit.*, p. 171; p. 42; for living costs and wages see Soule, *Prosperity Decade*, p. 321; *Wall Street Journal* is in Klein, *op. cit.*, p. 85; lack of unions is discussed in Ferrell, *Presidency of Calvin Coolidge*, p. 73; farm statistics are in Parrish, *op. cit.*, p. 83; for the Florida boom see Stewart, "The Madness That Swept Miami," in *Smithsonian*, January 2001, and Klein, *op. cit.*, pp. 88–95; "not little flakes" is in Stewart *op. cit.*, Galbraith is in Galbraith, *op. cit.*, p. 8; for Addison Mizner see Johnson, *The Amazing Mizners*; "Anyway" is in Stewart, *op. cit.*; coal industry conditions are in Abels, *In the Time of Silent Cal* p. 262, and Ferrell, *op. cit.*, p. 76; conditions in the Southern mills is based upon Bernstein, *The Lean Years*, "the strikes left" is in *ibid.*, p. 42; for the Klan march in Washington, see *Washington Star*, August 8–10, 1925; for the decline of the Klan see Slosson, *op. cit.*, pp. 311–14, and Goldberg, *Discontented America*, p. 138; Stephenson's story is also told in Abels, *op. cit.*, pp. 58–60; Coolidge on the Klan is in Ferrell, *op. cit.*, p. 112; for the outcome of the 1926 election see Sobel, *Coolidge*, pp. 328–29, and Hicks, *Republican Ascendancy*, pp. 128–29.

CHAPTER 14: SEVEN AGAINST THE WALL

For Jimmy Walker and his era see Fowler, *Beau James*, and Mitgang, *Once Upon a Time in New York*; for Mastbaum see Mitgang, *Ibid.*, p. 150; "I violate" is in Kobler, *Capone*, p. 209; "Prosecuting criminals" is in Leinwand, *1977*, p. 141; for Rothstein see Katcher, *The Big Bankroll*; "Prohibition is" is in Allsop, *The Bootleggers and Their Era*, p. 37; for Texas Guinan and the nightclub era see Morris, *Incredible New York*, pp. 326–30; for the New York gangsters see *ibid.*, pp. 343–44; Moley's comments are in Abels, *op. cit.*, p. 87; the best biographies of Capone are Kobler, *Capone*, and Bergreen, *Capone*; Loesch's account is in Kobler, *Capone*, pp. 13–17; statistics on crime in Chicago are in Leinwand, *op. cit.*, p. 142, and Allsop, *op. cit.*, p. 15; Capone's take is estimated in *ibid.*, pp. 33–34; physical description of Capone is in Kobler, *op. cit.*, p. 15; "I'm no Italian" is in *ibid.*, p. 23; "It's your funeral" is in Wendt and Kogan, *Lords of the Levee*, p. 340; "Sure, I know" is in Kobler, *op. cit.*, p. 137; "Hymie Weiss is dead" is in Allsop, *op. cit.*, pp. 122–23; Capone's take is in Bergreen, *op. cit.*, p. 236; Brother Ralph is in Kobler, *op. cit.*, 142; for Chicago and jazz see Allsop, *op. cit.*, pp. 180–86 and Ogren, *The Jazz Revolution*, pp. 54–56; for Bix Beiderbecke see Ogren, *op. cit.*, pp. 151–52; for the St. Valentine's Day Massacre see Allsop, *op. cit.*, pp. 137–49; for the murders of Scalise, Anselmi, and Giunta see Kobler, *op. cit.*, pp. 17–18; "I directed" is in Hoover, *Memoirs*; "Al is as nutty" is in Kobler, *op. cit.*, p. 373; for post-Prohibition gangsters see Russo, *The Outfit*.

CHAPTER 15: "YOU AIN'T HEARD NOTHIN' YET!"

Basic sources on Lindbergh are Berg, *Lindbergh*, and Lindbergh, *"We"* and *The Spirit of St. Louis*; "So Long" is in *New York Times*, May 21, 1927; for the flight of the NC-4 see Smith, *First Across!*; for U.S. government and air mail see Slosson, *The Great Crusade*, p. 400; Hoover's comment is in Hicks, *Republican Ascendancy*, p. 177; for military and naval air developments see Miller, *The U.S. Navy*, pp. 198–202; for Billy Mitchell, see Davis, *The Billy Mitchell Affair*; "in all great" is in Hicks, *op. cit.*, p. 175; profile of Lindbergh is based upon Berg, *op. cit.*; "I did not find" is in *ibid.*, p. 42; "You could see" is in *ibid.*, p. 43; "It is impossible" is in Berg, *ibid.*, p. 49; "I shall never" is in *ibid.*, p. 72; passenger who wanted to urinate is in *ibid.*, p. 83; "No attempt" is in *ibid.*, p. 121; "It seems always" is in *ibid.*, p. 124;

"I first saw" is in "*We*"; "is our Prince" is in Berg, *op. cit.*, p. 143; "You are the prophet" is in *ibid.*, p. 143; number of newspapers is in Slosson, *op. cit.*, pp. 348–49; for background on the tabloids see Stevens, *Sensationalism in the New York Press*, and Rutland, *The Newsmongers*; for Winchell see Gabler, *Winchell*; for the death of Valentino see Marberry, "The Overloved One," in *American Heritage*, August 1965; for the Snyder-Gray case see Abels, *In the Time of Silent Cal*, pp. 209–13; for the new leisure see Duffus, "The Age of Play," *Independent*, December 20, 1924; for Stuart Chase's comment see Slosson, *op. cit.*, p. 270; for costs of golf see *ibid.*, p. 280; for sports as big business see *ibid.*, Chapter 10; Taft is quoted in Klein, *Rainbow's End*, p. 118; for Babe Ruth see Wagenheim, *Babe Ruth*; for Jack Dempsey see Kahn, *A Flame of Pure Fire*; MacNamee's broadcast is in Churchill, *The Year the World Went Mad*, p. 263; "Harvard, I trust" is in Abels, *op. cit.*, pp. 156–57; for the coming of sound movies see Sklar, *Movie Made America*, and Griffith, *The Movies*.

CHAPTER 16: "THE FINAL TRIUMPH OVER POVERTY"

For Coolidge's statement see Sobel, *Coolidge*, pp. 369–74; Capper's account is in White, *A Puritan in Babylon*, p. 361; for Kent's column see Abels, *In the Time of Silent Cal*, p. 267; for Hoover's situation in 1927 see Burner, *Herbert Hoover*, pp. 190–93; Agnes Meyer's comment is in Barry, *Rising Tide*; my account of the Great Mississippi Flood is based upon *ibid.*, which is by far the best account; "For thirty-six hours" is in *ibid.*, pp. 278–79; "I urgently request" is in *ibid.*, pp. 286–87; for Hoover's activities see Burner, *op. cit.*, p. 193; "I came here" is in Barry, *op. cit.*, pp. 277–78; "There was no" is in *Crisis*, January 1928; Hoover and blacks is in Burner, *op. cit.*, pp. 195–96; Cleveland's comment is in Barry, *op. cit.*, p. 269; newspaper comments are in *ibid.*, p. 373; "We'll show 'em" is in Kennedy, *Freedom from Fear*, p. 236; "The people" is in Barry, *op. cit.*, p. 375; for Joan Hoff Wilson's comment see Wilson, *American Business and Foreign Policy*, p. x; for foreign affairs under Coolidge see Sobel, *op. cit.*, pp. 339–58; for Sandino see Macaulay, *The Sandino Affair*; for the election of 1928 see Lichtman, *Prejudice and the Old Politics*, and Moore, *A Catholic Runs for President*; segregation of blacks at the Democratic convention is in Burner, *op. cit.*, p. 208; for Hoover's early years see Burner, *op. cit.*, and for a shorter version see McCoy, "To the White House," in *The Hoover Presidency*; for the influence of his religion on Hoover see Fausold, *The Presidency of Herbert C. Hoover*, pp. 1–3; "no one could replace" is in Nash, *The Life of Herbert Hoover*, Vol. I, p. 11; "For the rest of his life" is in Hofstadter, *The American Political Tradition*, p. 283; "We have a young lady," is in Burner, *op. cit.*, p. 21; for the Boxers see Preston, *The Boxer Rebellion*; "You have saved" is in *ibid.*, p. 41; Keynes's comments are in Keynes, *The Economic Consequences of the People*, p. 247; for Hoover's acceptance speech see Smith, *op. cit.*, pp. 3–5; for the stock market bubble see Sobel, *The Great Bull Market*, and Klein, *Rainbow's End*, pp. 145–64; "The mass escape into" is in Galbraith, *The Great Crash*, pp. 16–17; White is in Fausold, *op. cit.*, p. 29; "Watch the trains!" is in Moore, *op. cit.*, p. 145; "I have been" is in Mencken, *A Carnival of Buncombe*, p. 138; for FDR and the 1928 campaign see Miller, *F.D.R.*, pp. 220–25; increases in stock prices is in Galbraith, *op. cit.*

CHAPTER 17: "WALL STREET LAYS AN EGG"

For Groucho Marx's comments see Klein, *Rainbow's End*, pp. 189–94; for women in brokerage offices see *ibid.*, p. 148, and Barnard, "Ladies of the Ticker," in *North American Review*, April 1929; Mitchell and Sloan are in Klein, *op. cit.*, p. 13, Fisher is quoted on p. 201; Galbraith is in Galbraith, *The Great Crash*, p. 83; for ownership of U.S. wealth see Daniels, *The Time Between the Wars*, p. 198, and *Washington Post Outlook*, May 26, 2002; "Well, Grace" is in Sobel, *Coolidge*, p. 402; for the telephone on the presidential desk, see Smith, *Shattered Dream*, p. 11; "I have no dread" is in Burner, *Herbert Hoover*, p. 211; for the first months of Hoover's presidency see *ibid.*, pp. 212–44, and Burner, "Before the Crash," in *The Hoover Presidency*, pp. 50–68; for Goddard and Lindbergh see Berg, *Lindbergh*, pp. 210–14; "We like to feel" is in Hall and Nelson, "How Unemployment Strikes Home," *Survey*, April 1, 1929; for insiders getting out see Klein, *op. cit.*, pp. 192–93; Hoover's concern over speculation is in Burner, *Herbert Hoover*, p. 245; for the stock market crash see Galbraith, *op. cit.*, Chapter 5, Soule, *Prosperity Decade*, Chapter 14, and Klein, *op. cit.*, Chapter 10; detailed accounts of events on the Exchange floor and off it are in Thomas and Morgan-Witts, *The Day the Bubble Burst*, and *New York Times*, October 24–30, 1929; the presence of Churchill is noted in Galbraith, *op. cit.*, p. 105; for Evangeline Adams see Thomas and Morgan-Witts, *op. cit.*, p. 370; "little flurry" is in Miller, *F.D.R.*, p. 239; Mellon's comments are in Hoover, *Memoirs*, Vol. III, p. 10; for Hoover and the global aspects of the Depression see Burner, *Herbert Hoover*, pp. 300–305, and Hoover, *Memoirs*, Vol. III; "a nightmare" is in Hoover, *Memoirs*, Vol. III, p. 82; Depression conditions are based on my own memories of the mid-1930s when conditions were similar, Bird, *The Invisible Scar*, and Wecter, *The Age of the Great Depression*; for blacks and the Depression see *The Nation*, April 22, 1931, and Chandler, *America's Greatest Depression*, p. 40; for writers and the crash see Hoffman, *The 1920's*, for the return of the exiles see Cowley, *Exile's Return*, pp. 385–86; for the Menckens' visit to the Fitzgeralds see Mencken, *My Life As Author and Editor*, pp. 262–63, and *The Diary of H. L. Mencken*, pp. 56–57; for the decline of Mencken's reputation see Manchester, *Disturber of the Peace*, pp. 256–63; for the decline in Fitzgerald's royalties see Mizener, *The Far Side of Paradise*, p. 232, and Turnbull, *Scott Fitzgerald*, p. 205; "If we start" is in Myers, *The Hoover Administration*, p. 63; "Hoover could not" is in Feis, *1933*, for the Democratic convention and campaign of 1932 see Miller, *F.D.R.*, pp. 265–90; for the Lindbergh kidnapping see Fisher, *The Lindbergh Case*; for Long and Coughlin see Brinkley, *Voices of Protest*; "There's the same goulash" is in John Dos Passos, "The Veterans Come Home to Roost," *New Republic*, June 29, 1932; for the crushing of the Bonus Army see the fine account by Lee McCardell in *Baltimore Evening Sun*, which was reprinted in Snyder and Morris, *A Treasury of Great Reporting*; FDR's reaction to Depression America is in Tugwell, *The Brain Trust*, pp. 357–59; "You know, Jimmy" is in James Roosevelt, *Affectionately, F.D.R.* p. 189.

Bibliography

GOVERNMENT DOCUMENTS

President's Research Committee on *Recent Social Trends in the United States*. Westport, Conn.: Greenwood Press, 1970, originally published, 1933.

U.S. Bureau of the Census. *Historical Statistics of the United States to 1957*. Washington, D.C.: Government Printing Office, 1960.

U.S. Commerce Department. *Statistical Abstract of the United States*. Washington, D.C.: Government Printing Office, 1919–1933.

Wickersham, George W. *U.S. National Commission on Law Observance and Enforcement Report*. Washington, D.C.: Government Printing Office, 1931.

BOOKS AND ARTICLES

Abels, Jules. *In the Time of Silent Cal*. New York: Putnam, 1989.

Abernathy, Lloyd M. "Washington Race War of July 1919." *Maryland Historical Magazine*, December 1963.

Adams, Samuel Hopkins. *The Incredible Era: The Life and Times of Warren Gamaliel Harding*. Boston: Houghton Mifflin; 1939.

Addams, Jane. *The Second Twenty Years at Hull-House*. New York: Macmillan, 1930.

Affron, Charles. *Lillian Gish: Her Legend and Her Life*. New York: Scribner, 2001.

Allen, Frederick Lewis. *Only Yesterday: An Informal History of the 1920's*. New York: Perennial, 1964.

Allsop, Kenneth. *The Bootleggers and Their Era*. Garden City, N.Y.: Doubleday, 1961.

Anthony, Carl Sferrazza. *Florence Harding*. New York: William Morrow, 1998.

Asbury, Herbert. *Chicago: Gem of the Prairie*. New York: Alfred A. Knopf, 1940.

———. *The Gangs of New York: An Informal History of the Underworld*. Garden City, New York: Doubleday, 1924.

———. *The Great Illusion: An Informal History of Prohibition*. Garden City, N.Y.: Doubleday, 1950

Bagby, Wesley N. *Road to Normalcy: The Presidential Campaign of 1920*. Baltimore: Johns Hopkins Press, 1962.

Bailey, Thomas A. *A Diplomatic History of the American People*. Prentice-Hall, 1980.

———. *Woodrow Wilson and the Great Betrayal*. Chicago: Quadrangle, 1963.

———. *Woodrow Wilson and the Lost Peace*. Chicago: Quadrangle, 1963.

Baldwin, Neil. *Henry Ford and the Jews: The Mass Production of Hate*. New York: Public Affairs, 2001.

Barnard, Eunice Fuller. "Ladies of the Ticker." *North American Review*, April 1929.

Barnard, Harry. *Independent Man: The Life of Senator James Couzens*. New York: Scribner, 1958.

Barnouw, Erik. *A Tower of Babel: A History of Broadcasting in the United States.* New York: Oxford University, 1966.

Barry, John M. *Rising Tide: The Great Mississippi Flood of 1927.* New York: Simon and Schuster, 1997.

Barton, Bruce. *The Man Nobody Knows: A Discovery of the Real Jesus.* Indianapolis: Bobbs-Merrill, 1925.

Baruch, Bernard M. *The Public Years.* New York: Holt, Rinehart & Winston, 1960.

Bassinger, Jeanine. *Silent Stars.* Middletown, Connecticut: Wesleyan University Press, 2001.

Bent, Silas. *Ballyhoo: The Voice of the Press.* New York: Boni and Liveright, 1927.

Berg, Scott. *Lindbergh.* New York: Putnam, 1998.

Bergreen, Laurence. *Capone: The Man and the Era.* New York: Simon and Schuster, 1992.

Bernstein, Irving. *The Lean Years: A History of the American Worker, 1920–1933.* Boston: Houghton Mifflin, 1960.

"Big Business Now Sweeps Retail Trade." *New York Times,* July 28, 1928.

Bird, Caroline. *The Invisible Scar.* New York: David McKay, 1966.

Breger, Louis. *Freud: Darkness in the Midst of Vision.* New York: John Wiley, 2000.

Brinkley, Alan. *Voices of Protest: Huey Long, Father Coughlin, and the Great Depression.* New York: Random House, 1982.

Britton, Nan. *The President's Daughter.* New York: Elizabeth Ann Guild, 1931.

Brody, David. *Labor in Crisis: The Steel Strike of 1919.* Philadelphia: Lippincott 1965.

Broer, Lawrence, and John D. Walther, eds. *Dancing Fools and Weary Blues: The Great Escape of the Twenties.* Bowling Green, Ohio: Bowling Green University Press, 1990.

Brooks, John, *Once in Golconda: A True Drama of Wall Street, 1920–1938.* New York: Allworth, 1997.

Brownlow, Kevin. *The Parade's Gone By.* New York: Alfred A. Knopf, 1968.

Bundles, A'Leila. *On Her Own Ground: The Life and Times of Madame C. J. Walker.* New York: Scribner, 2001.

Burchard, John, and Albert Bush-Brown. *The Architecture of America: A Social and Cultural History.* Boston: Little, Brown, 1961.

Burner, David. "Before the Crash: Hoover's First Eight Months in the Presidency." In Fausold and Mazuzan, *The Hoover Presidency.*

———. *Herbert Hoover: A Public Life.* New York: Knopf, 1978.

———. *The Politics of Provincialism.* New York: Knopf, 1968.

Carr, Virginia Spencer. *Dos Passos: A Life.* Garden City, N.Y.: Doubleday, 1984.

Cashman, Sean Dennis. *America in The Twenties and Thirties.* New York: New York University Press, 1989.

Cather, Willa. *Not Under Forty.* Lincoln: University of Nebraska Press, 1988.

CBS *MarketWatch.* January 12, 2002.

Chafee, Zechariah. *Freedom of Speech.* New York: Harcourt, Brace & Hall, 1920.

Chalmers, David. *Hooded Americanism: The History of the Ku Klux Klan.* Durham: Duke University Press, 1987.

Chandler, Lester. *America's Greatest Depression.* New York: Harper and Row, 1970.

Chaplin, Charles S. *Autobiography.* New York: Simon & Schuster, 1964.

Champney, [Madame] Marcia. "When an Astrologer Ruled the White House." *Liberty,* April 9, and June 11, 1938.

Chernow, Ron. *The House of Morgan.* New York: Atlantic Monthly Press, 1990.

Chesler, Ellen. *Woman of Valor: Margaret Sanger and the Birth Control Movement*. New York: Simon and Schuster, 1992.

Churchill, Allen. *The Year the World Went Mad*. New York: Crowell, 1990.

Clark, Norman H. *Deliver Us from Evil: An Interpretation of American Prohibition*. New York: W.W. Norton 1976.

Coffman, *War to End All Wars*. New York: Oxford University Press 1968.

Cohen, Stanley. *A. Mitchell Palmer: Politician*. New York: Columbia University Press, 1963.

Colby, Gerard. *Du Pont Dynasty: Behind the Nylon Curtain*. Secaucus, N.J.: Lyle Stuart, 1984.

Coolidge, Calvin. *Autobiography*. New York: Cosmpolitan, 1929.

Coolidge, Grace. *An Autobiography*. Worland, Wyo: High Plains, 1992.

Coughlan, Robert. "Konklave in Kokomo." In *The Aspirin Age*, ed., Isabel Leighton. New York: Simon and Shuster, 1966.

Cowley, Malcolm. *Exile's Return*. New York: Viking, 1951.

——. *A Second Flowering*. New York: Viking, 1973.

Cramer, Clarence. *American Enterprise: Free and Not So Free*. Boston: Little, Brown, 1972.

Crunden, Robert M. *Body and Soul: The Making of American Modernism*. New York: Basic Books, 2000.

——. *From Self to Society: Transition in American Thought, 1919–1941*. Englewood Cliffs, N.J.: Prentice Hall, 1972.

Daniels, Jonathan. *The Time Between the Wars*. Garden City, N.Y.: Doubleday, 1966.

Darrow, Clarence. *The Story of My Life*. New York: Scribner, 1932.

Daugherty, Henry M. *The Inside Story of the Harding Tragedy*. New York: Churchill, 1923.

Davis, Burke. *The Billy Mitchell Affair*. New York: Random House, 1967.

de Camp, L. Sprague. *The Great Monkey Trial*. Garden City, N.Y.: Doubleday, 1968.

Degler, Carl. "The Ordeal of Herbert Hoover." *Yale Review*, Summer 1963.

DeGregorio, William A. *Complete Book of United States Presidents*. New York: Dembner, 1984.

Dinnerstein, Leonard. *Antisemitism in America*. New York: Oxford University Press, 1994.

Dobson, John M. *A History of American Enterprise*. Englewood Cliffs, NJ: Prentice Hall, 1988.

Donaldson, Scott. *Hemingway vs. Fitzgerald: The Rise and Fall of a Literary Friendship*. Woodstock, N.Y: Overlook 2001.

Dorwart, Jeffrey M. *Conflict of Duty*. Annapolis: Naval Institute Press, 1983.

Dos Passos, John. *Mr. Wilson's War*. Garden City, N.Y.: Doubleday, 1962.

——. *Three Soldiers*. New York: Modern Library, 1932.

——. *U.S.A.* New York: Library of America, 1996.

——. "The Veterans Come Home to Roost." *The New Republic*, June 29, 1932.

Douglas, Ann. *Terrible Honesty: Mongrel Manhattan in the 1920s*. New York: Farrar, Straus and Giroux, 1995.

Douglas, Paul. *Real Wages in the United States, 1890–1926*. Boston: Viking 1930.

Downes, Randolph C. *The Rise of Warren Gamaliel Harding: 1865–1920*. Columbus: Ohio State University Press, 1970.

Draper, Theodore. *The Roots of American Communism*. New York: 1957.

Dray, Philip. *At the Hands of Persons Unknown: The Lynching of Black America*. New York: Random House, 2002.

Dubofsky, Melvyn. *We Shall Be All: A History of the IWW*. New York: Quadrangle, 1969

Dubofsky, Melvyn, and Warren Van Tine. *John L. Lewis: A Biography.* New York: 1977.

Duffus, R. L. "The Age of Play." *The Independent,* December 20, 1924.

Dumenil, Lyn. *The Modern Temper: American Culture and Society in the 1920s.* New York: Hill and Wang, 1995.

Eliot, T. S. *Collected Works.* New York: Harcourt Brace, 1936.

Ellsworth, Scott. *Death in a Promised Land: The Tulsa Race Riot of 1921.* Baton Rouge: Louisiana State University Press, 1982.

Epstein, Daniel M. *Sister Aimee: The Life of Aimee Semple McPherson.* New York: Harcourt, 1993.

Ernest, Robert. *Weakness Is a Crime: The Life of Bernard MacFadden.* Syracuse, N.Y.: Syracuse University Press, 1991.

Evans, Hiram Wesley. "The Klan's Fight for Americanism." *North American Review,* March 1926.

Fass, Paula, S. *The Damned and the Beautiful.* New York: Oxford University Press, 1977.

Faulkner, William. *The Sound and Fury.* In *The Portable William Faulkner,* ed., Malcolm Cowley. New York: Viking 1947.

Fausold, Martin, ed. *The Hoover Presidency* State University of New York Press, 1974.

———. *The Presidency of Herbert C. Hoover.* Lawrence: University Press of Kansas 1985.

Fecher, Charles. *Mencken: A Study of His Thought.* New York: Knopf, 1978.

Feis, Herbert. *1933: Characters in Crisis.* Columbia: University of Missouri, 1996. Boston: Little, Brown, 1966.

Ferrell, Robert H. *"Dear Bess."Letters from Harry to Bess Truman 1910–1959.* New York: W.W. Norton, 1983.

———. *The Presidency of Calvin Coolidge.* Lawrence: University Press of Kansas, 1998.

———. *The Strange Deaths of President Harding.* Columbia: University of Missouri, 1996.

Fisher, Jim. *The Lindbergh Case.* New Brunswick, NJ: Rutgers University Press, 1994.

Fitzgerald, F. Scott. *The Beautiful and Damned.* New York: Library of America, 2000.

———. *The Crack-Up,* ed., Edmund Wilson. New York: New Directions, 1945.

———. *The Great Gatsby.* New York: Scribner 1993.

———. *The Letters of F. Scott Fitzgerald,* ed., Andrew Turnbull. New York: Scribner, 1963.

———. *The Stories of F. Scott Fitzgerald,* ed., Malcolm Cowley. New York: Scribner, 1951

———. *This Side of Paradise.* New York: Library of America, 2000.

Flink, James J. *The Car Culture.* Cambridge: MIT Press, 1975.

Fogelson, Robert M. *Downtown: Its Rise and Fall, 1880–1950.* New Haven: Yale University Press, 2001.

Fowler, Gene. *Beau James: The Life and Times of Jimmy Walker.* New York: Viking, 1949.

———. *Good Night Sweet Prince.* Philadelphia: Blakiston, 1944.

Frankfurter, Felix, with Harlan B. Phillips. *Felix Frankfurter Reminisces.* New York: Reynal, 1960.

Franklin, John Hope, and Alfred A. Moss, Jr. *From Slavery to Freedom: A History of Black Americans.* New York: McGraw-Hill, 1994.

Friedheim, Robert L. *The Seattle General Strike.* Seattle: University of Washington, 1964.

Furnas, J. C. *Great Times: An Informal History of the United States, 1914–1929.* New York: Putnam, 1974.

Gabler, Neil. *An Empire of Their Own: How the Jews Invented Hollywood.* New York: Crown, 1988.

———. *Winchell: Gossip, Power and the Culture of Celebrity.* New York: Knopf, 1994.

Galambos, Louis, and Joseph Pratt. *The Rise of the Corporate Commonwealth: U.S. Business and Public Policy in the Twentieth Century.* New York: Basic Books 1988.

Galbraith, John Kenneth. *The Great Crash.* Boston: Houghton Mifflin, 1961.

Geisst, Charles R. *Wall Street: A History.* New York: Oxford University Press, 1999.

Gelb, Arthur, and Barbara Gelb. *O'Neill.* New York: Harper and Row, 1962.

Gerstle, Gary. *American Crucible: Race and Nation in the Twentieth Century.* Princeton: Princeton University Press, 2001.

Gilbert, Clinton. *"You Takes Your Choice."* New York: Putnam, 1924.

Ginger, Ray. *The Bending Cross: A Biography of Eugene Victor Debs.* New Brunswick, N.J.: Rutgers University Press, 1949.

Glabb, Charles N., in John Braemen, Robert H. Bremner, and David Body, eds. *Change and Continuity in Twentieth Century America: The 1920s.* Columbus: Ohio University Press, 1968.

Goldberg, David J. *Discontented America: The United States in the 1920s.* Baltimore: Johns Hopkins Press, 1997.

Goodfellow, Guy Fair. *Calvin Coolidge: A Study of Presidential Inaction.* Ann Arbor: University Microfilms, 1969.

Green, Harvey. *The Uncertainty of Everyday Life, 1915–1945.* New York: HarperCollins, 1992.

Griffith, Richard, Arthur Mayer and Eileen Bowser. *The Movies.* New York: Simon & Schuster, 1971.

Hager, Alice Rogers. "Occupations and Earnings of Women in Industry." *Annals of the American Academy of Political and Social Science,* May 1929.

Hale, Nathan G., Jr. *Freud and the Americans: The Beginnings of Psychoanalysis in the United States, 1876–1917.* New York: Oxford University Press, 1971.

———. *Freud and the Americans: The Rise and Crisis of Psychoanalysis in the United States.* New York: Oxford University Press, 1980.

Hall, Irene, and Irene H. Nelson. "How Unemployment Strikes Home." *Survey,* April 1, 1929.

Hall, Jacquelyn Dowd, et al. *Like a Family: The Making of a Southern Cotton Mill World.* Chapel Hill: University of North Carolina Press, 1987.

Hamilton, Virginia Van der Veer. *Hugo Black: The Alabama Years.* Baton Rouge: Louisiana State University Press, 1972.

Harrison, Morton. "Gentlemen from Indiana." *The Atlantic Monthly,* May 1928.

Haynes, John Earl. *Calvin Coolidge and the Coolidge Era: Essays on the History of the 1920s.* Washington, D.C.: Library of Congress, 1998.

Heckscher, August. *Woodrow Wilson: A Biography.* New York: Scribner, 1991.

Hemingway, Ernest. *Dateline: Toronto: Hemingway's Complete Toronto Star Dispatches, 1920–1924,* ed., William White. New York: Scribner, 1985.

———. *A Farewell to Arms.* London: Jonathan Cape, 1929.

———. *A Moveable Feast.* New York: Scribner, 1964.

———. *The Sun Also Rises.* In *The Portable Hemingway,* ed., Malcolm Cowley. New York: Viking, 1944.

Hemingway, Ernest, ed. *Men at War.* New York: Crown, 1942.

Hicks, John D., *Republican Ascendancy, 1921–1933.* New York: Harper Torchbooks, 1963.

Higdon, Hal. *Crime of the Century: The Leopold & Loeb Case.* New York: Putnam, 1975.

Higham, John. *Strangers in the Land: Patterns of American Nativism.* New York: Atheneum, 1965.

Hirsch, James S. *Riot and Remembrance: The Tulsa Race War and Its Legacy.* Boston: Houghton Mifflin, 2001.

Hobson, Fred. *Mencken: A Life.* New York: Random House, 1994.

Hoffman, Frederick J. *The 1920s: American Writing in the Postwar Decade.* New York: Free Press, 1965.

Hofstadter, Richard. *The American Political Tradition.* New York: Random House, 1973.

Hollingworth, Henry. "The Average Man." *Literary Digest,* May 28, 1927.

Holmes, Marian Smith. "Zora Neale Hurston: Out of Obscurity." *Smithsonian,* January 2001.

Hoover, Herbert C. *American Individualism.* Garden City, N.Y.: Doubleday, Page, 1923.

———. *The Memoirs of Herbert Hoover.* Vols. I, II, and III. New York: Macmillan, 1951–1952.

Hoover, Irwin W. *Forty-two Years in the White House.* Boston: Houghton Mifflin, 1934.

Hoyt, Edwin P. *Spectacular Rogue: Gaston B. Means,* Indianapolis: Bobbs-Merrill, 1963.

Huggins, Nathan I. *The Harlem Renaissance.* New York: Oxford University Press, 1971.

Jensen, Joan M. *The Price of Vigilance.* Chicago, Rand McNally, 1969.

Johns, Bud. *The Ombibulous Mr. Mencken.* San Francisco: Synergistic Press, 1958.

Johnson, Diane. *Dashiell Hammett: A Life.* New York: Random House, 1983.

Johnson, Paul. *Modern Times: The World from the Twenties to the Eighties.* New York: Harper and Row, 1983.

Johnston, Alva. *The Legendary Mizners.* New York: Farrar, Straus and Young, 1953.

Jones, Ernest, *The Life and Works of Sigmund Freud.* New York: Basic Books, 1961.

Jones, Laurie Beth, *Jesus, CEO.* New York: Hyperion, 1995.

Jones, Maxine. *A Documented History of the Incident Which Occurred at Rosewood, Florida in January 1923.* Submitted to the Florida Board of Regents, December 22, 1992.

Kahn, Roger. *A Flame of Pure Fire: Jack Dempsey and the Roaring 20s.* New York: Harcourt Brace, 1999.

Katcher, Leo. *The Big Bankroll: The Life and Times of Arnold Rothstein.* New York: Harper and Brothers, 1958.

Kazin, Alfred. *An American Procession.* New York: Knopf, 1984.

———. *On Native Grounds.* Garden City, N.Y.: Doubleday, 1956.

Kemler, Edgar. *The Irreverent Mr. Mencken.* Boston: Atlantic-Little, Brown, 1950.

Kennan, George F. *The Decision to Intervene.* Princeton: Princeton University Press, 1958.

Kennedy, David M. *Birth Control in America: The Career of Margaret Sanger.* New Haven: Yale University Press, 1970.

———. *Freedom from Fear: The American People in Depression and War, 1929–1945.* New York: Oxford University Press, 1999.

———. *Over Here: The First World War and American Society.* New York: Oxford University Press, 1970.

———. "Revisiting Frederick Lewis Allen's *Only Yesterday.*" *Reviews in American History,* June 1986.

Keynes, John Maynard. *The Economic Consequences of the People.* New York: Harcourt, Brace, 1922.

Kindleberger, Charles P. *Manias, Panics and Crashes.* 1978.

Kirkpatrick, Sidney D. *A Cast of Killers.* New York: Dutton, 1986.

Klein, Maury. *Rainbow's End: The Crash of 1929.* New York: Oxford University Press, 2001.

Klingman, William K. *1919: The Year Our World Began.* New York: Harper & Row, 1989.

Kobler, John. *Ardent Spirits.*

———. *Capone: The Life and World of Al Capone.* New York: Putnam, 1971.

Kyvig, David E. *Repealing National Prohibition.* Chicago: University of Chicago Press, 1979.

Lacey, Robert. *Ford: The Men and the Machine.* Boston: Little, Brown, 1986.

Larson, Edward J. *Trial and Error: The American Controversy Over Creation and Evolution.* New York: Oxford University Press, 1994.

Lasch, Christopher. *The American Liberals and the Russian Revolution.* New York Columbia University 1962.

Latham, Aaron. *Crazy Sundays: F. Scott Fitzgerald in Hollywood.* New York: Pocket Books, 1972.

Lears, Jackson. *Fables of Abundance: A Cultural History of Advertising in America.* New York: HarperCollins 1994.

Lefevre, Edwin. *Reminiscences of a Stock Operator.* New York: John Wiley, 1994. [Jesse Livermore's disguised autobiography]

Leff, Leonard J., and Jerold L. Simons. *The Dame in the Kimono: Hollywood, Censorship and the Production Code from the 1920s to the 1960s.* New York: Grove Weidenfeld, 1995.

Leffler, Melvyn P. *The Elusive Quest.* Chapel Hill: University of North Carolina Press, 1979.

Leighton, Isabel, ed. *The Aspirin Age.* New York: Simon and Schuster, 1963.

Leinwand, Gerald. *1927: High Tide of the 1920s.* New York: Four Walls Eight Windows, 2001.

Lichtman, Allan J. *Prejudice and the Old Politics: The Presidential Election of 1928.* Chapel Hill: University of North Carolina Press, 1979.

Levin, Phyllis Lee. *Edith and Woodrow: The Wilson White House.* New York: Scribner, 2001.

Lindbergh, Charles A. *The Spirit of St. Louis.* New York: Scribner, 1953.

———. *"We."* New York: Putnam, 1927.

Lisk, *Woodrow Wilson and the Progressive Era 1910–1917.* New York: Harper & Row, 1963.

Lowenthal, Max. *The Federal Bureau of Investigation.* New York: Harcourt Brace Jovanovich, 1950.

Longworth, Alice Roosevelt. *Crowded Hours.* New York: Scribner, 1933.

Lowry, Edward G. *Washington Close-ups.* Boston: Houghton Mifflin, 1921.

Lubell, Samuel. *The Future of American Politics.* New York: Harper and Row, 1952.

Lynd, Robert S., and Helen M. Lynd. *Middletown.* New York: Harcourt, Brace, 1929.

Lynn, Kenneth S. *Hemingway.* New York: Simon and Schuster, 1987.

Macaulay, Neill. *The Sandino Affair.* Durham: Duke University Press, 1985.

Madsen, Axel. *The Deal Maker: How William C. Durant Made General Motors.* New York: John Wiley, 1999.

Manchester, William. *Disturber of the Peace.* New York: Harper, 1951.

———. *The Glory and the Dream: A Narrative History of America, 1932–1972.* Boston: Little, Brown, 1974.

Marberry, M. M. "The Overloved One." *American Heritage,* August 1965.

Marchand, Roland. *Advertising the American Dream: Making the Way for Modernity, 1920–1940.* Berkeley: University of California Press, 1985.

Marsden, George. *Fundamentalism and American Culture: The Shaping of Twentieth Century Evangelism, 1870–1925.* New York: Oxford University, 1980.

McCoy, Donald R. *Calvin Coolidge: The Quiet President*. Lawrence: University Press of Kansas, 1988.

———. "To the White House: Herbert Hoover, August 1927–March 1929." In Fausold and Mazuzan, *The Hoover Presidency: A Reappraisal*.

McCutcheon, Marc. *Everyday Life from Prohibition Through World War II*. Cincinnati: Writer's Digest Books, 1995.

McDonald, Forrest. *Insull*, University of Chicago Press, 1962.

McGill, Ralph. *The South and the Southerner*. Boston: Little, Brown, 1964.

McKay, Claude. *Home to Harlem*. New York: Harper & Brothers, 1928.

McLean, Evalyn Walsh. *Father Struck It Rich*. Boston: Little Brown, 1936.

McLoughlin, William G., Jr. *Billy Sunday Was His Name*. Chicago: University of Chicago, 1955.

McWilliams, Carey. "Sunlight in My Soul." In *The Aspirin Age*, ed., Isabel Leighton. New York: Simon and Schuster, 1966.

Means, Gaston. *The Strange Death of President Harding*. New York: Guild Publishing, 1930.

Mencken, H. L. *A Carnival of Buncombe*, ed., Malcolm Moos. Baltimore: Johns Hopkins Press, 1956.

———. *The Days of H. L. Mencken*. New York: Knopf, 1947.

———. *The Diary of H. L. Mencken*, ed., Charles A. Fecher. New York: Knopf, 1989.

———. *The Editor, the Bluenose and the Prostitute: H. L. Mencken's Account of the "Hatrack" Censorship Case*, ed., Carl Bode. Boulder, Col.: Robert Rinehart, 1988.

———. *A Gang of Pecksniffs*, ed., Theo Lippman, Jr. New Rochelle, N. Y.: Arlington House, 1975.

———. *My Life As Author and Editor*, ed., Jonathan Yardley. New York: Knopf, 1993.

———. *A Mencken Chrestomathy*. New York: Knopf, 1948.

———. *A Second Mencken Chrestomathy*, ed., Terry Teachout. New York: Knopf, 1995.

———. *Thirty-five Years of Newspaper Work*, ed., Bradford Jacobs. Baltimore: Johns Hopkins Press, 1994.

Miller, Nathan. *F.D.R: An Intimate History*. Garden City, N.Y.: Doubleday, 1982.

———. *Spying for America: The Hidden History of U.S. Intelligence*. New York: Marlowe, 1997.

———. *Star-Spangled Men: America's Ten Worst Presidents*. New York: Touchstone, 1999.

———. *Stealing from America*. New York: Marlowe, 1996.

———. *Theodore Roosevelt: A Life*. New York: Morrow, 1992.

———. *The U.S. Navy: A History*. Annapolis: Naval Institute Press, 1997.

Mitgang, Herbert. *Once Upon a Time in New York: Jimmy Walker, Franklin Roosevelt and the Last Great Battle of the Jazz Age*. New York: Free Press, 2000.

Mizener, Arthur. *The Far Side of Paradise: A Biography of F. Scott Fizgerald*. Boston: Houghton Mifflin, 1951.

Moley, Raymond. *After Seven Years*. New York: Harper and Brothers, 1939.

Moore, Edward A. *A Catholic Runs for President: The Campaign of 1928*. New York: Ronald Press, 1956.

Morris, Lloyd. *Incredible New York*. New York: Random House, 1951.

———. *Postscript to Yesterday*. New York: Random House, 1947.

Murray, Robert K. *The Harding Era*. Minneapolis: University of Minnesota Press, 1969.

———. *The 103rd Ballot*. New York: Harper and Row, 1976.

———. *The Red Scare: A Study in National Hysteria, 1919–1920*. Minneapolis: University of Minnesota Press, 1955.

Myers, William S., and Walter H. Newton. *The Hoover Administration: A Documented Narrative*. New York: Scribner, 1936.

Nash, George H. *The Life of Herbert Hoover*. Vol. I. New York: Norton, 1983.

Nash, Roderick. *The Nervous Generation: American Thought, 1917–1930*. Chicago: University of Chicago Press, 1970.

Nevins, Allan, and Ernest F. Hill. *Ford: The Times, the Man, the Company*. New York: Scribner, 1954.

———. *Ford: Expansion and Challenge, 1915–1933*. New York: Charles Scribner, 1957.

Nicolson, Harold. *Peacemaking, 1919*. New York: Harcourt Brace, 1939.

Noggle, Burl. *Into the Twenties: The United States from Armistice to Normalcy*. Urbana: University of Illinois, 1974.

———. *Teapot Dome: Oil and Politics in the 1920's*. Greenwood: Publishing Group, 1980.

Conner, Harvey. *Mellon's Millions*. New York: Henry Day, 1933.

Ogren, Kathy J. *The Jazz Revolution: Twenties America and the Meaning of Jazz*. New York: Oxford University Press, 1989.

Oilen, Roger M., and Diana Davids Oilen. *Easy Money: Oil Promoters and Investors in the Jazz Age*. Chapel Hill: University of North Carolina Press, 1990.

Page, David, and John J. Koblas. *Scott Fitzgerald in Minnesota: Toward the Summit*. St. Cloud, Minn.: North Star, 1996.

Parrish, Michael E. *Anxious Decades: America in Prosperity and Depression*. New York: Norton, 1992.

Paterson, Thomas G., J. Garry Clifford, and Kenneth J. Hagan. *American Foreign Policy: A History—Since 1900*. Lexington, Mass.: D.C. Heath, 1991.

Paxson, Frederick L. "The American Highway Movement, 1916–1935." *The American Historical Review*, 1945.

Pecora, Ferdinand. *Wall Street Under Oath*. New York: Simon and Schuster, 1939.

Peel, Roy V., and Thomas C. Donnelly. *The 1932 Campaign*. New York: Farrar and Rinehart, 1935.

Peiss, Kathy. *Hope in a Jar: The Making of American Beauty Culture*. New York: Metropolitan Books, 1998.

Perret, Geoffrey. *America in the Twenties*. New York: Touchstone, 1982.

Pollard, James E. *The Presidents and the Press*. New York: Macmillan, 1947.

Potter, David M. *People of Plenty: Economic Abundance and the American Character*. Chicago: University of Chicago Press, 1954.

Pound, Ezra. *Patria Mia: A Discussion of the Arts, Their Use and Future in America*. Chicago: Ralph Fletcher Seymour, 1950.

Powers, Richard G. *Secrecy and Power: The Life of J. Edgar Hoover*. New York: Free Press, 1986.

Preston, Diana. *The Boxer Rebellion*. New York: Walker, 2000.

Quint, Howard H., and Robert H. Ferrell, eds. *The Talkative President: The Off-the-Record Press Conferences of Calvin Coolidge*. Amherst: University of Massachusetts Press, 1964.

Roosevelt, Eleanor. *This Is My Story*. New York: Harper, 1937.

Roosevelt, James, and Sidney Shalett. *Affectionately, F.D.R.*, 1959.

———. *My Parents: A Differing View*. New York: Harper & Row, 1976.

Rudwick, Elliott, M. *Race Riot at St. Louis, July 2, 1917*. Southern Illinois University Press, 1964.

Russell, C. P. "The Pneumatic Hegira," *The Outlook*, December 9, 1925.

Russell, Francis. "Bubble, Bubble." *American Heritage*, January 1973.

———. *A City in Terror: The Boston Police Strike*. New York: Viking, 1975.

———. *The President Makers: From Mark Hanna to Joseph P. Kennedy*. Boston: Little, Brown, 1976.

———. *The Shadow of Blooming Grove*. New York: McGraw-Hill, 1968.

———. *Three Studies in Twentieth Century Obscurity*. New York: Haskell House, 1966.

———. *Tragedy in Dedham*. New York: McGraw-Hill, 1962.

Russo, Guy. *The Outfit: The Role of Chicago's Underworld in the Shaping of Modern America*. New York: Bloomsbury, 2001.

Rutland, Robert. *The Newsmongers: Journalism in the Life of the Nation*. New York: Dial, 1973.

Salvatore, Nick. *Eugene V. Debs: Citizen and Socialist*. Urbana: University of Illinois Press, 1982.

Sanger, Margaret. *An Autobiography*. New York: Norton, 1938.

———. *Happiness in Marriage*. New York: Blue Ribbon Books, 1926.

Schlesinger, Arthur M. Jr., *The Crisis of the Old Order, 1919–1933*. Boston: Houghton Mifflin, 1955.

Schmidt, Hans. *Maverick Marine: General Smedley D. Butler and the Contradictions of American Military History*. Lexington: University Press of Kentucky, 1987.

Schwarz, Jordan A. *The Interregnum of Despair: Hoover, Congress and the Depression*. Urbana: University of Illinois Press, 1970.

Seymour, Harold. *Baseball: The Golden Age*. New York: Oxford Univ. Press, 1971.

Sheean, Vincent, *Personal History*. New York: Modern Library, 1940.

Shelby, Gertrude Mathews. "Florida Frenzy." *Harper's Monthly Magazine*, January 1926.

Sherman, Richard B. "The Harding Administration and the Negro: An Opportunity Lost." *Journal of Negro History*, July 1964.

Sidelsky, Robert. *John Maynard Keynes: Economist as Savior, 1920–1937*. New York: Penguin, 1994.

———. *John Maynard Keynes: Hopes Betrayed, 1883–1920*. New York: Viking, 1986.

Silver, Thomas. *Coolidge and the Historians*. Durham: North Carolina Academic, 1982.

Sinclair, Andrew. *The Available Man*. New York: Macmillan, 1964.

———. *Prohibition: The Era of Excess*. New York: Harper Colophon 1964.

Sklar, Robert. *Movie-Made America: A Cultural History of American Movies*. New York: Vintage, 1994.

Slayton, Robert A. *Empire Statesman: The Rise and Redemption of Al Smith*. New York: Free Press, 2001.

Sloan, Alfred P. *My Years with General Motors*. Garden City, N.Y.: Doubleday, 1963.

Slosson, Preston W. *The Great Crusade and After* New York: Macmillan, 1930.

Smith, Gene. *The Shattered Dream*. New York: Morrow, 1970.

———. *When the Cheering Stopped*. New York: Time-Life: 1966.

Smith, Richard. *First Across!* Annapolis: Naval Institute Press, 1973.

Snyder, Louis L., and Richard B. Morris, eds. *A Treasury of Great Reporting*. New York: Simon and Schuster, 1949.

Sobel, Robert. *Coolidge: An American Enigma*. Washington, D.C.: Regnery, 1998.

———. *The Great Bull Market: Wall Street in the 1920s*. New York: Norton, 1968.

————. *Herbert Hoover and the Onset of the Great Depression, 1929–1930*. Philadelphia: Lippincott, 1975.

Soule, George. *Prosperity Decade*. New York: Harper Torchbooks, 1947.

Stansell, Christine. *American Moderns*. New York: Metropolitan, 2000.

Starling, Edmund W. *Starling of the White House*. New York: Simon and Shuster, 1946.

Stashower, Daniel. *The Boy Genius and the Mogul: The Untold Story of Television*. New York: Broadway, 2002.

Stearns, Harold E., ed. *Civilization in the United States*.

————. *The Street I Know*. New York: Lee Furman, 1935.

Steel, Ronald. *Walter Lippmann and the American Century*. Boston: Altantic-Little, Brown, 1980.

Stevens, John D. *Sensationalism in the New York Press*. New York: Columbia University Press, 1991.

Stevenson, Elizabeth. *Babbitts and Bohemians: The American 1920s*. New York: Macmillan, 1967.

Stewart, Don. "The Madness That Swept Miami." *Smithsonian*, January 2001.

Stoddard, Lothrop. *The Rising Tide of Color Against White Supremacy*. With an Introduction by Madison Grant. New York: Scribner, 1930.

Sullivan, Mark. "The Stamp and the Porch." *Collier's*, October 9, 1920.

————. *The Twenties*. New York: Scribner, 1935.

————. *The War Begins*. New York: Scribner, 1932.

Susman, Warren I. *Culture As History: The Transformation of American Society in the Twentieth Century*. New York: Pantheon 1984.

Sward, Keith. *The Legend of Henry Ford*. New York: Rinehart, 1948.

Thomas, Gordon, and Max Morgan-Witts. *The Day the Bubble Burst*. Garden City, N.Y.: Doubleday, 1979.

Thomas, Lately. *Storming Heaven: The Lives and Turmoil of Minnie Kennedy and Aimee Semple McPherson*. New York: Morrow, 1970.

Tindall, George B. "The Bubble in the Sun." *American Heritage*, August 1965.

Trani, Eugene P., and David L. Wilson, *The Presidency of Warren G. Harding*. Lawrence: Regents Press of Kansas, 1977.

Tugwell, Rexford. G. *The Brain Trust*. New York: Viking, 1968.

Turnbull, Andrew. *Scott Fitzgerald*. New York: Scribner, 1962.

Tuttle, William M. *Race Riot: Chicago in the Red Summer of 1919*. New York: Atheneum, 1972.

Wagenheim, Karl. *Babe Ruth: His Life and Legend*. Chicago: Olmstead Press, 2001.

Ward, Geoffrey, and Ken Burns. *Jazz: A History of America's Music*. New York: Knopf, 2000.

Warren, Harris G. *Herbert Hoover in the Great Depression*. New York: Oxford University Press, 1999.

Waskow, Arthur I. *From Race Riot to Sit-in*. New York: Anchor, 1967.

Watson, James E. *The Memoirs of James E. Watson*. Indianapolis: Bobbs-Merrill, 1936.

Wecter, Dixon. *The Age of the Great Depression*. New York: Macmillan, 1948.

————. *The Hero in American History*. New York: Scribner, 1941.

————. *When Johnny Comes Marching Home*. Cambridge: Harvard University Press, 1944.

Weinstein, Edwin. *Woodrow Wilson: A Medical and Psychological Biography*. Princeton: Princeton University Press, 1981.

Weisberger, Bernard A. *The Dream Maker: William C. Durant, Founder of General Motors.* Boston: Little, Brown, 1979.

Wendt, Lloyd, and Herman Kogan. *Lords of the Levee: The Story of Bathhouse John and Hinky Dink.* Garden City, N.Y.: Doubleday, 1944.

Weiner, M.R., and John Starr. *Teapot Dome.* New York: Norton, 1965.

Wexler, Alice. *Emma Goldman: An Intimate Life.* New York: Random House, 1984.

White, E. B. "Farewell My Lovely." In *Second Tree from the Corner.* New York: Harper and Brothers, 1954.

White, Walter. *Rope and Faggot.* New York: Knopf, 1929.

White, William Allen. *The Autobiography of William Allen White.* New York: Macmillan, 1946.

———. "The Other Side of Main Street." *Collier's,* July 30, 1921.

———. "Portrait of a Typical Farmer." *New York Times Magazine,* January 30, 1927.

———. *A Puritan in Babylon: The Story of Calvin Coolidge.* New York: Macmillan 1938.

Wik, Raymond W. *Henry Ford and Grass-Roots America.* Ann Arbor: University of Michigan Press, 1972.

Williams, William Appleman. *The Tragedy of American Diplomacy.* Cleveland: World Publishing 1959.

Wilson, Edith Bolling. *My Memoir.* Indianapolis: Bobbs-Merrill, 1938.

Wilson, Edmund. *The American Earthquake.* Garden City, N.Y.: Doubleday, 1958.

———. *To the Shores of Light.* New York: Farrar, Straus, 1952.

Wilson, Joan Hoff. *American Business and Foreign Policy, 1920–1933.* Boston: Beacon, 1973.

———. *Herbert Hoover: A Public Life.* Boston: Beacon, 1984.

Wiseman, Carter. *Shaping a Nation: Twentieth Century American Architecture and Its Makers.* New York: Norton, 1999.

Yagoda, Ben. "Hollywood Cleans Up Its Act." *American Heritage,* February 1980.

NEWSPAPERS AND MAGAZINES

The American Mercury

Amsterdam News

The Atlantic Monthly

Baltimore Evening Sun

Baltimore Sun

Chicago Daily News

Chicago Tribune

Collier's

Current History

Current Opinion

Freeman

Liberty

Literary Digest

The Nation

The New Republic

New York Daily News

New York Herald Tribune

New York Mirror

New York Times

New York Tribune

New York World

The New Yorker

The North American Review

The Outlook

Popular Science Monthly

The Saturday Evening Post

The Smart Set

Survey

Time

Washington Evening Star

Washington Post

Index